Praise for *The Software IP Detective's Handbook*

"As a frequent expert witness myself, I found Bob's book to be important and well written. Intellectual property and software plagiarism are complicated subjects, as are patents and copyrights. This book explains the key elements better than anything else I have seen. The book is highly recommended to anyone who develops software and also to those who need to protect proprietary software algorithms. The book should also be useful to attorneys who are involved with intellectual property litigation."

—*Capers Jones, president, Capers Jones & Associates, LLC*

"Intellectual property [IP] is an engine of growth for our high-tech world and a valuable commodity traded in its own right. Bob Zeidman is a leading authority on software IP, and in this book he shares with us his expertise. The book is comprehensive. It contains clear explanations of many difficult subjects. Businesspeople who study it will learn how to protect their IP. Lawyers will use it to understand the specifics of how software embodies IP. Judges will cite it in their decisions on IP litigation."

—*Abraham Sofaer, George P. Shultz Senior Fellow in Foreign Policy and National Security Affairs, Hoover Institution, Stanford University*

"Bob has done a fantastic job in making computer science forensics understandable to mere mortals: attorneys, engineers, and managers. This is the ultimate handbook for expert witnesses, due diligence execution, and developing a baseline for software valuation. Buy it before your competitors do!"

—*Don Shafer, CSDP, chief technology officer, Athens Group, LLC*

"Bob has considerable experience in dealing with issues associated with unauthorized use of software code. His insights in this book are particularly helpful for those seeking to provide expert analysis with respect to software code."

—*Neel I. Chatterjee, partner, Orrick, Herrington & Sutcliffe, LLC*

"This readable book perfectly bridges the jargon divide between software engineers and IP attorneys. It helps each group finally understand exactly what the other is talking about. As a software developer and expert witness I will definitely keep a copy handy and recommend it to others on my team."

—*Michael Barr, president, Netrino, LLC*

"This book makes intellectual property law understandable and accessible to programmers by combining discussions of the law with discussions of computer science, and interweaving case studies to elucidate the intersection of these disciplines."

—*Robert C. Seacord, Secure Coding Manager, Sof*

THE SOFTWARE IP
DETECTIVE'S HANDBOOK

The Software IP Detective's Handbook

MEASUREMENT, COMPARISON, AND INFRINGEMENT DETECTION

Robert Zeidman
Software Analysis and Forensic Engineering Corporation

PRENTICE
HALL

Upper Saddle River, NJ • Boston • Indianapolis • San Francisco
New York • Toronto • Montreal • London • Munich • Paris • Madrid
Capetown • Sydney • Tokyo • Singapore • Mexico City

The publisher offers excellent discounts on this book when ordered in quantity for bulk purchases or special sales, which may include electronic versions and/or custom covers and content particular to your business, training goals, marketing focus, and branding interests. For more information, please contact:

> U.S. Corporate and Government Sales
> (800) 382-3419
> corpsales@pearsontechgroup.com

For sales outside the United States please contact:

> International Sales
> international@pearson.com

Visit us on the Web: informit.com/ph

Library of Congress Cataloging-in-Publication Data is on file with the Library of Congress

ISBN-13: 978-0-13-703533-5
ISBN-10:   0-13-703533-0

Text printed in the United States on recycled paper at Courier in Westford, Massachusetts.
First printing, April 2011

Editor-in-Chief
Mark L. Taub

Acquisitions Editor
Bernard Goodwin

Managing Editor
John Fuller

Full-Service Production Manager
Julie B. Nahil

Copy Editor
Barbara Wood

Indexer
Lenity Mauhar

Proofreader
Linda Begley

Cover Designer
Anne Jones

Compositor
LaurelTech

This book is dedicated to all those who attempt to do things that others say are wrong or impossible, and to all those who encourage them.

CONTENTS

PREFACE

WHAT IS THIS BOOK ABOUT?

This book is generally about software intellectual property and specifically about the field of software forensics. While you may never testify in a courtroom, attempt to deduce the true owner of a valuable program, or measure the intellectual property (IP) value of software source code, if you are at all involved with software you need to know how to protect your rights to that software. This book will give you an understanding of those rights, their limitations, how to protect those rights, and how to take action against someone or some organization that you believe has infringed on those rights.

Unlike digital forensics, which studies the bits and bytes on a digital storage medium, such as a hard disk or DVD-ROM, without a deep understanding of what those ones and zeros represent, software forensics studies the software code that instructs a computer to perform operations. Software forensics discovers information about the history and usage of that software for presentation in a court of law. It combines information and techniques from computer science, mathematics, and law in a way that is unique and, I believe, particularly interesting.

HOW IS THIS BOOK ORGANIZED?

This book contains overviews as well as in-depth information about law, mathematics, and computer science. The book is organized into chapters that can be categorized as follows: those primarily about intellectual property law, those about computer science, those about mathematics, and those about business and business procedures. There is, of course, overlap. Chapter 1 describes the organization of the book in detail and allows you to choose those chapters that are most relevant to your career and your interests.

WHO SHOULD READ THIS BOOK?

This book is for anyone interested in software intellectual property. Specifically, I believe the book will appeal to computer scientists, computer programmers, business managers, lawyers, engineering consultants, expert witnesses, and software entrepreneurs. While the focus is on software IP measurement, comparison, and infringement detection, the book also has useful information about many issues related to software IP, and I believe that many people involved with software will find the book valuable and interesting.

SUPPORT AND COMMENTS

Thank you for purchasing my book. Please send me feedback on corrections and improvements. Of course, I also like to hear about the things I did right, the things you like about the book, and how it has helped you in some way.

Bob Zeidman
bob@SAFE-corp.biz
www.SAFE-corp.biz
Cupertino, California
March 2011

ACKNOWLEDGMENTS

When I finished my last book, back in 2002, I swore I'd never write another one. They say that pregnancy is the same way. Ask a woman right after delivering a child whether she'd do it again and, if she's coherent, she'll give you an emphatic, "Never!" Yet within months, if not days, she forgets the pain of birth and only remembers the pleasure of spending time with her baby, then her infant, then her toddler, then her kid. (By the time the child is a teenager, some of the pain of birth may have returned to her memory, though.)

So it took me seven years to forget the pain of giving birth to my last book. Actually, I remembered that pain (though the memory had softened over the years) but really felt I had something worthwhile to say once again. I'm proud of all of my books (a parent isn't supposed to favor one child), but this one is different. Those other books were intended to explain areas of engineering that many others had invented, developed, and explored before me. I explained some of my own discoveries here and there, but the bulk of the creativity is correctly credited to the pioneers who preceded me. For this book, most of the work is original. The techniques, the mathematics, the algorithms, and the procedures in this book are being adopted fairly well, and that's exciting. I hope that others can take what I've done and build upon it. I continue to do that myself and am finding lots of unexplored areas that are being revealed, offering plenty of opportunities, I believe, for mathematicians, lawyers, programmers, computer scientists, and entrepreneurs.

Many people helped me with this book, some explicitly and some implicitly. First, I'll mention the lawyers who, despite their unbelievably full schedules, still found time to review my work and offer suggestions and corrections. This was particularly important because I'm not a lawyer, but I wanted this book to be accurate. Thanks to Joe Zito, Ed Kwok, Tait Graves, and Neel Chatterjee. Next are the mathematicians and computer scientists who gave me suggestions for representations for the formulas in the book. Thanks to John Wakerly, Kelvin Sung, and Ron Summers, and to the engineers who looked over my definitions and explanations and suggested numerous improvements. Thanks to Robert Seacord, Tom Quilty, Capers Jones, Jack Grimes, and Michael Barr. Special thanks go to Don Shafer and Chuck Pfleeger. Don did some scathing critiques of early versions of the manuscript that really pushed me to improve the book. Chuck did such detailed reviews and gave me such in-depth feedback that at times I was afraid that he understood the material better than I did. The employees at my companies have also provided a lot of great research and development, especially Nik Baer who, among other things, united the concepts of CLOC into one concise set of equations and nomenclature. Other employees who supplied a lot of great ideas and input include Jim Zamiska, Ilana Shay, Larry Melling, Tim Hoehn, and Michael Everest. I also want to thank Grace Seidman for setting up and taking the great photograph that became the cover art, and Jessica Yates for taking the flattering pictures of me.

I have a great, supportive editor at Prentice Hall: Bernard Goodwin. Sometimes I think that if I went to Bernard and said I want to do a book on the engineering principles of navel lint and dust bunnies, he'd give me the okay. As long as it was about engineering. I've heard horror stories about tough editors who put a lot of pressure on their writers, but that certainly wasn't the case with Bernard. And when I told him the schedule was slipping, but I felt I needed more time to make some important improvements, he responded, "Better trumps the schedule." I hope this is the "better" book we planned.

I want to thank Mike Flynn, Professor Emeritus of Electrical Engineering at Stanford. Mike has supported every one of my business and engineering endeavors, and this book is no exception. The concepts in this book took root in his office when he suggested I create a theory about source code correlation and spent a day working on it with me. Before that, I had a very useful program; after that, I had a new area of study including a set of axioms, theorems, and equations, and a vision about how to create something pretty big.

Finally, I want to thank my wife, Carrie. She has always been supportive of every crazy thing I decide to do, no matter how much time it takes me away from her. In this case, she gave up many weekends we wanted to spend together because I just had to get a few more pages written. I promise to spend all the weekends with her from now on, though she knows I'll find some other project that will keep me busy and that I'll keep on promising. I love her and thank her for her patience and also for the great artwork on the book cover and the figures inside the book, which she created.

ABOUT THE AUTHOR

 **Bob Zeidman** is the president and founder of Zeidman Consulting (www.ZeidmanConsulting.com), a premiere contract research and development firm in Silicon Valley that focuses on engineering consulting to law firms handling intellectual property dispute cases. Since 1983, Bob has designed computer chips and circuit boards for RISC-based parallel processor systems, laser printers, network switches and routers, and other complex systems. His clients have included Apple Computer, Cisco Systems, Cadence Design Systems, Facebook, Intel, Symantec, Texas Instruments, and Zynga. Bob has worked on and testified in cases involving billions of dollars in disputed intellectual property.

Bob is also the president and founder of Software Analysis and Forensic Engineering Corporation (www.SAFE-corp.biz), the leading provider of software intellectual property analysis tools. Bob is considered a pioneer in the field of analyzing software source code, having created the CodeSuite program for detecting software intellectual property theft, which is sold by SAFE Corp, founded in 2007.

Previously, Bob was the president and founder of Zeidman Technologies (www.zeidman.biz) where he invented the patented SynthOS program for automatically generating real-time software. Before that, Bob was the president and founder of The Chalkboard Network, an e-learning company that put high-end business and technology courses from well-known subject matter experts on the web. Prior to that, Bob invented the concept of remote backup and started Evault, the first remote backup company.

Bob is a prolific writer and instructor, giving seminars at conferences around the world. Among his publications are numerous articles on engineering and business as well as three textbooks—*Designing with FPGAs and CPLDs*, *Verilog Designer's Library*, and *Introduction to Verilog*. Bob holds numerous patents and earned two bachelor's degrees, in physics and electrical engineering, from Cornell University and a master's degree in electrical engineering from Stanford University.

Bob is also active in a number of nonprofits. He also enjoys writing novels and screenplays and has won a number of awards for this work.

PART I

INTRODUCTION

"From a drop of water . . . a logician could infer the possibility of an Atlantic or a Niagara without having seen or heard of one or the other. So all life is a great chain, the nature of which is known whenever we are shown a single link of it. Like all other arts, the Science of Deduction and Analysis is one which can only be acquired by long and patient study nor is life long enough to allow any mortal to attain the highest possible perfection in it. Before turning to those moral and mental aspects of the matter which present the greatest difficulties, let the enquirer begin by mastering more elementary problems."
—Sherlock Holmes in *A Study in Scarlet*

What is intellectual property and why is it important? According to the World Intellectual Property Organization (WIPO):

Intellectual property (IP) refers to creations of the mind: inventions, literary and artistic works, and symbols, names, images, and designs used in commerce.

Intellectual property is divided into two categories: Industrial property, which includes inventions (patents), trademarks, industrial designs, and geographic indications of source; and Copyright, which includes literary and artistic works such as novels, poems and plays, films, musical works, artistic works such as drawings, paintings, photographs and sculptures, and architectural designs. Rights related to copyright include those of performing artists in their performances, producers of phonograms in their recordings, and those of broadcasters in their radio and television programs.

Software is obviously a creation of the mind—simply ask any programmer who has spent numerous hours racking his brain trying to implement some complex function or trying to debug a piece of computer code that just will not work. Software embodies intellectual property in the human-readable source code. Software also embodies intellectual property in the machine-executable binary code that is produced from the source code.

Intellectual property is intangible property, but nonetheless it is valuable. Like other property, IP can be sold, traded, or simply held on to. It can also be stolen. Just as you would not want someone to take the fruits of your physical labor—for example, the boat that you built or the blueprints for that water-powered combustion engine—so you would not want someone to take the fruits of your mental labor. That constitutes theft. Similarly, if you paid for your television, it belongs to you and taking it is theft, just as taking software source code, software object code, or software patents that you purchased is theft, though not intellectual property theft.

At the beginning of each major part of this book is a short description of the content to be found in the chapters. You will also find two headings in each part-opening description: **Objectives** and **Intended Audience**. Under the *Objectives* heading you will find a very brief summary of the content of the chapters in the part. Under the *Intended Audience* heading you will find the type of reader who will find those chapters most valuable to her area of expertise. Feel free to read any part you want, though; no one is keeping track (at least that I am aware of).

OBJECTIVES

The objective of this book is to define ways of measuring and analyzing software intellectual property in order to value that intellectual property or to determine, in as precise and objective a manner as possible, whether software intellectual property has been misappropriated or infringed.

The objective of this part is to introduce you to the book, explain why the concepts described within it are important, and guide you through the chapters to understand which ones will be most useful to you.

INTENDED AUDIENCE

This book is intended for *computer scientists, computer programmers, corporate managers, lawyers, technical consultants and expert witnesses for litigation*, and *software entrepreneurs*.

- *Computer scientists* will be able to use the mathematical framework described in this book for measuring and comparing software IP. They will be able to use the mathematical definitions to quantify software IP, which until now has often been described in vague and sometimes conflicting terms. The mathematical framework described in this book can be expanded to take additional forms of software IP into account. This set of mathematical axioms and equations is certainly applicable to other aspects of software, and computer scientists should be able to find new and interesting applications of them.

- *Computer programmers* will find the chapters on implementation and application of the mathematical theories particularly useful. They will be able to create programs to measure and analyze software IP. They will be able to optimize existing applications, and they will find new areas in which to apply these algorithms in programs for other purposes. This book will also give programmers an idea of the different forms of intellectual property, how each is embodied in their programs, how that IP is protectable, and how to avoid unintentional IP infringement or misappropriation.

- *Corporate managers* will get a better understanding of the ongoing debate in Congress, in the courts, and among software developers and high-tech companies regarding software patents, a dispute that promises to affect the form and extent of protection of software intellectual property. These managers will also understand the legal concept of software IP and how the legal protections afforded to it can be used to protect their companies from competition and outright IP theft. Obviously the same concepts allow managers to avoid unintentional IP infringement or misappropriation and to understand how to protect themselves from false accusations of IP infringement and theft.

- *Lawyers* will better understand how to detect software IP theft or measure software IP changes and how to best present their positive or negative findings in court. Because software IP issues are changing very quickly, with courts defining and redefining IP specifics and IP protections all the way to the U.S. Supreme Court, this book cannot impart in-depth legal knowledge. What it can do, however, is to define the basics and the precedents up until now. This book also gives lawyers the ability to understand the mathematical concepts involved in determining software IP in order to do a better job of choosing consultants and expert witnesses, contemplating the potential for success in any litigation, and interrogating and cross-examining expert witnesses for the opposing party.

- *Technical consultants and expert witnesses for litigation* will be able to further their careers with a better understanding of how to detect software IP theft and infringement and how to best present their positive or negative findings in court. This book gives them a solid method for drawing conclusions about IP infringement and misappropriation that has been tested in court and in peer-reviewed studies. While many software IP cases still rely simply on a subjective contest of credibility between the expert witnesses of parties to litigation, it is my hope that the information in this book will create a more fair, standard, and objective means of reaching a decision in court. Those experts who understand the methods and tools described in this book will be in high demand.

- *Software entrepreneurs* will be able to leverage all of the advantages just described for all of the other categories of readers and create new software programs and new businesses that incorporate the methods, algorithms, and implementations described herein to build successful businesses.

This book focuses on intellectual property and intellectual property rights in the United States. Much of this is applicable to other countries as well, though the specific laws and specific remedies may differ. In some places throughout the book I introduce information regarding other countries, but unless specifically stated otherwise, the legal issues refer to the practice and understanding of software intellectual property in the United States at the time of this writing.

ABOUT THIS BOOK

This book crosses a number of different fields of computer science, mathematics, and law. Not all readers will want to delve into every chapter. This is the place to start, but from this point onward each reader's experience will be different. In this chapter I describe each of the parts and chapters of the book to help you determine which chapters will be useful and appealing for your specific needs and interests.

I should make clear that I am not a lawyer, have never been one, and have never even played one on TV. All of the issues I discuss in this book are my understanding based on my technical consulting and expert witness work on nearly 100 intellectual property cases to date. My consulting company, Zeidman Consulting, has been growing over the years, and now the work is split between my employees and me. When I refer in the book to my experiences, in most cases that is firsthand information, but in other cases it may be information discovered and tested by an employee and related and explained to me.

In this book I also refer to forensic analysis tools that I have used to analyze software, in particular the CodeSuite tool that is produced and offered for sale by my software company, Software Analysis and Forensic Engineering Corporation (S.A.F.E. Corporation), and can be downloaded from the company website at www.SAFE-corp.biz. The CodeSuite set of tools currently consists of the following functions: BitMatch, CodeCLOC, CodeCross, CodeDiff, and SourceDetective. Functions are being continually added and updated. Each of these functions uses one or more of the algorithms described in later chapters.

Also, the CodeMeasure program uses the CLOC method to measure software evolution, which is explained in Chapter 12. It is also produced and sold by S.A.F.E. Corporation and can be downloaded from its own site at www.CodeMeasure.com.

Table 1.1 should help you determine which chapters will be the most helpful and relevant to you. Find your occupation at the top of the table and read downward to see the chapters that will be most relevant to your background and your job.

PART I: INTRODUCTION

The introduction to the book is just that—an introduction, intended to give you a broad overview of the book and help you determine why you want to read it and which chapters you will find most in line with your own interests and needs. This part includes a description of the other parts and chapters in the book. It also gives information and statistics about intellectual property crime, to give you an understanding of why this book is useful and important.

PART II: SOFTWARE

In this part I describe source code, object code, interpreted code, macros, and synthesis code, which are the blueprints for software. This part describes these important concepts, which are well known to computer scientists and programmers but may not be understood, or may not be understood in sufficient depth, by attorneys involved in software IP litigation. This part will be valuable for lawyers to help them understand how different kinds of software code relate to each other, and how these different kinds of software code can affect a software copyright infringement, software trade secret, or software patent case.

PART III: INTELLECTUAL PROPERTY

In this part I describe intellectual property, in particular copyrights, patents, and trade secrets. I have found that many of these concepts are unclear or only partially understood by many computer scientists, programmers, and corporate managers. In this part I define these terms in ways that I believe will be comprehensible to those with little or no legal background.

Table 1.1   Finding Your Way through This Book

Chapter	Title	Computer scientist	Computer programmer	Manager	Lawyer	Consultant/expert witness	Software entrepreneur
Part I	Introduction	X	X	X	X	X	X
Chapter 1	About This Book	X	X	X	X	X	X
Chapter 2	Intellectual Property Crime	X	X	X	X	X	X
Part II	Software	X	X	X	X	X	X
Chapter 3	Source Code			X	X		
Chapter 4	Object Code and Assembly Code			X	X		
Chapter 5	Scripts, Intermediate Code, Macros, and Synthesis Primitives			X	X		
Part III	Intellectual Property	X	X	X	X	X	X
Chapter 6	Copyrights	X	X	X		X	X
Chapter 7	Patents	X	X	X		X	X
Chapter 8	Trade Secrets	X	X	X		X	X
Chapter 9	Software Forensics	X	X	X	X	X	X
Part IV	Source Code Differentiation	X	X	X	X	X	X
Chapter 10	Theory	X	X			X	X
Chapter 11	Implementation	X	X			X	X
Chapter 12	Applications	X	X	X		X	X
Part V	Source Code Correlation	X	X	X	X	X	X
Chapter 13	Plagiarism Detection	X			X	X	X
Chapter 14	Source Code Characterization	X	X	X	X	X	X

Continues

Table 1.1   Finding Your Way through This Book (*Continued*)

Chapter	Title	Computer scientist	Computer programmer	Manager	Lawyer	Consultant/ expert witness	Software entrepreneur
Chapter 15	Theory	X				X	X
Chapter 16	Implementation	X	X			X	X
Chapter 17	Applications	X	X	X		X	X
Part VI	Object and Source/Object Code Correlation	X	X	X	X	X	X
Chapter 18	Theory	X				X	X
Chapter 19	Implementation	X	X			X	X
Chapter 20	Applications	X	X	X		X	X
Part VII	Source Code Cross-Correlation	X	X	X	X	X	X
Chapter 21	Theory, Implementation, Application	X	X	X		X	X
Part VIII	Detecting Software IP Theft and Infringement	X	X	X	X	X	X
Chapter 22	Detecting Copyright Infringement			X	X	X	X
Chapter 23	Detecting Patent Infringement			X	X	X	X
Chapter 24	Detecting Trade Secret Theft		X	X	X	X	X
Part IX	Miscellaneous Topics	X	X	X	X	X	X
Chapter 25	Implementing a Software Clean Room		X	X	X	X	X
Chapter 26	Open Source Software		X	X	X	X	X
Chapter 27	Digital Millennium Copyright Act		X	X	X	X	X
Part X	Past, Present, and Future	X	X	X	X	X	X

I also define the field of software forensics in this part. When I am asked to work on a case, there is sometimes confusion about the fields of software forensics and digital forensics. In some cases, engineers practicing digital forensics claim to practice software forensics and sometimes use the tools of digital forensics to attempt to draw conclusions about software IP, yielding incorrect or inconclusive results. Software forensics requires the specialized tools of the field and expertise in the field to extract relevant information from the tools, reach appropriate conclusions, and opine on those conclusions. In this part I offer definitions of the two fields. In fact, the definition of software forensics has, to this point, been somewhat vague. My explanation in this part will clarify the practice of software forensics, show how it fits into the field of forensic science, and differentiate it from digital forensics.

PART IV: SOURCE CODE DIFFERENTIATION

This part describes source code differentiation, a very basic method of comparing and measuring software source code. Source code differentiation is especially useful for finding code that has been directly copied from one program to another and for determining a percentage of direct copying. While there are many metrics for measuring qualities of software, source code differentiation has some unique abilities to measure development effort, software changes, and software intellectual property changes that are particularly useful for determining software intellectual property value for such applications as transfer pricing calculations.

In this part I introduce the mathematics of the theory of source code differentiation and explain implementations of source code differentiation for programmers who want to understand how to implement it. I also describe the "changing lines of code" or "CLOC" method of measuring software growth that is based on source code differentiation, and I compare it to traditional methods like "source lines of code" or "SLOC." I then discuss various applications of source code differentiation, though I believe that many more applications of this metric will be found in the future.

PART V: SOURCE CODE CORRELATION

This part starts by exploring the various methods and algorithms for "software plagiarism detection" that have been developed over the last few decades.

I describe the origins of these methods and algorithms, and I explain their limitations. In particular, there have been no standard definitions and no supporting theory for this work, so I introduce the theory of source code correlation and definitions for characterizing source code. This characterization of software source code is practical for determining correlation and, ultimately, for determining whether copying occurred. While the theory and definitions are broad enough to be useful in various areas of computer science, they are particularly valuable in litigation.

In this part I also describe practical implementations of the theory for those programmers who want to understand how to implement the algorithms. Additionally, I describe applications of the theory in the real world. This part is highly mathematical, though the chapter on source code characterization will be useful for lawyers in understanding how elements of software source code can be categorized, how these various elements relate, and how the elements can affect a software copyright infringement, software trade secret, or software patent case.

PART VI: OBJECT AND SOURCE/OBJECT CODE CORRELATION

In this part I introduce the theory and mathematics of object code correlation, which is used to compare object code to object code to find signs of copying. I also introduce the theory of source/object code correlation, which is used to compare source code to object code to find signs of copying. Both of these correlation measures are helpful before litigation when there is no access to source code from at least one party's software. I also describe practical implementations of the theory for those programmers who want to understand how to implement these correlation measures, and I describe applications of the methods and algorithms in the real world.

PART VII: SOURCE CODE CROSS-CORRELATION

In this part I introduce the theory and mathematics of source code cross-correlation, which is specifically used to compare functional source code statements to nonfunctional source code comments to find signs of copying. This correlation measure is effective, in certain cases, for finding copied code that has been disguised enough to avoid detection with one of the other correlation measures. I describe some ways of effectively implementing code to measure source code cross-correlation for those programmers who want to understand how to implement this measure, and I describe applications of source code cross-correlation in the real world.

PART VIII: DETECTING SOFTWARE IP THEFT AND INFRINGEMENT

All of the correlation measures described in previous parts are useful for detecting software intellectual property theft; however, expert review is still required. Previously developed algorithms often produced a measure that claimed to show whether code was copied or not. In reality, a mathematical measure in and of itself is not enough to make this determination, and that is one of the problems with previous work in this area. In this part I describe detailed, precise steps to be taken once correlation has been calculated. These steps are as important to the standardization and objectivity required for determining intellectual property theft and infringement as are the various correlation measurements described in the previous parts.

PART IX: MISCELLANEOUS TOPICS

This part covers areas that have come up in my involvement with intellectual property litigation. These subjects were also suggested by some of the experienced reviewers of this book who felt they deserved discussion. The issues described in this part often arise in software intellectual property cases and are also important for code developers and managers to understand. In particular, I discuss procedures for implementing a software clean room, I explain open source code, and I describe the Digital Millennium Copyright Act.

PART X: PAST, PRESENT, AND FUTURE

The topics discussed in this book are cutting-edge, and I find them to be very interesting and exciting. A lot of work remains to be done, including extending the theories, advancing the mathematics, standardizing the definitions, and promoting the methodologies. In this part I discuss what has been done to date, speculate on areas of future research that build on the concepts in this book, and look toward new applications in various aspects of law and computer science.

INTELLECTUAL PROPERTY CRIME

Intellectual property infringement and theft are problems of growing concern for two specific entities—universities and corporations. With the pervasiveness of the Internet and the effectiveness of search engines, students in programming courses can now easily find existing code that solves large sections of their homework and exam problems, if not all of it. While this can often be a legal use of the found code, it is often a case of plagiarism if the student does not disclose the source. Also, it may constitute copyright infringement if the owner of the code does not allow such copying. In corporations, source code theft is also a problem, particularly because of the mobility of employees and the ease with which code can be loaded onto a virtually undetectable flash drive or transferred via encrypted email over the Internet. Patent infringement and copyright infringement are also concerns. Intellectual property theft of any kind may be purposeful when performed to gain an unfair advantage over a competitor, or it may be unintended as in the case of a programmer who takes code from one project and uses it in another project without first obtaining the appropriate permissions. Patent infringement often occurs without any malice but is simply the result of someone coming up with a great solution to a tough problem without checking whether some other person or some other company already invented that solution and holds the rights to it.

2.1 THE EXTENT OF IP THEFT

Just how bad is IP theft? Pretty bad, according to a research report released from McAfee, Inc., in 2009. According to the report, companies surveyed estimated that they lost an average of $4.6 million worth of intellectual property in 2008. Forty-two percent said laid-off employees were the single biggest threat to their intellectual property and other sensitive data that they faced in the current economic climate.

The report also stated four key findings:

1. Increasing amounts of IP and sensitive customer data are being sent around the world, and a percentage is being lost.
2. The worsening economy is creating a "perfect information security risk storm" because laid-off employees stealing IP now constitutes the largest risk.
3. The countries that constitute the worst risks for IP loss are China, Pakistan, and Russia.
4. Cyber thieves have grown more sophisticated. Now, rather than steal credit card numbers, they steal the IP for creating the credit card processing programs.

2.1.1 UNINTENTIONAL LOSS

Let us examine each of these findings. The first one involves unintentional loss. A key takeaway from this fact should be that companies need to do more to protect their intellectual property, not just from criminal activity but also from mistakes, failures, and negligence. How many times have you hit the send button for an email and immediately realized that you sent the email to the wrong person? Rather than going to Robert Smith, the email went to Robert Smigel—not a good thing at all, especially if Mr. Smigel is known to be a jokester who likes to cause trouble. You do not want to see your software source code posted on some blogger's website. Companies need to take precautions to prevent even accidental loss of IP. Policies need to be in place regarding what information can be emailed, mailed, or otherwise transported off-site. Policies need to be in place regarding to whom the information can be emailed, mailed, or otherwise transferred. Policies need to be in place regarding categories of items; for example, software source code should be in the highest category, requiring the most care in its transfer. Policies need to be in place regarding who can do such transfers and how the code can be transferred. In my companies, for example, source code is always zipped up with a password before being emailed, even to another person within the company.

Note that I emphasize that policies need to be in place (the repetition of this phrase is not just to annoy you, but to drill it into your mind). To successfully defend a trade secret case, and sometimes a copyright case or a patent case, you must show that you made an effort to protect your IP. Allowing employees to arbitrarily and individually decide what precautions to take with your IP can bring a quick end to your case. *Policies need to be in place.*

2.1.2 POOR ECONOMY

The second item refers to the poor economy at the time the report was written. I hope that by the time you are reading this book the economy has improved significantly and we are all sipping champagne from our yachts or at least working at fulfilling, lucrative jobs. But in any economy there are laid-off employees and those who are disgruntled for any number of reasons. These employees pose a serious risk to every business. Disgruntled employees can do damage to a company in many ways, including the theft of IP. Another report from the Ponemon Institute confirms this conclusion from the McAfee report. According to the Ponemon report, more than half of workers who are let go from their employers take confidential data and intellectual property with them as they head out the door. Here are some interesting statistics from the Ponemon report:

- 945 individuals who were laid off, fired, or quit their jobs in the past 12 months were surveyed.
- 59 percent admitted to stealing company data.
- 67 percent used their former company's confidential information to help them get a new job.
- 61 percent of respondents who disliked their company took data.
- 26 percent of those who liked their company still took data.
- 79 percent of those who took data rationalized it rather than calling it wrong.
- 24 percent claimed to still have access to their former employer's computers after they left.

More important, actually, is the threat from greedy employees. The vast majority of cases of IP theft on which I have worked, where theft was determined to have actually taken place, involved employees leaving one company and deciding it was advantageous to take their work product with them to speed up their effort at the next company. Often that next company was their own start-up. There were cases where an employee did not understand intellectual property rights and did not understand that he was stealing. These cases are by far in the minority, however. In most cases the thief made efforts to disguise the theft because he knew it was wrong and wanted to avoid getting caught.

2.1.3 Cheap Labor

The third point is a serious issue that many companies simply do not take seriously. In their desire for cheap labor or their desire to open up large new markets, companies are embracing countries that have few laws protecting intellectual property and that in some cases—for example, China—actually encourage IP theft. The government of China has been accused of stealing IP, including allegedly breaking into Google's computers to steal proprietary data and critical source code in early 2010. It is believed by many who are familiar with the Chinese government, which controls most industries in China, that they actually encourage this kind of "competitive behavior." I have been informed that in China, the website for my software company, Software Analysis and Forensic Engineering, is blocked, almost certainly because China does not want anyone to have access to tools that detect IP theft.

In Russia, the government is known to take over profitable foreign businesses as well as local businesses once the investors have put in the money and the founders have struggled to create a market. This happened with the private Yukos oil company, whose founders, Mikhail Khodorkovsky and Platon Lebedev, were arrested in 2003, allegedly for fraud, tax evasion, and breaking antitrust laws (an irony given that the Russian government now has its own monopoly on gas and oil firms). In 2005 Khodorkovsky was sentenced to nine years in jail, which was later changed on appeal to eight years, but in a Siberian penal colony. In March of 2009 Khodorkovsky and Lebedev were tried on additional charges of embezzlement and money laundering and sentenced in December of 2010 to yet another six years. In December of 2006, the Russian government forced Shell Oil to hand over its stake in the $20 billion Sakhalin-2 project to the government-owned Gazprom after Shell had invested billions of dollars in the oil and gas development project.

In their quest for profits, U.S. companies have decided to ignore these facts or simply write them off as costs of doing business. I am a strong capitalist who believes in the value of business and the virtue of making a profit. It is for this reason, not in spite of it, that I believe many companies are tickling a tiger when doing business in countries that have a poor record of intellectual property protection. Instead, companies should be withholding business until these countries pass and enforce strong IP protection laws.

2.1.4 CRIMINAL OPERATIONS

The fourth reason in the McAfee study refers to cybertheft. Rogue programmers and their criminal operations are growing ever more sophisticated. While the tools for protecting data online are getting better, it is the human factor that remains the single greatest weakness of every online system. When greater numbers of people are involved in creating, operating, and using any online system, the probability of mistakes goes up geometrically. The solution to this problem relies on laws and law enforcement that evolve with the technology and keep up with the amount of cyber crime. The solution also requires better software for creating secure online sites and better software for detecting online security breaches and tracking down the culprits. The first part of the solution requires that frameworks be created to ensure that a system is secure. While there is much work in this area, most tools still give programmers way too much "flexibility" and ability to "be creative." This flexibility and creativity can result in faster, more efficient software. It often also results in more difficult-to-find bugs and security weaknesses. In my opinion, limiting flexibility and creativity in a way that ensures strong security is a good trade-off but one that will require company officers and stakeholders to convince programmers about the serious risks and significant costs of stolen intellectual property.

IS GOOGLING REPLACING PROGRAMMING?

Because we're on the topic of searching the Internet for code, this is a good place to discuss a serious concern of mine regarding the state of computer science education. Over the last ten years or so I've interviewed a number of computer science graduates for employment at my companies. These students came from well-respected universities. All of them had bachelor's degrees in computer science or information science or electrical engineering. Many of them had master's degrees. In the past couple of years I have been hiring at a time when unemployment was high and jobs were scarce, yet I could offer them a decent salary and some security. One thing that most of these recent graduates had in common was that none of them could program competently.

Continues

I found that these graduating students were very adept at finding open source or other third-party code on the Internet that fit a particular need. I would often give assignments to write up a particular algorithm and was seriously impressed with how quickly they were able to find the code online. When I asked them to modify the algorithm in a way that was required for our particular application, they struggled. Once the code was actually written, testing it and debugging it seemed beyond their abilities. One recent hire had never used a debugger but instead used print statements throughout the code. While this was standard practice in my early years of programming, when debuggers were not available, particularly for embedded software, nowadays very sophisticated debuggers exist that allow breaking on complex conditions, viewing call stacks, interactively examining variables, and other things that cannot be replaced with simple print statements.

Even with the use of the debugger, many recent computer science graduates seem unaware of debugging techniques that allow them to narrow in on the problem by using breakpoints to isolate chunks of code or setting break conditions that force certain code paths to be executed.

The art of commenting also seems to have been ignored in most computer science education programs as well as in many companies. An excellent way to write code is to provide a comment for nearly every line of code. While this may seem like overkill, it is actually faster to code this way because there is no need to stop and question whether any particular line of code is important enough to merit its own comment. In my company, our coding standard requires that every routine, no matter how small, have a header comment that describes the functionality of the routine, all input parameters, and the output of the routine and gives any other information that someone using the routine would need. Yet most programmers out of school, and many working in the industry, produce uncommented code that is difficult to understand, difficult to debug, and very difficult to maintain.

When I was in school I felt that a college education should be mostly theory because the practical knowledge could be gained in the field. However, when I entered college I had already been programming for four years and had learned many practical lessons from my own mistakes. I hadn't considered that someone with a bachelor's degree in computer science, much less someone with a master's degree, would not be able to use state-of-the-art debugging tools, would not know many debugging techniques, and would not understand the importance of commenting. Can you imagine a medical program that did not teach how to stitch up a patient after surgery or use the latest CT scanner? University computer science departments need to take a serious look at the skills they are teaching their students. I now require prospective employees, as part of the interview process, to sit down at a computer and write a program that works correctly according to a written specification, is fully commented, and is completely their own code.

PART II
SOFTWARE

> "These hieroglyphics have evidently a meaning. If it is a purely arbitrary one, it may be impossible for us to solve it. If, on the other hand, it is systematic, I have no doubt that we shall get to the bottom of it."
> —Sherlock Holmes in *The Adventure of the Dancing Men*

In this part I describe software and the code that represents the software. Software consists of the instructions that a computer follows to perform a task, whether it is calculating the square root of 2, accepting input from a user, running a hotel elevator system, displaying a Web page, or searching the Internet. The software code typically starts out as source code files, human-readable text files that are turned into machine-readable object code files by programs called "compilers" or "interpreters." Sometimes software starts out as graphical representations of flowcharts and logic functions such as the Unified Modeling Language (UML) diagrams from which human-readable source code files or machine-readable object code files are produced by other programs. In all cases, software is organized into multiple functions that are combined and logically organized into computer programs.

The process of writing computer source code, called "programming," is a difficult task that typically requires years of education or experience. Programming requires significant understanding of complex concepts in mathematics and computer science and a great deal of creativity. There is a huge number of ways, perhaps even an infinite number of ways, to write a computer program to perform any given task. Some ways produce programs that run faster; other ways produce programs that run more reliably; other ways use fewer computer resources such as memory or electrical power. Just as many novels can be easily described as "Boy meets girl, boy and girl fall in love, boy and girl die," there is a big difference in the implementation if the author is Charles Dickens or Stephen King. And just as novels can be copyrighted, computer source code can be copyrighted, which is discussed in a later part of this book.

OBJECTIVES

The objective of this part of the book is to define software in basic terms that are useful for measuring and comparing intellectual property. Another objective is to give the reader a basic understanding of the process of creating a program and how it is turned into something that controls a computer.

INTENDED AUDIENCE

Nontechnical corporate managers will find this part useful for understanding basic software concepts and terminology that will enable them to manage software projects and software engineers and to communicate with them intelligently. *Lawyers* will find this part useful for understanding basic software concepts and terminology that will enable them to work with consultants and expert witnesses on software IP litigation cases and also to allow them to explain these technical concepts to a nontechnical judge or jury.

SOURCE CODE

Computers execute tasks that they are directed to execute by a computer program. A computer program consists of as many as millions of instructions, each instruction causing a fairly small operation such as adding two numbers. The instructions are represented by ones and zeros stored in memory. A single one or zero is called a "bit." Eight bits together are called a "byte."[1] Several bytes are called a "word," though the number of bytes in a word depends on the particular processor that is used to execute the instructions.

To make these instructions easier for a human to create and understand, computer programs can be written using higher-level instructions that look like English.[2] These high-level, English-like instructions are called "source code." For example, consider this instruction:

```
total = (coffee + pastry) * (1 + tax_rate + tip_rate)
```

---

1. In the early days of computing, a byte was not well defined and could refer to a larger or smaller number of bits. For many years, though, the byte has been effectively standardized to mean exactly 8 bits.

2. Throughout this text, unless otherwise explicitly stated, I use source code examples from the C programming language, one of the most popular languages in use today. Other programming languages use similar syntax, though there are differences, and a few programming languages look very different, but the concepts still apply.

The plus (+) symbol means add, just as it does on a calculator or on a store receipt or in an algebraic equation. The asterisk (*) symbol means multiply. The names `total`, `coffee`, `pastry`, `tax_rate`, and `tip_rate` are variables. These names are given to sections of memory in the computer that are used to hold values, in this case numbers. The variable names simply make it easier for humans to understand what is being held in these locations in memory. The parentheses are used to group parts of a calculation together so that the calculations are performed in the correct sequence. The equals (=) symbol is used a little differently from what you may have learned in algebra class. This equals symbol is called an "assignment operator." In this case, the value of the equation to the right of the equals symbol gets calculated. Then this calculated value is assigned to the variable named on the left of the equals symbol. This instruction tells the computer to take the number stored in memory and represented by the variable `coffee`, add the number stored in memory and represented by the variable `pastry`, multiply that quantity by one plus `tax_rate` plus `tip_rate`, and store the result in memory represented by the variable `total`. Similarly, consider this instruction:

`printf``("Hello world!")`

This instruction tells the computer to print the sentence "Hello world!" to the computer screen. In this case, **`printf`** is a function that means "print formatted" and is used for printing text in an easy-to-read format.

3.1 PROGRAMMING LANGUAGES

There are many different programming languages around today and many new ones are being created. Each language has its own advantages and limitations. Some languages are designed to easily create graphical user interfaces. Others are designed to run from a Web page. Some are designed to manipulate strings of text, and others are designed to manipulate large databases of arbitrary data. Some languages are used to create integrated circuits. A list of some common programming languages is given in Table 3.1 along with some notes about each language. This table is not meant to be comprehensive but is meant only to give examples of programming languages and some of their uses.

Table 3.1   Some Example Programming Languages

Language	Notes about the language
BASIC	Stands for "**B**eginner's **A**ll-purpose **S**ymbolic **I**nstruction **C**ode." Created by John George Kemeny and Thomas Eugene Kurtz in 1964 at Dartmouth University to teach computer programming to non-science students.
C	Created by Dennis Ritchie at Bell Labs in 1972, it is one of the most popular programming languages in existence.
C++	Pronounced "C-plus-plus." Created in 1979 by Bjarne Stroustrup at Bell Labs as an object-oriented enhancement of C.
COBOL	Stands for "**Co**mmon **B**usiness **O**riented **L**anguage." One of the earliest high-level programming languages, it was developed in 1959 at a consortium of computer professionals called the Conference on Data Systems Languages (CODASYL). Because of its early use for critical programs on mainframe computers, such as banking and defense, it is said that more lines of COBOL currently execute every day than of any other language, despite the fact that few programs are developed in COBOL anymore.
Fortran	Stands for "**For**mula **tran**slation." Developed at IBM in 1957 by a team led by John W. Backus and used extensively by scientists for performing calculations. It is the oldest high-level programming language in use today, though its use is diminishing.
Java	Developed at Sun Microsystems in 1995 by James Gosling as a language that could be run on a wide variety of computers with different operating systems residing on a common network.
JavaScript	Developed by Brendan Eich of Netscape as a simple language that could be run from a Web browser.
LISP	Stands for "**LIS**t **P**rocessing." Created by Professor John McCarthy in 1958 at the Massachusetts Institute of Technology for artificial intelligence (AI) projects. Rarely used outside of academia.
PHP	Created by Rasmus Lerdorf in 1995 for producing "dynamic" Web pages that have content based on information in a database or input by a user. The code can be embedded in a Web page.
SQL	Stands for "**S**tructured **Q**uery **L**anguage" and is pronounced "sequel." Developed by Donald Chamberlin and Raymond Boyce at IBM in the 1970s, this language is used for manipulating information in a database.
Verilog	Invented in 1983 by Phil Moorby and Prabhu Goel, this language is a hardware description language (HDL) that does not run on a computer but is used to design integrated circuits.
Visual Basic	Created in 1991 by Alan Cooper and enhanced by Microsoft, this language extends BASIC by allowing programmers to draw graphical user interfaces (GUIs) rather than write code for them.

3.2 FUNCTIONS, METHODS, PROCEDURES, ROUTINES, AND SUBROUTINES

As for any large project in any field of endeavor, it makes sense to divide a project into small pieces that are easy to understand, easy to test, and easy to reuse in other projects. In computer programming, these basic building blocks are called "functions." They are also called "methods," "procedures," "routines," and "subroutines." Sometimes these terms have subtle differences. Sometimes certain programming languages or programming methodologies make use of one of these terms and not another. In "object-oriented programming" (OOP) languages, for example, the term "method" is preferred. Sometimes a programmer may prefer one term over another. For our purposes, though, they all represent a small piece of code, typically fewer than 100 lines of code though there is no set rule about the size, that performs some task. Usually a function takes in data, though that's not always necessary. For example, a function can produce an error message on the screen that states, "This program has failed!" Typically a function also outputs data, though a function that simply pauses for a certain amount of time may not have any output. Every function, though, performs some task.

The operation of a small sample function is diagrammed in Figure 3.1. This function, called `PutSortedElement`, puts a string into the correct place in an alphabetically sorted list of strings. A list of alphabetically sorted names is shown, and a new name needs to be put into the function. In Figure 3.1a the name is already in the list. Once that fact is determined, nothing else needs to be done. In Figure 3.1b the name must be inserted into the middle of the list. Each name that goes after the inserted name needs to be bumped down one position in the list to make room for the new name. In Figure 3.1c the name must be inserted into the first position of the list. Each name in the list needs to be bumped down one position in the list and the new name needs to be inserted into the first position. In Figure 3.1d the name must be inserted into the last position of the list. None of the names in the list needs to be changed, and the new name is simply added at the end of the list. A function to insert the name must handle all of these conditions.

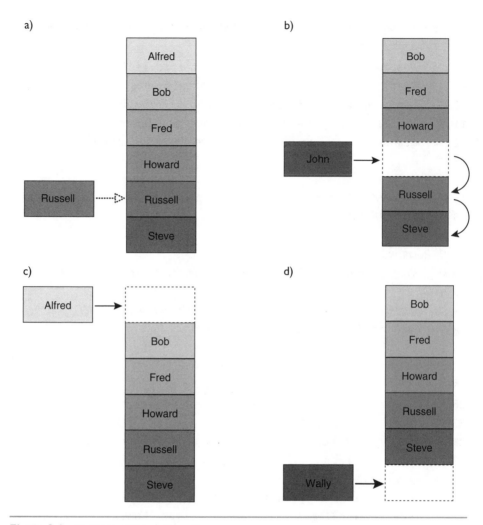

Figure 3.1 `PutSortedElement` routine

Listing 3.1 Source Code for a Small Function that Puts Strings into a Sorted List of Strings

```
1  ///////////////////////////////////////////////////////////////////////
2  //// PutSortedElement
3  //
4  // Purpose
5  //    Puts an element into a sorted list of elements.
6  //
7  // Parameters
```

Continues

Listing 3.1   Source Code for a Small Function that Puts Strings into a Sorted List of Strings
(Continued)

```
 8  //   NewElement      = element to put into list
 9  //   List            = sorted list of elements
10  //   NumElements     = current number of elements in list
11  //   MaxElements     = maximum number of elements in list
12  //   Csense          = case sensitive (true or false)
13  //
14  // Return Value
15  //   SUCCESS if no errors
16  //   not SUCCESS if errors
17  //
18  // Remarks
19  //   This function will not put duplicates into the list.
20  //
21  /////////////////////////////////////////////////////////////////////////
22  int PutSortedElement(char* NewElement,
23                       char* List[],
24                       int*  NumElements,
25                       int   MaxElements,
26                       bool  Csense)
27  {
28      int    CResult;         // Result of string comparison
29      int    Index;           // Index into list of elements
30
31      // Check if the element is already in the list.
32      Index = FindElement(NewElement, List, *NumElements, Csense);
33      if (Index < 0)
34      {
35         // It's not in the list, so put it there.
36
37         // Check that there's another array spot left.
38         if (*NumElements == MaxElements)
39            return(ERROR_TOO_MANY_ELEMENTS);
40
41         for (Index = (*NumElements)-1; Index >= 0; Index--)
42         {
43         if (Csense)
44             CResult = strcmp(NewElement, List[Index]);
```

```
45              else
46                  CResult = stricmp(NewElement, List[Index]);
47
48              if (CResult > 0)
49              {
50                  strcpy(List[Index+1], NewElement);
51                  break;
52              }
53              else
54                  strcpy(List[Index+1], List[Index]);
55          }
56      if (Index == −1)
57              strcpy(List[0], NewElement);
58
59      // Increment the element count.
60      (*NumElements)++;
61      }
62      return (SUCCESS);
63  }
```

The source code for PutSortedElement is shown in Listing 3.1. To give an idea of what source code does and how it is written, I will describe this particular small function in some detail. This is not meant to be a representative sample of all source code or even of particularly common source code. There are many aspects of source code that are not included in this example, but this will give you a good idea of the basic concept.

Lines 1 through 21 are comments that have no actual function but are written by the programmer to give information about the function to other programmers, or to refresh the original programmer's memory if she later forgets what she has written. These "header comments" are not required, but they are strongly recommended because they allow the code to be more easily debugged, tested, improved, and reused. In this example, the header of the function describes the basic purpose of the function, the inputs to the function, the output of the function (the "return value"), and any remarks, including information that is useful or required to better understand and use the function in a program.

Lines 22 through 26 comprise the function's "definition." The term int defines the output from this function as an integer. The name of the function is given as PutSortedElement. The inputs to the function, also known as input "parameters" or "arguments," are the "variables" NewElements, List, NumElements, MaxElements, and Csense. Variables are simply names that are given to data so that they can be identified easily. The data type for each input is given immediately preceding the variable name. For example, NewElements is a "char pointer" represented by char*. This means that NewElements is a "string" consisting of several characters such as the name of a person or a telephone number or any English-language word. The variable List has brackets at the end, meaning that it is a list of strings, also called an "array." The first string in the list would be List[0] (in most computer programming languages, the first element in a list has index 0), followed by List[1], List[2], List[3], and so on, until the end of the list is reached. The variable NumElements is an integer pointer (I won't go into why this is an integer pointer rather than an integer) and is the number of elements in the list. The variable MaxElements is an integer and is the maximum number of elements that can be put into the list. The variable Csense is a "Boolean" variable, meaning that it can have the value of true or false and determines whether we should differentiate between uppercase letters and lowercase letters when we put a new string into the list.

The bracket on line 27 indicates the beginning of the function. Lines 28 and 29 define two variables, CResult and Index, both integers. These variables are called "local variables" because they are defined within the function itself and are therefore "local" to the function. In other words, these variables represent temporary data locations that can be used only within the function. After the computer has executed the function, the data stored in these locations will no longer be accessible, will eventually be overwritten, and will effectively be lost. Also note the comments to the right of each variable definition that start with two slash characters. These comments describe the meaning of the variables.

Line 30 is blank and is just there to make the code easier to read. Line 31 is a comment that describes what the next line is doing. Line 32 is an instruction to execute a "call" of another function called FindElement that determines whether NewElement can be found in List. The FindElement function returns an integer that is placed in the Index variable. The FindElement function is defined somewhere else in the program. Line 33 checks whether Index is a negative number. The FindElement function is designed to return the index in the list where the element has been found or to return a negative number if the element cannot be found in the element list. If the index is negative, the code within the brackets on lines 34 and 61 is executed. If the index is positive, there is no need to put the element in the list because it is already in the list.

Line 35 has a comment that explains what the next lines of code are doing. Line 37 is a comment describing the `if` statement on line 38, which checks whether the number of elements in the list is already equal to the maximum number of elements in the list. Note that the double equals sign (==) is used in many programming languages to show that quantities are being tested for whether they are equal. If the maximum number of elements is already in the list, line 39 is executed where the function ends ("returns") and outputs the value `ERROR_TOO_MANY_ELEMENTS`, which is simply an integer that has already been defined. This integer is called a "constant" because once it is defined, it cannot change. The programmer could have written

return (1237);

but then every time the programmer sees the number 1237, he would have to remember that it is the error code for too many elements in a list. Instead, somewhere in the program is the line

#define ERROR_TOO_MANY_ELEMENTS 1237

which means everywhere the constant `ERROR_TOO_MANY_ELEMENTS` is used, it really represents the number 1237.

At line 41 there is a "loop," which is a section of code that is executed repeatedly until some condition occurs. In this case, the code instructs the computer to start with `Index` equal to 1 less than the number of elements in the list and execute the code between the brackets on lines 42 and 55. Line 41 also tells the computer to subtract 1 from `Index` (the − − operator) each time it completely executes the code between lines 42 and 55, as long as `Index` is greater than or equal to 0. When `Index` is less than 0, the computer exits or "breaks" out of the loop, and the code after the ending bracket on line 55 gets executed.

Lines 43 through 46 instruct the computer to test `NewElement` against the element of `List` determined by `Index`. If `Csense` is true, the program uses the built-in function `strcmp` that compares two strings while considering two strings with different-case letters as different strings. If `Csense` is false, the program uses the built-in function `stricmp` that compares two strings as if they were both lowercase (or both uppercase) strings. These two functions, `strcmp` and `stricmp`, are called "built-in functions" because they are part of the C programming language and are not defined in the program. Both of these functions provide an output that is stored in the variable `CResult`. The way the strcmp and stricmp functions work, if NewElement comes after the element in the list alphabetically, then the output will be 1. If NewElement comes before the element in the list alphabetically, then the output will be −1. If NewElement is identical to the element in the list, then the output will be 0. The test for the value of CResult is done on line 48. If CResult is positive, then NewElement belongs after the current element in the list, and it is placed after the current element by the instruction at line 50. Because the new element has been added to the list, the break instruction at line 51 instructs the computer to exit the loop, even though the loop has not reached its normal end, and begin executing the instruction outside the loop at line 56. If NewElement belongs before the current element in the list, the instruction at line 54 is executed, which moves a copy of the current element up in the list to make room for NewElement, which will eventually be put into the list.

At line 56, Index is tested to see if it equals −1. If so, that means the loop completed without ever finding a place in the list for the new element. In that case, the new element comes before the first element in the list alphabetically, so it is placed in the first spot in the list by the instruction at line 57.

The comment at line 59 describes the line of code at line 60, which increments the number of elements because there is now one more element in the list. At line 62, the constant SUCCESS is returned, which informs any function that called this function that this function completed without any errors.

3.3 FILES

Source code is stored in text files called "source code files" that can be opened, viewed, and modified using a simple text editor, though programmers prefer to use code editors that are smarter than text editors in that they understand the syntax of the language and can show different types of instructions in different colors and automatically cross-reference one part of code to a related part of code. The code in Listing 3.2 is from a code editor, which can typically be set to display the various code elements in unique fonts and colors. For example, it can be set to display comments in green, programming language keywords and symbols in bold blue, and function names in bold black. Although the files are simple text files, the code editor understands the programming language well enough to colorize the terms to make the code easier to read and understand, even when skimmed quickly.

Typically, one file contains one function or one set of closely related functions. There is no rule requiring this; it is just good programming practice. In object-oriented programming, a file may contain a single "class" that contains related data and functions.

There are often special source code files called "header files" or "include files" because they are explicitly included in other source code files. These header files contain definitions of variables and constants that are used throughout the other source code files. Typically header files contain no functional code, though they include "declarations" of routines that specify the type of data input to the routines and the type of data output from the routines. When one source code file needs to call a routine in another file or use a constant or variable that has been defined in another file, that source code file will explicitly ask for a header file to be included, for example:

```
#include "header_file.h"
```

This has the same result as if the contents of the source code file `header_file.h` were copied directly into the source code at the point where the `#include` statement is located. An example header file is shown in Listing 3.2. Again, it is useful to describe the source code in this example to give a flavor of what it is doing and how source code is written.

Line 1 is a comment that describes the contents of the file. Lines 4 through 13 define constants. Throughout the program, any time the constant `MAX_KEYWORDS` is used, for example, the result is the same as using the number 5,000. Similarly, the string `"zconsult.dll"` is effectively replaced in the code at all places where the constant `DLL_NAME` appears. You might wonder why this is done. Why use a name instead of a number? Suppose the program is designed to handle 5,000 keywords and many routines require this information, for example, to allocate memory for all 5,000 keywords or to know when to stop counting keywords. The programmer could use the number 5,000 in all of these cases. Now suppose the program is upgraded to handle 10,000 keywords. A programmer would have to search the code for all instances of the number 5,000 and change it to 10,000. Complicating matters, notice that the maximum number of special characters is also 5,000, and suppose that does not change in the upgraded version of the program. In this case, the programmer would need to evaluate each instance of the number 5,000 in the code to determine what it represents and whether to change it. This would require an in-depth understanding of the entire code and a time-consuming search-examine-replace process that is prone to errors. Setting the constant MAX_KEYWORDS to 5,000 in a single header file, then changing it to 10,000 in that one header file for the new, upgraded version, ensures that the correct value is used wherever the constant MAX_KEYWORDS is found within the code.

Listing 3.2   Source Code Header File

```
1  // zconsult.h : main header file for the zconsult DLL
2
3  // Constants
4  #define DLL_NAME          "zconsult.dll"   // Name of this DLL
5  #define GRAPHICS_FOLDER   "graphics"       // Name of folder
6  #define BITMATCH_VERSION  "1.0.1"          // BitMatch version
7  #define CODECROSS_VERSION "1.1.0"          // CodeCross version
8  #define CODEDIFF_VERSION  "4.0.0"          // CodeDiff version
9  #define CODEMATCH_VERSION "5.3.1"          // CodeMatch version
10
11 #define MAX_KEYWORDS      5000  // Maximum number of keywords
12 #define MAX_ESCAPE_CHARS  4     // Max number of escape chars
13 #define MAX_SPECIAL_CHARS 5000  // Max no. of special chars
14
15 enum ELEMENT_TYPE               // Enumerate element types
16 {
17      STATEMENT_ELEMENT,          // Examining statements
18      COMMENT_ELEMENT,            // Examining comments
19      IDENTIFIER_ELEMENT          // Examining identifiers
20 };
21
22 // User-defined structures
23 struct CS_DirInfo               // Info about a directory
24 {
25      char*   DirName;            // Directory name
26      long    FileSize;           // Total size of files compared
27      long    FileNumber;         // Total number of files
28      char*   FileTypes;          // String of types to search
29 };
30
31 // Routine declarations
32 long     AddToSortedLists(long, int[], long[], bool);
```

```
33 void      AlphaNum(char*);
34 double    CompareByIdentifier(FILE*, char**, long);
35 int       CompareStrings(char*, char*, char*, bool);
36 float     ComputeScore(char*, float, float);
37 long      FindUnsortedLine(char*, char*[], long, bool);
38 char*     GetErrorMessage(int, char*);
39 void      PrintHTML(FILE*, char*);
40 int       round(double);
```

Lines 15 through 20 define an enumeration, which means a simple way of defining a sequence of constants. Using an enumerator, the constant STATEMENT_ELEMENT is given a value of 0, the constant COMMENT_ELEMENT is given a value of 1, and the constant IDENTIFIER_ELEMENT is given a value of 2.

Lines 23 through 29 define a data structure. When the code uses the structure CS_DirInfo, that always refers to four data elements that belong together— DirName, FileSize, FileNumber, and FileTypes.

Lines 32 through 40 are called "function declarations" or "prototypes." These declarations show how each routine in the program accepts data as inputs, what kind of data it accepts, and what kind of values are output from the routine. This kind of data is used as a form of error checking. If the programmer writes code that uses a routine in the wrong way—some way that does not match its declaration—then an error is detected. Either the declaration is wrong or, more likely, the code that uses the routine is wrong.

There are no requirements for header files; they are just good programming practice for organizing the source code, though some languages, such as Java, do not allow header files. Some automatic code generation programs, such as Microsoft Visual Studio, that can automatically generate code to create the screens, icons, drop-down lists, and so forth that are used in user interfaces generate their code in header files. Though this violates good programming practice, it is likely done simply to differentiate the human-generated source code from the software-generated source code.

3.4 PROGRAMS

Programs consist of one or many functions in one or many files that get executed by the computer to perform various tasks. A program may be a simple "utility program," such as a mortgage rate calculator embedded in a Web page where the user enters the amount of a loan, an interest rate, and a number of years and the program calculates the monthly payment. Such a program may be produced from a single file consisting of a dozen lines of source code. Or a program can be one that runs a search engine and is produced from millions of lines of source code in thousands of files and runs on a fast, specialized computer called a Web server that can handle many transactions at once.

3.5 EXECUTING SOURCE CODE

Somehow the human-readable code has to be converted into something that a computer processor can understand to control input and output devices and to perform calculations. The various tools for the conversion include compilers, interpreters, virtual machines, and synthesizers.

3.5.1 COMPILERS

For most computer programs, the source code gets changed into many logical ones and zeros that represent very basic instructions for the computer, also known as "machine language." The process of translating source code into this simple binary code is called "compiling" and is performed by a program called a "compiler." The computer can then directly execute these simple instructions. These very low-level instructions are called "object code," "binary code," or "executable code," described further in Chapter 4.

3.5.2 INTERPRETERS

Some programs are run directly from the source code by another program that interprets the source code. The programs that interpret the source code are known, not surprisingly, as "interpreters." Rather than convert the source code to binary object files, each line of source code is interpreted and the computer is instructed by the interpreter program. In a sense, the source code is still being turned into binary instructions for the computer, but in an indirect way. Source code that is interpreted is sometimes called a "script" rather than a program, especially if it is written in a simple, limited-functionality language called a "scripting language." Scripts and interpreters are discussed in more detail in Chapter 5.

3.5.3 VIRTUAL MACHINES

Another way to execute a program involves a compiler and an interpreter for a "virtual machine." The program source code is turned into intermediate code that can be run on a virtual machine, which is not a physical machine but a hypothetical computer that executes a well-defined set of instructions that make up the intermediate code instructions. In this way, code can be written and executed on many different kinds of computer hardware because the virtual machine compiler translates the source code into intermediate code for the virtual machine, and the virtual machine interpreter then can execute the code. Interpreted code and virtual machines are described further in Chapter 5.

3.5.4 SYNTHESIZERS

A relatively new process is software synthesis. With software synthesis a programmer writes code in a normal programming language but includes special statements called "primitives" that look like function calls but really represent complex operations. A program called a "synthesizer" goes through the source code and replaces all of the primitives with the appropriate set of programming language instructions. If the program is written in the C programming language plus primitives, the output is pure C programming language source code. Primitives and synthesis are discussed further in Chapter 5.

OBJECT CODE AND ASSEMBLY CODE

The computer processor, the brains of the computer, requires sequences of ones and zeros that represent very basic commands to control input and output devices and to perform calculations. The raw sequences of ones and zeros are called "object code." The mnemonics that are used to make these low-level instructions somewhat readable to humans constitute "assembly code." These kinds of code are described in more detail in this chapter.

4.1 OBJECT CODE

For most computer programs, the source code gets changed into many logical ones and zeros that represent very basic instructions for the computer, also known as "machine language." One such instruction may be to add two integers. Another such instruction may be to load data from memory into the microprocessor's internal register or to display a single character on the computer screen. A single line of human-readable source code may end up being translated into tens or hundreds of these simple binary instructions. The process of translating source code into this simple binary code is called "compiling" and is performed by a program called a "compiler." The computer can then directly execute these simple instructions. These very low-level instructions are called "object code," "binary code," or "executable code." Not all source code is compiled to create a program; source code can also be interpreted, as described in the next chapter.

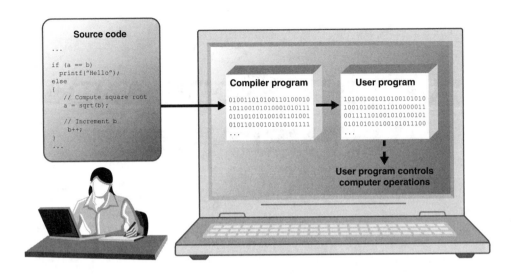

Figure 4.1   Compiler diagram

A diagram of how a compiler works is shown in Figure 4.1. A programmer types source code to create a program. The source code files are input to a compiler program running on a computer. The output from the compiler program is another program called the "user program" that performs the functions specified by the source code. When the user program is run on the computer, the user program controls the computer. A compiler can take a long time to produce an optimized user program. The compiler can look at the entire program to decide which functions can be optimized for high speed or small memory usage or small file size, though usually there is a trade-off such that optimizing for one results in less-than-optimal code for the others.

The kind of binary code that is produced by the compiler is called "native code" because it is created to run directly only on the type of processor for which the compiler is designed. In order for this program to run on a different processor, the original source code would have to be recompiled into a binary format that is understood by that processor. A compiler that runs on one computer but creates native code for another computer is called a "cross compiler."

4.2 ASSEMBLY CODE

Before the advent of high-level programming languages and compilers, code was entered into a computer in the raw form of bytes. Physical switches on the front of the computer were toggled, each switch representing a one or a zero, and when an entire word was ready, another switch was pressed to enter that word into the computer's memory. In the 1950s, assembly code was developed, which is a way of representing these binary numbers using mnemonics that describe their functionality. The code written using these mnemonics is called "assembly code." One high-level source code statement corresponds to multiple computer instructions. One line of assembly code generally corresponds to exactly one computer instruction, though assembly code has gotten more sophisticated over the years. For example, commonly used sequences of code may be placed in a single-line "macro" that may be used throughout the program whenever that sequence of assembly code is needed.

It is rare for programmers to write in assembly code anymore. Some years ago, for example, in the early days of the personal computer, programmers needed to fit programs into the tiny memories of the machines,[1] and so they wrote assembly code and tweaked it until it fit in the limited memory space. Now computers generally have much more memory and compilers are much better at shrinking code than people are. Some programmers who write code for embedded systems still write some code in assembly language. Embedded systems are hardware systems that have computers designed into them for controlling the system, but the user is unaware of the computer. The software in an embedded system is fixed at the time the product is shipped and can be changed only by a company representative using appropriate tools. An example of an embedded system is a computer-controlled electronic thermostat. A programmer might write some code for such a system in assembly language in order to conserve memory and therefore reduce the cost of the device. Or a programmer might write in assembly code when the timing of an operation must meet certain strict requirements, as in the case of a pacemaker or other critical medical device.

Listing 4.1 Source Code for a Small Routine that Examines Registers and Displays their Values

```
1   ;******************************************************************
2   ;*  TS1_TEST
3   ;*
4   ;*  Purpose
5   ;*  Perform tests on internal processor registers.
6   ;*
```

Continues

---

1. The first IBM PC came equipped with 16 kilobytes of memory, expandable to 256 kilobytes. This compares to today's machines that have gigabytes, more than 1 million times the amount of those original machines.

Listing 4.1 Source Code for a Small Routine that Examines Registers and Displays their Values (Continued)

```
7  ;**************************************************************
8  .MODEL large
9  .486P              ; uses Use16 attribute because .MODEL is first
10
11 ;**************************************************************
12 ;*           Include definitions, constants, macros
13 ;**************************************************************
14 INCLUDE defs.inc
15
16 ;**************************************************************
17 ;*               Public variables
18 ;**************************************************************
19 PUBLIC     TS1_TEST
20
21 TS1_TEST:
22     ; Display the value of the AC bit
23     CALL_BY_GATE0 GATE_GET_EFLAGS      ; get the value of EFLAGS
24     and     eax, AC_BIT                ; Get the value of AC bit
25     jnz     LAB1
26     DISPLAY_PM    MSG_AC0              ; Display message AC = 0
27     jmp     LAB2
28 LAB1: DISPLAY_PM MSG_AC1               ; Display message AC = 1
29 LAB2:
30     iretd                              ; return from task
```

The source code for an assembly routing called TS1_TEST is shown in Listing 4.1, written in the MASM language created by Microsoft for use on Intel processors. To give an idea of what assembly code does and how it is written, I will describe this small routine in some detail. This is not meant to be a representative sample of all assembly code or even a representative of particularly common source code. There are many aspects of assembly code that are not included in this example, but this will give you a good idea of the basic concepts.

Lines 1 through 7 are comments that describe the functionality of the routine. In MASM, comments begin with a semicolon character and continue until the end of the line. Line 8 defines the memory model to be used. Line 9 defines the processor that will be running this program. Various processors access memory in different ways, and the assembler needs to know which process is being used and how the processor running the code will access memory.

Line 10 is blank and is used for easier reading of the code. Lines 11 through 13 are comments. Line 14 signals to include code in another file, defs.inc, at this point in the file. This file includes code that defines constants and macros that are used throughout the program.

Line 19 declares that the TS1_TEST routine can be accessed by other routines, and line 21 is the beginning of the TS1_TEST routine.

Line 23 calls routine ***CALL_BY_GATE0***, which is used to get the value of a register inside the processor. The parameters of the routine are defined by the constant GATE_GET_EFLAGS. A register in a processor is a very small memory, as small as a byte, that is used to store information about the state of the processor. These registers can contain information that, if modified, can cause the program being run to fail. Similarly, reading some registers can cause security breaches. Because of this the methods of reading these bits often require complex routines.

Line 24 performs a logical "AND" operation between the contents in the *eax* register and a constant called AC_BIT that masks everything except a single bit in the register. Line 25 tests the result of the AND operation with a "jump not zero" instruction. If the result of the operation is not zero, execution continues at line 28, which has the label LAB1, where a message is displayed to the user that the AC bit is equal to 1. Otherwise, line 26 is executed, where a message is displayed to the user that the AC bit is equal to 0, and then a jump instruction is executed so that in both cases, program execution continues at line 29, which has the label LAB2.

Line 30 has a return instruction that signals the processor to resume execution at the point after this routine was called in the program.

4.3 FILES

As part of the compilation process, object code files are created. There is not a one-to-one mapping of source code files to object code files. It may be the case that each source code file is compiled into a single object code file. More commonly, multiple source code files are compiled into a smaller number of object code files. Often all of the source code files of a program are compiled into a single object code file called an "executable file" because it is this file that is executed by the computer to run the program.

4.4 PROGRAMS

In modern software systems, though, multiple executable files are usually needed to run a program, though one file is the main executable file that is run to start execution of the program. Most modern programs need to call functions in other executable files. For example, in the Microsoft Windows operating system there are "dynamic link libraries" or "DLLs" that contain functions such as those needed to create a dialog box that asks a user which file to open. Each programmer could create such a dialog box for her own program, but then each program would have a distinct look and feel that might be confusing to users and would require them to learn different ways to open files when running each program. Instead, because a common library of these kinds of functions is provided, each program has a consistent look and feel, and when users understand basic operations of one program, they do not need to relearn those operations for every other program running on the same operating system.

Scripts, Intermediate Code, Macros, and Synthesis Primitives

Scripts are source code programs that are interpreted rather than compiled. Intermediate code is code that is human-readable like source code but is simple and intended to be interpreted rather than compiled into object code. Macros consist of one or a few user-defined source code statements that represent large sets of source code instructions and are used for convenience by programmers. Synthesis primitives are simple statements representing high-level functionality that get translated in a non-fixed manner that is dependent on how the primitives are used in the program. These kinds of code are described in more detail in this chapter.

5.1 Scripts

Some programs are run directly from the source code by another program that interprets the source code. The programs that interpret the source code are known, not surprisingly, as "interpreters." Rather than converting the source code to binary object files, each line of source code is interpreted, and the interpreter program tells the computer what to do. In a sense, the source code is still being turned into binary instructions for the computer, but in an indirect way.

A diagram of how an interpreter works is shown in Figure 5.1. A programmer writes source code to create a program. The source code files are input to an

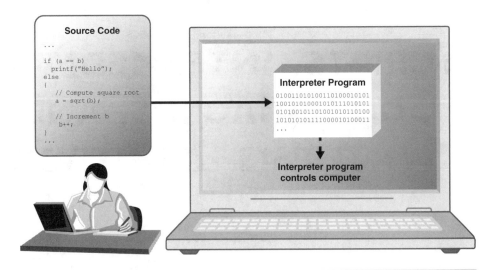

Figure 5.1 Interpreter diagram

interpreter program running on a computer. When the interpreter is directed to run the user program, each line of source code is interpreted, but it is still the interpreter program that runs on the computer and directly controls it. The BASIC programming language is one well-known example of an interpreted language. Many interpreted languages are very simple, performing only limited functionality. These simple programming languages are called "scripting languages" and the programs are called "scripts." Examples of scripting languages include JavaScript (not to be confused with the programming language Java), which is run from client-side Web pages. JavaScript performs manipulations of the page elements based on the user's mouse and keyboard actions and communicates simple strings over the Internet to the Web server that serves the Web pages to the user. Perl and Python are more recent scripting languages that run on Web servers and are used to manipulate Web pages before being sent to users and also for more complex communications between the Web client and Web server.

An interpreter cannot optimize the source code as well as a compiler because it does not know what code is being used in other parts of the program, only the code that has already been run and the code it is currently interpreting. Interpreted programs always run slower than equivalent compiled programs because the interpreter always has the extra step of parsing and understanding the source code before it can direct the operation of the computer. However, if interpreters are available that run on different processors, the same source code program can be run on all of these processors without change, because it is the interpreter that handles the differences between the processors. That is why Web servers typically use interpreters to run programs—there are many different processors on different computers distributed throughout the Internet, and it would be difficult to compile every program once for each processor available. It is more efficient to create interpreters for every possible machine and to run each user program using an interpreter.

5.2 INTERMEDIATE CODE

Some systems combine compiling and interpreting by first compiling source code into intermediate code consisting of simple instructions that are not native to any particular processor, as illustrated in Figure 5.2. Another way of stating this is that the instructions are native to a "virtual machine" that does not really exist as a piece of hardware. For each real processor, a virtual machine interpreter must exist to read each instruction and interpret it for the real processor. This combination of compiling and interpreting keeps many of the advantages of both systems. The compiling process allows the code for the entire program to be optimized. The interpreting process allows one program to be run on many different kinds of machines. The Java programming language is implemented using this combination of interpreting and compiling. The intermediate code produced during compilation of Java source code is called "bytecode."

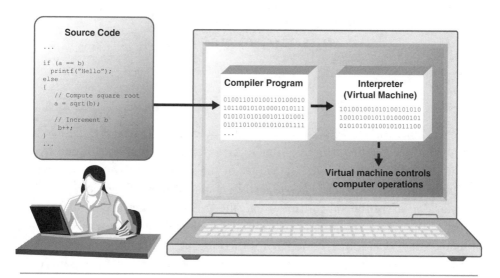

Figure 5.2 Compiler/interpreter diagram

5.3 MACROS

Macros consist of one or a few lines of source code that are defined by the user for convenience. If several lines of source code are commonly used together, the programmer can define a macro such that each time that macro is used, the compiler knows to substitute the appropriate lines of code. Listing 5.1 gives an example of a definition of a macro called EndCompare. Whenever the statement EndCompare is used in the source code, the programming statements shown on lines 2 through 13 are substituted. In addition, whatever argument is supplied to the routine is substituted for the placeholder argument SV in the macro. The backslashes at the end of lines are called "continuation characters." They signal that the macro is defined on several lines. The first line names the macro. Lines 2 through 13 are the macro definition. The macro ends at line 13 because there is no continuation character at the end of that line.

Listing 5.1 A Macro Consisting of Several Lines of Source Code

```
1   #define EndCompare(SV)                                  \
2       {                                                   \
3           RemoveDir(TemporaryDir);                        \
4           StatusValue = SV;                               \
5           ComparisonRunning = FALSE;                      \
6           if (UpdateStatus)                               \
7           {                                               \
8               if (StatusTextHandle)                       \
9                   SendMessage(StatusTextHandle,           \
10                      WM_SETTEXT, 0, (LPARAM)"Done");      \
11          }                                               \
12          return;                                         \
13      }
```

You might wonder why a programmer would use a macro rather than a subroutine. A subroutine requires many operations that are hidden from the programmer to occur. The values of the subroutine arguments are "pushed onto the stack" (i.e., placed in a special part of memory called a "stack") before the subroutine is executed. These values are then "popped off of the stack" (i.e., read back from the stack memory) when the subroutine ends. Other operations to prepare for the subroutine execution can also take place. These operations take extra time and thus slow down a program if a subroutine is used many times. A macro is just a shortcut for writing the same code many times throughout the program; no extra operations take place. However, regardless of how many times a subroutine is called throughout a program, the code for the routine exists in only one place in memory and the processor executing the program jumps to that place each time the routine is executed. If a macro is used 1,000 times within the program, then 1,000 copies of that code exist, which can be difficult to debug, can use up significant amounts of disk space, and can require code to be repeatedly swapped in and out of memory, which can also slow down performance.

5.4 SYNTHESIS PRIMITIVES

Synthesis is the process of turning a high-level description into a lower-level description that, in the case of software, can be compiled or interpreted directly. By working at a higher level, the programmer is kept uninvolved with implementation details. Synthesis involves automatic code generation (ACG) but there is more to it than that. Some very popular and useful code generation tools already exist. Microsoft Visual Studio and HTML layout tools like Macromedia Dreamweaver allow users to create graphics and buttons with little or no knowledge of the underlying code. These kinds of ACG tools are indispensable for creating a user interface.

The concept of software synthesis is derived from that of hardware synthesis. With hardware synthesis a programmer writes a description in a high-level language such as Verilog or VHDL, and the hardware synthesis tool creates a low-level description that is still in Verilog or VHDL. Similarly, with software synthesis the programmer writes code in a high-level language like C using high-level primitives that look like function calls but really represent complex functionality. For example, primitives may represent operating system interfaces like thread creation and destruction, message-passing mechanisms, and mutexes and semaphores. The output code, after synthesis, is still in the original programming language, but the synthesis tool handles all of the implementation details.

Figure 5.3 is a graphic representation of the process of software synthesis. The programmer writes a program consisting of source code, as usual, plus high-level primitives that represent complex functions. The programmer also creates a configuration file that controls the synthesis tool. The configuration file may specify the particular computer processor being used, or it may be related directly to the application being created. For example, if the user is creating a self-contained embedded system, the configuration file may specify the operating

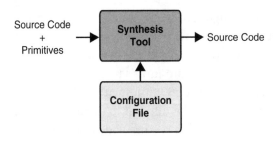

Figure 5.3 Synthesis diagram

system scheduling algorithm and the priorities of the various tasks being controlled by the operating system.

Listing 5.2 shows a sample section of source code that includes a primitive on line 12. In this case the primitive is SynthOS_call, which looks like a simple function call. The resulting source code after synthesis is shown in Listing 5.3, where line 12 has been replaced by lines 12 through 25.

Listing 5.2 Source Code with Primitives

```
1  for (i = 0; i < maxCount; i++)
2  {
3      // Check whether the task completed.
4      if (taskDone)
5          break;
6
7      // Wait 1 second (1,000 milliseconds).
8      sleep(1000);
9  }
10
11 // Blink the LED to signal that the task completed.
12 SynthOS_call(taskLed(g_input, irotation));
13
14 Increment the counter
15 count++;
```

Listing 5.3 Synthesized Code without Primitives

```
1  for (i = 0; i < maxCount; i++)
2  {
3      // Check whether the task completed.
```

```
4      if (taskDone)
5          break;
6
7      // Wait 1 second (1,000 milliseconds).
8      sleep(1000);
9  }
10
11 // Blink the LED to signal that the task completed.
12 // SynthOS: begin generated code.
13 // original statement: SynthOS_call(taskLed(g_input , irotation));
14 // Create a new TCB.
15 {
16     struct SYNTHOS_TCB *stcpNewTcb;
17     stcpNewTcb = getFreeTcb( g_stcpTcbQ__taskLed );
18     ASSERT (stcpNewTcb != NULL); // make sure we get a free TCB
19     stcpNewTcb->u32TaskState = 1;
20     stcpNewTcb->pTaskId = NULL;
21     stcpNewTcb->u32Params[0] = g_input;
22     stcpNewTcb->u32Params[1] = irotation;
23      (taskLed__type *)stcpNewTcb->u32pReturnVal = &taskLed__dummy;
24 }
25 // SynthOS: end generated code.
26
27 Increment the counter
28 count++;
```

Another name used for synthesis primitives is "context-dependent macros."
Macros are always transformed into the same set of source code statements,
regardless of where they are placed in the program or what function the
program performs. Synthesis primitives are transformed in a more complex
manner that depends on context, including such factors as the configuration
file settings and the number and types of primitives in the program as well
as the relationships between the sections of code in which the primitives are
embedded.

PART III
INTELLECTUAL PROPERTY

"Life is infinitely stranger than anything which the mind of man could invent."
—Sherlock Holmes in *A Case of Identity*

Property rights are essential to any capitalistic society and are recognized by most societies in existence today. When we think of property, we typically think of land, though we may also think of other physical goods that are owned, bought, sold, and traded such as homes, automobiles, jewelry, and household appliances. Intellectual property (IP) refers to property that is abstract rather than physical. Specifically, it refers to anything created by the human mind. This includes music compositions, novels, movies, works of art, inventions, and of course software.

While the concept of physical property rights goes back as far as human history, intellectual property is not a completely new idea. The origins of intellectual property law are a bit tangled and difficult to pin down. One early legal IP ruling occurred about 500 BC in the Greek colony of Sybaris, a city that was well known for its prosperity and opulence. The Sybarites made a law that when a chef created a particularly superb dish, no one else could make that dish for one year so that the chef could profit from his creation and to encourage others to create and share their delicacies.

The first documented use of the term "intellectual property" is from the 1818 collection of writings by Benjamin Constant, the French liberal theorist, who actually argues against the concept:

> However, the property which is called intellectual is only a matter of opinion. If it is permitted to anyone to assign it to himself, all will no doubt claim it, since political rights will become not only a social prerogative, but also an attestation of talent, and to deny them to oneself would indeed be a rare act both of disinterestedness and of modesty. If it is the opinion of others which must confer this *intellectual property*, this opinion manifests itself only by the success and fortune which are its necessary outcome. Property will be the natural lot of every kind of distinguished man.

Constant was writing shortly after the French Revolution. Although the French Revolution is often credited with creating the modern concept of intellectual property rights, it was actually concerned with spreading the products of intellectual endeavors rather than limiting them. Before the revolution, publishing books and other works that challenged royal authority or disturbed the "tranquility of the state" was an act punishable by death. Fully 35 to 40 percent of those imprisoned in the famous Bastille of Paris had been sentenced for crimes related to the book trade. With the French Revolution and the Declaration of the Rights of Man in 1789, printers no longer had to obtain permission from the king.

One early codification of the modern-day concept of intellectual property rights came from the United States Constitution in 1787. The founding fathers believed that intellectual property rights were among the most basic, fundamental rights of men and that their protection would allow innovation and prosperity for the young, new nation. These rights were not an afterthought, not an amendment like the Bill of Rights, but central to the Constitution in Article I, Section 8:

> Congress shall have power … To promote the progress of science and useful arts, by securing for limited times to authors and inventors the exclusive right to their respective writings and discoveries.

In general, modern intellectual property can be divided into four categories: trademarks and service marks, copyrights, trade secrets, and patents. The owners of these creations are entitled to certain exclusive rights, and intellectual property law is intended to enforce these rights.

The Cornell University Legal Information Institute defines a trademark as follows:

> A trademark is any word, name, symbol, or design, or any combination thereof, used in commerce to identify and distinguish the goods of one manufacturer or seller from those of another and to indicate the source of the goods.

In other words, a trademark is used by a manufacturer to identify its products and differentiate them from the products of other manufacturers. Service marks are identical to trademarks except that they identify services rather than products. The product may be a software product, and there have been lawsuits involving software trademarks, for example the 1997 lawsuit between Sun Microsystems and Microsoft involving the Java trademark. However, trademark issues involve product branding, and branding software is not much different from branding other products. It typically does not involve the internal workings of the software, other than the fact that the source code may have branding information inside it. For this reason trademarks will not be discussed in this book. The other three categories of intellectual property—copyrights, trade secrets, and patents—will be discussed in the following chapters.

OBJECTIVES

The objective of this part is to define in basic terms those forms of intellectual property that are relevant to software and to explain their similarities, differences, and uses.

INTENDED AUDIENCE

Computer scientists, computer programmers, corporate managers, and *software entrepreneurs* will find this part of the book useful for understanding basic concepts of intellectual property law and how it can be used to protect their software. *Technical consultants and expert witnesses for litigation* will find this part useful for understanding intellectual property issues in order to analyze software for intellectual property misappropriation and infringement, and to understand the issues that will come up in a lawsuit that they may need to opine about in an expert report, deposition, and trial. *Lawyers whose practice is not intellectual property* will also find this part interesting and useful for understanding the basics of intellectual property law as it relates to software.

COPYRIGHTS

6.1 THE HISTORY OF COPYRIGHTS

The invention of the printing press by Johannes Gutenberg in Germany around 1440 made it possible for written works to be copied on a large scale. Initially, there was no problem with unauthorized copying, because there was a limited number of printers and they were well known to one another. In England, the first government regulation of printing was not to prevent unauthorized copying but to prevent publication of works critical of the Crown. In 1557 a royal charter for exclusive publishing rights was given to the Worshipful Company of Stationers of London, a group of printers. Every printer who was a member of the group had to register the work to be printed with the Stationers' Company. Registration gave the printer the exclusive perpetual right to publish the work after it was purchased from the author.

The copyright's origins can also possibly be traced to seventeenth-century Jewish law. The prayers in Jewish prayer books had been in existence for centuries and in some cases millennia by that time and thus would be considered, in modern terms, to be "in the public domain" and not protectable. In other words, the original author or authors no longer had any claim to the material. Rabbinic laws were enacted, however, to protect the publisher of a prayer book, not the author. Competition among publishers for such a small market, it was felt, could cause the publishers to go out of business and make these important prayer books unavailable. Thus the publishers were granted IP rights in the form of limited monopolies, though there was much debate as to the time period for the IP right (3 to 25 years), the owner of the IP right (printer or purchaser), and the geographical extent of the IP right (printer's country or worldwide).

The author had no rights after the initial purchase, was not given royalties, and was not allowed to join the group simply to self-publish, so these two examples of exclusive rights were unlike the modern copyright, which initially gives the rights to the author of the work, not the publisher. However, by the late 1600s, independent printers began to compete with the Stationers, who asked the British Parliament for legislation to curtail competition. In March of 1710,[1] Parliament passed "An act for the encouragement of learning, by vesting the copies of printed books in the authors or purchasers of such copies, during the times therein mentioned." The Statute of Anne, named for Queen Anne during whose reign it was enacted, was the first copyright law of the Kingdom of Great Britain (see Figure 6.1).

Stationers were not happy with the Statute of Anne for a number of reasons. Rather than providing perpetual rights to a work, the law granted protection for new works for 14 years from the date of publication and allowed authors to renew the protection for another 14 years if they were alive at the end of the initial protection period. Existing works were protected for 21 years from the effective date of the law. More important, this protection was granted not to the publisher but to the author. Publishers could print a book only if given the authority by its author. One thing the Stationers got, though, was the requirement of registration with the Stationers' Company before publication to prevent publication without authorization. So the Statute of Anne created the modern concept of copyright protection and also of copyright registration.

The first Copyright Act in the United States was passed in 1790 and protected only "maps, charts and books." Subsequently, Copyright Acts were passed in 1909 and 1976 as well as the International Copyright Act of 1891 and the Digital Millennium Copyright Act (DMCA) in 1998. These copyright acts, as well as Copyright Office interpretations and judicial decisions regarding copyrights, have broadened the scope of creative works that are protected by U.S. copyright law. Today federal copyright law protects almost all types of creative works that meet the criteria of "original works of authorship fixed in

---

1. The date on the statute indicates that it was passed in March 1709. At that time, March 25 was considered the first day of the calendar year. Beginning in 1752, the formal New Year was moved back to January 1; dates in the early months of prior years were by convention identified as if they fell under the new calendar. So March 1709 became March 1710.

(261)

Anno Octavo

Annæ Reginæ.

An Act for the Encouragement of Learning, by Vesting the Copies of Printed Books in the Authors or Purchasers of such Copies, during the Times therein mentioned.

Whereas Printers, Booksellers, and other Persons have of late frequently taken the Liberty of Printing, Reprinting, and Publishing, or causing to be Printed, Reprinted, and Published Books, and other Writings, without the Consent of the Authors or Proprietors of such Books and Writings, to their very great Detriment, and too often to the Ruin of them and their Families : For Preventing therefore such Practices for the future, and for the Encouragement of Learned Men to Compose and Write useful Books ; May it please Your Majesty, that it may be Enacted, and be it Enacted by the Queens most Excellent Majesty, by and with the Advice and Consent of the Lords Spiritual and Temporal, and Commons in this present Parliament Assembled, and by the Authority of the same, That from and after the Tenth Day of April, One thousand seven hundred and ten, the Author of any Book or Books already Printed, who hath not Transferred to any other the Copy or Copies of such Book or Books, Share or Shares thereof, or the Bookseller or Booksellers, Printer or Printers, or other Person or Persons, who hath or have Purchased or Acquired the Copy or Copies of any Book or Books, in order to Print or Reprint the same, shall have the sole Right and Liberty of Printing such Book and Books for the Term of One and twenty Years, to Commence from the said Tenth Day of April, and no longer ; and that the Author of any Book or Books already Composed and not Printed and Published, or that shall hereafter be Composed, and his Assignee, or Assigns, shall have the sole Liberty of Printing and Reprinting such Book and Books for the Term of Fourteen

. 6   Ttt 2   teen

Figure 6.1   The first page of the six-page Statute of Anne (from the British Library)

any tangible medium of expression, now known or later developed, from which they can be perceived, reproduced, or otherwise communicated, either directly or with the aid of a machine or device."

Obviously this includes software, but the Computer Software Copyright Act of 1980 amended the Copyright Act of 1976 to specifically address aspects of software copyright. Three aspects are particularly interesting. First, it defined a computer program as a "set of statements or instructions to be used directly or indirectly in a computer in order to bring about a certain result." Second, it allowed small sections of computer programs to be submitted for registration to protect trade secrets within the code. Third, it allowed copying in certain circumstances that are specific to computer programs. For example, when a program is loaded onto a hard drive in order to be run, technically a copy is being made. Similarly, when a program is run, copies of sections of code are loaded into memory. These copies are allowable. Another set of circumstances is making temporary copies while a computer is being repaired. A third set of circumstances involves selling, leasing, or transferring the software. A fourth allowable circumstance for software copying is making backup copies.

6.2 COPYRIGHT PROTECTIONS

The World Intellectual Property Organization (WIPO) defines a copyright simply as follows:

> Copyright is a legal term describing rights given to creators for their literary and artistic works (including computer software).

Each government that recognizes intellectual property rights gives similar but slightly different copyright protections. In the United States, the protections given to copyrighted works are as follows, according to Circular 1, *Copyright Basics,* published by the U.S. Copyright Office:

> Copyright is a form of protection provided by the laws of the United States (title 17, U.S. Code) to the authors of "original works of authorship," including literary, dramatic, musical, artistic, and certain other intellectual works. This protection is available to both **published** and **unpublished** works. Section 106 of the 1976 Copyright Act generally gives the owner of copyright the **exclusive right** to do and to authorize others to do the following:
>
> - To **reproduce** the work in copies or phonorecords;
> - To **prepare derivative works** based upon the work;

- To **distribute copies** or phonorecords of the work to the public by sale or other transfer of ownership, or by rental, lease, or lending;

- To **perform the work publicly**, in the case of literary, musical, dramatic, and choreographic works, pantomimes, and motion pictures and other audiovisual works;

- To **display the work publicly**, in the case of literary, musical, dramatic, and choreographic works, pantomimes, and pictorial, graphic, or sculptural works, including the individual images of a motion picture or other audiovisual work; and

- In the case of sound recordings, to perform the work publicly by means of a digital audio transmission.

I have put key concepts in bold to help you understand copyrights. Essentially, as the owner of a copyright, you have the right to reproduce the work, enhance the work, distribute the work, and perform it or display it in public.

To understand what copyright protects, it is important to understand what it does not protect. This is spelled out explicitly in Circular 1, *Copyright Basics,* published by the U.S. Copyright Office:

> Several categories of material are generally not eligible for federal copyright protection. These include among others:
>
> - Works that have not been fixed in a tangible form of expression (for example, choreographic works that have not been notated or recorded, or improvisational speeches or performances that have not been written or recorded)
>
> - Titles, names, short phrases, and slogans; familiar symbols or designs; mere variations of typographic ornamentation, lettering, or coloring; mere listings of ingredients or contents
>
> - Ideas, procedures, methods, systems, processes, concepts, principles, discoveries, or devices, as distinguished from a description, explanation, or illustration
>
> - Works consisting entirely of information that is common property and containing no original authorship (for example: standard calendars, height and weight charts, tape measures and rulers, and lists or tables taken from public documents or other common sources)

Note that a copyright exists at the moment the work is created. In other words, despite some common misunderstandings about copyrights, a work does not need to be published to have a copyright. Also, the copyright does not need to be registered with the U.S. Copyright Office. It is simply a right given to the person who created the work. However, there are four very strong reasons why you should register the copyright of any work you create very soon after it is created.

First, in the United States copyright registration is required to initiate a copyright infringement lawsuit. A copyright owner cannot proceed with a copyright infringement lawsuit unless the work has been registered. Although you may not anticipate anyone copying your creative work without permission, it happens, and if you wait until infringement has occurred you may have a more difficult time in court because of the second and third reasons for registering a copyright.

The second reason you should register a copyright soon after creating it is that you will then be eligible to receive "statutory damages" and "legal costs and attorneys' fees" from a copyright infringer. According to the law, the copyright registration must be filed prior to an infringement taking place or within three months of the publication date of the work. Otherwise the copyright owner will not be entitled to receive statutory damages and legal costs and attorneys' fees. The effective date of copyright registration is the date when the Copyright Office receives the completed copyright registration application, all fees, and copies of the work to be deposited with the Copyright Office.

"Statutory damages" is a legal term that refers to damages that are determined not by the amount of money that the copyright holder lost because of the infringement, but by using some predetermined calculation. Normally a copyright holder must prove how much the copyright infringement cost in terms of lost profits. For example, if the copyright holder of a record album can obtain the number of bootleg albums sold, that number would represent the number of lost legitimate sales. In many cases, these sales numbers are unavailable and so the copyright holder can get statutory damages instead. A judge or jury has the ability to increase statutory damage awards to punish the infringer if it is determined that the infringer was "willful" (knew she was infringing) or particularly harmful.

Legal fees associated with litigation can be extremely high and difficult for individuals or small companies to afford. Often a copyright infringer takes the bet that a small company or individual does not have the resources to fight in court. Thus the ability to win back legal costs and attorneys' fees can be a big advantage to a copyright holder.

The third reason why you should register a copyrighted work is that registration serves as "prima facie" evidence that the work is original and is owned by the registrant. This term is Latin for "first face" and is used to mean a self-evident fact that needs no further proof. In other words, in court a copyright registration is taken as proof that the registrant is the owner of the work and the alleged infringer would need to prove otherwise. Registration can allow the copyright owner to get a preliminary injunction that will force the alleged infringer to stop distribution of the work. This presumption of validity applies only if the work has been registered within five years from the publication date.

The fourth reason to register a copyright soon after its creation is that it is inexpensive. Today the fee is around $30 and the paperwork can be downloaded from the Web and completed in only a few minutes. The U.S. government gives all of these advantages to registered copyright owners to encourage people to register their copyrights and to deter others from stealing them.

6.3 SOFTWARE COPYRIGHTS

The first computer program submitted for copyright registration was the SCOPAC-PROG.63 program from North American Aviation. The submission was done on November 30, 1961, in the form of a magnetic tape. While the Copyright Office was trying to determine whether such a deposit could be registered, two short computer programs were submitted on April 20, 1964, by John Francis Banzhaf III, a Columbia University Law School student assigned to research and draft a note for the *Columbia Law Review* on whether computer programs and other software could be protected under U.S. copyright law. One computer program was submitted as a printout published in the *Columbia Law Review Notes*, and the other was submitted on magnetic tape. The copyrights for both student computer programs were registered in May 1964, and North American Aviation's computer program was registered in June 1964.

The Copyright Office was actually not certain whether computer programs were copyrightable and whether a machine-readable version of a program qualified as a "copy" under the 1909 Copyright Act. However, it granted the software copyright based on the "rule of doubt"—an office-created policy that resolves uncertain cases in favor of the applicant.

The number of software copyrights in the United States was not significant because the Copyright Act of 1909 required publication of the work, and works deposited with the Copyright Office were made public, resulting in a fear of disclosing trade secrets encompassed in the program. In the 14 years from May 1964 to January 1, 1978 (the general effective date of the 1976 Copyright Act), only about 2,000 programs were registered. Nearly that many machine-readable works were submitted in just the first two years under the 1976 Copyright Act. The Computer Software Copyright Act of 1980 changed the submission requirements for software, allowing "redacted" or "blocked out" copies of only small sections of code to be deposited with the Copyright Office, fully addressing the concern about disclosing trade secrets.

6.3.1 COPYRIGHTING CODE

With regard to software, copyright protection is given to the source code, assembly code (which can be considered another form of source code), and object code. It seems obvious that source code should be protected since few, if any, programmers would argue that source code does not fit the criterion of "original works of authorship fixed in any tangible medium of expression." The protection of object code under copyright law may not seem as clear. It was determined in several cases in the late 1970s and early 1980s, the most significant of which were the case of *Williams Electronics v. Artic International* (see sidebar) and the case of *Apple Computer Inc. v. Franklin Computer Corp.* (see sidebar), that object code is indeed protected by copyright.

WILLIAMS ELECTRONICS, INC. V. ARTIC INTERNATIONAL, INC.

Around October 1979, Williams Electronics put together a team consisting of Eugene Jarvis, Larry DeMar, Sam Dicker, and Paul Dussault to design a new video game that eventually came to be called Defender, in which a spaceship is flown over a planet's surface while destroying various enemy spaceships that fire at it. The game was introduced at an industry trade show in 1980, and sales were initially slow, but it eventually became a big hit, with estimates of having produced in excess of $1 billion in revenue.

Williams obtained three copyright registrations relating to its Defender game: one covering the computer program, the second covering the audiovisual effects displayed during the game's "attract mode," and the third covering the audiovisual effects displayed during the game's "play mode."

Artic International, Inc., sold kits that allowed customers to make a custom video game. The Artic kits included circuit boards, various electronic components, a microprocessor, and a read-only memory (ROM) with a game called Defense Command that was practically identical to Defender. As it turned out, the object code program in ROM was a copy of the Defender ROM code. Williams sued Artic for copyright infringement.

Artic did not deny that it copied the ROM code but rather argued that the object code was not protected by copyright because a ROM is part of a machine. If the "copy" is not intelligible to human beings and not intended to be a medium of communication to human beings, then it cannot be protected by a copyright.

Judge Dolores Sloviter disagreed and ruled in favor of Williams against Artic, stating that copyright defines a "copy" to include a material object in which a work is fixed "by any method now known or later developed, and from which the work can be perceived, reproduced, or otherwise communicated, either directly or with the aid of a machine or device." Congress had anticipated new technologies for containing the code. Furthermore, Judge Sloviter rejected any interpretation of copyright that would "severely limit the copyrightability of computer programs which Congress clearly intended to protect." Further, Judge Sloviter could not accept Artic's argument because it would create an "unlimited loophole" for avoiding infringement of a computer program by enabling the copying of any silicon chip in which it was stored.

Note that copyright does not protect "ideas, procedures, methods, systems, processes, concepts, principles, discoveries, or devices, as distinguished from a description, explanation, or illustration." A copyright protects the actual code but not the concepts or inventions embodied by the code. A copyright can protect the specific instructions used to implement an LZS method for compressing files but does not stop anyone from creating a file compression program or even from creating an LZS file compression program as long as the software is different and not derived from the copyrighted software. For protecting those things, you need patents and trade secrets, discussed in the following chapters. However, while copyright protects the expression of an idea, but not the idea itself, the distinction can get a little fuzzy and is open to interpretation by judges. For example, structural expressions and abstract expressions are protected. In the case of *Salinger v. Colting* in July of 2009, Judge Deborah Batts of the U.S. District Court, Southern District of New York, ruled that Fredrik Colting's sequel to J. D. Salinger's novel *The Catcher in the Rye* was a derivative work and therefore copyright infringement, even though no significant literal text was copied from the original. The judge found essentially that the main characters in both novels were similar and that a "lay observer" would recognize the sequel as a copy and "would regard the aesthetic appeal of the two works as the same."

In the same way, the organization of routines, the organization of data, the user interfaces, the "architecture" of a program, and various other abstractions of program code can be protected by copyright if they are not determined by outside requirements such as an interface standard or another program. However, as I describe in more detail later in this book, these abstract expressions are more difficult to define and to defend in court.

APPLE COMPUTER INC. V. FRANKLIN COMPUTER CORP.

Apple Computer introduced the Apple II personal computer in 1977. In 1979, the spreadsheet program called VisiCalc was introduced for the Apple II. Created by Dan Bricklin and Bob Frankston for their company, Software Arts, and distributed by Personal Software, this "killer app" caused sales of the Apple II to skyrocket. In 1982, seeing an opportunity, Franklin Computer Corporation came out with its own personal computer, the ACE 100. So that it would be 100 percent compatible with the Apple II and run the hundreds of application programs that had been developed for the Apple II, Franklin copied the object code for the operating system of the Apple II; the operating system controls the hardware and the application programs running on it. Like other computer programs, the operating system started out as source code and was compiled into object code. The operating system was then written to a ROM integrated circuit chip that was inserted into the Apple II motherboard. This kind of code that is fixed inside a machine and cannot be easily changed is called "firmware." However, a ROM chip can easily be physically removed, and the ones and zeros of the object code can easily be copied.

In court, Franklin did not dispute that it had copied Apple's object code but rather claimed that firmware was not protectable by copyright. Essentially there were three parts to Franklin's argument. Franklin argued that the ROM was a piece of hardware and thus was part of the machine, and machines are not protected by copyright. Franklin also argued that the operating system was a method for controlling hardware and software, and methods are not protected by copyright. They also argued that the firmware existed only in machine-readable form, and not in printed form or any form that could be understood by a human, and thus was not protected by copyright.

The court agreed with Franklin. Three days later, however, on appeal from Apple, the United States Court of Appeals overruled the lower court and created an important precedent ruling. Judge Dolores Sloviter, who also presided over the case of *Williams Electronics v. Artic International*, specifically stated that (1) object code is copyrightable, (2) computer software embedded in a ROM is copyrightable, and (3) operating system code is copyrightable.

6.3.2 COPYRIGHTING SCREEN DISPLAYS

There have been a number of cases involving alleged copyright infringement of one program's visual display by another program, rather than the code. The Copyright Office is very clear that it considers a computer program's visual display to be a "visual arts work" that is protectable by copyright. When registering computer code and visual display, the Copyright Office allows both to be copyrighted with one submission. You can choose to call that submission a "literary work," which is the common categorization for computer code, or a "visual arts work." In either case, both the code and the visual display are protected, even if screen shots or any other depiction of the displays generated by the computer program are not submitted with the copyright application.

One of the most famous computer display copyright disputes involved Apple and Microsoft and Xerox (see the sidebar). A screen shot of the Windows 2.0 desktop from Microsoft is shown in Figure 6.2. For comparison, a screen shot of

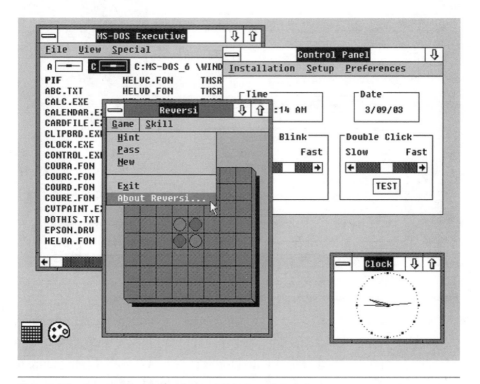

Figure 6.2 Screen shot of the Microsoft Windows 2.0 desktop

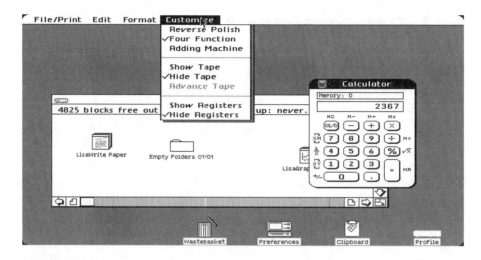

Figure 6.3   Screen shot of the Apple Lisa Office System 1 desktop

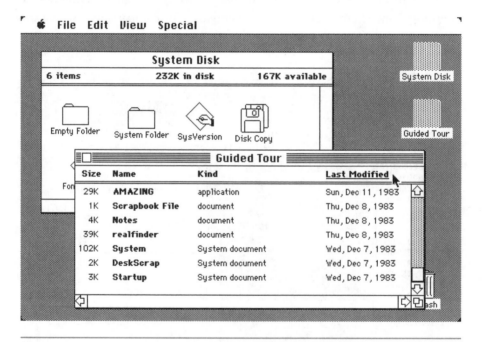

Figure 6.4   Screen shot of the Apple Macintosh OS System 1.0 desktop

Apple's Lisa Office System 1 desktop is shown in Figure 6.3, and a screen shot of Apple's Macintosh OS System 1.0 desktop is shown in Figure 6.4. In Figure 6.5 is the original Xerox 8010 Star desktop that is considered the ancestor of all of today's windowed operating systems.

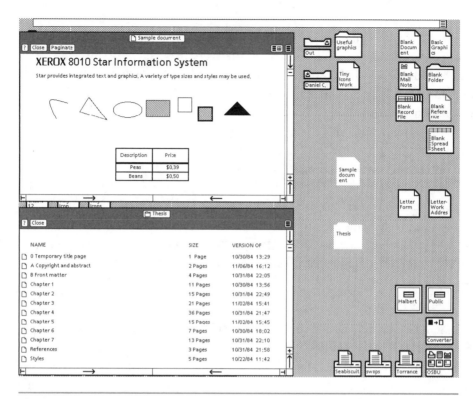

Figure 6.5   Screen shot of the Xerox 8010 Star desktop

APPLE SUES AND GETS SUED OVER GUIS

Apple Computer introduced the Apple Lisa in January 1983 and the Macintosh computer a year later in January 1984. These were the first commercially successful personal computers to use a graphical user interface (GUI) that included icons and overlapping windows. In November of 1983, Microsoft announced Windows 1.0 and introduced it to the market in 1985. It was a clunky GUI with nonoverlapping windows, ugly fonts, and simple icons. In January 1988, Microsoft released Windows 2.0, which had overlapping windows and a much more Macintosh-like GUI.

Shortly after that, in March 1988, Apple sued Microsoft in federal court for copyright infringement of the "look and feel" of the Macintosh operating system, asking for $5.5 billion in damages. The judge insisted on a specification of specific GUI elements that Apple claimed were infringing, and Apple produced a list of 189 such elements.

Continues

What is not commonly known is that when Apple first released the Mac, it felt it needed the support of Microsoft's applications to make it successful. Bill Gates, CEO of Microsoft, wanted the rights to duplicate the Macintosh GUI and said so to Apple CEO John Sculley. After some brutal negotiations, the two parties signed an agreement that granted Microsoft a "non-exclusive, worldwide, royalty-free, perpetual, nontransferable license to use these derivative works in present and future software programs, and to license them to and through third parties for use in their software programs." Clearly Microsoft had the right to create a Macintosh-like GUI. U.S. District Judge Vaughn R. Walker determined that 179 of the GUI elements had been licensed to Microsoft in their agreement, and of the remaining 10 elements, all except the "trash can" icon and file folder icons were not copyrightable. The case lasted four years, the decision was upheld on appeal in 1994, and the U.S. Supreme Court refused to hear the case.

Interestingly, Apple had derived the Lisa and Macintosh GUIs from the Alto computer developed at Xerox when Xerox invited Apple employees into its Palo Alto Research Center. During the conflict between Apple and Microsoft, Bill Gates told Steve Jobs, founder of Apple, "Hey, Steve, just because you broke into Xerox's house before I did and took the TV doesn't mean I can't go in later and take the stereo." But another fact not commonly known is that Apple paid Xerox to get a look at the Alto, and Xerox in return invested in Apple.

Midway through Apple's suit, Xerox filed its own copyright infringement lawsuit against Apple for the GUI, but the Xerox case was dismissed because the three-year statute of limitations had passed.

6.3.3 REGISTERING A SOFTWARE COPYRIGHT

To register a copyright, it is normally necessary to file a copy of the work being protected with the U.S. Copyright Office as proof. However, software is treated differently from other works. If the software does not contain trade secrets (discussed in Chapter 8), the Copyright Office requires that only the first 25 and last 25 printed pages of source code need to be submitted along with a section of code containing a copyright notice. If the program is fewer than 50 lines long, the entire program must be submitted. There are no guidelines as to what constitutes "first" and "last" in something consisting of many independent files and a complex interconnect of routines. The Copyright Office is fairly lax about this, allowing the owner to designate the first and last 25 pages for registration.

If the software does contain trade secrets, the Copyright Office requires a letter stating so. In this case, the submission must still include the first 25 and last 25 printed pages of source code and a section of code containing a copyright notice. However, you can "redact" or block out sections of code that constitute trade secrets. If this is not feasible for some reason, you can submit the first and last 10 pages of source code with no redactions, or you can submit the first and last 25 pages of object code and 10 sequential pages of source code without redactions. You can even submit a registration of the object code without any source code, but this registration occurs under the Copyright Office's "rule of doubt," which means that the Copyright Office vouches for the date of registration but not the contents or copyrightability since the object code cannot be read. Registration of object code is not recommended except when source code is unavailable, because it reduces the protection of a copyright registration.

There are many other variations of requirements for copyright, depending on whether the program is original or a revision of an existing copyrighted program or a revision of a public domain program. It is best to check with the Copyright Office for the latest requirements.

6.3.4 TERM OF COPYRIGHT PROTECTION

The term of protection for copyrighted software is the same as that for any other literary work. The Copyright Act of 1976, effective January 1, 1978, changed the length of the term, so copyrights obtained before 1978 have a shorter term. A work that was created on or after January 1, 1978, is protected from the moment of its creation and is normally protected for the author's life plus 70 years after the author's death, except in the following cases:

- In the case of "a joint work prepared by two or more authors who did not work for hire," the protection lasts for 70 years after the last surviving author's death.

- For works made for hire, and for anonymous and pseudonymous works, the duration of copyright is 95 years from publication or 120 years from creation, whichever is shorter. If the author's real name appears in the Copyright Office records, then the work is not considered anonymous or pseudonymous.

6.4 ALLOWABLE AND NONALLOWABLE USES OF COPYRIGHTED CODE

There are allowable and nonallowable uses of copyrighted code. It is important to understand these issues completely before using copyrighted code.

6.4.1 FAIR USE

U.S. copyright law does allow certain kinds of copying without permission from the copyright holder. This kind of copying is called "fair use" and is described in Title 17 of the U.S. Code as follows:

> Notwithstanding the provisions of sections 106 and 106A, the fair use of a copyrighted work, including such use by reproduction in copies or phonorecords or by any other means specified by that section, for purposes such as criticism, comment, news reporting, teaching (including multiple copies for classroom use), scholarship, or research, is not an infringement of copyright. In determining whether the use made of a work in any particular case is a fair use the factors to be considered shall include—
>
> (1) the purpose and character of the use, including whether such use is of a commercial nature or is for nonprofit educational purposes;
>
> (2) the nature of the copyrighted work;
>
> (3) the amount and substantiality of the portion used in relation to the copyrighted work as a whole; and
>
> (4) the effect of the use upon the potential market for or value of the copyrighted work.
>
> The fact that a work is unpublished shall not itself bar a finding of fair use if such finding is made upon consideration of all the above factors.

Fair use often depends on the particular circumstances of the use of the copyrighted work. Some common fair uses of software include

- Making backup copies
- Modifying a program in order to get it to run on your machine
- Making a copy from a CD-ROM or DVD-ROM onto a hard disk
- Making a copy from the hard disk into memory when the program runs

6.4.2 REIMPLEMENTATION

I have consulted on cases where programmers have reimplemented computer programs by rewriting them to replace the source code with their own code in the belief that this did not constitute copyright infringement. Unfortunately, that belief is wrong. First, if the programmer had access to the source code of the original program without authorization, that may not be copyright infringement, but it is theft.

Second, derivative works that are substantially similar to the copyrighted work constitute copyright infringement. Rewriting the original program in a new programming language still does not help. Imagine taking a novel in English and translating it into Hebrew. Even though every word is different, the translated book, like the translated computer program, is an infringing derivative.

If the programmer were to completely replace every line of the original code with a new line of code, there are still nonliteral elements—abstract elements including data structures, file organization, and overall architecture—that exist in both programs, thus making the new program infringing.

It is permissible to study software for the purpose of learning from it and then creating a similar program using the ideas encompassed in the software. For more information on this, see section 6.4.5 on reverse engineering. One way to reimplement a program without infringing the copyright is to set up a clean room, which is discussed in Chapter 25.

6.4.3 VERSIONS, MODIFICATIONS, AND DERIVATIVES

Because programming consists of writing and rewriting code, a program can be considered to be a series of programs, each covered by a copyright. Each revision of a program can be considered to be a derivative work. If the original program is registered with the Copyright Office, each new version is covered by the copyright registration as long as the changes to the original are not "substantial." Unfortunately there is no commonly accepted legal definition of the term "substantial," particularly in relation to software. A few lines of code can be substantial if they are important to the functionality of the program. It is a good idea to register each major revision to the program.

6.4.4 COMPILATIONS

It is often the case that a program incorporates libraries of source code and object code that are themselves copyrighted computer programs. A "compilation" is the legal term for when two or more preexisting works are combined to form a new work. A good example of a literary compilation is an anthology of poetry. Each poem may have its own copyright and may not be reproduced in the anthology without the author's permission. However, the anthology can also be copyrighted for the choice of poems, the order presented in the book, footnotes, annotations, quizzes, and any other materials that required some intellectual effort when the collection was put together.

The copyright for a software compilation is limited to the new code contributed by the author of such a compilation. The copyright for a compilation does not provide any exclusive right to the preexisting copyrighted code. It does not affect the copyright protection of the preexisting code, and the author of the compilation does not get any special rights to the preexisting code. This means that to distribute the new computer program, the author must get permission from the copyright owners of all the software components. So as not to infringe on the copyrights of any code libraries used in the new program, it is necessary that the library's usage license allow the redistribution of the library in the new program.

There are cases when code libraries are not distributed with the program but are used at run time. For example, dynamically linked libraries (DLLs) are application programs that are part of the operating system on which the program runs. Because these DLLs are not being distributed with the application program, no permission is needed from the copyright owner of the library for distribution to users. Users are the ones who are combining the programs, but this falls within the fair use of the program—modifying it in order to run on their computers.

6.4.5 REVERSE ENGINEERING

Copyrights protect expression of ideas, but not ideas themselves. For example, a novel about two young, star-crossed lovers in Italy can be copyrighted, but that does not prevent others from reading the book and getting an idea for a different novel about two young, star-crossed lovers in Italy. For this reason, software can be reverse engineered for the purpose of learning the ideas it embodies but not to copy the code itself. Two early video game cases enforced this idea: *Atari Games Corp. v. Nintendo of America Inc.* in September 1992 and *Sega Enterprises Ltd. v. Accolade Inc.* in October 1992.

In the first case, Nintendo very tightly controlled access to its successful NES video game system and did not release the specifications for creating a game cartridge for use in the system. To produce a game for the Nintendo NES system, companies had to pay a license fee to Nintendo and had to agree not to produce the licensed game for any other system for two years. The Nintendo

NES system incorporated a computer program called 10NES to check whether a particular game had been licensed before it would run. Atari obtained the source code for 10NES, reverse engineered it, and figured out how to bypass the 10NES program by using its own program called Rabbit. Atari sued Nintendo for, among other things, unfair competition and monopolistic practices, and Nintendo countersued for, among other things, copyright infringement. Atari lost the case and appealed to the U.S. Court of Appeals. While the appeals court determined that Atari did indeed infringe on Nintendo's copyright when it created its own program based on Nintendo's program, it also overruled part of the lower court's decision and determined that reverse engineering is allowed as fair use. Reverse engineering a product to understand how it works—to understand the ideas and concepts that are not protected by copyright—is perfectly legal. While creating a copy of the specific implementation of these ideas is not legal, reverse engineering is not only legal but is to be encouraged if ideas are to be propagated and built upon. The decision by Judge Randall Rader specifically states:

> The district court assumed that reverse engineering (intermediate copying) was copyright infringement. … This court disagrees. Atari did not violate Nintendo's copyright by deprocessing computer chips in Atari's rightful possession. Atari could lawfully deprocess Nintendo's 10NES chips to learn their unprotected ideas and processes. This fair use did not give Atari more than the right to understand the 10NES program and to distinguish the protected from the unprotected elements of the 10NES program. Any copying beyond that necessary to understand the 10NES program was infringement. Atari could not use reverse engineering as an excuse to exploit commercially or otherwise misappropriate protected expression.

In the case of *Sega v. Accolade*, Sega produced the Genesis game console and allowed other manufacturers to license the design to create competing video game consoles that could accept Sega video games. All Sega video game cartridges, according to the license, had to be manufactured by Sega. Rather than pay the license fee, Accolade decided to reverse engineer the Genesis console software to determine how to create its own game cartridges for Genesis. Sega sued for copyright infringement. The part of the ruling by Judge Stephen Reinhardt of the U.S. Court of Appeals that dealt with reverse engineering was short and clear:

> We conclude that where disassembly is the only way to gain access to the ideas and functional elements embodied in a copyrighted computer program and where there is a legitimate reason for seeking such access, disassembly is a fair use of the copyrighted work, as a matter of law.

One way to look at this is to consider a book instead of a software program—the rules are essentially the same. If you copy a book and sell it, that constitutes copyright infringement. If you make changes to a book and sell it, that is still copyright infringement. If you read a book in order to understand it and even write your own book, where no elements of the book are copied, that is a fair use. If you did not have permission to take the book (for example, you shoplifted it from a bookstore), then it is theft whether you read the book or copy the book or do nothing with the book.

ATARI'S UNCLEAN HANDS

According to the court ruling, Atari did some things that made it much more difficult for the company to win in court. According to the judge, Atari came to court with "unclean hands," an actual legal term meaning that the party did something unlawful or unethical and cannot win a lawsuit because of it. What did Atari do?

Atari's engineers tried everything they could think of to understand Nintendo's 10NES program code in the Nintendo NES system, including monitoring the communication between the chips and chemically peeling layers from the chips to allow microscopic examination of the transistors to determine the object code, but to no avail.

In December 1987, Atari became a Nintendo licensee. Atari paid Nintendo to gain access to the NES for its video games, but the license strictly controlled Atari's access to Nintendo's technology, including the 10NES program. Under the license, Nintendo would take Atari's games, place them in cartridges containing the 10NES program, and resell them to Atari, so Atari was no closer to understanding the internals of the NES system.

In early 1988, Atari's attorney applied to the Copyright Office to obtain a copy of the registered, copyrighted 10NES program. The application stated that Atari was a defendant in an infringement action and needed a copy of the program for that litigation. In fact, there was no lawsuit at that time. It was not until December 1988 that Atari sued Nintendo for antitrust violations and unfair competition. Nintendo did not file an infringement suit against Atari until nearly a year after that.

After obtaining the 10NES source code from the Copyright Office, Atari again tried to read the object code from peeled chips. Through microscopic examination, Atari's engineers transcribed the 10NES object code into a handwritten representation of zeros and ones. Atari then used the information from the Copyright Office to correct errors in this transcription.

Atari then set out to create its own program to duplicate the 10NES program. During the lawsuit, the judge was made aware of the deception of the Copyright Office and declared that Atari's unclean hands prevented the company from winning the case regardless of the judgment.

PATENTS

While copyrights protect expressions but not ideas, patents cover ideas but not expressions. According to the United States Patent Office:

> A patent is an intellectual property right granted by the Government of the United States of America to an inventor "to exclude others from making, using, offering for sale, or selling the invention throughout the United States or importing the invention into the United States" for a limited time in exchange for public disclosure of the invention when the patent is granted.

A slightly more generic definition can be found on the World Intellectual Property Organization (WIPO) website:

> A patent is an exclusive right granted for an invention, which is a product or a process that provides a new way of doing something, or offers a new technical solution to a problem. A patent provides protection for the invention to the owner of the patent for a limited period, generally 20 years.

Essentially, a patent is meant to allow an inventor to share his invention with the world yet have it be protected from use by others without the inventor's approval and, of course, compensation. Some call a patent a government-approved monopoly. The owner of a patent can use the invention without restriction; all others, even if they create the same invention independently, can use the invention only if licensed to do so by the patent holder.

The idea behind patents is that without them, inventors would keep the principles of their inventions secret to prevent competition. When the inventor dies, the principles behind the invention might also die. Technology could stagnate. By granting patents, governments tell inventors that they must describe to the public exactly how their invention works so that others can use the principles and further the technology. In return, the government gives the inventor a limited amount of time to completely control the use of the invention.

7.1   THE HISTORY OF PATENTS

In medieval times in many European countries, rulers granted exclusive intellectual property rights in return for a fee. Not all of these grants were for inventions, as we think of patents today; some were for innovations in such areas as mining and the production of textiles. The first recorded case of granting limited-term monopolies to inventors as a form of economic policy seems to have been in Venice in 1474. This law came about during a long war between Venice and the Turks during which Venice's great trading empire suffered. As a result, Venice began to establish success in manufacturing and passed laws to protect that success.

The first English patent, a direct predecessor to today's modern patent, was granted to John of Utynam on April 3, 1449. He was an artist skilled in a technique for making colored glass that he learned in Flanders but that was not known or practiced in England. King Henry VI was founding Eton College and King's College, Cambridge. He wanted John of Utynam to create stained-glass windows for these colleges and to teach others how to create them. In return for John's services the king commanded that none of his subjects could use such arts for a term of 20 years without John's consent. The original meaning of the word *patent* was a document that was open to general inspection. The patent for John of Utynam was a letter with the king's royal seal on the outside, with the writing open for inspection. John of Utynam went on to create the stained-glass windows, which unfortunately have not survived. It was more than 100 years before a second patent was granted, this one to Henry Smyth on April 26, 1552, for making Normandy glass.

In America, prior to independence from England, the king of England officially owned all the intellectual property created by the colonists. In 1790, only two years after the U.S. Constitution was ratified, Congress passed the first United States Patent Act entitled "An Act to Promote the Progress of Useful Arts." George Washington signed the first U.S. patent grant; the patent examiner was Thomas Jefferson. The inventor was Samuel Hopkins of Pittsford, Vermont; the invention was a new method of making potash, an industrial chemical used to make soap, glass, fertilizers, and gunpowder. The fee for a patent at that time was $4.

7.2 Types of Patents

In the United States there are three kinds of patents: utility patents, design patents, and plant patents.[1] Design patents cover how something looks as opposed to how it functions, as described in U.S. Code Title 35, Part II, Chapter 16, and summarized on the U.S. Patent and Trademark Office (PTO) website:

> Design Patent—Issued for a new, original, and ornamental design for an article of manufacture, it permits its owner to exclude others from making, using, or selling the design for a period of fourteen years from the date of patent grant.

Ornamental designs of jewelry, furniture, and buildings are examples of objects that can be covered by design patents. Perhaps the most famous design patent is number 11,023, filed January 2, 1879, by Auguste Bartholdi of Paris, France. This was the design patent for the Statue of Liberty, the diagram of which is shown in Figure 7.1. Graphics generated by software, such as computer screens and icons, can be protected by design patents, but software code cannot be protected by them, because code is functional.

Plant patents cover new breeds of plants as described in U.S. Code Title 35, Part II, Chapter 15, and summarized on the PTO website:

> Plant Patent—Issued for a new and distinct, invented or discovered asexually reproduced plant including cultivated sports, mutants, hybrids, and newly found seedlings, other than a tuber propagated plant or a plant found in an uncultivated state, it permits its owner to exclude others from making, using, or selling the plant for a period of up to twenty years from the date of patent application filing.

Obviously plant patents are not relevant to software. Utility patents cover how something functions as described in U.S. Code Title 35, Part II, Chapter 10, and summarized on the PTO website:

> Utility Patent—Issued for the invention of a new and useful process, machine, manufacture, or composition of matter, or a new and useful improvement thereof, it generally permits its owner to exclude others from making, using, or selling the invention for a period of up to twenty years from the date of patent application filing.

In general, utility patents cover apparatuses, methods, and compositions of matter, though the latter kind of utility patent does not apply to software. An apparatus is a physical thing, whereas a method is a series of steps for producing something. Utility patents do apply to software.

---

1. In other countries, there is another kind of patent called a "utility model" or "petit patent," given mostly to cover a useful industrial design.

DESIGN.

A. BARTHOLDI.
Statue.

No. 11,023.   Patented Feb. 18, 1879.

LIBERTY ENLIGHTENING THE WORLD.

Figure 7.1 Statue of Liberty design patent

7.3 PARTS OF A PATENT

The structure of a patent generally consists of these sections, though there is ongoing debate about what is actually required by law:

1. **Abstract**. This is a one-paragraph description of the invention.

2. **Drawings**. These are carefully labeled figures that are used to illustrate points that are described in the patent.

3. **Background of the invention**. This section describes the field of the invention, inventions that predate this invention ("prior art"), and inventions related to this invention. This section often gives the reasoning for why the invention is needed.

4. **Summary of the invention**. This is a paragraph to a page description of the invention (not legally required by law).

5. **Brief description of the drawings**. One sentence briefly describes each drawing.

6. **Detailed description**. This section explains the invention as completely as possible, referencing the drawings. It describes the "embodiment" of the invention that differentiates it from existing inventions and allows "one of ordinary skill in the art" to replicate it. According to the patent office's *Manual of Patent Examining Procedure* § 1.71, the description must explain "[t]he best mode contemplated by the inventor of carrying out his invention. . . ."

7. **Claims**. This is the essence of the invention. Each claim is a single sentence, though it is usually a very long sentence broken into multiple parts, that describes the invention in wording that is as precise as possible. A claim can be an apparatus claim that describes a physical thing, a method claim that describes a process, or a combination of these.

Examples of the two kinds of claims can be found in claims 2 and 3 of patent 174,465, issued to Alexander Graham Bell in 1876 for the telephone:

> **2.** The combination, substantially as set forth, of a permanent magnet or other body capable of inductive action, with a closed circuit, so that the vibration of the one shall occasion electrical undulations in the other or in itself, and this I claim, whether the permanent magnet be set in vibration in the neighborhood of the conducting-wire forming the circuit, or whether the conducting-wire be set in vibration in the neighborhood of the permanent magnet, or whether the conducting-wire and the permanent magnet both simultaneously be set in vibration in each other's neighborhood.
>
> **3.** The method of producing modulations in a continuous voltaic current by the vibration or motion of bodies capable of inductive action, or by the vibration or motion of the conducting-wire itself, in the neighborhood of such bodies, as set forth.

Some drawings from Bell's patent of the telephone are shown in Figure 7.2.

Note how Bell wrote his telephone patent not only to cover how his invention was actually implemented ("permanent magnet") but also to cover modifications that he or others might make in the future ("or other body capable of inductive action"). This is one important aspect of the art of writing patents. A claim should be written to cover not only the current implementation but also functionally equivalent future implementations. There are dangers, though. By reaching too far, specifying technologies that do not work ("inoperative") or that do not currently exist, a patent claim can be determined to be invalid. For example, claiming a "transporter device that instantaneously moves an

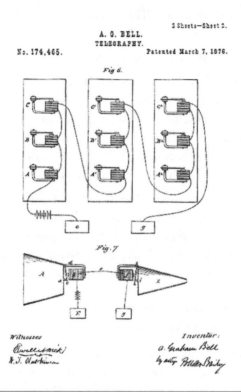

Figure 7.2   Telephone patent drawings

object from one location in the galaxy to another" may seem like a great way to get a patent on an invention that will not show up for 100 years, but in reality it is a way to, at best, get a patent that is unenforceable. Also, not providing a description of the invention in enough detail that someone can actually produce it ("non-enabling") results in an invalid patent.

Also note that Bell's patent has multiple claims so that more of the invention is protected. This also has its risks, though, as patent examiners these days are more likely to insist that multiple modes of operation are actually descriptions of multiple inventions. In this case, the examiner will insist that the claims be divided up and distributed in multiple patent applications, each one called a "divisional" patent. Whether the examiners are doing this to focus each patent on a single invention or this is an attempt by the patent office to collect more patent fees is debatable. However, the gray area between an overly broad patent that will be found to be invalid and a narrow patent that does not provide protection is the reason that an inventor should always use a skilled patent attorney or patent agent to draft these very important documents.

7.4 PATENTING AN INVENTION

In the United States, as in most countries, for an invention to be patentable it must meet the three criteria of novelty, utility, and nonobviousness at the time of filing, as defined here:

1. **Novelty:** The invention must be new and different from any other invention that is publicly known. If someone has already produced your invention and made it public, whether that person patented it or not, you lose the right to patent the same invention.

2. **Utility:** The invention must be useful for some legitimate purpose such that people would want to have it to make their lives easier in some way.[2] An invention that looks pretty but performs no useful function can get a design patent but not a utility patent. It also cannot be a computer program that produces results that are as good as, but no better than, some other well-known method.

3. **Nonobviousness:** The invention cannot be something that is obvious to "one of ordinary skill in the art" but never produced, or produced but never made public. For example, it cannot be a computer program method that is obvious to an ordinary programmer.

During the application process for a patent, the examiners in the patent office rarely challenge the criterion of utility. The patent must be "enabling," which means that the description must be correct and allow one who reads it to actually produce the invention. Failing that criterion is known as "non-enabling," and patent litigation can be lost if it can be shown that the patent-in-suit (the patent being asserted in litigation) is missing some key piece of apparatus or step in the method or actually describes the step or piece incorrectly.

The novelty aspect of a patent application is often challenged by the patent examiner who attempts to find prior art that invalidates the patent. In other words, the examiner tries to find some public document, whether in an earlier

---

2. The subject matter of an apparatus claim is seldom if ever rejected for lack of utility. The threshold is low for usefulness in apparatus claims, unless the claimed subject matter is inoperable or can be used only for an illegitimate purpose. There are more instances where composition of matter claims and method claims are rejected for lack of utility. A method for evading taxes is per se lacking utility. Drug claims that broadly describe synthesis of all kinds of compounds in the lab, just to prevent people from generating compounds that someone else may find a use for, require a showing of some modicum of usefulness before they are allowed. Of course, even in these situations, clever patent attorneys have discovered magical incantations that get around the requirements.

patent or patent application or in some magazine article or Web page, that describes the same invention. In patent litigation, the defendant will try to invalidate a patent by finding prior art that shows that the patent was not actually novel and should not have been issued in the first place.

The nonobviousness of a patent application is the vaguest aspect, and the courts have been defining and redefining this criterion. Clearly, there is a lot of room for interpretation. What is obvious to me may not be obvious to another. That is why obviousness is defined with respect to "one of ordinary skill in the art" ("OOSITA"). However, it is not clear who is considered one of ordinary skill. A self-taught computer programmer who has been working for more than ten years? A recently graduated programmer with a bachelor's degree in computer science from a prestigious university? A person with a PhD in computer science who has spent her entire career in academia? It is this criterion that patent examiners often challenge when reviewing a patent application, and it is this criterion that requires the most patience and perseverance to overcome.

Note that U.S. patent law is a first-to-invent system, which means that the person who invents something first, and can prove it, is entitled to the patent rights. U.S. patent law allows a person to apply for a patent no later than one year after a public disclosure of the invention. That public disclosure could be a published paper or article or a public offer to sell the product that encompasses the invention. All other countries that grant patent rights have first-to-file patent laws, which means that the first person to file a patent gets those rights, even if someone else came up with the invention first. This means that once a public disclosure is made, the rights to foreign patents are lost unless a U.S. filing has been made within the preceding year.

7.5 SPECIAL TYPES OF PATENT APPLICATIONS

There are several types of patent applications that can be filed in special cases. These are provisional, divisional, continuations, and continuations-in-part (CIP) patents. Each of these types of applications is described in the following sections.

7.5.1 PROVISIONAL

A provisional patent application is intended to be a way to reduce the initial application cost and to postpone the effort required to fully define the claims that make up the essence of the invention. A provisional patent application is typically filed by someone who believes he has an invention worth patenting but either does not currently have the money to pay for an attorney or patent agent to write the application or does not have the time to write a full patent application because, for example, he must get the invention to market right away or believes a competitor may come out with the invention very soon.

The provisional application does not need to contain claims. The applicant may then wait up to a year before filing the full patent application. The 20-year patent term begins on the date of the subsequent patent application, so a provisional patent has the advantage of postponing the start of the 20-year patent term by up to one year. The provisional application also has the disadvantage of postponing the examiner's examination of the patent for up to a year until the full patent application is submitted to the patent office.

Under U.S. patent law, the provisional application, like the subsequent full patent application, must be complete enough to enable one skilled in the art to create the invention (i.e., it must be enabling) and must completely describe the subsequent full patent application. If the details of the full patent application cannot be traced back to the provisional patent application, the full patent application could be considered a new invention without any timing benefit from the provisional application. The typical strategy for a provisional patent application is therefore to use an everything-plus-the-kitchen-sink approach by including all available technical information about the invention. The potential disadvantage to this approach is that the entire workings of the invention are released in the provisional application that will eventually be made public by the patent office.[3] If the patent is not eventually granted, all technical details of the invention will be known to your competitors.

7.5.2 DIVISIONAL

When a single patent application (called the "parent application") is divided into multiple patents, those resulting patents are called "divisional patents." Typically this occurs because the patent examiner believes that the claims of the parent patent actually describe multiple inventions. When this occurs, the patent examiner divides the patent claims into groups, each representing a different invention. The inventor can then decide which claims should continue with the original application and which should become claims for new, divisional patent applications. Each divisional application is entitled to the filing date of the parent application as its priority date.

---

3. Public disclosure can be avoided by waiving all foreign rights, and therefore the patent application is not published unless the patent is granted. This applies to both the provisional application and the nonprovisional application.

Unfortunately, whether some claims represent a separate invention or simply a different way of describing the same invention is open to many subjective considerations on the part of the patent examiner. There is also little recourse if an examiner decides to force division of a patent. Whether this division is for the correct reasons or not, the patent office ends up getting multiple application, issuance, and maintenance fees when a patent is divided, and so it seems that there has been pressure in recent years for examiners to create more "restriction requirements" that force divisional patent applications.

7.5.3 CONTINUATION

Sometimes an inventor may realize that the device described in a patent application comprises additional novel, useful, and nonobvious inventions that she had not previously realized. Under U.S. patent law, the inventor can file a continuation patent application that claims priority from its parent application and also receives the priority date of its parent application. The continuation must be filed after the parent application is filed but before the parent patent is issued or abandoned.

7.5.4 CONTINUATION-IN-PART (CIP)

A continuation-in-part (CIP) patent application is an application that contains some matter in common with a previous patent application but also contains new matter. When the CIP patent is issued, some claims share a priority date of the parent patent if those claims can be shown to be found in the parent patent. Other claims have the priority date of the CIP application if those claims are new to the CIP. Note that in order to get the earlier filing date, the entire claim must be traced back to the parent patent. Like a continuation, the CIP must be filed after the parent patent application is filed but before the parent patent is issued, when the parent application is pending.

WHO REALLY INVENTED THE COMPUTER?

The invention of the digital computer is usually credited to two professors at the University of Pennsylvania, J. Presper Eckert and John Mauchly. Funded by the United States Army, the ENIAC computer was designed to calculate tables for launching artillery shells accurately in World War II but was not completed until after the war in 1946. Unlike earlier computers that had a fixed purpose, ENIAC (meaning "Electronic Numerical Integrator and Computer") could be reprogrammed to handle many different purposes. But were Eckert and Mauchly really the pioneers of today's modern digital age?

Actually, no. The real inventors of the digital computer were physics professor John Atanasoff and his student Clifford Berry, who created the first digital computer in a laboratory at Iowa State University. The ABC ("**Atanasoff-Berry Computer**") was built in 1939, yet by the time of ENIAC's introduction to the world, the ABC had been forgotten. What had happened? World War II broke out and the University of Iowa as well as Atanasoff and Berry simply didn't realize the power of what they had created. Atanasoff was called up by the navy to do physics research, eventually participating in the atomic bomb tests at Bikini Atoll.

When Atanasoff returned to Iowa State, he found that his invention had been dismantled to make room for other equipment—because the ABC was built piece by piece in the laboratory, it was too big to move out. Iowa State had decided that a patent was too expensive and so never filed one. John Atanasoff went on to gain recognition for a number of inventions involving physics, but the ABC was mostly forgotten.

In the 1950s and 1960s a handful of companies saw the great potential in the electronic computer. Sperry Rand Corporation, which was formed through a series of mergers and acquisitions including the Eckert-Mauchly Computer Corporation, held U.S. Patent 3,120,606 for the digital computer. In 1973, Sperry Rand sued Honeywell, Inc., and Honeywell reciprocated. Thus began one of the most important intellectual property cases in history.

During the research for this case, Honeywell found out about John Atanasoff and the ABC, which became pivotal information. The case was tried for seven months, after which Judge Earl R. Larson handed down his decision, which stated, among other things, that the Eckert-Mauchly patent was invalid.

Some people have disputed this finding, arguing that this was a "legal" finding or a "loophole" or that a lawyer or a judge simply couldn't understand the complex engineering issues involved. Here's my take on this:

1. Both sides had sufficient time and access to technical experts to make the best case they could.
2. So much was at stake, and a huge amount of money was spent to bring out the truth. Both sides had very significant resources. If a case with this much

Continues

at stake could not convince a judge after seven months, then there is little hope for any IP case.

3. Evidence was found and witnesses verified that John Atanasoff had attended a conference in Philadelphia where he met John Mauchly and described his work. He then invited Mauchly to Iowa, where Mauchly spent several days examining Atanasoff's computer and many late nights reading Atanasoff's technical specifications. Letters were produced, signed by Mauchly, that thanked Atanasoff for his hospitality and for the tour of his amazing invention.

4. Mauchly testified at the trial. He admitted that he had met Atanasoff and eventually admitted that he had examined the ABC and read its specifications.

5. Mauchly and Sperry Rand Corporation were challenged to produce a single piece of evidence that Mauchly or Eckert had written about or researched digital electronics before Mauchly's meeting with Atanasoff. The best Mauchly could do was to produce a circuit for a model railway flasher that he claimed was a binary counter—it counted from 0 to 1 and then back to 0.

In fact, it became clear that Mauchly and Eckert attempted to claim much more credit than they deserved and tried to deny credit to others. They had actually greatly improved on Atanasoff's original design. Had Eckert and Mauchly been more humble, had they added Atanasoff's name to their patent, had they patented their own improvements instead of the entire invention, they might have given Sperry Rand the most powerful IP in technology history. Instead, the invention of the computer entered the public domain without restriction, and the rest is history.

For a good book on the subject, read *The First Electronic Computer: The Atanasoff Story* by Alice R. Burks and Arthur W. Burks.

7.6 SOFTWARE PATENTS

The idea that software can be patentable is a fairly recent one, and still a somewhat controversial one. The PTO considers patents to cover processes, machines, articles of manufacture, and compositions of matter but not scientific truths or mathematical expressions. In the 1970s, the PTO gave no protection for an invention that used a calculation made by a computer. In the 1980s, the U.S.

Supreme Court ruled on the case *Diamond v. R. Diehr* where a process used, as one of its steps, a computer program. This forced the PTO to accept that some computerized inventions are patentable. In the 1990s, the U.S. Federal Circuit Court ruled in *State Street Bank & Trust Co. v. Signature Financial Group* that almost all software is patentable. Given that methods have always been patentable, this seems to be a reasonable conclusion because software is a computer method.

The patentability of software varies from country to country. In the United States any kind of software is patentable. In the European Union software that solves technical problems is patentable but not software that solves business problems. In Japan software is patentable if it solves technical problems in a nonobvious way (though nonobviousness is a requirement for patentability of an invention in any country). In India, a change was proposed to the patent system to allow software patents, but it was killed by the Indian Parliament in April 2005. In Australia, as in the United States, any software that solves technical problems or business problems is patentable.

7.7 SOFTWARE PATENT CONTROVERSY

A number of arguments have been put forward by many groups both for and against software patents. The debate is heated, and many are pushing for laws in the United States to disallow software patents. The main arguments for and against software patents are summarized in the next two sections.

7.7.1 ARGUMENTS FOR SOFTWARE PATENTS

The main arguments for software patents are as follows.

7.7.1.1 Promoting Development

The patent system in the United States, as well as in other countries, has served these countries well by promoting research and development of new ideas. There is no reason not to promote the same kind of effort in software research and development.

7.7.1.2 Public Disclosure

Software patents require that software be made public, allowing for a wider distribution than would otherwise occur and allowing other programmers to build on the concepts.

7.7.1.3 Protection

Inventors who spend mental effort coming up with something new and useful are allowed to protect their intellectual property. This protection should apply to software inventors just as it does to other kinds of inventors.

7.7.1.4 Economic Benefit

The United States in particular has reaped economic benefits by allowing inventors to patent their inventions, and now that software has become a major worldwide industry, economic benefits will be gained by allowing software patents. Also, the only way for a small inventor to succeed against large software companies with influence and money is by allowing them to patent their software and start companies, license their software inventions to large companies, or, as a last resort, sue companies for incorporating their patented ideas.

7.7.1.5 International Law (TRIPs Agreement)

Internationally, the World Trade Organization (WTO) has created an agreement on Trade-Related Aspects of Intellectual Property Rights (TRIPS) that is generally interpreted to allow software patents. The WTO includes 153 member nations and was created to deal with the rules of trade between these countries.

7.7.1.6 Patent Challenges

Patents can be challenged and invalidated. So there exist mechanisms for revoking patents that are found to be obvious or were in use before the patent was granted. Many of the arguments against software patents focus on some notoriously bad software patents, but there have always been bad patents and there have always been ways to challenge them.

7.7.2 ARGUMENTS AGAINST SOFTWARE PATENTS

The main arguments against software patents are as follows.

7.7.2.1 Cost and Loss of R&D Funds

The costs of examining software to find out if it contains patented methods are too high. Software code is so large and so complex that for most programs, such a search would be prohibitively expensive. Although this may be true, software analysis can be automated to significantly speed up and lower the cost of such efforts, whereas mechanical devices must be examined manually to find potential infringement.

There is also an argument that because the distribution costs of software are so low compared to the distribution costs of physical inventions, patents should not apply to software. Although this is an argument against software patents, it seems that it actually promotes software patents because physical inventions have a manufacturing cost that already provides the inventor with a barrier to competition, whereas software does not.

7.7.2.2 Copyright

Some argue that software is already covered by copyrights and so patent protection is unnecessary. However, in the United States at least, copyrighted software does not have to be disclosed publicly, whereas patents must be disclosed. Patents are designed to give protection in return for this full public disclosure. Also, because copyrights protect the implementation (the actual code) but not the concept, copyrights do not prevent someone from implementing an algorithm in a different programming language or with a different set of routines, for example, offering almost no protection for something as complex and flexible as software.

7.7.2.3 Trivial Patents

Some argue that most software patents cover trivial, obvious developments. When software patents began being issued, the PTO had few people qualified to examine software. That is changing, but there is still a lack of qualified software examiners. However, this is a problem with the patent office, not with the patents. The patent office has always issued some number of trivial patents; these can always be challenged by the public and a reexamination can be requested. Also, there is typically little incentive for the owner of a poor patent, software or otherwise, to attempt to enforce it because that would require large legal fees, and if the patent is truly trivial the chances of success are small. Of course, there have been inventors with very deep pockets who, through litigation, have forced major companies to pay fees for licenses to their trivial patents. But these situations involving the litigation of trivial patents are not limited to software patents; they are an issue with all kinds of patents. The PTO has been attempting to put into place rules to prevent this kind of thing, though not all of the rules have been successful, and some have had unintended effects.

7.7.2.4 Open Source Movement

Advocates of open source software are concerned that the open source movement may be destroyed by patent claims against open source code. Of course, all developers of any kind of software should be aware of the issues concerning patents and other intellectual property. The open source community actually has organizations like the well-funded Electronic Frontier Foundation (EFF), which hires major law firms to fight for their rights in court, and they have had a number of recent successes. In addition, it would be difficult for an inventor to sue a developer of free software because open source programmers often have little money (they give away their code for free), and thus any award would have little chance of ever being paid.

7.7.2.5 Ideas and Mathematical Expressions

Software simply represents ideas and mathematical expressions. This is where those who are against software patents make their best point. However, software does not consist simply of ideas; they are specific implementations of those ideas in a manner that a physical machine—a computer—can execute. They are also not simply mathematical expressions, but a series of steps that include mathematical expressions. Steps of a method have always been patentable.

7.7.3 THE SUPREME COURT RULES?

One of the most famous, and important, intellectual property cases of recent years involves patent application 08/833,892, entitled "Energy Risk Management," filed in 1997 by Bernard Bilski and Rand Warsaw. Their invention was a method for hedging risks in commodities trading. The first claim of their patent reads as follows:

> (1) A method for managing the consumption risk costs of a commodity sold by a commodity provider at a fixed price comprising the steps of:
>
>> (a) initiating a series of transactions between said commodity provider and consumers of said commodity wherein said consumers purchase said commodity at a fixed rate based upon historical averages, said fixed rate corresponding to a risk position of said consumer;
>>
>> (b) identifying market participants for said commodity having a counter-risk position to said consumers; and
>>
>> (c) initiating a series of transactions between said commodity provider and said market participants at a second fixed rate such that said series of market participant transactions balances the risk position of said series of consumer transactions.

This type of invention that describes a process but no physical object is called a "business method patent," and it is closely related to a software patent because a software patent is also a process, albeit one that directs computer operations. This patent was rejected by the patent office, which stated that "the invention is not implemented on a specific apparatus and merely manipulates [an] abstract idea and solves a purely mathematical problem without any limitation to a practical application, therefore, the invention is not directed to the technological arts." Mathematical concepts are not patentable. The applicants appealed the rejection to the Board of Patent Appeals and Interferences (BPAI), which affirmed the rejection, although on different grounds. The board held that the examiner erred to the extent that he relied on a "technological arts" test because the case law does not support such a test. Bilski and Rand then appealed again, this time to the Court of Appeals for the Federal Circuit (CAFC).

The CAFC decided that the invention was not patentable because patents must be tied to a particular machine or transform an article from one thing or state to another. This "machine-or-transformation test" was a new test for patentability and was confusing to inventors and attorneys. The applicants once again appealed, this time to the United States Supreme Court.

On June 28, 2010, the Supreme Court decided against Bilski and Rand, but not because of the machine-or-transformation test. Abstract ideas have never been patentable, and that's what this patent was, according to the Supreme Court. The court also ruled that the machine-or-transformation test is only one test for patentability, not the only test, as the CAFC had stated. In addition, it ruled that business methods are patentable, as long as they are not abstract ideas.

Confused? So are many others—except for Bilski and Rand, who now know for sure that they do not have a patent. The Supreme Court has maintained a broad scope of patent protection but has made the test for patentability muddier. Software is still patentable. Business methods are patentable but only under certain conditions that are not completely clear at this time.

7.8 PATENT INFRINGEMENT

Software patent infringement can generally mean four different things—using a patented method or incorporating code for a patented method ("direct infringement"), contributing to infringement by another party ("contributory infringement"), forcing another party to infringe a patented method ("induced infringement"), or cooperating with another party on patent infringement ("divided infringement")—as described in the next sections.

7.8.1 DIRECT INFRINGEMENT

Software infringes on a software patent if it performs some function using a method that the software patent describes, and the software has not been licensed from the owner of the patent.

Software also infringes on a software patent if the patent claims an apparatus and the infringing software incorporates code for the patented apparatus without permission from the patent owner. In other words, patents can be methods or apparatuses. If the patent claims an apparatus as the invention, then it is claiming the code that implements a particular function. Therefore, if some software includes that function, even if it is rarely or never used, that software infringes the patent. Of course, the damages that can be collected for infringing a patent by code that is never executed are probably very small.

7.8.2 CONTRIBUTORY INFRINGEMENT

Contributory infringement of a software patent occurs if a party provides a component of patented software, and another party who receives the component then uses that component to directly infringe the patent. However, the following conditions also apply: (1) the component must be a significant part of the invention; (2) the component must be specially made or adapted for use in a way that infringes at least one claim of the patent, and the supplier knows that the component is especially made for that use; and (3) the component must not have a significant non-infringing use.

So if a computer program meets the first two criteria but has many different uses, and only one of them causes infringement, the program is not contributing to another party's infringement. The party using the program may still be directly infringing, though.

7.8.3 INDUCED INFRINGEMENT

Software can infringe on a software patent by inducing its users to infringe when the software has not been licensed from the owner of the patent. In other words, if the only way to use a supplier's software is in a way that infringes on a software patent, the supplier is inducing infringement, but only if the supplier knows, or should know, about the patent. Similarly, if the supplier instructs its customers to run software in a way that infringes on a patent, the supplier can be held liable for infringement.

One consequence of this type of infringement is that members of standards groups need to be careful. If a member of a standards group promotes a standard that forces those who abide by the standard to infringe a patent, the members of the group can be accused of inducing patent infringement.

Another consequence is that software manufacturers can be accused of inducing infringement by selling software that infringes or software components that when combined infringe on a patent. Software producers can sell inexpensive programs, such as word processors, to millions of customers who are each infringing on a software patent. Without this type of infringement, the patent owner would need to force millions of end users to pay several dollars each in royalties. Instead, the inventor can request that the software producer pay royalties on the order of millions of dollars, or take that software producer to court if necessary.

7.8.4 DIVIDED INFRINGEMENT

Divided infringement occurs when two parties conspire to infringe a patent. This means that one party makes information available to a second party, instructs a second party, or somehow facilitates a second party's involvement in the infringement, but the two parties must have what is called an "agency relationship." This means that the two parties are actively working together.

If the software of two parties each inadvertently infringes on claim elements of a patent such that the combination of the software combines to infringe, the parties themselves cannot normally be held liable. Divided infringement, particularly after the CAFC's 2006 decision in the case of *On Demand Machine Corporation v. Ingram Industries, Inc. et al.*, has been defined to ensure that companies do not conspire to infringe on a patent by attempting to look as if they do not have a close relationship.

THE UNRECOGNIZED FATHER OF REMOTE BACKUP

When people ask me the value of a patent, I relate the following story. In the early 1990s I had the idea to back up data over phone lines to a remote location and was the first to implement such a system and bring it to market. I had been working as an independent engineering consultant and was growing concerned about all of the data on my computer that was critical to my business. If there had been a fire or theft, my hard drive and backup disks and tapes could all be gone, along with my business.

So I came up with the idea of remote backup. I set up a server and developed client software to automatically zip, encrypt, and send my files over the phone to the server. My supportive friends thought the idea was "interesting," though none was willing to actually try it. Other, more blunt friends and colleagues told me this idea was ridiculous. No one would send important files over wires to an unknown location. Remember, this was before Netscape and the Internet boom— most people had not heard of the Internet.

Continues

Disregarding the strong advice, I started my backup company, eVault Remote Backup Service. I put ads and wrote articles in magazines, gave talks at conferences, and made a name for the company. Unfortunately, there was nearly zero business. Someone suggested that I file for a patent, so I went to an attorney and on June 13, 1994, filed U.S. Patent Application 08/259,256, entitled "A Remote Backup System."

In the meantime, eVault was running out of money—all of which had been a loan from me personally. Venture capitalists initially told me there was no market for this kind of service, and later, after other remote backup companies had sprung up, they told me I was too late in the game. I went to a lecture by a professor at the Stanford Business School who made the point that patents were unnecessary in the new high-tech world. Technology changed so quickly, he said, that patents couldn't protect the inventions.

When the U.S. Patent Office rejected my patent (I found out later that they almost always reject the initial filing), it would have cost me the rest of the company's money to pay the attorney to craft a response. Instead I abandoned the patent and put a full-page ad in a monthly magazine, hoping to get just a few more customers and a little more revenue.

eVault went out of business. Two months after my filing, U.S. Patent 5,537,533, entitled "System and Method for Remote Mirroring of Digital Data from a Primary Network Server to a Remote Network Server," was filed on August 11, 1994, and subsequently issued on July 6, 1996 (also after being initially rejected). Since that time, remote backup has become a huge industry of which I could have had a piece.

Since that time I turn every good idea of mine into a patent, and several have paid off nicely. The story ending was not completely bad. The people at the last company I approached for funding before closing eVault liked the idea so much that they started their own remote backup company. Since mine was dead, and I had done a lot of publicity for it, they took the name Evault. I had been smart enough to register the trademark, and when Evault sought venture capital, the investors found out that the company didn't own the trademark. Not owning your IP is a sure way not to get funded. So they came to me, and after a little negotiation, they walked away with the trademark registration and I walked away with cash and stock. I was even happier when in 2007 Seagate purchased Evault.

7.9 NPEs and Trolls

This is a good place to discuss "non-practicing entities," otherwise known as "NPEs" and "patent trolls." The latter term comes from the concept that these companies "troll" for patents—in other words, they go around looking to buy patents wherever they find them. It is also derogatorily used to equate them with the mean, ugly monsters of fairy tales that prevent innocent people from crossing bridges to their intended destinations.

NPEs are typically large, well-funded entities, usually corporations or other business entities, that own patents which they attempt to license to corporations that produce products that infringe on those patents. These patents may have been created by one or more inventors who then form the business entity to license the patents, just as they might incorporate in order to manufacture the invention. When these licensing efforts fail, NPEs take the infringing business entities to court.

In the American system, one does not lose the right to intellectual property just because one cannot commercialize it successfully. A company is not allowed to infringe a patent just because the patent owner is not manufacturing the invention, just as someone cannot steal your car just because you no longer drive it. An NPE formed by an inventor is just a common legal entity that allows that inventor to attempt to collect licensing fees that he is owed under the law. An NPE that buys patents from individual inventors who do not have the extensive resources required to negotiate license agreements with large companies or to go to court is similar to an art gallery owner who markets and sells artwork for artists who do not have the resources, the desire, or the skills and connections to market the artwork themselves.

Of course, some NPEs own, license, and sue companies over bad patents that should not have been granted in the first place or companies that do not actually infringe. There are, I am sure, unethical NPEs just as there are unethical operators in all businesses. Unethical behavior by some NPEs should not form the basis for legislation to eliminate all NPEs, as some have suggested. The unethical practices of Enron and WorldCom and numerous other companies throughout history have resulted in criminal prosecution, better scrutiny, and sometimes further regulation of business practices, but they have not (yet) resulted in the outlawing of businesses in general. Problems with the practices of NPEs should be viewed as the possible result of inefficiencies in the patent system, inequities in the civil court system, unethical behavior by some NPEs, or combinations of these things. However, the solution is not the elimination of the patent system, the civil court system, or NPEs, but rather the improvement of these things through laws and free markets so that inventors maintain the rights to sell or license their inventions freely.

I AM A TROLL

I should state that I myself am a non-practicing entity. In fact, I would guess that a large percentage of patent owners are NPEs. The fact is that I have many more inventions than I can produce with the time and money that I have. Also, there are inventions that I've created and sold, but I was unable to generate enough revenue from them to support continued production. But I shouldn't lose the right to my intellectual property just because I couldn't commercialize it successfully.

Some years ago I invented software I called Molasses that was used to connect a hardware emulator to a live network. A hardware emulator is a specialized computer that can be programmed to work like a semiconductor chip, or a set of chips, before manufacture. The emulator could be connected to a live system to see how the actual hardware would behave under real conditions. Emulators run at a fraction of the speed of the actual chip, and connecting them to networks posed some problems because networks have timing constraints that require them to run at full speed. My Molasses software slowed down packets coming from the network (as if slogging through molasses) to a speed that the emulator could handle.

After I had been selling Molasses software to several emulator companies over a period of several years, one of them approached me with a request to purchase the software and the patents. The negotiations fell through because the company demanded terms that included my waiving my right to sue them for infringement of any patent I ever came up with in perpetuity—a condition I was never going to accept. At that time, the company representative simply told me the company would create its own product and that the company had decided my patent was invalid—essentially daring me to go after it.

A year later I noticed one sentence in a brochure on that company's website that described a product that replaced Molasses. Usually the company issued press releases about its new products, but this one was kept quiet. I contacted a friend at the company who confirmed that it had indeed copied Molasses, infringing my patent and killing any more sales for me.

I approached lawyers about hiring them to help me license the patent or, if necessary, take this company to court for willful infringement, but the law firms required a retainer of $100,000 just to begin work. They warned me that litigation could cost as much as $1 million, which I just didn't have available at the time.

It was the NPEs that came to my rescue. I contacted several firms, and they saw an opportunity. I sold my patents to one of them and walked away with cash. I hear from representatives of the NPE once in a while, but I don't know what they did with my patents. Perhaps they negotiated license deals with the emulator companies. Perhaps they are still planning to take legal action. In either case, I got something for my efforts. The NPE got something it wanted, including the potential to make back much more than it had paid me for the patents. And the emulator company will most likely pay a fair price for something it tried to get, unethically, for free.

TRADE 8 SECRETS

The precise language by which a trade secret is defined varies by jurisdiction, as do the particular types of information that are subject to trade secret protection. The World Intellectual Property Organization (WIPO) defines trade secrets as follows:

> Trade secrets/undisclosed information is protected information which is not generally known among, or readily accessible to, persons that normally deal with the kind of information in question, has commercial value because it is secret, and has been subject to reasonable steps to keep it secret by the person lawfully in control of the information.

8.1 THE HISTORY OF TRADE SECRETS

Some claim that the earliest intellectual property laws were to protect trade secrets. In ancient Roman times there were laws that afforded relief against a person who corrupted one person's slave to extract secrets about the master's business. Some see these as trade secret protection laws. During the Renaissance, guilds in Europe made great efforts to protect their trade secrets. The laws that arose to protect these guilds' secrets evolved into trade secret laws during the Industrial Revolution in England in the early nineteenth century and eventually into modern trade secret laws. In fact, trade secret laws predate patent laws because trade secrets tend to disappear when businesses fold or the people who own them die. Patent laws were created as a means to disseminate great concepts and inventions in return for a limited-time monopoly, ensuring that these ideas were promulgated rather than terminated.

The earliest trade secret case in the United States was the case of *Vickery v. Welch* in 1836, which involved "a bond to convey and to assure to the obligee the obligor's chocolate-mill, 'together with his exclusive right and art or secret manner of making chocolate and all information pertaining to his said manner of making chocolate....'" In the case of *Peabody v. Norfolk* (98 Mass. 452 [Mass. 1868]) in 1868, the Supreme Judicial Court of Massachusetts wrote a ruling that strongly anticipated modern trade secret laws:

> ... a process of manufacture, whether a proper subject for a patent or not, ... has a property in it, which a court of chancery will protect against one who in violation of contract and breach of confidence undertakes to apply it to his own use, or to disclose it to third persons.

In total, the court determined that a secret manufacturing process

1. Is the property of the business that developed it
2. Is protectable against theft
3. Must be kept secret by employees even after employment ends
4. May be disclosed confidentially to others who need to use it
5. Cannot be used by a recipient who received it without authority

Modern U.S. trade secret law eventually became codified in 1939 in the Restatement of Torts, Sections 757 and 758, and later in the Uniform Trade Secrets Act in 1979.

8.2 UNIFORM TRADE SECRETS ACT (UTSA)

In the United States, whereas copyrights and patents are protected by federal laws, trade secrets are protected by state laws. Different states have different trade secret laws, but they generally adhere to the Uniform Trade Secrets Act (UTSA) that was drafted by the National Conference of Commissioners on Uniform State Laws (NCCUSL), a nonprofit, unincorporated association in the United States that consists of commissioners appointed by each state and territory. The NCCUSL was established to attempt to effect uniformity among similar laws in different jurisdictions. The acts created by this association are presented as "model acts" or "uniform acts" that each jurisdiction can decide whether to adopt.

The UTSA was originally enacted in 1979 and amended in 1985. It has been adopted by 46 states, the District of Columbia, and the U.S. Virgin Islands. As of this writing only Massachusetts, New Jersey, New York, and Texas have not adopted it. According to the UTSA, the definition of trade secret is as follows:

> "Trade secret" means information, including a formula, pattern, compilation, program device, method, technique, or process, that: (i) derives independent economic value, actual or potential, from not being generally known to, and not being readily ascertainable by proper means by, other persons who can obtain economic value from its disclosure or use, and (ii) is the subject of efforts that are reasonable under the circumstances to maintain its secrecy.

8.3 ECONOMIC ESPIONAGE ACT

Although trade secrets are determined by state law, on October 11, 1996, President Clinton signed the Economic Espionage Act of 1996 into law, covering commercial espionage in general and trade secret theft in particular. The Economic Espionage Act made trade secret theft involving multiple states or foreign entities punishable under federal law, though it also caps fines at $10 million or $5 million for organizations, depending on the nature of the crime, and caps fines for individuals at $500,000. The specific sections that are relevant to trade secrets are § 1831 and § 1832, which state the following:

§ 1831. Economic espionage

(a) In General. Whoever, intending or knowing that the offense will benefit any foreign government, foreign instrumentality, or foreign agent, knowingly

(1) steals, or without authorization appropriates, takes, carries away, or conceals, or by fraud, artifice, or deception obtains a trade secret;

(2) without authorization copies, duplicates, sketches, draws, photographs, downloads, uploads, alters, destroys, photocopies, replicates, transmits, delivers, sends, mails, communicates, or conveys a trade secret;

(3) receives, buys, or possesses a trade secret, knowing the same to have been stolen or appropriated, obtained, or converted without authorization;

(4) attempts to commit any offense described in any of paragraphs (1) through (3); or

(5) conspires with one or more other persons to commit any offense described in any of paragraphs (1) through (4), and one or more of such persons do any act to effect the object of conspiracy,

shall, except as provided in subsection (b), be fined not more than $500,000 or imprisoned not more than 15 years, or both.

(**b**) Organizations. Any organization that commits any offense described in subsection (a) shall be fined not more than $10,000,000.

§ 1832. Theft of trade secrets

(**a**) Whoever, with intent to convert a trade secret, that is related to or included in a product that is produced for or placed in interstate or foreign commerce, to the economic benefit of anyone other than the owner thereof, and intending or knowing that the offense will injure any owner of that trade secret, knowingly

(**1**) steals, or without authorization appropriates, takes, carries away, or conceals, or by fraud, artifice, or deception obtains such information;

(**2**) without authorization copies, duplicates, sketches, draws, photographs, downloads, uploads, alters, destroys, photocopies, replicates, transmits, delivers, sends, mails, communicates, or conveys such information;

(**3**) receives, buys, or possesses such information, knowing the same to have been stolen or appropriated, obtained, or converted without authorization;

(**4**) attempts to commit any offense described in paragraphs (1) through (3); or

(**5**) conspires with one or more other persons to commit any offense described in paragraphs (1) through (3), and one or more of such persons do any act to effect the object of the conspiracy, shall, except as provided in subsection (b), be fined under this title or imprisoned not more than 10 years, or both.

(**b**) Any organization that commits any offense described in subsection (a) shall be fined not more than $5,000,000.

8.4 ASPECTS OF A TRADE SECRET

I prefer to think of trade secrets in terms of three characteristics, although only two are expressly stated. The implied characteristic is that a trade secret is, in fact, a secret. So these are the three characteristics:

1. The trade secret is not generally known to the public.
2. It confers some sort of economic benefit on its holder where the benefit derives from the trade secret not being known to the public.
3. The owner of the trade secret makes reasonable efforts to maintain its secrecy.

Figure 8.1 shows the changing face of one of the most closely guarded trade secrets in the world. The recipe for making Kentucky Fried Chicken (Colonel Sanders' "Secret Recipe of 11 Herbs & Spices") is definitely not known to the public. According to their website, KFC Corporation is the world's most popular chicken restaurant chain, and their parent company, Yum! Brands, Inc., is the world's largest restaurant company. This secret recipe confers significant economic benefit on the company. And KFC Corporation goes to great lengths to guard this secret. For years, Colonel Sanders is said to have guarded his valuable recipe by keeping it entirely in his own brain, not revealed to anyone. Today, the recipe is locked in a safe in Louisville, Kentucky. Very few people know that multimillion dollar recipe, and each is obligated to strict confidentiality by his or her employment contract. Also, no single supplier knows the entire recipe. One supplier blends a part of the recipe and another supplier blends the other part. A system controlled by a computer program is used to blend these parts into the famous recipe so that neither a company, nor any human, can easily reproduce it.

Figure 8.1   Kentucky Fried Chicken: The recipe is a trade secret; the logo is a trademark.
Source: Copyright © KFC Corporation. All Rights Reserved.

8.4.1 NOT GENERALLY KNOWN

With regard to software trade secrets, many aspects of the source code can be trade secrets. For example, there can be unique algorithms, special organizations of the software, or unique sequences of code to implement functions. Most software comprises many trade secrets because most software, other than that taken from third-party sources, contains unique implementations.

Algorithms that are known to the public cannot be trade secrets in isolation, though they can be trade secrets if used in an unusual way or to solve a problem for which the particular algorithm is not known to be useful. For example, a sorting algorithm found in a textbook or in an application note on a website is, or can be, known to the public and cannot be a trade secret by itself. However, if the algorithm is used to sort a list of words in a file where such sorting makes file compression more effective, and this compression technique is not generally known, then the algorithm can be a trade secret as part of the compression technique. Also, it is possible that the specific code to implement the algorithm can be a trade secret. If it can be shown that there is something in the code that is not generally known, such as the specific source code instructions or sequences of instructions for implementing the algorithm faster than otherwise, then it can be argued that the specific implementation of the well-known algorithm is a trade secret.

These days there is a growing use of open source code that is available to anyone who agrees to the licensing terms put forth by the owner of the code. Open source code, by its nature, cannot be considered a trade secret itself. However, it is possible that a unique modification to open source code, assuming the modification is not made public, can constitute a trade secret. Similarly, the use of open source code in a unique manner may constitute a trade secret. Open source code is discussed in more detail in Chapter 26.

8.4.2 ECONOMIC BENEFIT

Even if an algorithm or technique is not generally known, there must be an economic benefit to the trade secret holder, and that benefit must be due to the fact of its being secret. So a proprietary sorting algorithm that can be easily replaced with a well-known sorting algorithm to give equivalent results (and equivalent economic benefit) may not be a trade secret. Similarly, some code that is secret but that can easily be re-created at little or no cost may not be a trade secret. Companies typically keep all of their critical software source code secret. It can be argued that any software code takes a significant amount of time and expense to write, compile, test, integrate, and maintain. Thus all of a company's critical code could be considered to be a trade secret because it would give a competitor an economic advantage simply by significantly speeding up the entire development process. However, a recent decision in *Yield Dynamics, Inc. v. TEA Systems Corporation* determined that this is not necessarily the case. The court's opinion on the matter of economic benefit was as follows:

> No evidence was admitted relating to their value to a competitor nor was there any evidence that these functions, in and of themselves, would provide a competitive advantage to a competitor. Although plaintiff may have kept its source code confidential after receiving it from defendants there was no evidence that the functions at issue were unknown in the industry. There was no evidence presented regarding the length of time that it would take a program[m]er familiar with metrology devices and experienced in the lithography industry to create such functions. The testimony on this point from Elena Dehtyar (who was a percipient witness and not an expert) was that the source code procedures in question would provide "some help" to a program[m]er in creating new routines or a similar function or save time in programming: Ms. Dehtyar was unfamiliar with the formatting of the data produced by the metrology devices in question. As a result, she used [Yield]'s source code to assist her in formatting the data. The data formats are not trade secrets of [Yield] as they are the result of the particular vendor's design of their product. There was no credible evidence that creating import functions to import data formats that have been and continue to be available to any one purchasing the vendor's products is a trade secret. Further, the evidence established that defendant Zavecz created similar import functions for KLA which were not shown to be a trade secret.
>
> The functions or procedures in question did not perform any of the applications which make these programs commercially attractive. The evidence was that import functions or procedures are common to virtually every type of software program that can be conceived of. The evidence was that import functions may be obtained from the internet. The defendant Terrence Zavecz had written similar import routines in the past for his prior employer, KLA Systems. Plaintiff's expert testified that the use of the old routines would provide some help or would be helpful in writing new routines. He did not testify that the import routines contained in the Yield programs involved any new or innovative advances in software programming. In fact, plaintiff's expert was unfamiliar with the semiconductor industry in general and with the fields of Lithography and Metrology specific to it and was not able to compare content and functionality to other similar programs written by other manufacturers having similar function. He was, however, certain that other metrology measuring programs existed and that they would also use similar import routines.

One lesson from the judgment in *Yield Dynamics v. TEA Systems* is that in order for source code to be considered a trade secret, the economic benefit of the source code should be strongly quantified in terms of the costs to reproduce it for someone who has no knowledge of it.

8.4.3 SECRECY

Individuals or companies that develop source code should take reasonable precautions to protect its secrecy. There should be written policies that dictate how to handle software source code, who has access to it, where it is to be stored, under what conditions it can leave the facility in which it is stored, and where and how it can be transferred. Not only do these policies make sense for protecting valuable assets, but putting them in writing is essential if the owner of the source code has to litigate a trade secret theft case. Without these written policies, a defendant can argue that reasonable precautions were not taken to protect the secrecy of the software and thus the software does not comprise trade secrets. For this reason, company employees should be required to sign nondisclosure agreements (NDAs), and they should be trained in handling all confidential materials, including software. Companies should mark their software as confidential, in the source code comments and on any documents that describe the internal workings of the software.

Companies must make reasonable efforts to implement these policies and implement them consistently. A reasonable effort does not mean that the security measures are impossible to overcome. Any employee can violate a policy and take source code home or copy it without notifying the company, for example. Stopping this kind of activity is impossible. A reasonable policy means that the employee is informed that this activity is wrong and enough checks are in place that the employee must make a conscious effort to avoid detection.

I have met with individuals and start-up companies that do not make a reasonable effort to protect their secrets. In some cases they do not use NDAs or, if they do, they are not consistent. For example, they may ask certain business partners whom they do not know well to sign NDAs while revealing proprietary, valuable code or other information to friends without requiring an NDA to be signed. This is a mistake. As much as possible, no valuable proprietary information should be shared without a signed NDA. Otherwise, a defendant in a trade secret theft case will argue that reasonable precautions were not taken at all times and thus the information cannot be considered a trade secret. This argument can be persuasive.

Essentially, if the owner of proprietary source code allows programmers to share code, or does not put notices of confidentiality in the source code, and does not take other reasonable steps to ensure that employees do not take the code home with them, then that source code cannot be a trade secret.

8.5 Trade Secret Theft

The UTSA defines "misappropriation" as follows:

"Misappropriation" means:

(1) acquisition of a trade secret of another by a person who knows or has reason to know that the trade secret was acquired by improper means; or

(2) disclosure or use of a trade secret of another without express or implied consent by a person who

(A) used improper means to acquire knowledge of the trade secret; or

(B) at the time of disclosure or use, knew or had reason to know that his knowledge of the trade secret was

(i) derived from or through a person who had utilized improper means to acquire it;

(ii) acquired under circumstances giving rise to a duty to maintain its secrecy or limit its use; or

(iii) derived from or through a person who owed a duty to the person seeking relief to maintain its secrecy or limit its use; or

(C) before a material change of his [or her] position, knew or had reason to know that it was a trade secret and that knowledge of it had been acquired by accident or mistake.

Trade secret theft is, obviously, when a trade secret is stolen. The difficulty in proving trade secret theft is that the owner must prove that (1) the IP was stolen and (2) the IP has the three characteristics of a trade secret. For example, if someone independently discovers the algorithms embodied in the software that constitutes one company's trade secret, without ever having seen the original code, then there is no theft involved.

In the case of trade secrets, there can be multiple independent inventors who are all entitled to use the same inventions freely. This is the significant difference between trade secrets and patents, where only one party—the owner of the patent—can use the invention without restriction. All others, even if they create the same invention independently, can use the invention only if licensed to do so by the patent holder.

8.6 PATENT OR TRADE SECRET?

When you have a useful invention, should you file for a patent or maintain it as a trade secret? A comparison of the advantages and disadvantages of patents and trade secrets is given in Table 8.1.

Table 8.1   Patent versus Trade Secret

Characteristic	Patents	Trade secrets
Public or private?	**Public.** A patent can be kept secret for 18 months after it is filed, after which it must be published.	**Private.** Trade secrets must never be made publicly available.
Owner's legal action	**Easier.** The government has put its stamp of approval on the invention.	**Harder.** The owner must prove that the invention qualifies as a trade secret and that the defendant did not independently invent it.
Cost	**High.** There is a significant cost to "prosecute" a patent, which includes the attorney costs, filing costs, and costs to address all patent office rejections and actions.	**Low.** There is some cost for maintaining secrecy, such as producing, enforcing, and maintaining secrecy procedures such as NDAs. There may also be a cost for ensuring the secrets do not get stolen, but usually this is a marginal cost of doing business.
Protection from theft	**Harder.** The invention is described in detail to the public.	**Easier.** The invention is kept secret.
Time	**Limited.** The government grants rights for 17 to 20 years, after which anyone can produce the invention.	**Unlimited.** There is no limit as long as the invention is kept secret and not developed independently.
Ownership	**Restricted.** The owners are only the patent holders who are on record with the patent office.	**Unrestricted.** If the invention is created independently, any number of inventors and owners can exist.

SOFTWARE FORENSICS

The word *forensic* comes from the Latin word *forensis* meaning "of or before the forum." In ancient Rome, an accused criminal and the accusing victim would present their cases before a group in a public forum. In this very general sense it was not unlike the modern U.S. legal system where plaintiffs and defendants present their cases in a public forum. Of course, the rules and procedures of the presentation, of which there are very many, differ from those days. Also, whether in a civil trial or a criminal trial, all parties can be represented by lawyers trained in the intricacies of these rules and procedures.

At these ancient Roman forums, both parties would present their cases to the forum and one party would be declared a winner. The party with the better presentation skills, regardless of innocence or guilt, would often prevail. The modern system relies on the fact that attorneys representing the parties make the arguments rather than the parties themselves. The entire system relies on the assumption that lawyers, trained in law and skilled at presenting complex information, will present both parties' cases in the best possible manner and that ultimately a just outcome will occur. I don't want to say that the truth will prevail, not only because that's a cliché but because there is often some amount of truth in the arguments of both parties. Rather, more often than not, justice will be served.

This model works very well—not perfectly, but very well. With regard to highly technical cases, however, the percentage of cases where justice is served is lower because the issues are difficult for judges and juries to grasp. Technical experts can throw around highly technical terms, sometimes without realizing it and other times to purposely confuse a judge or jury. This is why two things are required to improve the analysis of software for the legal system:

1. Create a standard method of quantizing software comparisons.
2. Create a standard methodology for using this quantization to reach a conclusion that is usable in a court of law.

These two things are embodied in what is called "software forensics." Before we arrive at a working definition, let us look at the definitions of related terms: "forensic science," "forensic engineering," and "digital forensics."

THE NEED FOR SOFTWARE FORENSICS

Some years ago, when I had just begun developing the metrics described in this book, the software to calculate the metrics, and the methodology to reach a conclusion based on the metrics, I was contacted by a party in a software copyright dispute in Europe. A software company had been accused of copying source code from another company. The software implemented real-time trading of financial derivatives. A group of software engineers had left one company to work for the other company; that's the most common circumstance under which software is stolen or alleged to have been stolen.

The plaintiff hired a well-known computer science professor from the Royal Institute of Technology, Stockholm, Sweden, to compare the source code. This respected professor, who had taught computer science for many years, reviewed both sets of source code and wrote his report. His conclusion could be boiled down to this: "I have spent 20 years in the field of computer science and have reviewed many lines of source code. In my experience, I have not seen many examples of code written in this way. Thus it is my opinion that any similarities in the code are due to the fact that code was copied from one program to another."

Unfortunately for the plaintiff, the defendant responded by hiring another well-known computer science professor. This person was the head of the computer science department at the very same Royal Institute of Technology, the first professor's boss. This professor compared the source code from the two parties, and essentially her conclusion was this: "I have spent 20 years in the field of computer science and have reviewed many lines of source code. In my experience, I have seen many examples of code written in this way. Thus it is my opinion that any similarities in the code are due to the fact that these are simply common ways of writing code."

The defendant did some research and came across my papers and my CodeSuite software. The defendant hired me, and I ran a CodeMatch comparison and then followed my standard procedure. CodeMatch revealed a fairly high correlation between the source code of the two programs. However, there were no common comments or strings, there were no common instruction sequences, and when I filtered out common statements and identifier names I was left with only a single identifier name that correlated. Because the identifier name combined standard terms in the industry, and both programs were written by the same programmers, I concluded that no copying had actually occurred.

After writing my expert report, what struck me was how much a truly standardized, quantified, scientific method was needed in this area of software forensics, and I made it my goal to bring as much credibility to this field as there is in the field of DNA analysis, another very complex process that is well defined and accepted in modern courts.

9.1 FORENSIC SCIENCE

According to the *Merriam-Webster Online Dictionary*, science is defined as "knowledge or a system of knowledge covering general truths or the operation of general laws especially as obtained and tested through scientific method." Forensic science is the application of scientific methods for the purpose of drawing conclusions in court (criminal or civil). The first written account of using this kind of study and analysis to solve criminal cases is given in the book entitled *Collected Cases of Injustice Rectified*, written by Song Ci during the Song Dynasty of China in 1248. In one case, when a person was found murdered in a small town, Song Ci examined the wound of the corpse. By testing different kinds of knives on animal carcasses and comparing the wounds to that of the murder victim, he found that the wound appeared to have been caused by a sickle. Song Ci had everyone in town bring their sickles to the town center for examination. One of the sickles began attracting flies because of the blood on it, and the sickle's owner confessed to the murder.

This groundbreaking book discussed other forensic science techniques, including the fact that water in the lungs is a sign of drowning and broken cartilage in the neck is a sign of strangulation. Song Ci discussed how to examine corpses to determine whether death was caused by murder, suicide, or simply an accident.

In modern times, the best-known methods of forensic science include fingerprint analysis and DNA analysis. Many other scientific techniques are used to investigate murder cases—to determine time of death, method of death, instrument of death—as well as other less criminal acts. Some other uses of forensic science include determining forgery of contracts and other documents, exonerating convicted criminals through ex post facto examination of evidence that was not considered at trial, and determining the origins of paintings or authorship of contested documents.

9.2 FORENSIC ENGINEERING

Forensic engineering is the investigation of things to determine their cause of failure for presentation in a court of law. Forensic engineering is often used in product liability cases when a product has failed, causing injury to a person or a group of people. A forensic engineering investigation often involves examination and testing of the actual product that failed or another copy of that product. The examination involves applying various stresses to the product and taking detailed measurements to determine its failure point and mode of failure. For example, a plate of glass at a very high temperature, when hit by a small stone, might chip, shatter, or crack in half. This kind of examination would be useful for understanding how a car or airplane windshield failed. The investigation might start out to replicate the situation that led to the failure in order to understand what factors might have combined to cause it.

Forensic engineering also encompasses reverse engineering, the process of understanding details about how a device works. Thus forensic engineering is critical for patent cases and many trade secret cases.

Two of the most famous cases of forensic engineering involved the *Challenger* and *Columbia* space shuttle disasters. On January 28, 1986, the space shuttle *Challenger* exploded on takeoff, killing its crew. President Ronald Reagan formed the Rogers Commission to investigate the tragedy. A six-month investigation concluded that the O-rings—rubber rings that are used to seal pipes and are used in everyday appliances like household water faucets—had failed. The O-rings were designed to create a seal in the shuttle's solid rocket boosters to prevent superheated gas from escaping and damaging the shuttle. Theoretical physicist Richard Feynman famously demonstrated on television how O-rings lose their flexibility in cold temperatures by placing rubber O-rings in a glass of cold water and then stretching them, thus simplifying a complex concept for the public. Further investigation revealed that engineers at Morton Thiokol, Inc., where the O-ring was developed and manufactured, knew of the design flaw and had informed NASA that the low temperature on the day of the launch created a serious danger. They recommended that the launch be postponed, but NASA administrators pressured them into withdrawing their objection.

On February 1, 2003, the space shuttle *Columbia* disintegrated over Texas during reentry into the Earth's atmosphere. All seven crew members died. Debris from the accident was scattered over sparsely populated regions from southeast of Dallas, Texas, to western Louisiana and southwestern Arkansas. NASA conducted the largest ground search ever organized to collect the debris, including human remains, for its investigation. The Columbia Accident Investigation Board, or CAIB, consisting of military and civilian experts in various technologies, was formed to conduct the forensic examination.

Figure 9.1 *Challenger* space shuttle: the crew, the launch, and physicist Richard Feynman demonstrating the breakdown of the O-ring that was determined to be the cause

Amazingly enough, *Columbia*'s flight data recorder was recovered in the search. *Columbia* had a special flight data OEX (**O**rbiter **Ex**periments) recorder, designed to record and measure vehicle performance during flight. It recorded hundreds of different parameters and contained extensive logs of structural and other data that allowed the CAIB to reconstruct many of the events during the last moments of the flight. The investigators could track the sequence in which the sensors failed, based on the loss of signals from the sensors, to learn how the damage progressed.

Six months of investigation led to the conclusion that a piece of foam that covered the fuel tank broke off during launch and put a hole in the leading edge of the left wing, breaching the reinforced carbon-carbon (RCC) thermal protection system that protected the shuttle from the extreme heat (2,700°C or 5,000°F) during reentry.

Figure 9.2   *Columbia* space shuttle: the crew and a scene during reentry from the recovered on-board shuttle video

9.3 DIGITAL FORENSICS

"Digital forensics" is the term for the collection and study of digital data for the purpose of presenting evidence in court. Most typically, digital forensics is used to recover data from storage media such as computer hard drives, flash drives, CDs, DVDs, cameras, cell phones, or any other device that stores information in a digital format, for the purpose of determining important characteristics of that data that are useful in solving a crime or resolving a civil dispute. These characteristics might include the type of data (e.g., pictures, emails, or letters) or the owner of the data, or the date of creation or modification of the data. Digital forensics does not involve examining the content of the data, because that requires skills that are not necessarily computer science. For example, a digital forensic examiner may be able to recover a deleted email from an investment banker about a publicly traded company. However, it would take someone familiar with banking and banking regulations to determine whether the content of the email constituted illegal insider trading.

Digital forensics often involves examining metadata, which is the information about the data rather than the content of the data. For example, while the content of an email may give facts about insider trading by an investment banker and thus be useful evidence for criminal proceedings against that banker, the metadata might show the date that the email was created. If the banker was on vacation that day, this digital forensic information might be evidence that the banker was being framed by a colleague. Proving or disproving such an issue is a key component of the investigative part of digital forensics.

Digital forensic examiners often inspect large and small computer systems to look for signs of illicit access or "break-ins." This can involve examining network activity logs that are stored on the computers. It may involve searching for suspicious files that meet certain well-known profiles and that are used to attack a system, or it may involve looking at files created at the time of a known break-in. It may also involve actively monitoring packets traveling around a network.

Techniques employed by digital forensic examiners include methods for recovering deleted and partially deleted files on a computer hard disk. They also include comparing files and sections of files to find sections that are bit-by-bit identical. Other techniques include recovering and examining metadata that gives important information about the creation of a file and its various properties. Automatically searching the contents of files and manually examining the contents of files are also important techniques in digital forensics.

Digital forensic examiners must be very careful about how data is extracted from a computer so that the data is not corrupted while the extraction is taking place. Operating systems typically maintain important metadata about files, and any modification of a file, such as moving or copying it for the purpose of examining it, will change the metadata. For this reason, special techniques and special hardware have been developed to preserve the contents of computer disks prior to a forensic examination. This can be particularly tricky when the system being examined is used in an active business, such as an online retailer, or in a critical system, such as one that controls a medical device and must operate 24/7. In these cases, special techniques, special hardware, and special software have been developed to extract data from such a live system.

Evidence procedures, such as how an item or information is acquired, documented, and stored, are very important. An examiner should be able to show what procedures were used or not used, to collect the evidence, and to show how the evidence was stored and protected from other parties. Digital forensic examiners must also be very concerned about documenting the chain of custody, which is the trail of people who handled the evidence and the places where it has been stored. In order to reduce the chance of evidence tampering, and to relieve any doubts in the mind of a judge or jury, the chain of custody must be well documented in a manner that can be verified.

9.4 SOFTWARE FORENSICS

Software forensics is the examination of software for producing results in court; it should not be confused with digital forensics. There are times when digital forensic techniques are used to recover software from a computer system or computer storage media so that a software forensic examination can be performed, but the analysis process and the methodology for finding evidence are much different. Unlike digital forensics, software forensics is involved with the content of the software files, whether those files are binary object code files or readable text source code files.

The objective of software forensics is to find evidence for a legal proceeding by examining the literal expression and the functionality of software. Software forensics requires a knowledge of the software, often including things such as the programming language in which it is written, its functionality, the system on which it is intended to run, the devices that the software controls, and the processor that is executing the code.

Whereas a digital forensic examiner attempts to locate files or sections of files that are identical, for the purpose of identifying them, a software forensic examiner must look at code that has similar functionality even though the exact representation might be different. In patent and trade secret cases, functionality is key, and two programs that implement a patent or trade secret may have been written entirely independently and look very different. In copyright and trade secret cases, software source code may have been copied but, because of the normal development process or through attempts to hide the copying, may end up looking very different. Digital forensic processes will not find functionally similar programs; software forensic processes will. Digital forensic processes will not find code that has been significantly modified; software forensic processes will.

9.5 THOUGHTS ON REQUIREMENTS FOR TESTIFYING

In recent years I have been frequently disturbed by the poor job done by some experts on the opposing side of cases I have worked on. Sometimes the experts do not seem to have spent enough time on the analysis, most certainly because of some cost constraints of their client. Other times the experts do not actually have the qualifications to perform the analysis. For example, I have been across from experts who use hashing to "determine" that a file was not copied because the files have different hashes. If you are familiar with hashes, changing even a single space inside a source code file will result in a completely different hash. While hashing is a great way to find exact copies, it cannot be used to make any statement about copyright infringement.

Most disturbing is when an expert makes a statement that is unquestionably false and the only reason it could be made is that the expert is knowingly lying to support the client. In one case an expert justified scrubbing all data from all company disks (overwriting the data so that it could not be retrieved), the weekend after a subpoena was received to turn over all computer hard drives, as a normal, regular procedure at the company. Another time an experienced programmer—the author of several programming textbooks—claimed that she could determine that trade secrets were implemented in certain source code files simply by looking at the file paths and file names. Yet another time a very experienced expert, after hours at deposition trying to explain a concept that was simply and obviously wrong, finally admitted that the lawyers had written his expert report for him. Although I was often successful, working with the attorneys for my client, in discrediting the results of the opposing expert, there were times when the judge simply did not understand the issues well enough to differentiate the other expert's opinions from mine.

Is there a way to ensure that experts actually know the areas about which they opine and a way to encourage them to give honest testimony and strongly discourage them from giving false testimony? Following are a few ideas about this, though each one carries with it potential problems. Perhaps not all of these ideas can definitely be implemented, but if some or all of them were adopted in the current legal system, we might have just results a higher percentage of the time. And applying these ideas to criminal cases might be a good idea, where an expert's opinion can be the difference between life and death for a person accused of a crime.

9.5.1 CERTIFICATION

Certain states require that experts be certified in a field of engineering before being allowed to testify about that field in court. My understanding is that few states require certification, and it is rare in those states that an expert is actually disqualified from testifying because of lack of certification. Perhaps if certification were required, there would be fewer "experts" who are simply looking for ways to do extra work on the side. Similarly, it might be more difficult for attorneys to find "experts" who support their case only because they are not sophisticated enough to understand the technical issues in depth.

One important question would be who runs the certification program? There would certainly be some competition and fighting among organizations to implement the certification. Organizations definitely exist, such as the Association for Computing Machinery (ACM) and the Institute of Electrical and Electronics Engineers (IEEE), that could set certification standards for computer scientists and electrical engineers respectively. Other engineering groups could set standards for their own engineers. Perhaps the American Bar Association (ABA) or the American Intellectual Property Law Association (AIPLA) as well as state and federal government offices could also be involved.

A very important consideration would be under what circumstances certification could be revoked. There would have to be a hierarchy of actions and ramifications ranging from fines to revocation. In reality, many penalties short of revocation would almost certainly result in the end of an expert's career. Few attorneys would want to put an expert on the stand who had a record of having been found to be unqualified or dishonest. Also, would any behaviors lead to criminal charges against the expert? Perhaps unethical behavior in a criminal trial should carry stronger punishment, including criminal charges, than similar behavior in a civil trial.

There should be a no-tolerance policy for dishonest, unethical, or illegal behavior by an expert. At a recent conference on digital forensics, a professor gave an example of a student who cheated on a test. The professor discovered the cheating and confronted the student. The student was sufficiently remorseful, according to the teacher (in my experience most criminals are remorseful once they are caught), and so the professor gave the student a second chance. This was simply a wrong decision. Remember that digital forensics is the study of sophisticated ways to hack into systems, so this professor could very well be training a criminal. Unfortunately, only about half of the faculty members at the conference agreed with me, and not all of the colleges had official policies regarding cheating. For sure, all forensics education programs must have zero-tolerance policies, in writing, and any certification program must, too.

One issue that is sure to arise is what to do if no certified expert in a particular field is available to work on the case. Perhaps the technology is very new or specialized. Or perhaps all of the certified experts are conflicted out or simply have no time. It seems that a judge could create an exception, allowing someone with experience in the field to testify in cases where certified experts are not available.

Many experts themselves resist certification requirements because they are already earning a living that they would not want to interrupt in order to study for and take a test that they feel is unnecessary. I also used to think the certification was unnecessary, but having seen the shoddy or unethical work of some experts, I am changing my mind. The government requires that a lawyer pass a bar exam before practicing law, yet experts require no similar test despite their importance to the legal process.

9.5.2 NEUTRAL EXPERTS

Another way of dealing with this problem is to require neutral experts who are contracted either by the court or jointly by the parties in the case and whose costs are shared by both parties. Currently, there are typically two situations when neutral experts are used. One situation is when the judge decides that the issues involved are too complex for the judge or the jury to understand without an expert in the field to explain them, and a neutral expert can cut through any biases that the experts hired by the parties may have. Another situation is when the parties agree on an expert and jointly cover the expert's fees. Hiring only one expert saves time and money in coming to a resolution, and it gives each party a limited ability to persuade the expert. Perhaps neutral experts should be required for every case. The parties could split the cost, or the loser could be required to pay. This seems to be a good solution, particularly if the neutral expert has been certified in her area of expertise. One drawback of having a neutral expert that should be considered carefully is that a biased expert, or one whose skills are less than ideal, could draw an incorrect conclusion, and there would be little ability for a party to challenge it on technical grounds. Of course, having a neutral expert does not preclude the possibility that each party could additionally employ its own expert, though this might further obscure the issues rather than clarify them, given that there could potentially be three different opinions.

9.5.3 TESTING OF TOOLS AND TECHNIQUES

It also seems that tools and techniques used by experts should be tested and certified by an official body. There have been instances of experts using the wrong tools, either accidentally because they did not really understand what the tool did, or possibly on purpose to confuse the issues before the judge or jury. It would be good to require that tools be tested, that their results be rigorously verified, and that experts be certified in the use of the tools before testimony can be introduced in court that relies on the results of the tools.

PART IV

SOURCE CODE DIFFERENTIATION

"Data! Data! Data!" he cried impatiently. "I can't make bricks without clay."
—Sherlock Holmes in *The Adventure of the Copper Beeches*

In this part I cover some basic methods of comparing and measuring software. In particular, I define software source code differentiation, which is a mathematical method for comparing software source code to find basic similarities and differences. The technique of differentiation is particularly useful for finding code that has been directly copied from one program to another. While other methods exist for finding copying, as will be described later in this book, source code differentiation is better at determining not only what has been copied but also the percentage of copying that has taken place.

There are many different metrics for measuring qualities of software, but source code differentiation has some unique abilities to measure development effort as well as software changes and software intellectual property changes.

In Chapter 10, I introduce the theory of differentiation, which will get a little mathematical, but anyone with an understanding of basic algebra should be able to follow. In Chapter 11, I discuss implementations of source code differentiation, including the "changing lines of code" or "CLOC" method of measuring software growth, and compare it to traditional methods like "source lines of code" or "SLOC." In Chapter 12, I discuss various applications of source code differentiation, including measuring software intellectual property growth and also its use in copyright infringement litigation.

Much of the mathematics and algorithms described in this section are utilized in the CodeDiff and CodeCLOC functions of the CodeSuite program developed and distributed by S.A.F.E. Corporation.

OBJECTIVES

The objective of this part of the book is to give a theoretical, mathematical foundation for software source code differentiation as well as its applications and implementations. In particular, software differentiation is used to compare basic characteristics of software source code and also to measure software development effort as well as software growth and software intellectual property growth during product development.

INTENDED AUDIENCE

Computer scientists, computer programmers, and *technical consultants and expert witnesses for litigation* will find this part useful for understanding the theory, implementation, and applications of source code differentiation, particularly with respect to measuring code to quantify development progress on a software project. *Intellectual property lawyers* and *corporate managers* with an understanding of algebra will find this section interesting and useful, especially to get a deep understanding of this method and the associated tools that can be used in software IP litigation, and to give them an idea of how this method and the tools should not be used because of their limitations. *Tax lawyers, economists, accountants*, and *corporate managers* with an understanding of algebra will find this section useful for understanding a technique that can be used to measure software changes for transfer pricing calculations. *Software entrepreneurs* will find this section useful for understanding source code differentiation in order to apply it to new software products and new businesses.

10 THEORY

Source code differentiation is the measure of the similarity of two sets of source code based on the number of lines of code that match completely as a fraction of the total number of lines of code. There are other ways of measuring the similarities and differences between sets of source code, and each way has its own advantages and disadvantages. Source code correlation, for example, is discussed in detail in Part V of this book. Source code differentiation is particularly useful for finding and measuring the amount of code that has been directly copied from one program to another, or one program version to another version, without modification.

In addition to measuring the similarity of two sets of code, source code differentiation has been shown to be a very useful software metric for the following applications:

- Measuring software development effort
- Measuring software changes in an evolving software project
- Measuring software intellectual property changes in an evolving software project

These applications are discussed in Chapter 11.

10.1 DIFF

The most common method for measuring the similarity of two sets of source code is the *diff* command that is built into the UNIX operating system and into UNIX-like operating systems such as Linux. The UNIX operating system, developed in the early 1970s at AT&T Bell Labs, incorporated a number of utilities that were useful for programmers including *diff*, which prints out the differences between the lines of two text files. The *diff* utility was developed by Douglas McIlroy and was shipped in the fifth edition of UNIX in 1974. The algorithm behind *diff* was published in a 1976 paper by McIlroy and James W. Hunt, who developed an initial prototype of *diff* at Stanford University. *Diff* was not the first utility program for finding differences in text files, but it was considered to be the first reliable one.

10.1.1 DIFF THEORY

Diff produces a list of the smallest number of changes that must be applied to one file to make it identical to a second file. The changes can be one of three kinds: add a line, delete a line, or change a line. Consider the two text files in Table 10.1. Note that the line numbers shown in the table are only for identifying lines and for describing the steps that *diff* takes; they have no other meaning and do not exist in the files.

Table 10.1 Two Files for Measuring Similarity with *Diff*

File A		File B	
Line no.	Text	Line no.	Text
1	aaaaaaa	1	1111111
2	bbbbbbb	2	aaaaaaa
3	ccccccc	3	bbbbbbb
4	ddddddd	4	2222222
5	eeeeeee	5	3333333
6	fffffff	6	4444444
7	ggggggg	7	eeeeeee

The operations that can be performed to change File A to File B are:

1. Add a line 0 at the beginning of File A: 1111111.
2. Change File A, line 3, from ccccccc to 2222222.
3. Change File A, line 4, from ddddddd to 3333333.
4. Change File A, line 5, from eeeeeee to 4444444.
5. Delete File A, line 6: fffffff.
6. Delete File A, line 7: ggggggg.

Converting File B to File A requires the following operations:

1. Delete File B, line 1.
2. Change File B, line 4, from 2222222 to ccccccc.
3. Change File B, line 5, from 3333333 to ddddddd.
4. Change File B, line 6, from 4444444 to eeeeeee.
5. Add a line at the end of File B: fffffff.
6. Add a line at the end of File B: ggggggg.

The number of operations to convert one file to another can be used as a measure of the differences between the two files. There are a few things to note about this example. First, the smallest number of steps to convert a file to itself is 0. I call the first property the **identity property**, which says that this measure confirms that a file is identical to itself. This is one important property of any source code measurement technique.

Second, the smallest number of steps to convert File A to File B is equal to the smallest number of steps to convert File B to File A. I call the second property the **commutativity property**, which says that comparing File A to File B is exactly the same as comparing File B to File A.

These two properties are necessary for any algorithm to produce a useful number for measuring software or software intellectual property. It can be seen that comparing a file to itself should always result in the minimal measurement value (or maximal value, depending on whether similarity or difference is being measured). Also, measuring two files should yield the same result regardless of which file is the first in the pair being compared.

Therefore the *diff* theory results in a value—the number of steps required to change one file to another—that can be used to provide a measurement of the difference between the two files.

There is a third property that should be added to this list. I call this property the **location property**. This means that the location of the files in a file system should have no bearing on the measurement of the similarities or differences between the files. While this may seem obvious, some measurement algorithms do not meet the requirements of the identity and commutativity properties. Also, one well-known algorithm, at least as it is implemented, gives different values depending on the locations of the files in the file system. The algorithms and their implementations that do not have these three critical properties are not useful for measuring source code differences or similarities.

ORIGIN OF THE LOCATION PROPERTY

When I first created CodeMatch for comparing source code, I wasn't aware that there were any other programs that did something similar. When CodeMatch became commercially available, some customers told me about other programs, and I decided to see how mine compared to the others. I didn't know about them because they were all from universities, and their developers hadn't done much to commercialize them or advertise them outside the academic community.

So I downloaded two available programs and contacted the professors about two others. Of these other two, one program had been a pure research project that no longer existed. Once the program was run and the paper written about it, the program and its source code were deleted or lost. I was able to obtain the second of these unavailable programs, but everything had been hard-coded into the program, even things like file names, number of files, and file locations, rather than using constants defined in a header file as good programming practice would dictate. I decided that it wasn't worth the effort to try to find all these references, make the appropriate changes, and recompile the code, especially since tinkering with the code could break the algorithm and would thus produce results that didn't really show the algorithm's effectiveness.

Each of the other two programs had both a Web version and a stand-alone version. I contacted both professors to obtain the stand-alone version for testing, and only one complied. I then ran CodeSuite and the two other "plagiarism detection" programs on our test cases, consisting of files and modified files, to see which programs correctly determined that the modified files were "plagiarized" copies of the original files. The one stand-alone program from academia produced results that were so poor, I was sure something had gone wrong. Perhaps I had received the wrong version of the program, or perhaps I was missing some initialization step.

I called the professor and emailed him the results. His answer came back a short time later, addressing me like a student who hadn't read the assigned class material. Of course the results would be wrong, he said. The files in my test cases were distributed in all kinds of nested folders. When professors assign programming problems to students, he explained, each student's work is put in a folder with the student's name. The program expects to compare files in one folder to files in folders at the same level of the directory tree.

When I rearranged the files into this directory structure, the results were much better, though still not as good as those with CodeMatch. Two thoughts occurred to me. First, in my line of work—litigation consulting—I can't dictate to the opposing parties how they should distribute their files. Second, I thought that writing a program to look only in certain directory structures seemed like a limitation that required extra thought and extra coding. I marveled at not only why someone would put this limitation into the program, but also how much time that programmer must have spent implementing the limitation.

When writing this book, I decided to include the location property to discourage others from putting this strange and restrictive limitation into their algorithms or programs.

10.1.2 DIFF IMPLEMENTATION

What I have described is the theory behind the *diff* utility. Different versions of the utility are implemented differently, and I will not go into the details of these implementations here. All of these implementations, though, have the requirement that *diff* must work in a reasonable amount of time even on very large files. These implementations speed up the basic comparison algorithm, but they also introduce some drawbacks that are described in the following sections.

10.1.3 FALSE POSITIVES

Diff uses a hashing algorithm to convert each line of text into a single number. Hashing algorithms convert strings into numbers so that rather than comparing each line character by character, only two numbers must be compared to determine whether the lines are equal, significantly speeding up the comparison. The hashing algorithm used in *diff* may hash two lines of unequal length to the same value, something Hunt and McIlroy refer to as a "jackpot." According to their original paper, on their state-of-the-art 16-bit computer, they estimated that these jackpots should happen less than 10 percent of the time for 5,000-line files and less than 1 percent of the time for 500-line files. So in any comparison using *diff* there is a small but nonzero number of cases of false positives where *diff* reports lines as matching that do not actually match.

10.1.3 FALSE NEGATIVES

Diff is a great utility, in both theory and implementation, for comparing general text files. There are some limitations, though, when used to compare computer source code files. Consider, for example, the files in Table 10.2.

The two source code files are functionally equivalent. The lines have been rearranged, but this rearrangement results in no functional difference. The operations to convert File A to File B are[1]:

1. Delete File A, line 1.
2. Change File A, line 3: a = 5.
3. Change File A, line 5: aa = 13.
4. Delete File A, line 6.
5. Delete File A, line 7.
6. Add after File A, line 8: ccc = a + b;.

Table 10.2 Two Files Showing Limitations of *Diff*

File A		File B	
Line no.	Text	Line no.	Text
1	a = 5;	1	b = 6;
2	b = 6;	2	a = 5;
3	aa = 13;	3	bb = 12;
4	bb = 12;	4	aa = 13;
5	aaa = 99;	5	ddd = aa / a;
6	bbb = 2;	6	ccc = a + b;
7	ccc = a + b;	7	bbb = 2;
8	ddd = aa / a;	8	aaa = 99;
9	xxxx = aa * bb;	9	xxxx = aa * bb;
10	yyyy = 0;	10	yyyy = 0;

---

1. Several equivalent operations can be used to convert the strings in this example, all with the same number of steps.

7. Add after File A, line 8: bbb = 2;.

8. Add after File A, line 8: aaa = 99;.

Using *diff* to produce a difference measure, the number of steps needed to convert one file to another would produce the number 8. For source code, this measure would not be accurate because source code can be rearranged without affecting functionality.

10.2 DIFFERENTIATION

Source code differentiation is the measure of the number of lines of code that match completely as a fraction of the total number of lines of code. Unlike documents, where the order of the text can be critical to its meaning, lines of software source code can be reordered and entire sections cut and pasted into other locations within a file or into another file without changing the functionality of the program. For source code differentiation, the order of the statements is not considered, so comparing a file to an identical copy where the statements were all in a different order would still result in a similarity score of 1. This is done to recognize simple reordering of lines that can confuse other similarity-measuring algorithms.

To calculate a similarity score we first count the number of lines in File A and File B, *LA* and *LB*. Then we must determine the number of matching lines, *mA,B*. Note that the number of matching lines is one to one. In other words, a line in File A is counted as matched to a line in File B if and only if they are considered matching and neither line has already been counted as matched to another line. This is illustrated in the code in Table 10.3. There are six lines of code in File B that match a line in File A. However, the number of matching lines is 1 because once line 1 of File A is matched to line 1 (or line 2, 3, 4, or 5) of File B, it cannot again be counted as matching another line in File B.

Table 10.3   Two Files for Measuring Similarity with Differentiation

File A	File B
`a = a + 1;`	`a = a + 1;`
`for (i = 0; i < 10; i++)`	`a = a + 1;`
`{`	`a = a + 1;`
`    a = a * 1;`	`a = a + 1;`
`    printf("The answer is`	`a = a + 1;`
`    %i\n", a);`	`a = a + 1;`
`}`	

10.2.1 DEFINITIONS

Source code differentiation defines a measure of similarity between two source code files, represented by the Greek letter sigma. The symbols of source code differentiation and their meanings are as follows:

F^n	= file number n
$\sigma(F^n, F^m)$	= source code similarity between two files
D^n	= location of file number n (e.g., directory path)
L_n	= the number of lines in file n
$M(F^n, F^m)$	= the number of lines that match between two files
$m_{i,j}$	= match score, with a value between 0 and 1, for lines i and j
$l(i)$	= the length of (i.e., number of characters in) line i
$w(c)$	= a character-weighting function for character c
$w(i)$	= the weighted length of line i
c_k^i	= character k of line i
$LCS(i,j)$	= longest common subsequence of lines i and j
$LCCS(i,j)$	= longest common contiguous subsequence (substring) of lines i and j
$WR(i)$	= whitespace reduction of line i

10.2.2 AXIOMS

Source code differentiation must meet the three properties described previously—identity property, commutativity property, and location property—for source code differentiation to be a consistent and usable measure. These properties are axioms because they are fundamental properties to which any comparison measure must adhere for the measurement to be useful.

10.2.2.1 Commutativity property

Similarity must not be dependent on the order of comparing two files. In other words, the similarity measure between files F^n and file F^m must be commutative:

$$\sigma\left(F^n, F^m\right) = \sigma\left(F^m, F^n\right) = 1 \tag{10.1}$$

10.2.2.2 Identity property

The similarity measure between two files must be equivalent to the identity similarity measure. In other words, a file cannot be more similar to another file than it is to itself:

$$\sigma\left(F^n\right)=\sigma\left(F^n,F^n\right)=1 \tag{10.2}$$

10.2.2.3 Location property

The similarity measure of two files must be independent of the location of the files:

$$\sigma\left(F^n,F^m\right)=\sigma\left(F^n,F^m\right)\forall\, D^n,D^m \tag{10.3}$$

10.3 Types of Similarity

There are two ways to measure similarity: mutual similarity and directional similarity. These measurements are useful for different applications, and each is described in the following sections. Mutual similarity is useful for creating a measure of how much code is shared by two source code files. Calculating the mutual similarity of all of the source code files in two different programs is useful for determining how much code the two programs have in common. Directional similarity is useful for determining how much code from one file came from another file. Calculating the directional similarity of all of the source code files in two different programs is useful for determining how much of one program was derived from another program. Directional similarity is particularly useful for measuring, for example, how much of one program's code is open source code. Directional similarity is also useful for calculating how much of one version of a program was derived from a previous version. The "changing lines of code" (CLOC) method for calculating software evolution, described in detail in Chapter 12, relies on directional similarity.

10.3.1 Mutual Similarity

Mutual similarity is twice the total number of matching lines in file n and file m, divided by the total number of lines in file n and file m. It is calculated according to Equation 10.4. Mutual similarity is useful as a measure of the number of lines in common between two files.

$$\sigma\left(F^n,F^m\right)=\frac{2M\left(F^n,F^m\right)}{L_n+L_m} \tag{10.4}$$

The factor of 2 is simply for the purpose of normalizing the similarity number. If both files are identical, then both files contain the same number of lines L, and M is equal to L, but the denominator is $2L$.

10.3.2 DIRECTIONAL SIMILARITY

Directional similarity is the total number of matching lines in two files divided by the total number of lines in one of the files. There are two ways to calculate directional similarity, which are shown in Equations 10.5a and 10.5b. Equation 10.5a shows similarity in the direction of file n, while Equation 10.5b shows similarity in the direction of file m. Directional similarity is most useful for measuring how much code in one file was used in another file. In particular, this method is used in the CLOC method of measuring changes to software IP, described in Chapter 12.

$$\sigma_n\left(F^n, F^m\right) = \frac{M\left(F^n, F^m\right)}{L_n} \tag{10.5a}$$

$$\sigma_m\left(F^n, F^m\right) = \frac{M\left(F^n, F^m\right)}{L_m} \tag{10.5b}$$

Note that the commutativity property still holds with directional similarity because the direction is associated with one of the files. If the order of the files is swapped, the direction is still associated with the same file as before, and the similarity is the same.

10.4 MEASURING SIMILAR LINES

Up until this point we have not defined a "matching line." There are a number of ways of measuring m, all of which are legitimate and have different uses. The methods include

- Simple matching
- Whitespace-reduced matching
- Case-insensitive matching
- Fractional matching
- Weighted fractional matching

10.4.1 SIMPLE MATCHING

Simple matching means, as its name implies, that lines either match completely or don't match at all. Equation 10.6 describes simple matching in mathematical terms, stating that $m_{i,j}$ equals 1 if and only if lines i and j are the same length and all characters are identical.

$$m_{ij} = \left\{ 1 \Leftrightarrow l(i) = l(i) \text{ and } c^i_k = c^j_k \ \forall \ 1 \le k \le l(i) \atop 0 \text{ otherwise} \right. \tag{10.6}$$

Simple matching results in a lemma, the associative property, that is described mathematically in Equation 10.7. This states that if line i matches line j and line j matches line k, then line i matches line k. This should be obvious—if one line exactly matches a second line and that second line exactly matches a third line, then the first line must exactly match the third line.

$$m_{i,j} = 1, m_{j,k} = 1 \Rightarrow m_{i,k} = 1 \tag{10.7}$$

This associativity property can be used to simplify and speed up the calculation of similarity scores between file pairs, as discussed in section 10.5 on measuring file similarity.

10.4.2 FRACTIONAL MATCHING

Fractional matching means that the match scores between strings have a value ranging from 0 to 1, depending on the amount of similarity of the strings. Calculating fractional match scores can rely on finding the longest common subsequence or the longest common contiguous subsequence, more commonly known as the longest common substring.

We are interested in the longest common subsequence with regard to characters in two strings—in particular the longest sequence of characters that occurs in both strings. As shown in Figure 10.1, when the string abcdefghijklmnop is compared

Figure 10.1 Comparing strings using longest common subsequence

to the string `abc123456mn66op95014`, the longest common subsequence is abcmnop because this sequence of characters can be found in both strings.

As shown in Figure 10.2, when the same string `abcdefghijklmnop` is compared to the same string `abc123456mn66op95014`, the longest common contiguous subsequence is abc because this is the longest unbroken sequence of characters in both strings.

Equations 10.8 and 10.9 represent these concepts mathematically, stating that the match score is the length of the longest common subsequence (shown in Equation 10.8) or longest common contiguous subsequence (shown in Equation 10.9) divided by the length of the larger string.

$$m_{i,j} = \frac{l(LCS(i,j))}{\max(l(i), l(j))} \tag{10.8}$$

$$m_{i,j} = \frac{l(LCCS(i,j))}{\max(l(i), l(j))} \tag{10.9}$$

Note that the match score is divided by the larger of the lengths of the two strings. This is done so that getting a match score of 1 requires that all characters match and that both strings be the same length.

Longest common contiguous subsequence (LCCS) finds identical, uninterrupted sequences of characters in the lines. It can be calculated, on average, in linear time $O(l(i)+l(j))$ using what is known as the Rabin-Karp algorithm. Longest common subsequence (LCS) considers strings to have some degree of matching even when differences exist within the matching sequences of characters. The computation time for longest common subsequence can be calculated in quadratic time $O(l(i) \cdot l(j))$, much longer than that for longest common contiguous subsequence. However, consider the following source code statements:

```
z = param1 /* temp */ + param2 /* dist */ + param3; /* length */
z = param1 + param2 + param3; /* temp + dist + length */
```

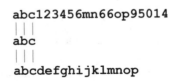

Figure 10.2   Comparing strings using longest common contiguous subsequence (substring)

While both statements are functionally identical, and they convey the same information in the comments, calculating LCCS would find a maximum sequence of only 12 characters:

```
+ param3; /*
```

Calculating LCS would find a maximum sequence of 29 characters, which seems to be more indicative of the amount of matching of these two lines:

```
z = param1 + param2 + param3;
```

10.4.3 Weighted Fractional Matching

Weighted fractional matching involves weighting some characters more than others in a comparison. This is done because some characters are more significant than others when matching. For example, when source code is compared, numerals might be given less weight than alphabetic characters because numbers are generic and are used throughout programs. As an illustration, it may be considered that while the following three lines all fractionally match, they have different meanings:

```
a = res100;
a = 100;
a = res;
```

The first line assigns the value of variable res100 to variable a. The second line assigns a value of 100 to the variable a, which seems to be a fairly generic line of code and has little functionality in common with the first line. The third line assigns the value of variable res to variable a, which seems to have more in common with the first line and may be a copied and modified version of the first line. Other characters that can be weighted lower are symbols, particularly those that are required by the programming language, such as the semicolon.

Equation 10.10 shows how the weighting of an entire line $w(i)$ is simply the sum of the weights of each character in the line. The character-weighting function w gives greater weights to some characters and lesser weights to others.

$$w(i) = \sum_{k=1}^{l(i)} w\left(c^i_k\right)$$

(10.10)

Equations 10.11 and 10.12 express weighted fractional matching mathematically based on the line-weighting function and using either longest common subsequence (shown in Equation 10.11) or longest common contiguous subsequence (shown in Equation 10.12). Fractional matching can be thought of as weighted fractional matching where the weights for all characters are equal.

$$m_{i,j} = \frac{w(LCS(i,j))}{\max(w(i), w(j))} \qquad (10.11)$$

$$m_{i,j} = \frac{w(LCCS(i,j))}{\max(w(i), w(j))} \qquad (10.12)$$

10.4.4 CASE INSENSITIVITY

Case insensitivity considers two characters to be equal if they are equivalent or one is a lowercase letter and the other is the equivalent uppercase letter (e.g., letter z is equivalent to letter z and to letter Z). Case insensitivity can be combined with any form of matching. Simple matching combined with case insensitivity would be called "case-insensitive simple matching."

10.4.5 WHITESPACE REDUCTION

Whitespace reduction removes all whitespace from the right and left ends of the string and converts all contiguous sequences of whitespace within a string to a single space. For example, whitespace reduction of the following line

```
    Variable1     =         5*      (aaa +      bbb   );
```

would result in this line:

```
Variable1 = 5* (aaa + bbb);
```

Whitespace reduction can be combined with any other form of matching by performing the whitespace reduction on lines before comparing them. Simple matching combined with whitespace-reduced matching would be called "whitespace-reduced simple matching," for example.

10.5 MEASURING FILE SIMILARITY

Once match scores have been determined for each pair of lines in a file, those match scores are used to determine the similarity of a pair of files. To calculate the similarity of a pair of files, we want to pair up lines of code in each file such

Table 10.4   Calculating File Pair Similarity from Simple Match Scores

Match score		File I			
		Line I	Line 2	Line 3	Line 4
File 2	Line I	0	1	0	0
	Line 2	0	0	0	1
	Line 3	0	0	0	1
	Line 4	1	0	0	1
	Line 5	1	0	0	1
	Line 6	0	1	0	0

Table 10.5   Calculating File Pair Similarity from Fractional Match Scores

Match score		File I			
		Line I	Line 2	Line 3	Line 4
File 2	Line I	0.2	1.0	0.0	0.0
	Line 2	0.0	0.0	0.0	1.0
	Line 3	0.0	0.9	0.0	0.4
	Line 4	0.0	0.0	0.0	0.2
	Line 5	0.0	0.0	0.0	0.1
	Line 6	0.0	0.0	0.0	0.0

that we optimize the total of all of the match scores. Table 10.4 shows an example for simple match scores. The lines of File 1 are represented across the top of the table, and the lines of File 2 are represented at the left of the table. Each line can be paired only once. In this case line 3 of File 1 and lines 5 and 6 of File 2 are not paired. The total for the two files is 3. This value would be plugged into Equation 10.4 to result in a mutual similarity value of 0.60, or plugged into Equation 10.5a to result in a similarity value of 0.75 in the direction of File 1 or into Equation 10.5b to result in a similarity value of 0.50 in the direction of File 2. Other combinations of lines could have been chosen, but no combination results in a match score higher than 3.

Table 10.5 shows an example for fractional match scores. In this case line 3 of File 1 and lines 4, 5, and 6 of File 2 are not paired. The total for the two files is 2.1.

This value would be plugged into Equation 10.4 to result in a mutual similarity value of 0.42, or plugged into Equation 10.5a to result in a similarity value of 0.525 in the direction of File 1 or into Equation 10.5b to result in a similarity value of 0.35 in the direction of File 2. Other combinations of lines could have been chosen, but no combination results in a match score higher than 2.1.

Mathematically this maximization of the file pair match score is represented by Equation 10.13, whether weighted matching is used or not.

$$M\left(F^n, F^m\right) = \max\left(\sum_{i,j} m_{i,j}\right) \forall\{i, j\} \in \left\{F^n, F^m\right\} \tag{10.13}$$

Equation 10.13 states that the total match M between two files F^n and F^m is the maximum sum of match scores between pairs of lines in the two files. Lines can be paired in many different ways to produce many possible similarity values. For F^n with i lines and F^m with j lines, there are $i \cdot j$ possible line pairings. The total number of possible combinations of lines is given by Equation 10.14 (note that $0! = 1$).

$$Total\ line\ pairs = \frac{j!}{(j-i)!}\ for\ i \leq j \tag{10.14}$$

This number is very large for large files because it is on the order of the factorial of the number of lines in the smallest file. For example, 10! is 3,628,800 and 20! is 2,432,902,008,176,640,000, yet files of only 20 lines are tiny and rare. Fortunately, there is a fast algorithm for calculating the similarity when simple matching is used, because many line pairs do not need to be examined. This significantly speeds up the computation. When using fractional matching, the algorithm is much slower, but there are still algorithm shortcuts that speed up the calculation. These algorithms for calculating the similarity of two files, using simple matching or fractional matching, are discussed in the next chapter.

10.6 MEASURING SIMILAR PROGRAMS

Once similarity is determined for each pair of files, those similarity scores are used to determine the similarity of an entire program (for our purposes I refer to sets of files as "programs" even though it may be the case that the files represent only subsets of programs or even multiple programs).

For determining the similarity of two programs, the similarities of the file pairs are not summed, because it is important to consider the file pairs individually. We want to know more than just how the programs are similar; we want to know which files are most similar and which are least similar. However, we can maximize based on individual files or maximize based on the entire program.

10.6.1 MAXIMIZING BASED ON FILES

Maximizing based on files means we want to select the file pairs with the highest similarity values, even if we end up pairing files more than once. In other words, we want to determine the most similar files within two programs. If File 1 of Program 1 and File 2 of Program 2 have a similarity of 1.0, and File 1 of Program 1 and File 3 of Program 2 have a similarity of 1.0, we want to consider both file pairs even though this references File 1 of Program 1 twice. Of course, we have two programs, so we can choose the maximum similarity scores based on the first program or based on the second program. It makes sense that if we want to maximize the similarity scores based on the first program, we should also calculate the similarity in the direction of the first program. Similarly, if we want to maximize the similarity scores based on the second program, we should calculate the similarity in the direction of the second program.

Table 10.6 shows how files are selected if based on the files in the first program. Note how the largest value in each column is chosen. If there are multiple values in a column with the same value, one is chosen arbitrarily.

Table 10.6   Measuring Program Similarity Based on the First Set of Files

		Program 1			
Match score		File 1	File 2	File 3	File 4
Program 2	File 1	0.2	1.0	0.0	0.0
	File 2	0.1	0.0	0.0	1.0
	File 3	0.9	0.9	0.0	0.5
	File 4	0.8	1.0	0.0	0.2
	File 5	0.2	0.1	0.1	0.1
	File 6	0.0	0.0	0.0	0.5

Table 10.7 Measuring Program Similarity Based on the Second Set of Files

Match score		Program 1			
		File 1	File 2	File 3	File 4
Program 2	File 1	0.2	1.0	0.0	0.0
	File 2	0.1	0.0	0.0	1.0
	File 3	0.9	0.9	0.0	0.5
	File 4	0.8	1.0	0.0	0.2
	File 5	0.2	0.1	0.1	0.1
	File 6	0.0	0.0	0.0	0.5

Table 10.7 shows how files are selected if based on the files in the second program. Note how the largest value in each row is chosen. If there are multiple values in a row with the same value, one is chosen arbitrarily. Note also that the resulting file pairs that are selected to represent the programs are different for both methods. Also note that in this example, maximizing based on the second program results in files in the first program being used more than once.

We represent this maximization using Equation 10.15a (maximizing program similarity based on first set of files) or Equation 10.15b (maximizing program similarity based on second set of files):

$$\max\left(\sigma_n\left(F^n, F^m\right)\right) \forall\, m \tag{10.15a}$$

$$\max\left(\sigma_m\left(F^n, F^m\right)\right) \forall\, n \tag{10.15b}$$

10.6.2 MAXIMIZING BASED ON PROGRAMS

Maximizing based on programs means we want to select the file pairs such that each file is paired at most once, and the overall sum of similarity values for file pairs is maximized. It makes sense that we should calculate the mutual similarity of the files in this case so that neither program is given more weight than the other.

This problem is the same one we encountered when measuring file similarity using fractional match scores. Again, the number of file pairs that must be examined is given in Equation 10.16 and is on the order of the factorial of the number of files in the program with the fewest files. In Chapter 11 I describe an

Table 10.8 Measuring Program Similarity Based on Programs

Match score		Program 1			
		File 1	File 2	File 3	File 4
Program 2	File 1	0.2	1.0	0.0	0.0
	File 2	0.1	0.0	0.0	1.0
	File 3	0.9	0.9	0.0	0.5
	File 4	0.8	1.0	0.0	0.2
	File 5	0.2	0.1	0.1	0.1
	File 6	0.0	0.0	0.0	0.5

algorithm used to select these files that reduces computation time by taking into account certain characteristics of the similarity measurement.

$$Total\ file\ pairs = m! \cdot (n-m+1)\ for\ m \leq n \tag{10.16}$$

Table 10.8 shows how files are selected if based on programs. Because Program 1 has four files and Program 2 has more files, the total number of pairs is four. Each file is matched at most once, but some files are not matched at all. Note that File 2 of Program 1 is paired with File 1 of Program 2, but it could have been paired with File 4 of Program 2 because both pairs have a similarity of 1. With this method, sometimes file pairs are still chosen arbitrarily.

We represent this maximization using Equation 10.17:

$$\max\left(\sigma\left(F^n, F^m\right)\right) \forall \{n,m\} \tag{10.17}$$

$\underset{\text{11}}{\textbf{IMPLEMENTATION}}$

Now that I have discussed the theory behind source code differentiation, I will discuss ways of practically and efficiently implementing that theory.[1] The particular implementation discussed in this chapter is based on the implementation used in the commercial CodeDiff tool that is a function of the CodeSuite program, available from S.A.F.E. Corporation.

11.1 CREATING AND COMPARING ARRAYS

To implement source code differentiation, it is first necessary to put each line into an array. Source code differentiation is not programming-language-aware. In other words, all programming languages are treated identically. There is no discrimination between statements and comments. Multiple statements on a line separated, for example, by a semicolon are treated as a single line. All text from the beginning of the line to the end of the line is treated as a single line.

To compare the lines to each other, it is necessary to put the lines of code into arrays. Table 11.1 shows two example source code files. The arrays for these files are shown in Table 11.2, where File A is used to create Array A, and File B is used to create Array B.

---

1. Note that some of the concepts discussed in this chapter may be covered by patents that have been issued or are pending.

Table 11.1   Two Source Code Files for Comparison

File A		File B	
Line no.	Text	Line no.	Text
1	a = 5;	1	b = 6;
2	b = 6;	2	a = 5;
3	aa = 13;	3	bb = 12;
4	bb = 12;	4	aa = 13;
5	aaa = 99;	5	ddd = aa / a;
6	b = 6;	6	ccc = a + b;
7	ccc = a + b;	7	bbb = 2;
8	ddd = aa / a;	8	aaa = 99;
9	b = 6;	9	xxxx = aa * bb;
10	yyyy = 0;	10	yyyy = 0;

Table 11.2   Brute-Force Arrays for the Two Source Code Files

Array A	Array B
a = 5;	b = 6;
b = 6;	a = 5;
aa = 13;	bb = 12;
bb = 12;	aa = 13;
aaa = 99;	ddd = aa / a;
b = 6;	ccc = a + b;
ccc = a + b;	bbb = 2;
ddd = aa / a;	aaa = 99;
b = 6;	xxxx = aa * bb;
yyyy = 0;	yyyy = 0;

The brute-force method of comparing the lines is to simply iterate through Array A, and for each line of Array A iterate through Array B to compare each line of Array B. This is easily done using one loop nested within another. The computation time for this calculation is $O(i \cdot j)$, where i and j are the number of lines in Array A and Array B respectively. In other words, it will take on the order of i times j comparisons. If we are using fractional matching, there is not much we can do to speed up the comparison, because we cannot predict which characters will match and which will not match. If we are using simple matching and looking for identical lines, we can speed up the comparisons by sorting lines, ordering lines, hashing lines, and saving arrays to memory.

11.1.1 SORTING LINES

To speed up this comparison, it makes sense to sort the lines of only one file, because the other file must be examined line by line and compared to the sorted file. In Table 11.3 Array B is sorted alphanumerically. Note that we must now keep a second array containing the original line numbers if we are to report back to the user which lines match now that we have changed the line order.

When one file is sorted, the comparisons now have a comparison time $O(i \cdot \log_2 j)$. Of course the sorting time is $O(j \cdot \log_2 j)$, so the total computation time is $O((i+j) \cdot \log_2 j)$. A little more efficiency is squeezed out by sorting the larger file because $i \cdot \log_2 j < j \cdot \log_2 i$ when $i < j$.

11.1.2 ORDERING LINES

We can gain a little more computational efficiency by ordering the lines of the file that is not sorted. Notice that in File A, lines 2, 6, and 9 are identical. In actual source code files this is a common occurrence where common simple instructions like do or a single beginning bracket { or closing bracket } on a line may occur in many places in the same file.

Table 11.4 shows that an ordered array can be created from File A. After the first instance of a line, all identical lines are placed immediately after it. Again we

Table 11.3 Creating Arrays for Source Code Files with a Sorted Array

Array A	Array B	Line no. B
a = 5;	a = 5;	2
b = 6;	aa = 13;	4
aa = 13;	aaa = 99;	8
bb = 12;	b = 6;	1
aaa = 99;	bb = 12;	3
b = 6;	bbb = 2;	7
ccc = a + b;	ccc = a + b;	6
ddd = aa / a;	ddd = aa / a;	5
b = 6;	xxxx = aa * bb;	9
yyyy = 0;	yyyy = 0;	10

need to keep track of original line numbers in a new array. We also need to keep track of which lines are identical in another new array. I call this the "same_as_previous" array. Each line that is identical to the one before it has a value of `true` in the same_as_previous array. Each time a line in Array A is compared to a line in Array B and found to match, we simply need to look at the next value in the same_as_previous array. For each `true` value, we know there is another identical line without needing to do the comparison.

Ordering lines can squeeze even a little more performance out of the calculation time if there are duplicate lines of code in many files, as is typical. The ordering itself involves, in the worst case, $\frac{1}{2} \cdot (i^2 - i)$ comparisons or $O(i^2)$ computation time. This could actually slow down the computation time altogether, but source code differentiation typically compares multiple files of one program to multiple files of another program. In this case, the ordering operation can be done only once for a file in the first program and the comparison operation performed many times on each file in the second program. When dealing with a large number of files, the ordering can speed up the overall computation time.

11.1.3 HASHING LINES

Another technique for speeding up the computation time is to hash the lines. The array would then consist of a list of hashes rather than a list of text characters. Hashes can be compared very quickly, and the arrays would have the added advantage of requiring significantly less memory. Hashes run the risk of hashing two different lines to the same value, but a hashing algorithm can be chosen to

Table 11.4   Creating Arrays for Source Code Files with an Ordered Array

Array A	Line no. A	Same	Array B	Line no. B
a = 5;	1	false	a = 5;	2
b = 6;	2	false	aa = 13;	4
b = 6;	6	true	aaa = 99;	8
b = 6;	9	true	b = 6;	1
aa = 13;	3	false	bb = 12;	3
bb = 12;	4	false	bbb = 2;	7
aaa = 99;	5	false	ccc = a + b;	6
ccc = a + b;	7	false	ddd = aa / a;	5
ddd = aa / a;	8	false	xxxx = aa * bb;	9
yyyy = 0;	10	false	yyyy = 0;	10

make that possibility extremely small for all reasonably sized source code files. As an extra reassurance, when two lines have identical hashes, the original lines can be compared to see whether they are indeed identical.

Of course, hashing algorithms also take some computational time. If most lines of code in the files are short or different lines differ significantly, then hashing may not save much time.

11.1.4 SAVING ARRAYS TO DISK

Because source code differentiation involves comparing multiple files against each other, it can help to save some arrays to disk. For example, if all files from program P^1 are being compared to all files from program P^2, you might create arrays for the first file of program P^1 and then create arrays for each file of program P^2 as the comparison is done. Because these arrays can be very large, it may be impractical to maintain them in memory, but they can be saved to disk. Then when the second file in program P^1 is being compared, each array for files in program P^2 can be read from disk rather than re-created.

Reading from disk and, even more so, writing to disk are typically relatively slow processes. Saving arrays to disk only makes sense if the files are long. For short files the arrays can be re-created faster than they can be read from disk. Whether to save arrays to memory depends on the size of the files being examined, the amount of RAM available, and file I/O performance, to name a few factors.

11.2 NUMBER OF OPTIMAL MATCH SCORE COMBINATIONS

When measuring file similarity, we want to choose line pairs such that totaling the match scores for each line pair results in the largest possible value. First we should understand how many line pairs there are. Table 11.5 shows the match scores for two files, File 1 with four lines and File 2 with six lines. Let $m_{i,j}$ be the value of the cell at column i and row j that represents the match score between line i and line j. Let us create a function called $Opt()$ that selects unique line pairs such that each line is paired at most once and the sum of the match scores is maximized. In particular, $Opt(M_{i,j})$ optimizes a matrix with i rows and j columns. Let us use the notation $M[-p,-q]$ to represent the matrix $M_{i-1,j-1}$ where row p and column q have been removed.

Because we are matching lines one to one, we know that every line in the smaller file can be matched with one in the larger file (though the match score may be 0), but some lines in the larger file remain unmatched. We can therefore test each line in the smaller file. If line 1 in File 1 is matched with line 1 in File 2, then those lines cannot be matched with other lines, leaving a matrix $M[-1, -1]$ of the lightly shaded cells at the bottom right of Table 11.5, also shown in Table 11.6. The best possible total score in this case would be the value of the match score for these lines plus the best total score for the remaining lines, or

$$m_{1,1} + Opt(M[-1,-1])$$

Because we know that line 1 of File 1 must be matched to one of lines 1 through 6 of File 2, we can try each combination and just see which total is larger. The solution to this particular problem, then, is given by Equation 11.1:

$$opt\left(M_{6,4}\right) = max \begin{pmatrix} m_{1,1} + Opt\left(M_{6,4}[-1,-1]\right), m_{2,1} + Opt\left(M_{6,4}[-2,-1]\right) \\ m_{3,1} + Opt\left(M_{6,4}[-3,-1]\right), m_{4,1} + Opt\left(M_{6,4}[-4,-1]\right) \\ m_{5,1} + Opt\left(M_{6,4}[-5,-1]\right), m_{6,1} + Opt\left(M_{6,4}[-6,-1]\right) \end{pmatrix} \quad (11.1)$$

Table 11.5   Matrix $M_{6,4}$ of File Match Scores

		File 1			
Match score		**Line 1**	**Line 2**	**Line 3**	**Line 4**
File 2	**Line 1**	$m_{1,1}$	$m_{2,1}$	$m_{3,1}$	$m_{4,1}$
	Line 2	$m_{1,2}$	$m_{2,2}$	$m_{3,2}$	$m_{4,2}$
	Line 3	$m_{1,3}$	$m_{2,3}$	$m_{3,3}$	$m_{4,3}$
	Line 4	$m_{1,4}$	$m_{2,4}$	$m_{3,4}$	$m_{4,4}$
	Line 5	$m_{1,5}$	$m_{2,5}$	$m_{3,5}$	$m_{4,5}$
	Line 6	$m_{1,6}$	$m_{2,6}$	$m_{3,6}$	$m_{4,6}$

Table 11.6   Matrix $M[-1,-1]$ of File Match Scores

		File 1		
Match score		**Line 2**	**Line 3**	**Line 4**
File 2	**Line 2**	$m_{2,2}$	$m_{3,2}$	$m_{4,2}$
	Line 3	$m_{2,3}$	$m_{3,3}$	$m_{4,3}$
	Line 4	$m_{2,4}$	$m_{3,4}$	$m_{4,4}$
	Line 5	$m_{2,5}$	$m_{3,5}$	$m_{4,5}$
	Line 6	$m_{2,6}$	$m_{3,6}$	$m_{4,6}$

The optimal value for this 6×4 matrix involves maximizing the value in each cell plus the optimal value for a matrix that has one less column and one less row. Generalizing this result gives us Equation 11.2, where there are two choices, depending on which is smaller, the row or the column:

$$Opt\left(M_{i,j}\right) = max\left(m_{1,k} + Opt\left(M_{i,j}[-1,-\kappa]\right)\right)\forall\{1 \le k \le j\} \text{ for } i \le j$$

$$Opt\left(M_{i,j}\right) = max\left(m_{k,1} + Opt\left(M_{i,j}[-\kappa,-1]\right)\right)\forall\{1 \le k \le i\} \text{ for } j \le i$$

(11.2)

In the generalized case we continue looking at smaller matrices until we get to one that is of size

$$|i-j| + 1 \times 1$$

which has $|i-j|+1$ cells to consider. Thus the number of computed sums of match scores to be considered in Equation 11.1 is given by Equation 11.3, which is a very large number even for small numbers of lines in a file (note that $0! = 1$, making this true even when $i = j$).

$$\frac{j!}{(j-i)!} \text{ for } i \le j$$

(11.3)

11.3 CHOOSING OPTIMAL MATCH SCORES FOR CALCULATING FILE SIMILARITY

Given that the number of comparisons grows factorially, this section gives algorithms for efficiently choosing the line pairs that give the match scores that result in the correct, maximum similarity value for a pair of files.

11.3.1 SIMPLE MATCHING

This is a fairly simple process when using simple matching where two lines either match or do not match. The match score value for any pair of lines is either 0 or 1. Table 11.7 gives match scores between lines in File 1 and File 2. File 1 has four lines, shown across the top row, and File 2 has six lines, shown across the left columns. The cells show the simple match scores between the lines of the files, either 0 or 1.

A simple algorithm for calculating the file similarity involves comparing line 1 of File 1 to each line of File 2 until a match is found. In this case, File 1, line 1,

Table 11.7   Simple Match Scores for File 1 and File 2

Match score		File 1			
		Line 1	Line 2	Line 3	Line 4
File 2	Line 1	0	1	0	1
	Line 2	0	0	0	0
	Line 3	0	0	0	0
	Line 4	1	0	0	0
	Line 5	1	0	0	0
	Line 6	0	1	0	1

Table 11.8   Matching File 1, Line 1

Match score		File 1			
		Line 1	Line 2	Line 3	Line 4
File 2	Line 1	0	1	0	1
	Line 2	0	0	0	0
	Line 3	0	0	0	0
	Line 4	1	0	0	0
	Line 5	1	0	0	0
	Line 6	0	1	0	1

matches File 2, line 4, shown highlighted in Table 11.8. Once the match is found, the column for File 1, line 1, is grayed out because a match has been found for File 1, line 1. Similarly, the row for File 2, line 4, is grayed out because a match has been found for File 2, line 4.

Table 11.9 shows that File 1, line 2, is then compared against every line in File 2, and immediately a match is found with File 2, line 1. That cell is highlighted; the column for File 1, line 2, is grayed out; and the row for File 2, line 1, is grayed out.

File 1, line 3, is then compared against all lines in File 2, but any grayed-out lines need not be compared because they have already been found to match another line. When programming this algorithm, keeping track of which lines have already been found to match another line can be done by using a shadow array that corresponds to the array of lines in the file and has a flag that signals whether the corresponding line has been matched or not. For File 1, line 3, no lines in File 2 match, and so the entire column gets grayed out, as shown in Table 11.10.

Table 11.9 Matching File 1, Line 2

Match score		File 1			
		Line 1	Line 2	Line 3	Line 4
File 2	Line 1	0	1	0	1
	Line 2	0	0	0	0
	Line 3	0	0	0	0
	Line 4	1	0	0	0
	Line 5	1	0	0	0
	Line 6	0	1	0	1

Table 11.10 Matching File 1, Line 3

Match score		File 1			
		Line 1	Line 2	Line 3	Line 4
File 2	Line 1	0	1	0	1
	Line 2	0	0	0	0
	Line 3	0	0	0	0
	Line 4	1	0	0	0
	Line 5	1	0	0	0
	Line 6	0	1	0	1

Table 11.11 Matching File 1, Line 4

Match score		File 1			
		Line 1	Line 2	Line 3	Line 4
File 2	Line 1	0	1	0	1
	Line 2	0	0	0	0
	Line 3	0	0	0	0
	Line 4	1	0	0	0
	Line 5	1	0	0	0
	Line 6	0	1	0	1

File 1, line 4, is then examined, skipping grayed-out cells where matches have already been found. File 1, line 4, matches File 2, line 6, and now the entire table is grayed out except for the matching line pairs, as shown in Table 11.11.

For the files in this example, the number of matched lines $M(F^1,F^2) = 3$. When we plug this into Equation 10.4 from the previous chapter, the mutual similarity score is calculated as

$$\sigma = (2 \times 3)/(4 + 6) = 0.60$$

When we plug this into Equation 10.5a, the directional similarity score in the direction of File 1 is calculated as

$$\sigma_1 = 3/4 = 0.75$$

When we plug this into Equation 10.5b, the directional similarity score in the direction of File 2 is calculated as

$$\sigma_2 = 3/6 = 0.50$$

11.3.2 FRACTIONAL MATCHING

Table 11.12 shows File 1 containing four lines across the top row and File 2 containing six lines across the left columns. The cells show the fractional match scores between the lines of the files where two lines may partially match.

To find the similarity value for these files, we use the same kind of algorithm discussed previously to determine the number of optimal match score combinations. Create a recursive function called `MatrixCalc()` as shown in Listing 11.1 (in pseudocode).

Table 11.12 Calculating File Pair Similarity from Fractional Match Scores

		File 1			
Match score		Line 1	Line 2	Line 3	Line 4
File 2	Line 1	0.2	1.0	0.0	0.0
	Line 2	0.0	0.0	0.0	1.0
	Line 3	0.0	0.9	0.0	0.4
	Line 4	0.0	0.0	0.0	0.2
	Line 5	0.0	0.0	0.0	0.1
	Line 6	0.0	0.0	0.0	0.0

Listing 11.1   Recursive Routine for Determining the Number of Optimal Match Score Combinations

```
float MatrixCalc(
  float matrix[][],        // Matrix containing pair match scores
  int nRows,               // Number of rows in matrix
  int nCols)               // Number of columns in matrix
{
  float simVal;            // Maximized similarity value of line pairs
  float tempVal;           // Temporary value
  float subMatrix[][];     // Submatrix of matrix
  int Index;               // Index into a row or column
  // Initialize variables
  simVal = 0.0;
  tempVal = 0.0;
  // Calculate along the longest direction — row or column.
  if (nRows >= nCols)
  {
    for (Index = 0; Index < nRows; Index++)
    {
      tempVal = matrix[Index][0];

      // If the number of columns is 1, there are no more submatrices
      if (nCols > 1)
      {
        // Create subMatrix excluding column 0
        // and the current row being examined.
        subMatrix = ...;

        tempVal = tempVal + MatrixCalc(subMatrix, nRows-1, nCols-1);
      }

      // If this value is greater than the current value, this
      // becomes the new value.
      if (tempVal > simVal)
        simVal = tempVal;
```

Continues

Listing 11.1 Recursive Routine for Determining the Number of Optimal Match Score
Combinations *(Continued)*

```
    }
  }
  else
  {
    // Do the same but for the column instead of the row.

    .

    .

    .

  }
  return(simVal);
}
```

This `MatrixCalc` function takes as input the matrix and the number of columns
and rows in the matrix. It initializes the `simVal` variable that it will eventually
return as the similarity score for the two files represented by the matrix.

There are two nearly identical sections of code, depending on which is smaller: the
number of rows or the number of columns. I show only the code for the case when
the number of rows is smaller; the corresponding code for when the number of
columns is smaller is identical except that rows and columns are interchanged.

The `Index` variable is incremented along the rows of the matrix. The value at the
indexed row and column 0 is stored in the `tempVal` variable. If the number of
columns is greater than 1, we create a submatrix that is the full matrix excluding
the indexed row and column 0. To get the similarity score if we were to select the
current cell, we must add the value in the cell to the value for the submatrix. We
do this by recursively calling this `MatrixCalc` routine on the submatrix and
adding the similarity value for the submatrix.

Then we compare the similarity value to the largest value we have found so far.
If the value when selecting this cell is larger, we replace the previous similarity
value with this one.

Once we have gone through each cell in the row (or the column if the column
was larger) and examined all possibilities by using `MatrixCalc` recursively, we
return the maximized similarity value, which is the true similarity value.

This `MatrixCalc` function correctly calculates the file pair similarity value in an efficient manner, but it still requires all combinations of cells to be examined, and as we have seen, the number of combinations grows factorially. We can introduce some optimizations that will speed up the process, using our knowledge of similarity, as shown in the pseudocode in Listing 11.2.

Listing 11.2   Optimized Recursive Routine for Determining the Number of Optimal Match Score Combinations

```
float MatrixCalcOptimized(
    float matrix[][],      // Matrix containing pair match scores
    int nRows,             // Number of rows in matrix
    int nCols)             // Number of columns in matrix
{
    float simVal;          // Maximized similarity value of line pairs
    float tempVal;         // Temporary value
    float subMatrix[][];   // Submatrix of matrix
    int Index;             // Index into a row or column

    // Initialize variables
    simVal = 0.0;
    tempVal = 0.0;

    // Calculate along the longest direction – row or column.
    if (nRows >= nCols)
    {
        for (Index = 0; Index < nRows; Index++)
        {
            tempVal = matrix[Index][0];

            // If the number of columns is 1, there are no more submatrices
            if ((nCols > 1) && (simVal < tempVal + nCols - 1))
            {
                // Create subMatrix excluding column 0
```

Continues

Listing 11.2 Optimized Recursive Routine for Determining the Number of Optimal Match Score Combinations *(Continued)*

```
        // and the current row being examined.
        subMatrix = ...;

        tempVal = tempVal + MatrixCalc(subMatrix, nRows-1, nCols-1);
      }
      // If this value is greater than the current value, this
      // becomes the new value.
      if (tempVal > simVal)
          simVal = tempVal;

    }
  }
  else
  {
    // Do the same but for the column instead of the row.
      .

      .

      .

  }
  return(simVal);
}
```

In this new routine, `MatrixCalcOptimized`, I have added an additional condition for calling the routine on the submatrix. This additional condition is `simVal < tempVal + nCols - 1`. We know that in the best case, there can be exactly one full match for each column in the submatrix (or for each row in the case where there are more columns than rows). In other words, in the best case each remaining line of File 1 can exactly match one line of File 2, resulting in a value of 1.0 for each remaining line of File 1. If the value in the cell (`tempVal`) is so small that even if every column in the submatrix matches some row it could still not be larger than the current value (`simVal`), then there is no reason to even consider the submatrix.

11.4 CHOOSING FILE SIMILARITY SCORES FOR REPORTING PROGRAM SIMILARITY

Typically, program similarity does not result in a single score, because that score would hide a lot of interesting information. Instead, program similarity is defined by the distribution of file similarity scores, such as that shown in Figure 11.1. From this distribution, different useful properties can be measured, including the average, maximum, and minimum similarity scores as well as the standard deviation of the similarity scores.

11.4.1 CHOOSING FILE PAIRS FOR OPTIMALLY DETERMINING PROGRAM SIMILARITY

However, which file pairs should be considered as matching? This problem is identical to the one for determining the file pair similarity based on choosing the line pair match scores. In other words, we can use the `MatrixCalcOptimized` routine where the matrix represents files and file similarity scores rather than lines and line-matching scores.

The number of files that can be found in a typical program can be in the thousands or even tens of thousands. Running the `MatrixCalcOptimized` routine on a matrix of this size can be prohibitively time-consuming because the computation time still grows factorially. In cases of large files the following approximations can be used.

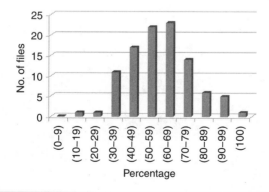

Figure 11.1   Distribution of similarity values of file pairs in two programs

11.4.2 CHOOSING FILE PAIRS FOR APPROXIMATELY DETERMINING PROGRAM SIMILARITY

Table 11.13 shows Program 1 containing four files across the top row and Program 2 containing six files across the left columns. The cells show the similarity values between the files.

There are more rows than columns, so we must go through each column to find the largest similarity value in that column because each column needs to be matched to one row. If there were more columns than rows, we would go through each row. While going through the columns, we select the largest value in the first column, as shown in Table 11.14. Whenever there are two equal values in a column, we select the first one.

Now we have a problem because we have paired up File 1 in Program 2 twice and File 2 in Program 2 twice. We need to choose only one file in Program 2 to match

Table 11.13   Similarity Values for Program 1 and Program 2

Similarity values		Program 1			
		File 1	File 2	File 3	File 4
Program 2	File 1	0.2	1.0	0.0	0.0
	File 2	0.0	0.0	0.3	1.0
	File 3	0.0	0.9	0.1	0.9
	File 4	0.0	0.0	0.0	0.2
	File 5	0.1	0.0	0.0	0.1
	File 6	0.0	0.2	0.1	0.0

Table 11.14   Traversing Files in Program 1

Similarity values		Program 1			
		File 1	File 2	File 3	File 4
Program 2	File 1	0.2	1.0	0.0	0.0
	File 2	0.0	0.0	0.3	1.0
	File 3	0.0	0.9	0.1	0.9
	File 4	0.0	0.0	0.0	0.2
	File 5	0.1	0.0	0.0	0.1
	File 6	0.0	0.2	0.1	0.0

with each file in Program 1. We do this by unselecting the smallest of the selected similarity values for each file in Program 2. This results in the pairs shown in Table 11.15. Because File 1 of Program 2 paired with File 1 of Program 1 with a similarity value of 0.2 and with File 2 of Program 1 with a much larger similarity value of 1.0, the first pairing was unselected and that pairing was grayed out so it would not be attempted again. Similarly, the pairing of Program 2, File 2, with Program 1, File 4, was kept while the other pairing with Program 1, File 3, was removed and grayed out. The process of "graying out" can be handled by a shadow matrix with true/false or 1/0 values so that in the next pass these pairs are not considered.

The process of going through each column starts over. All grayed-out cells cannot be considered, and all columns that have a selected cell can be skipped. Now the largest pairing with Program 1, File 1, is Program 2, File 5. The largest pairing of Program 1, File 3, is 0.1 with Program 2, File 3. The resulting matrix is shown in Table 11.16, which has four distinct file pairs. The next part of the

Table 11.15   Eliminating Duplicate Selections

Similarity values		Program 1			
		File 1	File 2	File 3	File 4
Program 2	File 1	0.2	1.0	0.0	0.0
	File 2	0.0	0.0	0.3	1.0
	File 3	0.0	0.9	0.1	0.9
	File 4	0.0	0.0	0.0	0.2
	File 5	0.1	0.0	0.0	0.1
	File 6	0.0	0.2	0.1	0.0

Table 11.16   Resulting File Pairs

Similarity values		Program 1			
		File 1	File 2	File 3	File 4
Program 2	File 1	0.2	1.0	0.0	0.0
	File 2	0.0	0.0	0.3	1.0
	File 3	0.0	0.9	0.1	0.9
	File 4	0.0	0.0	0.0	0.2
	File 5	0.1	0.0	0.0	0.1
	File 6	0.0	0.2	0.1	0.0

Table 11.17 Optimal File Pairs

Similarity values		Program 1			
		File 1	File 2	File 3	File 4
Program 2	**File 1**	0.2	1.0	0.0	0.0
	File 2	0.0	0.0	0.3	1.0
	File 3	0.0	0.9	0.1	0.9
	File 4	0.0	0.0	0.0	0.2
	File 5	0.1	0.0	0.0	0.1
	File 6	0.0	0.2	0.1	0.0

algorithm would be to go through the rows as before, looking for multiple pairings, and the result would be that there are none and so we are done.

While this approximate algorithm does a good job, the optimal algorithm produces a slightly different selection of file pairs, shown in Table 11.17.

Other approximations can be used for selecting the file pairs of two programs. Also note that other applications of file pair similarity can be valid for other uses besides producing statistics about program similarity. Some of these uses are described in Chapter 12. Other uses will likely be found as these techniques are better understood.

APPLICATIONS

Initially source code differentiation was developed as a quick and simple way to look for source code copying. Since then, other important uses have been found for it. In this chapter I discuss some of these applications, though others will certainly emerge in the future.

12.1 FINDING SIMILAR CODE

The initial reason for the development of source code differentiation was to find code that had been copied with no changes or with an insignificant number of changes. Source code differentiation points the software forensic examiner to those files with high similarity values, which represent files with identical lines of code. There are a number of scenarios where source code differentiation can be used to find similar code as part of a more involved examination. Some examples are given in the following sections.

12.1.1 COMPARING MULTIPLE VERSIONS OF POTENTIALLY COPIED CODE

In many cases where code has been copied, it will go through normal modifications during the development process and after a time look very different from the original code. If a software forensic examiner needs to compare two programs that are separated by significant development time, then source code differentiation is not the right tool. In that case, source code correlation, which I discuss in Part V, can compare source code after it has gone through modifications. Similarly, if the software forensic examiner suspects that code has been modified to disguise copying, source code correlation is the correct measure, not source code differentiation. In cases where modification is not suspected, such as where the two sets of code files represent programs developed around the same time, source code differentiation is a useful tool, especially because the computation time is much less than that for source code correlation.

In some cases, a software forensic examiner may be given two "original" programs to compare to a third, "suspect" program. Perhaps the two original programs are slightly different versions of a single program and it is believed that code from one of the versions was misappropriated and included in the suspect program. Source code correlation can be calculated between one original program and the suspect program. After the results are obtained, correlation can be calculated between the other original program and the suspect program. These two calculations are graphically represented in Figure 12.1.

However, rather than calculating source code correlation between the second original program and the suspect program, it can make sense to simply calculate source code similarity, using source code differentiation, between both sets of original code to determine how much code has changed and in which files. If both original sets of code are substantially identical, no further work needs to be done. If there are differences between the two original sets of code, source code correlation can be performed between only the original files containing the substantial differences and the suspect code. This second, more efficient

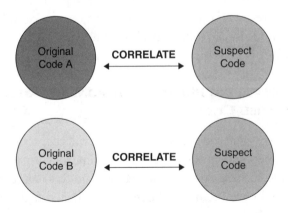

Figure 12.1 Correlation of two original programs to a suspect program

method is shown graphically in Figure 12.2, where A is one original program, B is the other original program, A∩B is the code that is common to both programs, A-B is the code in A that is not in B, and B-A is the code in B that is not in A. In addition to comparing the code in A to the suspect code, only the code represented by B-A needs to be compared to the suspect code because the rest of the code was already compared.

12.1.2 Use of Third-Party Code

Source code differentiation is also useful for determining whether a program uses third-party source code. Companies need to understand whether their source code uses third-party libraries. For example, it is possible that a commercial third-party library was used without payments being made to the owner of the library, and it would be beneficial for the company to know if a programmer used such code without the company's knowledge. Source code differentiation can be part of a due diligence process during a merger, acquisition, or an investment in a company, to determine which third-party libraries are being used. It can also play a part in litigation when a company is accused of incorporating third-party code into its own code; source code differentiation can be used to make that determination by comparing the code from the program in question to code from third-party libraries. The difficulty is knowing which third-party libraries to compare with the program code. This information may come from copyright notices in the program's source code or acknowledgment from the programmer who incorporated the library in the first place.

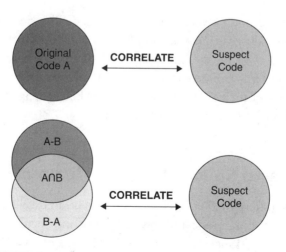

Figure 12.2   Correlation of two original programs to a suspect program using source code differentiation

12.1.3 USE OF OPEN SOURCE CODE

Similarly, source code differentiation can be used to determine whether open source code is being used in a program. This use of source code differentiation is somewhat easier than finding third-party libraries because open source code is freely available on the Internet. The source code for the program in question can be searched against a database of open source code, some of which exists online, to find any incorporated open source code. If found, it can be separately determined whether the party incorporating the open source code has adhered to the appropriate licensing agreements.

A difficulty with using source code differentiation to find open source code, when there are no clues as to which particular open source programs may have been used, is that there is a very large number of programs to compare. Other solutions exist that involve hashing and indexing large sections of the programs being compared. These solutions are particularly good at finding similarities within a large set of programs. The advantage is that the comparison is significantly sped up. The disadvantage is that even minor modifications of the source code within the program in question can result in completely different hashes that would result in the comparison completely missing the copied code. The size of the sections that are hashed and indexed can be varied to produce more accurate results or faster execution times, but not both. These variations produce trade-offs involving false positives, false negatives, and execution times with these kinds of hashing algorithms; you should be aware of these trade-offs, and how they affect your results, before using such methods.

In cases of searching for very specific source code libraries within a program, whether open source or proprietary libraries, source code differentiation is useful because typically the third-party code is unchanged or insignificantly changed in order to preserve its functionality. If the library source code has been changed, or there is suspicion that it has been changed, then source code correlation is a better method for finding it.

12.2 MEASURING SOURCE CODE EVOLUTION

Source code differentiation has been found to be an excellent basis for measuring changes to source code and to source code intellectual property (see the sidebar entitled "Transfer Pricing and the Origins of CLOC"). In particular, source code differentiation is the basis of the changing lines of code (CLOC) method that is described in this section.

There are a number of common software metrics, including the Halstead measures, lines of source code, cyclomatic complexity (also known as the McCabe measure), function point analysis, bugs per line of code, and code coverage. Each metric is designed to quantify the amount of work involved in producing or maintaining software. Each metric quantifies a single software characteristic in an attempt to measure the software as a whole. Some of these methods, such as cyclomatic complexity, focus on the complexity of the software, and some, such as lines of source code, focus on the size of the software. None of these methods provides a useful measurement of the effort involved in changing the software, something that CLOC performs very well. Each of the following sections describes one of these methods and its drawbacks for measuring code changes.

12.2.1 LINES OF CODE

The simplest way to measure software is to count the source lines of code (SLOC) to determine the size of the software. Although the SLOC metric does not take into account the complexity of the code, it is a good metric for very roughly estimating the effort involved in the initial production of code and for roughly comparing the relative effort involved in creating two programs. The closer the functionality of the programs, the better an SLOC measurement turns out to be. Also, SLOC works best on programs having the same mix of programming languages because some languages are compact and use statements representing significant complexity while others are more verbose or use simpler statements and consequently require more of them.

There are two kinds of SLOC measurements: physical SLOC (often simply abbreviated "LOC") and logical SLOC (often abbreviated "LLOC"). Physical SLOC measures lines of code, starting at the first character on the line and ending at the newline character or characters, the same way that source code differentiation considers lines. One significant difference is that SLOC counts blank lines unless the blank lines of code in a section constitute more than 25 percent of the lines, in which case the blank lines above 25 percent are not counted. Counting blank lines is odd because it is hard to make any kind of argument that the number of blank lines shows any kind of work or measures any kind of complexity other than perhaps the organizational skill or visual skill of the programmers to make the code more readable. Also, the 25 percent mark seems arbitrary, and I am not aware of any studies on this subject. I suspect that many SLOC counting programs actually do not count blank lines at all, which makes more sense.

Logical SLOC understands the syntax of the programming languages being examined well enough to count only functional lines of code but not comments.

Not only does logical SLOC ignore comments, but when multiple statements are on a single line, separated typically by a semicolon, logical SLOC counts each statement on the line as a separate line. One disadvantage of logical SLOC is that it ignores comments. Any manager knows how difficult it can be to get programmers to comment their code, so obviously there is work involved in writing comments that logical SLOC ignores. Also, logical SLOC has even less relevance when comparing programs in different programming languages, though it can be argued that logical SLOC is better than physical SLOC when comparing programs in the same programming language.

An advantage of the SLOC metric, both physical SLOC and logical SLOC, is that it is simple to measure and computationally fast, as it is $O(n + m)$ for comparing a program with n lines to a program with m lines.

12.2.2 HALSTEAD MEASURES

One of the earliest methods of measuring software was developed by Maurice H. Halstead in his 1977 book *Elements of Software Science*. Halstead created a quantitative measurement of software source code that counted the number of unique operators, operands, operator occurrences, and operand occurrences in the code being measured. He labeled these quantities as follows:

$n1$ = number of unique operators

$n2$ = number of unique operands

$N1$ = number of operator occurrences

$N2$ = number of operand occurrences

Halstead combined these quantities in various ways. He defined measures that he called program length, program vocabulary, volume, difficulty, effort, and time, as shown in Table 12.1.

Table 12.1   Halstead Measures

Measure	Formula
Program length	$N = N1 + N2$
Program vocabulary	$n = n1 + n2$
Volume	$V = N \cdot \log_2 n$
Difficulty	$D = (n1 \cdot N2)/(2 \cdot n2)$
Effort	$E = D \cdot V$
Time	$E/18$

While the Halstead measures are simple to implement, involving simply counting operators and operands and applying some simple math, their usefulness is questionable. Many of the calculations seem arbitrary and difficult, if not impossible, to justify. For example, why is time defined with a divisor of 18? It turns out that Halstead was influenced by the work of psychologist John Stroud, who wrote in 1949 that he believed that human beings could detect between 5 and 20 "moments" or discrete events per second. This number became known as the "Stroud number," and Halstead chose 18 as a representative value because it conformed to his experimental data. Stroud's work has mostly disappeared in the years since he wrote his paper entitled "The Psychological Moment in Perception," so it is difficult to know how he came to his conclusion.

Halstead ignores comments in code and in fact ignores everything about code other than operands and operators. Because of this, modern programming languages cannot easily be measured using Halstead measures. Consider the following lines of code:

```
1    i = i + 1;
2    i += 1;
3    a = sqrt(i);
4    int i;
5    *ptr = &abc;
6    public class MyClass
```

It is easy to count that there are three operands and two operators in line 1. How about line 2? Are there two operands and one operator, as a cursory evaluation would indicate? But lines 1 and 2 are functionally equivalent. In line 3 there is a function call. Does the function call count as an operator? If not, but the function call were instead expressed using a symbol, would that turn it into an operator? Are there any operators in lines 4, 5, and 6? It should be obvious why it is that although Halstead broke ground with his concepts, his metrics are no longer in use today in industry (though academia continues to use them, building on what I believe is a very shaky foundation for some areas of computer science).

12.2.3 CYCLOMATIC COMPLEXITY

In 1976 Thomas McCabe proposed a complexity measure known as "cyclomatic complexity," also known as the "McCabe measure." This method counts the number of individual execution paths through the code. For example, a conditional statement, such as an if statement in the C programming language, would count as two distinct paths through the code: the first path for the condition being true and a second path for the condition being false. Cyclomatic complexity can be calculated by creating graphs of source code and counting the number of execution paths. This can be a long, computationally time-consuming process, as just a few lines of code can result in many distinct paths.

The usefulness of the McCabe measure is also questionable. For example, by the McCabe measure a 10,000-line program with five if statements is less complex than a 100-line program with six if statements. While this is an extreme example, it illustrates the difficulty with the measurement. It seems that something is missing. In fact, the McCabe metric seems too simple in that it reports a single number to describe the complexity of a program. Today's programs are made up of many pieces—some simple, some complex—a fact that is not reflected in the single number given by the McCabe metric.

12.2.4 FUNCTION POINT ANALYSIS

Function point analysis was developed by Allan Albrecht at IBM in 1979. Function point analysis divides code into categories:

- Outputs
- Inquiries
- Inputs
- Internal files
- External interfaces

Once the code is categorized, it is assessed for complexity and assigned a number that is then further examined and given adjustments and weights. Performing function point analysis requires a person trained in the concepts. It is very labor-intensive and can be very expensive. It requires that a fairly complete set of software requirements be available in order to analyze the code. It is also subjective rather than quantitative. Over the years, a number of different function point methods have been developed, each with its own advocates:

- IFPUG function points
- Backfired function points
- COSMIC function points
- Finnish function points
- Engineering function points
- Feature points
- Netherlands function points
- Unadjusted function points
- Function points light

12.2.5 HOW SOURCE CODE EVOLVES

When attempting to understand the effort involved in the growth of code for a single project, or the change in IP for a single project, we want to compare subsequent versions of source code for the same program. Comparing SLOC values of subsequent versions is not a good measurement of the evolution of source code because it does not properly measure the efforts involved in refactoring, debugging, or trimming existing source code. SLOC equates productivity to the development of more code and is inaccurate when the activities involve deletion or alteration of code. As Bill Gates of Microsoft famously stated, "Measuring programming progress by lines of code is like measuring aircraft building progress by weight." The SLOC metric is valuable, but comparing SLOC measurements between versions does not properly measure the progress of normal software maintenance and development. Optimization of code often involves reducing the lines of code by substituting more efficient algorithms for inefficient ones. It often also involves the process of clone detection and refactoring whereby multiple sections of code that perform substantially the same function (i.e., "clones") are replaced with a single function, making maintenance and debugging of the program easier. If one were to take SLOC as a measure of effort or change to a software program, then an optimization that reduces the number of lines of code would result in a smaller SLOC number and thus appear to be negative work or negative growth.

Similarly, a change to the cyclomatic complexity of the code is not a clear indicator of source code evolution. There are several forms of source code maintenance that may simplify the execution paths of a program. The fixing of bugs, deletion of outdated code, clone detection, and refactoring of code can all take a significant amount of work and have a significant impact on the functionality of a program but may decrease or have no effect on the cyclomatic complexity measurement. If one were to take cyclomatic complexity as a measure of effort or change to a software program, then an optimization that reduces the complexity of the code would result in a smaller cyclomatic complexity and thus appear to be negative work or negative growth.

The Halstead measures may or may not have been useful at one point in computer history, but they are definitely not useful now. And function point analysis is complex, costly, and somewhat subjective. What is needed is a measure that is objective and can be easily automated.

Because we want to measure source code evolution, it is necessary to first understand how the source code of a software project evolves. Figure 12.3 shows

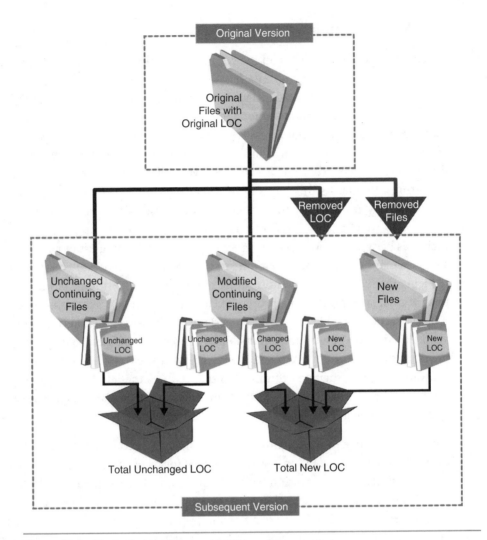

Figure 12.3   The evolution of files and LOC in software projects

how the LOC and files of a software project evolve from an original version to a subsequent version. Some of the original files may get removed. Other files may continue without any change to the LOC inside. There may also be files that continue from the original version but that do contain changes. The modified continuing files are files that continue from the original version but are composed of a mix of unchanged LOC, changed LOC, and new LOC. Finally, there may be new files that are completely composed of new LOC.

During each revision of a program, lines are added, edited, and deleted. This illustrates why simply counting SLOC is not accurate enough to measure software evolution. One can reasonably conclude that a 400-file program with 100,000 lines of code takes more effort than a program consisting of only 2 files with only 500 lines of code, but what about the evolution of that large program? Perhaps the first version had 399 files and 99,750 lines of code. The SLOC method would measure a .25 percent change between the first and final version. This might seem reasonable at first, but what about all of the lines that were changed or removed? Perhaps entire algorithms consisting of 60,000 lines were removed and other algorithms of 60,750 lines were added during development. Those modifications represent a significant amount of change and effort on the part of the programmers, and at .25 percent a simple SLOC comparison grossly underestimates that change.

12.2.6 CHANGING LINES OF CODE MEASURE (CLOC)

The CLOC metric, however, is a useful software evolution measurement. CLOC examines the changes in source code instead of the static size or complexity. The CLOC method counts the number of lines of code that have been modified, added, or remain constant from one version of a software project to subsequent versions. These measurements are then analyzed to determine the percentage growth of the software. The CLOC method can be used to show either the growth of the software or the continuity (or decay, which is 1 minus the continuity) of the original source code from version to version of a program. The CLOC method properly measures the intricacies of source code maintenance and provides a quantitative metric for software evolution.

First we count the number of files and non-blank lines in the software project's directory tree. Next we perform source code differentiation to compare files from the original version to subsequent versions of a software project. In the CLOC method the source code differentiation is limited to comparing files with the same name. Typically file names are not changed from version to version, and a movement of source code between files or a file name change represents work being performed.

The data about the file similarities from the source code differentiation is combined with the file count and line count to generate the software evolution results. This combination can be performed in a simple spreadsheet, though the calculation is automated in the CodeMeasure program from S.A.F.E. Corporation.

12.2.6.1 Definition of Terms

The terms used in the calculation of CLOC are defined here. Note that the number *n* represents version *n* of the program, and *m* represents an earlier version *m* of the program. If only one version is given, that represents the later version and the previous version is assumed to be version *0*, the first version of the program.

Note that the term "continuing file" means a file that existed in a previous version and also exists in a subsequent version. While there may be different ways to determine that a file is continuing, one easy and useful way is by considering the name of the file. Because it is rare that a file name is changed in a project, a continuing file may be considered to be one that has the same name in the original version and in the subsequent version. If a mapping of files from one version to another is available, then that mapping can be used to determine continuing files. It is also possible that all files in a project were renamed because the project was renamed. A determination dependent on such a mapping would be very specific to that project and difficult to generalize about here, so using the name of the file is a good general principle.

$TF(n)$	= total files—the total number of files in version n of the program
$NF(n,m)$	= new files—the number of new files in version n compared to previous version m
$TL(n)$	= total LOC—total lines of code in version n
$TNL(n,m)$	= total new LOC—total new lines of code in version n compared to previous version m
$TCF(n,m)$	= total continuing files—total files in version n that also existed in previous version m
$TLCF(n,m)$	= total LOC in continuing files
$NLCF(n,m)$	= new LOC in continuing files—LOC in continuing files that are in the file in new version n but not in the file in previous version m
$CL(n,m)$	= continuing LOC—LOC present in the files in previous version m and in the continuing files in version n
$MCF(n,m)$	= modified continuing files—number of files in version n that also existed in previous version m but have changed
$UCF(n,m)$	= unchanged continuing files—number of files in version n that also existed in previous version m without changes

CLOC Growth(n,m)   = ratio of new LOC in version n to LOC in previous version m

File Continuity(n,m)   = ratio of continuing files in version n from version m to total files in version n

File Decay(n,m)   = ratio of files in version n that are not continuing from version m to total files in version n (1 − File Continuity)

Line Continuity(n,m)   = ratio of continuing LOC in version n from version m to total LOC in version n

Line Decay(n,m)   = ratio of LOC in version n that are not continuing from version m to total LOC in version n (1 − Line Continuity)

Unchanged File Continuity(n)   = ratio of unchanged continuing files in version n to total files in version n

SLOC Growth(n,m)   = ratio of total LOC in version n minus total LOC in previous version m to LOC in previous version m

12.2.6.2 SLOC Growth

Equation 12.1 gives the traditional measure of software growth based on the SLOC method:

$$\text{SLOC Growth}(n) = (TL(n) - TL(0)) / TL(0) \qquad (12.1)$$

12.2.6.3 CLOC Growth

The growth of each version is the ratio of total new LOC (*TNL*) to the total LOC (*TL*) in the original version, shown in Equation 12.2. The *TNL* is the number of LOC that do not exist in the original version, including lines that have changed, along with completely new lines in either continuing files or completely new files. The *TNL* is represented by the box at the bottom right in Figure 12.3.

$$\text{CLOC Growth}(n) = TNL(n) / TL(0) \qquad (12.2)$$

12.2.6.4 File Continuity

The continuity can also be represented in terms of either the file continuity or the unchanged file continuity. The file continuity is the ratio of original files that are still remaining (*TCF*) to the total number of files in the subsequent version (*TF*), shown in Equation 12.3. The file decay is the ratio of files that are new files in the subsequent version to the total number of files in the subsequent version, or simply 1 minus the file continuity, as shown in Equation 12.4.

$$\text{File Continuity}(n) = TCF(n) \ / \ TF(n) \tag{12.3}$$

$$\text{File Decay}(n) = 1 - (TCF(n) \ / \ TF(n)) \tag{12.4}$$

The unchanged file continuity is the ratio of the continuing files that are unchanged in the subsequent version (*UCF*) to the total number of files in the subsequent version, shown in Equation 12.5.

$$\text{Unchanged File Continuity}(n) = UCF(n) \ / \ TF(n) \tag{12.5}$$

12.2.6.5 LOC Continuity

It can also be important to know how the original code and the IP it represents has continued as a software project evolves. The LOC continuity is the ratio of total continuing LOC (*CL*) to the total LOC (*TL*) in each version, shown in Equation 12.6. The total continuing LOC is the count of LOC that are present in the original version as well as in the files that have continued into the subsequent version and is shown as the box at the bottom left in Figure 12.3. The line decay is the ratio of lines that are new lines in the subsequent version to the total number of lines in the subsequent version, or simply 1 minus the line continuity, as shown in Equation 12.7.

$$\text{Line Continuity}(n) = CL(n) \ / \ TL(n) \tag{12.6}$$

$$\text{Line Decay}(n) = 1 - (CL(n) \ / \ TL(n)) \tag{12.7}$$

12.2.6.6 Measured Results

An example of a CLOC spreadsheet that has been populated with data from an analysis of the popular Mozilla Firefox Web browser is shown in Table 12.2. The data that was measured from the source code differentiation, or from counting files, is shown in normal text, and the data calculated from those results is shown in bold text. Table 12.2 reports the growth according to the SLOC method in the last row.

The graphical representation of the two growth measurements of the Mozilla Firefox software project in Figure 12.4 shows the superiority of the CLOC method to the traditional SLOC method. It is safe to assume that the Firefox project is continually evolving, even though the SLOC measurement shows the project to be "devolving." The CLOC measurement correctly shows a steady

Table 12.2   CLOC Analysis of the Mozilla Firefox Browser

Data from Firefox browser	Version 0.1	Version 1.0	Version 2.0	Version 3.0
Total files: $TF(n)$	10,302	10,320	11,042	9,429
New files: $NF(n)$	**0**	**175**	**1,455**	**2,399**
Total LOC: $TL(n)$	3,169,530	3,180,268	3,570,712	3,288,983
Total new LOC: $TNL(n)$	**0**	**40,922**	**843,683**	**1,530,918**
Total continuing files: $TCF(n)$	10,302	10,145	9,587	7,030
Total LOC in continuing files: $TLCF(n)$	3,169,530	3,148,460	3,125,785	2,288,903
New LOC in continuing files: $NLCF(n)$	0	9,114	398,756	530,838
Continuing LOC: $CL(n)$	**3,169,530**	**3,139,346**	**2,727,029**	**1,758,065**
Modified continuing files: $MCF(n)$	0	281	8,577	6,543
Unchanged continuing files: $UCF(n)$	**10,302**	**9,864**	**1,010**	**487**
SLOC Growth(n)	**0%**	**0%**	**13%**	**4%**
CLOC Growth(n)	**0%**	**1%**	**27%**	**48%**
File Continuity(n)	**100%**	**98%**	**87%**	**75%**
Unchanged File Continuity(n)	**100%**	**96%**	**9%**	**5%**
LOC Continuity(n)	**100%**	**99%**	**76%**	**53%**

growth of the project. In contrast, the SLOC measurements rise and fall. The SLOC method measures only the total LOC of each version instead of the dynamically changing total new LOC that the CLOC method measures, so it does not accurately portray the evolution of this popular open source project.

The ups and downs of the Firefox SLOC measurements are a drastic demonstration of the traditional method's shortcomings. An examination of another popular open source project, the Apache HTTP Server, is a less dramatic but perhaps clearer demonstration of why the CLOC method should be used. Figure 12.5 shows the measured growth according to the CLOC and SLOC methods.

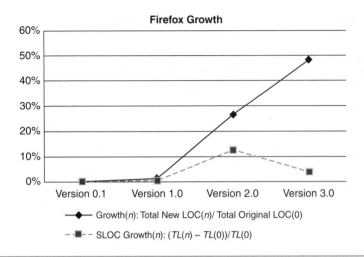

Figure 12.4 CLOC growth versus SLOC growth of the Mozilla Firefox software

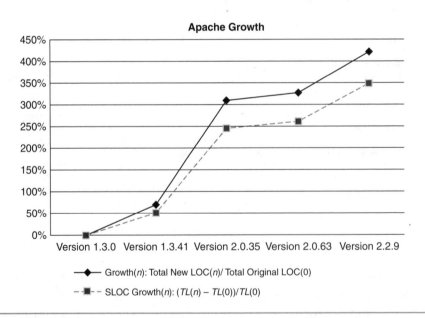

Figure 12.5 CLOC growth versus SLOC growth of the Apache HTTP Server software

Both follow the same basic trend, but the CLOC growth is more rapid than the SLOC growth. The SLOC method leaves out a large number of lines that were deleted and replaced as well as those that were modified. This leads to a gross under-representation of the software project's evolution.

12.2.7 NON-HEADER FILES

Header files typically contain definitions, declarations, and simple macros but not a significant amount of functional code. Header files can be added to a project to provide declarations for third-party library functions that are not part of the protectable intellectual property of a project. Many header files are automatically generated. A more accurate CLOC growth measure can be obtained when header files are eliminated from the CLOC analysis.

TRANSFER PRICING AND THE ORIGINS OF CLOC

A few years ago I invited an attorney to lunch in Palo Alto to get some ideas about how to grow my consulting and software businesses. He and I had worked together on a software copyright infringement case a couple of years earlier. He told me he worked mainly on tax cases, but he was glad to toss around ideas, especially in return for lunch at an expensive restaurant.

After talking for some time, he started asking me how I would measure software growth. He had worked on tax cases where the original version of software was taxed at one rate and a subsequent version of the same software was taxed at a different rate. As I understand it (which is certainly a simplification), when goods are transferred internally within a company, they can be expensed from one division and recorded as income to the other division. How the goods are priced is called the "transfer pricing." When the divisions are in different tax jurisdictions (e.g., different countries), different tax rates apply, and the Internal Revenue Service is vigilant about making sure that the transfer was not done simply to avoid paying the appropriate amount of U.S. taxes.

When intangible assets like intellectual property are transferred, determining an appropriate transfer price can be difficult. In the case of software there is the issue of valuing the intellectual property but also the fact that software is developed and improved, and there is not a clear demarcation showing which parts were developed at which times and in which tax jurisdictions. Companies and the IRS often battle it out in court to determine how much of the software can be traced back to the original code and how much is new. This attorney was working on just such a case, representing Symantec in *Symantec v. Commissioner of Internal Revenue.* Veritas, which was purchased by Symantec, transferred software between Veritas U.S. and its Irish subsidiary and paid taxes on software it valued at $118

Continues

million. The IRS valued the software at about $2.5 billion and calculated back taxes and penalties at about $1 billion. You can see the problem.

The problem was intriguing, and the attorney asked if our software analysis tools could be used to come up with an answer. Initially I thought we could use the software company's version control system to extract the information (my wife teases me when I do that—save my client money but at the same time lose potential revenue by directing the client away from an expensive custom solution and toward an inexpensive off-the-shelf solution). However, when I attempted to extract the information, it just wasn't possible. For example, if you remove 100 lines from the code and later put those lines back in, the version control system reports 200 lines changed even though the code is completely unchanged. Also, extracting specific statistics about the changes is difficult because the systems were not designed to do that.

So I began working with the attorney to use our CodeDiff program to generate the appropriate statistics. We also had to figure out what kind of statistics made sense. I had to make a number of modifications and additions to the functionality of the program but eventually came up with something that seemed very useful. My associate Nik Baer coined the term "CLOC."

In court, the IRS hired an expert who examined the code. Because there was too much code to analyze in detail, he claimed, he broke each version of the program into basic block diagrams. The diagrams consisted of little more than "read file from disk," "analyze file," "perform calculations," and "write results to disk." He presented the argument that since each block diagram looked about the same, there was no substantial change to the code from its initial version ten years ago to the present.

When I testified in court, I had all kinds of spreadsheets and charts showing the growth and continuity of the program. I testified that we had examined 95 million lines of code representing several versions of the program over a ten-year period and could present lots of statistics.

It took one and a half years for Judge Maurice Foley to come to a decision after the trial ended, but he concluded that the IRS valuation was "arbitrary, capricious and unreasonable." In the end we helped save Symantec about $550 million in back taxes and penalties in this precedent-setting case.

PART V

SOURCE CODE CORRELATION

"You know my methods, Watson. There was not one of them which I did not apply to the inquiry. And it ended by my discovering traces, but very different ones from those which I had expected."
—Sherlock Holmes in *The Crooked Man*

In this part we examine more complex methods of comparing software. In particular I define software source code correlation which, like source code differentiation, is a mathematical method of comparing software source code to find similarities. However, while differentiation finds literal similarities and is good for determining statistics about code changes, correlation finds similarities even though changes have occurred. Some of the kinds of things for which source code correlation is useful include

- Detecting plagiarism
- Detecting copyright infringement
- Determining common authors of code
- Finding code clones (refactoring)
- Identifying third-party code
- Locating common algorithms
- Detecting trade secret theft
- Detecting patent infringement

Correlation is designed to produce large scores even when only a small portion of code is correlated or only specific elements of code are correlated, such as identifiers or even comments. This is done purposely because it is more like a detective's tool. It is designed to lead the user to suspicious sections of code regardless of how small those sections are. Code may have been copied from one program into another program. As part of the normal development process, or to disguise the copying, much of the code may have changed by the time it is examined. For example, identifiers may have been renamed, code reordered, instructions replaced with similar instructions, and so forth. However, perhaps one comment remains the same and it is an unusual comment. Or a small sequence of instructions is identical. Correlation is designed to produce a relatively high value based on that comment or that sequence, to direct the detective toward that similarity.

Like any detective's tool, source code correlation does not determine the reason for the correlation. It does not determine guilt or innocence. That determination is up to the detective, and ultimately up to the courts in a case of intellectual property theft or infringement. Some tool creators claim that their tools "detect plagiarism," but that cannot be the case. Those most guilty of this are in academia, where "software plagiarism detection" is considered a legitimate area of computer science. As I describe in Chapter 13, no mathematical tool or computer program can detect plagiarism. What it can do is calculate correlation, and then, through a series of filtering steps, some of which are quantitative and some of which are subjective, a person can make a determination of the reason for the correlation, including copying. Whether that copying constitutes plagiarism is dependent on factors outside of mathematics or computer science but falls in the realms of law and ethics.

In Chapter 13, I discuss the history of the study of software plagiarism detection in academia and point out its uses and its shortcomings. In Chapter 14, I discuss how to characterize source code according to basic elements that are necessary for measuring correlation. In Chapter 15, I explain the theory behind source code correlation, which will get a little mathematical, but anyone with an understanding of basic algebra should be able to follow. In Chapter 16, I discuss implementations of source code correlation, that is, algorithms for creating a program to measure source code correlation. In Chapter 17, I describe applications of source code correlation, including existing applications and potential future applications.

Much of the mathematics and algorithms described in this section are incorporated in the CodeMatch function of the CodeSuite program developed and distributed by S.A.F.E. Corporation.

OBJECTIVES

The objective of this part of the book is to give a theoretical, mathematical foundation for software source code correlation that can be used for basic comparisons of software as well as its applications and implementations. In particular, software source code correlation is used to compare elements of software source code to detect similarities that might be hidden from a basic literal comparison such as one involving source code differentiation.

INTENDED AUDIENCE

Computer scientists and *computer programmers* will find this part useful for understanding the theory, implementation, and application of source code correlation, and they will be able to build upon this theory and practice for a variety of uses, including detecting software plagiarism and performing software refactoring, code optimization, and software testing. *Technical consultants and expert witnesses for litigation* will find this part useful for understanding the theory, implementation, and application of source code correlation and will be able to use it in software IP litigation, particularly copyright infringement cases, certain kinds of trade secret theft cases, and possibly patent infringement cases. *Intellectual property lawyers* and *corporate managers* with an understanding of algebra will find this part useful, especially to get a deep understanding of the theory, implementation, and application of source code correlation and the associated tools that can be used in software IP litigation. *Software entrepreneurs* will find this part useful for understanding source code correlation to apply it to new software products and new businesses.

13

Software Plagiarism Detection

As mentioned previously, the unauthorized copying of software is a growing problem. In this chapter I discuss the field of study in computer science that has historically been called "software plagiarism detection." This is a good starting point for understanding what source code correlation is and what it is not.

13.1 The History of Plagiarism Detection

Software plagiarism has been an area of study within computer science at least since the 1970s. In 1987 J. A. W. Faidhi and S. K. Robinson of Brunel University published their paper entitled "An Empirical Approach for Detecting Program Similarity and Plagiarism within a University Programming Environment." Faidhi and Robinson characterize six levels of modifications to source code resulting in program plagiarism, illustrated in Figure 13.1. The inner circle, the most basic level, represents a category of programs where there are no changes made to the source code. Moving outward to more complex changes, the levels comprise software with comment changes, identifier changes, variable position changes, procedure combinations, program statement changes, and control logic changes.

While this categorization can be useful, it is somewhat arbitrary, particularly the rankings given to these program modifications. These categorizations rely on a value judgment. For example, does a program in which all identifiers have been

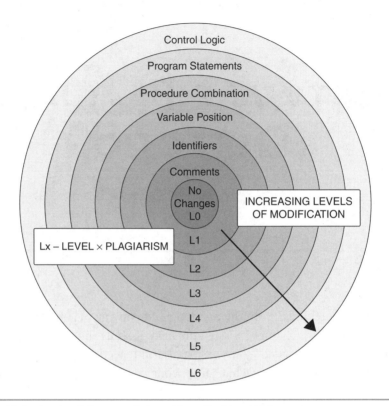

Figure 13.1   Levels of plagiarism (adapted from Faidhi and Robinson)

modified have a "lower level" of plagiarism than one in which one "control logic" routine out of many has been significantly rewritten? You can certainly make an argument that rewriting a routine takes more effort, ingenuity, understanding of programming in general, and knowledge of the specific program being plagiarized. On the other hand, some routines are easy to rewrite, such as a small iterative loop. Some routines can be rewritten in trivial ways, such as decrementing a counter rather than incrementing it. Changing identifier names to better reflect their data types and their use in the program could take a significant amount of knowledge of programming and of the program being plagiarized and could be a very difficult task. Also, how are combinations of these modifications categorized? How does one categorize plagiarism that involves renaming identifiers and also modifying comments? Which category encompasses the rearrangement of significant chunks of code without modifying their functionality?

Later discussions and research sought to create measurements that could be used to determine whether plagiarism had occurred. Many of the measurements were based on the work of Maurice H. Halstead in his book *Elements of Software Science.* As discussed in Chapter 12, Halstead created a quantitative measurement of software source code that counted the number of unique operators, operands, operator occurrences, and operand occurrences in the code being measured. He labeled these quantities as follows:

$n1$ = number of unique operators

$n2$ = number of unique operands

$N1$ = number of operator occurrences

$N2$ = number of operand occurrences

Halstead was not considering plagiarism but rather ways of measuring the complexity of code and the effort required to create it. He defined a "volume" V of a program and the mental effort E required to create the program as follows:

$$V = (N1 + N2) \log2 (n1 + n2)$$
$$E = [n1 \ N2(N1 + N2) \log2 (n1 + n2)]/(2n2)$$

Alan Parker and James Hamblen of Georgia Tech presented one of the earlier summaries of "plagiarism detection" algorithms in existence at the time in their paper entitled "Computer Algorithms for Plagiarism Detection." Each algorithm assigned metrics to features within source code that each algorithm developer felt were most important. These features were variations of Halstead's quantities. Sometimes a programming language parser was used to create an abstract syntax tree to assist with finding these features. In some cases as many as 20 or more features were assigned metrics. One of these measurements was included in a tool to find plagiarism written up by Hugo Jankowitz of Southampton University in his paper entitled "Detecting Plagiarism in Student Pascal Programs." The algorithm for the program to calculate this measurement is shown in the flowchart in Figure 13.2.

13.2 PROBLEMS WITH PREVIOUS ALGORITHMS

All of these algorithms create a single metric for each program and compare metrics to identify plagiarism. Because a single metric is created for the entire program, small sections of plagiarized code can be missed entirely. These kinds of algorithms often reflect the creators' biases—they were all created by university professors looking for plagiarism in student programming projects. Computer programmers in industry, intellectual property lawyers, software project managers,

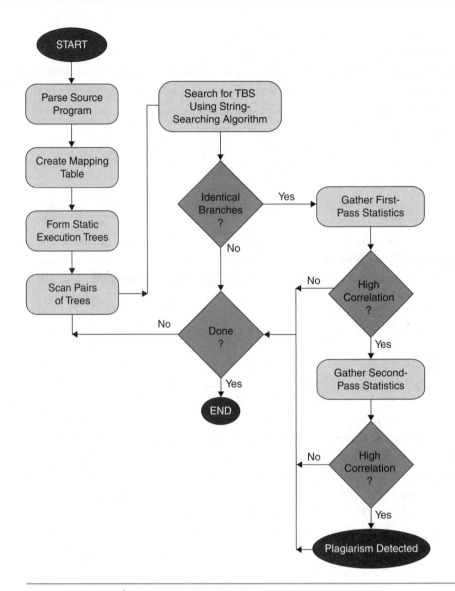

Figure 13.2   Jankowitz algorithm for plagiarism detection

and open source advocates have different perspectives and goals in identifying similar source code. In particular, note the oval block at the bottom right of Figure 13.2 labeled "Plagiarism Detected." Like many algorithms developed after this, Jankowitz's algorithm results in a single binary flag representing whether source code was plagiarized or not. This two-word block has exactly two problems. The first is the word *plagiarism* and the second is the word *detected*.

The term "plagiarism" has a bias because it means that maliciousness is involved. According to the *Random House Unabridged Dictionary*, the definition of plagiarism is

> The unauthorized use or close imitation of the language and thoughts of another author and the representation of them as one's own original work.

Essentially, plagiarism means unauthorized copying, and no software tool, algorithm, or measurement can determine whether authorization was given. Also, plagiarism can occur when only parts of a work have been copied, and so a single binary flag representing whether source code was plagiarized is impossible to create. How much copying would switch the flag from non-plagiarized to plagiarized? Whatever is being detected by these algorithms cannot result in a single true/false result. There can be many reasons for code to be similar, and as I will discuss in Chapter 15, finding similarity does not, in itself, enable one to make a determination of the reason for that similarity. Making a determination requires external information about the similarities, such as which elements are correlated and whether authorization was given to copy those elements. Ultimately, an assessment of plagiarism requires human judgment. With regard to IP theft, I discuss these reasons for similarities in detail in Part VII and give guidelines for making the appropriate judgment.

Another problem is that in the history of this field, there has been little if any theoretical basis for understanding what it means for programs to be similar. There have been attempts to measure "plagiarism," but even that term was never defined. Until recently there has been little exploration of a theoretical basis for what constitutes software source code correlation and how to measure it. Most researchers developed a program and then sought to validate that program. A strict definition of software source code correlation is needed, based on a language-independent definition of source code structure, so that these different correlation detection programs can be compared on an equal basis.

Finally, what is most disturbing about previous research is the sloppiness with which it has been performed. This is partly the result of the lack of common definitions and standard theoretical measures, as I stated previously. Starting at least with the paper by Geoff Whale at the University of New South Wales entitled "Identification of Program Similarity in Large Populations," one of the seminal papers in the field, experiments have all been performed without control groups. Whale created the Plague program for "detecting software plagiarism." Following in Whale's footsteps, Michael J. Wise at the University of Sydney created the YAP programs; Saul Schleimer, Daniel Wilkerson, and Alex Aiken at the

University of California at Berkeley created the MOSS program; and Lutz Prechelt, Guido Malpohl, and Michael Phlippsen at the University of Karlsruhe created the JPlag program. These researchers, like other less well-known researchers in the field, use interesting and in some cases complex and intricate algorithms. Yet their methodology leaves something to be desired. As a whole, they take sets of source code turned in by their students to solve homework problems or test problems. They then run their detection program to determine that a certain percentage of programs has been copied. They then assign graduate students to examine a small number of programs to decide how accurate their detection program has been.

Any undergraduate student of the scientific method should be able to see multiple problems with this methodology. First, there is no theoretical measure with which to compare the results. Second, the graduate students, working after the program has been run, are not unbiased examiners, especially without the necessary theoretical basis. Nor can they be consistent with each other because their examination is subjective. Third, there is no control group. It is impossible to know if the detection program and the grad students are actually reporting anything other than random numbers. And given that there are a number of different reasons for correlation, there is no guarantee that the correlation is not the result of factors other than copying.

13.3 REQUIREMENTS FOR GOOD ALGORITHMS

This poor methodology for running experiments and drawing conclusions has unfortunately been the accepted methodology for nearly all research in the field. It is absolutely mandatory that stricter, more controlled experiments be performed and precise definitions and theoretical measures be developed for this research to produce acceptable results. I have attempted to lay the groundwork in my own papers and in this book. A precise definition of what is being measured is needed. This may seem silly because all computer programmers and computer scientists know what software is, but in a true scientific field of study a precise definition is needed so that everyone is analyzing the same things, and different results can be examined and compared.

Also needed, ideally, is a reference that is well understood so that when measurements are made, it is easy and objective to determine whether they are correct and useful.

The first step in solving these problems is to define source code in a simple, language-independent way that is applicable to the problem being solved. The next step is to create a nonjudgmental, measurable quantity. And the final step is to apply this measure to known reference samples of code to determine if the measure is effective. The next chapters in this part describe how I did this to develop software source code correlation.

FROM LITTLE ACORNS ...

The development of this whole field of endeavor for me came about in a very unexpected way. I had been working on the concept of software synthesis and had started a company to automatically synthesize a real-time operating system (RTOS) from simple commands that a programmer would place in the source code of an embedded software program. I had been pumping money into this start-up venture—hiring programmers and sales and marketing people, renting office space, producing flyers and brochures, and renting booths at conferences—when I realized that my personal financial resources were running low (I was going broke). I turned back to the lucrative expert witness work I had done in the past, and I was hired to compare source code for a lawsuit involving code theft. Being paid by the hour, I should have relished the many hours I spent poring over pages and pages of code, but I didn't. So I thought about what I was doing manually and decided to automate it.

At meetings with colleagues I mentioned this little utility program I had created and got a lot of interest. I gave out free copies and asked for feedback, incorporating the best ideas into the program. Soon, colleagues were recommending me for this type of work, and lawyers were asking about the program and about my services. I found that I could charge for running the program, and the lawyers were OK with that because it still saved money, and got more accurate results, than hiring an expert on an hourly basis to use combinations of off-the-shelf and homegrown tools.

It took me about a year to realize that the software synthesis business to which I had devoted several years was losing money while the little utility program I had created for virtually nothing was actually making money (I guess I'm not the entrepreneur I think I am). I still think that software synthesis is a great idea that will eventually catch on, but I effectively closed down that company and refocused on my CodeMatch program.

Continues

I decided I wanted to have legitimacy in the field, so I performed a study comparing CodeMatch to plagiarism detection programs coming out of academia. I created a standard set of correlated files up front and ran each program to find which performed best—in other words, which program did the best job of spotting the correlated code. I was happy to find that CodeMatch performed significantly better, though with a longer run time, than any of the competitors. Of course, in litigation, the focus of my efforts, more accurate results are worth the extra time.

I submitted what I thought was a great paper, full of carefully documented tests and descriptions, and got one rejection after another. Although business was growing, I was disappointed and called my friend Mike Flynn, Professor Emeritus of Electrical Engineering at Stanford, for advice. Mike had been a mentor for years and always had time to talk to me. Many of the successes in my career can be traced back to some initial advice he gave me or a recommendation from him to a potential customer or employer.

"Mike, you've published hundreds of papers in academic journals and I can't get one published. What am I doing wrong?"

"Well, first, you don't have a PhD, and second, you're not teaching at a university. What kind of feedback are you getting from reviewers?"

"One thing I've heard several times is that I don't have a theory about plagiarism or program similarity. I don't think that's fair because I've read just about every paper in the field and none of them has a theory. Why am I the only one being held to this standard?"

"Well," he replied, "look at this as an opportunity. You can be the first in the field with a theory. Your paper will be the seminal paper in the field."

Mike invited me to meet him early one day at his office and bring all the textbooks I had on information theory, statistics, and computer science. He would have his own books there. We would shut ourselves in a conference room and not come out until we had a theory of program similarity.

We spent a good part of the day developing this theory of source code correlation. Mike refused to take credit for what he explained was my idea and implementation, which he had simply helped direct. I added the theory to my paper, and after yet a few more rejections it was finally accepted at an IEEE conference and published in the conference proceedings. After that, each subsequent paper became easier to get published, though initially they were accepted for workshops or dismissively labeled as "works in progress." I found that after a while, commercial success inevitably brings respect, even in academia where free-market forces have shown that source code correlation is a useful measure and that my CodeMatch program (now incorporated into my CodeSuite program) is a reliable means of performing that measurement.

14 SOURCE CODE CHARACTERIZATION

To a programmer, defining the various elements that constitute software source code may seem trivial and unnecessary. However, to measure software accurately, we need to have a common definition. As with anything else, the definition can vary according to our needs. It can vary depending on the level at which code is being examined. We could, for example, define software source code according to its functionality—embedded software, such as that embedded in your smart toaster or your digital watch, would look different from software in a desktop system. We could define software source code by considering the basic routines in the code. We could define software source code according to a program's "architecture," but that would require us to define the term because it is used loosely, and with different meanings, by computer scientists and programmers. To measure anything, we first need a precise definition of what is being measured. All of these definitions may in fact be legitimate and useful, and source code correlation is a general framework for measuring the similarity of different elements of software, so each of these could be included in the framework. That is one of the advantages of source code correlation: that it can be expanded or restricted as necessary for the task being considered.

For the specific purpose of finding copied code, we can consider that source code consists of three basic kinds of elements. These elements may not correspond to the way code elements are classified for other purposes. For our purpose, code consists of statements, from which we can derive a control structure; comments that serve to document the code; and strings that are messages to users. These elements are shown in Table 14.1. Statements can be further broken down into instructions and identifiers. Instructions comprise control words and operators. Identifiers comprise variables, constants, functions, and labels. A single line of source code may include one or more statements and one or more comments.

Listing 14.1 is a small sample routine that I will reference in the rest of this chapter to better illustrate the various elements of software source code.

Table 14.1   Source Code Elements

Software source code elements	Description
Statements	Cause the computer to perform actions
Instructions	Signify the actions to take place
Control words	Control the program flow (e.g., `if`, `case`, `goto`, `loop`)
Specifiers	Specify data allocations or compiler directives (e.g., `int`, `float`, `#include`)
Operators	Manipulate data (e.g., `+`, `-`, `*`, `/`)
Identifiers	Reference code or data
Variables	Identify changing data
Constants	Identify constant data
Functions	Identify code
Labels	Identify locations in the program
Comments	For documentation purposes only; cause no actions to occur
Strings	Messages to the user

Listing 14.1   Sample Routine to Illustrate the Source Code Elements

```
1   ////////////////////////////////////////////////////////////////////////
2   /* PrintHeader
3    *
4    * Purpose
5    *  Prints a header to a spreadsheet file
6    *
7    * Parameters
```

```
8    *  OutFile             = file to print to
9    *
10   * Return Value
11   *  optimal sum
12   *
13   * Remarks
14   *  none
15   */
16   ////////////////////////////////////////////////////////////////////
17   void PrintHeader(FILE* OutFile)
18   {
19     char date[128];        // Buffer to hold the date
20     int i;                 // Generic integer for various uses
21
22     // Set time zone from TZ environment variable.
23     _tzset();
24
25     _strdate_s(date, 128); fprintf(OutFile, "Date:\n\t%s\n", date);
26
27     for (i = 0; i < NumVersions; i++)
28     {
29       fprintf(OutFile, "Version %i dir: %s\n", i, Dir[i]);
30       if (SubdirList[i]) fprintf(OutFile, "and subdirs\n");
31     }
32
33     if (CompareInit)
34       fprintf(OutFile, "Comparing each version to the first\n");
35     else
36       fprintf(OutFile, "Comparing each version to the previous\n");
37   }
```

14.1 STATEMENTS

Statements are the functional elements of source code. If software were a
building, statements would be all of the structural components of the building
such as the bricks and mortar, the wood framing, the roof, and the floors.
It would not include any purely cosmetic components such as the paint, the
trim, or the façade. Statements do the work of the program and define the
functionality.

It is a mistake to think that the source code consists entirely of the statements. Just as the paint, the trim, and the façade of a building identify it and make it unique, the nonfunctional elements of a program also make it unique.

It is also easy to confuse a statement with an instruction. A statement typically includes an instruction but encompasses more than just the instruction itself. Listing 14.2 gives only the statements from Listing 14.1. (Note that strings have been removed from between the quotes.)

There are a few things to note about this listing of statements. First, all of the strings—specifically on lines 25, 29, 30, 34, and 36—have been removed. This is because strings are considered differently from statements. Strings are messages to be displayed to a user but do not affect the functionality of the program. In Listing 14.2, all that remains of the strings are the double quotes. These double quotes show that a string is being used in the statement at that specific place, but the content of the string is not important to the statement. There are other ways that strings can be represented in the statement. In a program designed to calculate source code correlation, other substitutions may be useful or necessary. Leaving double quotes works well from a representation (as opposed to an implementation) point of view.

Another thing to notice is line 25, where two statements are on the same line, separated by a semicolon. Remember that source code correlation considers lines of code, not how the lines are physically represented in the file. Line 25 represents two distinct statements, each with its own distinct functionality, and each should be considered as a full and separate statement.

Listing 14.2   Statements from the Simple Routine in Listing 14.1

```
17 void PrintHeader(FILE* OutFile)
19    char date[128];
20    int i;
23    _tzset();
25    _strdate_s(date, 128); fprintf(OutFile, "", date);
27    for (i = 0; i < NumVersions; i++)
29       fprintf(OutFile, "", i, Dir[i]);
30       if (SubdirList[i]) fprintf(OutFile, "");
33    if (CompareInit)
34       fprintf(OutFile, "");
35    else
36       fprintf(OutFile, "");
```

14.1.1 SPECIAL STATEMENTS

Some statements require special handling. These statements are programming-language-dependent. Here I show some statements in the C programming language, though many other languages use similar constructs and consequently require similar special consideration.

14.1.1.1 The for Statement

A question arises about how to consider the for statement on line 27. This example uses the C programming language, but most programming languages have a for statement that is similar, if not identical, in construction to that of the C programming language. Each language has its own unique cases that must be considered individually. For the for statement, it is best to consider the statement as actually three distinct statements, as shown in Listing 14.3.

Listing 14.3   Statements that Comprise the for Statement of Line 27

```
i = 0;
while (i < NumVersions){
  i++;
}
```

This way of dividing up a for statement makes logical sense as three statements. The first statement initializes the loop counter i. The second statement loops while the condition i < NumVersions is true. The third statement increments the loop counter i during each pass through the loop.

14.1.1.2 The if and else Statements

Yet another issue is the if statement. On line 30 the if statement and the statement executed when the conditional statement following the if statement, the fprintf statement, are on the same physical line. Later in the code, an if statement is on line 33, but the conditional statement is on the following line 34. Given the way I have described these statements, it should be clear that I consider the if statement to be a statement by itself and the conditional statement that follows the if statement to be a separate statement to be considered independently. Similarly, an else statement is a statement by itself and the statement following the else statement is also a separate statement to be considered independently.

14.1.2 INSTRUCTIONS

Instructions specify the actions that the computer must execute. Instructions can be further classified as control words, specifiers, and operators. Control words and specifiers can be grouped together as keywords.

14.1.2.1 Control Words

Control words are keywords that instruct the computer to take some action. The control words from Listing 14.1 are shown in Table 14.2.

Note that on line 27 three control words are listed: `for`, `(set)`, and `(set)`. This is because an equals sign in the C programming language, as well as in most other programming languages, though it may look like an operator, is an assignment operator; it essentially acts as a control word that tells the processor to set a variable to a specific value. I call this the "implied `set` control word," so the statement

```
index = 5;
```

is really shorthand for the statement

```
set index = 5;
```

Table 14.2   Control Words from the Simple Routine in Listing 14.1

Line number	Control words		
23	_tzset		
25	_strdate_s	fprintf	
27	for	(set)	(set)
29	fprintf		
30	if	fprintf	
33	if		
34	fprintf		
35	else		
36	fprintf		

Similarly, the statement

```
index ++;
```

is really shorthand for the statement

```
index = index + 1;
```

so the statement effectively includes the implied set control word (the = symbol) and the + operator.

14.1.2.2 Specifiers

Specifiers are keywords that instruct the compiler to take some action when it compiles source code into executable binary files. For example, specifiers can cause the compiler to allocate memory for variables, can define compile-time constants, and can conditionally leave in or leave out sections of code. The specifiers from Listing 14.1 are shown in Table 14.3.

14.1.2.3 Operators

Operators perform operations that manipulate data. The operators from Listing 14.1 are shown in Table 14.4.

Note that on line 33 there is an implied == operator because the line

```
if (CompareInit)
```

Table 14.3   Specifiers from the Simple Routine in Listing 14.1

Line number	Control words
17	void FILE
19	char
20	int

Table 14.4   Operators from the Simple Routine in Listing 14.1

Line number	Operators
27	< ++
33	(==)

is really shorthand for the statement

```
if (CompareInit == true)
```

so the statement effectively includes the implied equality test operator (the == symbol).

14.1.3 IDENTIFIERS

Identifiers are names used for referencing code or data. Usually these names are mnemonics that give information about the code or data so that they can be easily understood in the code. Identifiers can be further categorized as variables, constants, functions, and labels.

Variable names identify data that can change and be manipulated while the program is running. Constant names identify values that do not change while the program is running.

Function names identify groupings of lines of code that work together and can be executed using the function name. Functions are also called methods, procedures, routines, and subroutines. Sometimes these terms have subtle differences. Sometimes certain programming languages or programming methodologies make use of one of these terms and not another. In object-oriented programming (OOP) languages, for example, the term "method" is preferred.[1] Sometimes a programmer may prefer one term over another. For our purposes, though, they all represent a small piece of code that performs some task. Usually a function takes in data, though that's not always necessary. For example, a function can produce an error message on the screen that states, "This program has failed!" Typically a function also outputs data, though a function that simply pauses for a certain amount of time may not have any output. Every function, though, performs some task.

Labels are used to mark locations in the program for flow control and allow one statement to cause execution to continue at a different location in the program. Source code written in high-level programming languages like BASIC or C rarely uses labels, and many high-level programming languages do not include support for labels. Labels are most commonly found in assembly language programs such as that shown in Listing 14.4, where line 21 has the label TS1_TEST which defines the beginning of a function. This label could equally be considered a

---

1. The OOP paradigm is a bit different, but it is still possible to dissect an OOP program into its constituent elements and derive a canonical representation similar to the one we are developing here for this example C program.

function name, though that would take some knowledge of the structure of the code and how it is used. In assembly code, a function is preceded by a label that identifies the line and is also used to identify the beginning of the function. Lines 28 and 29 show labels LAB1 and LAB2. Note that lines 25 and 27 have instructions that direct execution to "jump" to the lines where these labels are located. Line 25 causes a jump only if the result of an operation is nonzero (jnz instruction). Line 27 causes a jump in all cases (unconditional jmp instruction).

Listing 14.4 Assembly Code Showing Labels

```
 1    ;********************************************************************
 2    ;* TS1_TEST
 3    ;*
 4    ;* Purpose
 5    ;* Perform tests on internal processor registers.
 6    ;*
 7    ;********************************************************************
 8    .MODEL large
 9    .486P      ; uses Use16 attribute because .MODEL is first
10
11    ;********************************************************************
12    ;*    Include definitions, constants, macros
13    ;********************************************************************
14    INCLUDE defs.inc
15
16    ;********************************************************************
17    ;*    Public variables
18    ;********************************************************************
19    PUBLIC TS1_TEST
20
21    TS1_TEST:
22      ; Display the value of the AC bit
23      CALL_BY_GATE0 GATE_GET_EFLAGS  ; get the value of EFLAGS
24      and  eax, AC_BIT               ; Get the value of AC bit
25      jnz  LAB1
26      DISPLAY_PM MSG_AC0             ; Display message AC = 0
27      jmp  LAB2
28    LAB1: DISPLAY_PM MSG_AC1         ; Display message AC = 1
29    LAB2:
30    iretd                           ; return from task
```

14.2 COMMENTS

Comments are nonfunctional lines of code that are intended to give information to the person reading the code. Typically comments give information about the functionality of the code. Functions also can contain information about the file in which the comments appear or the program as a whole, including the author of the code, the date it was created, the version, the copyright owner, how to use the program, and any licensing requirements. Sometimes even jokes and anecdotes can be found in the comments—essentially they can be any text the author wishes because they have no effect on the functionality of the code. Comments from the simple routine in Listing 14.1 can be seen in Listing 14.5.

Listing 14.5 Comments from the Simple Routine in Listing 14.1

```
 1   /////////////////////////////////////////////////////////////////
 2   /* PrintHeader
 3    *
 4    * Purpose
 5    *    Prints a header to a spreadsheet file
 6    *
 7    * Parameters
 8    *    OutFile                 = file to print to
 9    *
10    * Return Value
11    *    optimal sum
12    *
13    * Remarks
14    *    none
15    */
16   /////////////////////////////////////////////////////////////////
19                              // Buffer to hold the date
20                              // Generic integer for various uses
22   // Set time zone from TZ environment variable.
```

Comments are represented in different ways in different programming languages. In nearly all languages, though, a certain sequence of characters is used to signify that those characters to the end of the line constitute a comment that the compiler will ignore. Typically there are two other sets of characters that signify the beginning and end of a comment that can extend beyond a single line. In the C programming language, double slashes (//) signify a comment until the end of the line as shown in lines 1, 16, 19, 20, and 22. Also in the C programming language, a slash-star combination (/*) signals the beginning of a comment, and a star-slash (*/) combination signals the end of a comment. Note that this is used on line 2 and line 15 to signal that lines 2 through 15 are all comments to be ignored by the compiler. These character combinations are used in C, but they are common to many other programming languages as well.

Note that lines 19 and 20 contain a statement followed by a comment. This is a common way to make a note about a particular statement that allows a programmer to understand the statement. Any number of statements and comments can be combined on a single line. Interspersing comments in the middle of statements is not a good programming practice, because it reduces the readability of the statement, which is something the comments are intended to improve. Fortunately, comments are not often interspersed in the middle of statements, but it does happen.

14.3 Strings

Strings are used to hold character data that is almost always intended to be displayed to a user. The strings from the simple routine given in Listing 14.1 are shown in Listing 14.6. These strings are printed to a file while the program is running. Changing these strings would not affect the functionality of the program.

Listing 14.6   Strings from the Simple Routine in Listing 14.1

```
25  Date:\n\t%s\n
29  Version %i dir: %s\n
30  and subdirs\n
34  Comparing each version to the first\n
36  Comparing each version to the previous\n
```

Note the %s sequence in the strings. The %s is called a "format string" because the characters %s are not actually printed to the file but are used to format the output of data that is inserted into the string. Another string, held in a variable, is substituted into the string where the %s is located while the program is running. On line 25 of the original code, the date is held in a string variable called, appropriately, date.

Note the \n and \t character sequences in some strings. These are called "escape sequences," which are used to represent other characters that would otherwise cause confusion in the source code. The \n character sequence is the most common escape sequence, representing a newline. The \t character sequence represents a tab character.

If the date in the date string variable is January 18, 1960, then the string in line 25 would contain two newline characters (i.e., it would display on two lines) and include a tab as shown here:

```
Date:
        January 18, 1960
```

This dissection of source code lines into various well-defined elements is necessary for calculating source code correlation, as I will discuss in Chapter 15.

15
THEORY

In the previous chapter I defined source code as consisting of statements, from which we can derive a control structure, and comments and strings (see Table 14.1). Statements further consist of instructions, identifiers, and labels. Instructions comprise control words, specifiers, and operators. Identifiers comprise variables, constants, functions, and labels. A single line of source code may include one or more statements and one or more comments and strings.

Correlation in statistics is a measure of the relationship between two variables. A correlation ρ is 0 for completely unrelated variables, 1 for perfectly identical variables, and -1 for completely opposite variables. For our purposes, there is no such thing as source code that is completely opposite, so we should consider correlation values ranging from 0 to 1.

Any accurate measure of source code correlation should consider the actual program source code without requiring any significant changes to the code. It should divide the software into its essential elements. A correlation between 0 and 1 should be determined for each element individually. The correlation for a particular element should represent a single dimension of a multidimensional correlation that is orthogonal to the correlation of the other elements. The dimensions of source code correlation were chosen to correspond to the software source code elements defined in Table 14.1, though arguments can be made for dividing the code into different sets of elements. Regardless of which elements are chosen, the overall methodology is the same. The individual correlation scores can then be combined into a single overall correlation score between 0 and 1.

15.1 PRACTICAL DEFINITION

Before we get into a rigorous definition of source code correlation, here is a practical, easy-to-understand definition. Correlation is based on the amount of matching of the source code elements. We can consider three types of matches:

1. **Exact match:** Symbols and spaces match exactly after whitespace has been reduced.

2. **Partial match:** A substring in one element matches a substring in another element. There are many possible methods for determining partial match, and we do not require any particular one.[1]

3. **Transformational match:** A transformation can be established between element 1 and element 2. Element 2 can be predicted by knowing a corresponding element 1.

In this book I restrict the discussion to exact and partial matches. Correlation using transformational matches is still an area that has not been explored in much detail. The measurement of the correlation of a source code element is simply the ratio of matches and partial matches to the total number of elements examined, resulting in a maximum of 1. Given two sets of source code files, correlation can be determined between elements of the code, and that can be used to calculate an overall correlation. When a programmer changes one or several elements of source code from one program to another, intentionally or not, the overall measure of correlation between the programs diminishes. However, when correlation is measured for each different element, correlation of some elements may diminish while others can remain high.

The following four types of correlation, and a fifth overall correlation, cover the basic elements of source code and are described in practical terms in the

---

1. For example, we could find the longest common substring, which is the longest sequence of contiguous characters in both strings. Or we could find the longest common subsequence (LCS), which is the longest sequence of characters in both strings, though there may be other characters between them in the original string. The string ABC is a substring of the string ABCDEFG and is a subsequence of the string AxBxxCxxxDxxxExxFxG. Other methods may be useful for determining partial matches, but source code correlation is independent of the particular method.

following sections. In practice, each correlation is determined on a file-to-file basis because files are natural ways to isolate sets of source code and because programmers typically divide their source code into files in a logical manner. Nothing precludes comparing source code on a program-to-program basis or some other basis, but files are convenient and available.

- Statement correlation (ρ_S)
- Comment/string correlation (ρ_C)
- Identifier correlation (ρ_I)
- Instruction sequence correlation (ρ_Q)
- Overall source code correlation (ρ)

15.1.1 STATEMENT CORRELATION

The statement correlation ρ_S is the result of comparing functional lines in the source code of the file pair. This measure relates strongly to the functionality of the two files. Two files with high statement correlation can also have similar functionality, though statements may match because they are simply commonly used statements for the given programming language.

15.1.2 COMMENT/STRING CORRELATION

The comment/string correlation ρ_C is the result of comparing comments and strings from both files. Comments and strings are considered together because both have no functionality and both are intended to give information from the program developer to another person, though the audience is different. Comments are intended to give information to other programmers. Strings are intended to give information to users of the program. Matching comments and strings are often the result of a common author who tends to describe source code in certain ways using colloquialisms, slang, or unintentional misspellings.

It is conceivable that comments and strings could have their own correlation scores and that comment correlation would be one correlation element and string correlation would be another correlation element that could be combined into the overall correlation score as two separate elements rather than one. Experience has shown that combining them produces good results, but an argument can be made for separating them, and that would still fall within the general framework of multidimensional correlation.

COMMENTS ABOUT COMMENTS

In creating my original CodeMatch program to help detect software copyright infringement, I got some strong feedback about the fact that my program considered comments along with functional code. In all of the programs coming out of universities, comments were thrown out before the comparison started. In academia, professors are less concerned about whether students copied comments than about whether the students understood the functionality of the code. One can even argue that if a student copied a program and then modified it significantly, then the student must understand the program and there was no need to challenge him about plagiarism (I don't agree with this assessment, but I've heard the argument).

So one of the arguments I encountered when I was initially trying to publish papers on my technology was that there was no need to consider comments. The comments I received about comments were not always very nice. One test that I developed to determine the usefulness of CodeMatch stripped all functional code out of some files and left only comments, then compared those files to a large group of files, including the original files with functional code and comments. The purpose was to see whether the methodology worked, but several people had a good laugh about that one because, they explained, it was pretty ridiculous to examine source code files consisting only of comments. I was surprised that they didn't see the value of considering corner cases that, of course, were extremes but that would be most likely to expose problems in the algorithm or the implementation.

I knew from experience that comments can be very significant when trying to find clues to copying, particularly in litigation. In the case of *Cadence Design Systems Inc. v. Avant! Corporation*, Avant! was found guilty of stealing code from Cadence. The code for Avant!'s ArcCell and Aquarius programs included a word in a comment that was misspelled in the same way and in the same place in an identical comment in the code for Cadence's Symbad program. It appeared that sections of the code had been copied and significantly rewritten, which isn't surprising considering what was at stake in the case, but at least some comments had not been touched. Finding these copied comments led to the discovery of tens of thousands of lines of copied code, forming a proof that Avant! had not started its code development from scratch but had gotten a head start by illegally appropriating source code. The civil and criminal cases against Avant! resulted in hundreds of millions of dollars in fines and jail time for the company's executives.

Nowadays, most plagiarism detection programs, even those coming out of universities, compare comments.

15.1.3 IDENTIFIER CORRELATION

The identifier correlation ρ_I is the result of comparing identifiers in the source code of the file pair. This correlation measure is high for code where common identifier names are used for variables, constants, functions, and labels. Correlation of identifiers includes both exact matches and partial matches such as MyName and MyName2. Such similar identifiers can point to code that has been purposely masked, using a global search and replace, either to hide its origin or because of natural changes to the code during the development process. Matching identifier names may be the result of a common author who prefers certain words and naming conventions, though it may also be the result of common specifications or terms commonly used by programmers in general or by programmers within the industry served by the program.

15.1.4 INSTRUCTION SEQUENCE CORRELATION

The instruction sequence correlation ρ_Q is the result of comparing instruction sequences in the file pair. This measure finds the longest common sequence of instructions in two files. Note that comments and strings are ignored for determining instruction sequences because those elements do not contribute to the functionality. Also, note that this correlation measure considers sequences of instructions, not sequences of statements. In the statements, variable names may have been modified; even operations may be replaced with identical or equivalent operations that are represented differently. Instruction sequence correlation considers only the instructions in the statements.

Instruction sequence correlation finds functionally similar programs that perform sequences of operations in a similar way. Given the sequential nature of software source code, this correlation is an important, though not exhaustive, measure of functional similarity between two programs.

15.1.5 OVERALL SOURCE CODE CORRELATION

Finally, an overall source code correlation ρ is calculated as a measure of the similarity of the file pairs. The exact mathematical method of combining the individual correlation scores into a single overall correlation score is described later in this chapter.

15.2 COMPARING DIFFERENT PROGRAMMING LANGUAGES

Nothing in the definition of source code correlation precludes comparing programs in different languages. All modern programming languages can be divided into the elements we have been considering. Comparing programs in different languages may result in lower overall correlation scores because it is difficult to have exact matches if the programming languages use significantly different syntax. However, relative correlation scores, which are all we are really interested in, will still be significant. Also, comparing different programming languages may require the use of transformational matches, defined previously, to transform elements of one program into elements of another program or into a third standard format for more accurate comparisons. This transformational matching is particularly important for statement correlation and instruction sequence correlation.

15.3 MATHEMATICAL DEFINITIONS

In this section, I take a more rigorous mathematical look at correlation. The following are the mathematical definitions of terms and symbols used throughout this chapter that you need to understand to calculate correlation:

F^n = the nth source code file in a set of files being compared

$\rho_S(F^n, F^m)$ = statement correlation between files F^n and F^m

$\rho_C(F^n, F^m)$ = comment/string correlation between files F^n and F^m

$\rho_I(F^n, F^m)$ = identifier correlation between files F^n and F^m

$\rho_Q(F^n, F^m)$ = instruction sequence correlation between files F^n and F^m

$\rho(F^n, F^m)$ = overall source code correlation between files F^n and F^m

The following are definitions that apply to all elements being examined for correlation. These are described in more detail later in this chapter. I define a generic code element X, where X can be a statement or a comment/string or some other element that may be defined in the future.

X_i = the ith element of type X of a source code file

$N^n(X_i)$ = the number of times the ith element X_i appears in source code file n

$\mu(X_i, X_j)$ = element match score, a measure of the similarity between the ith X-type element of a source code file and the jth X-type element of a source code file, not necessarily the same files

$\mu(X_i)$ = element identity match score, the match score for the ith X-type element of a source code file; in other words, the match score if that element is also exactly found in another file

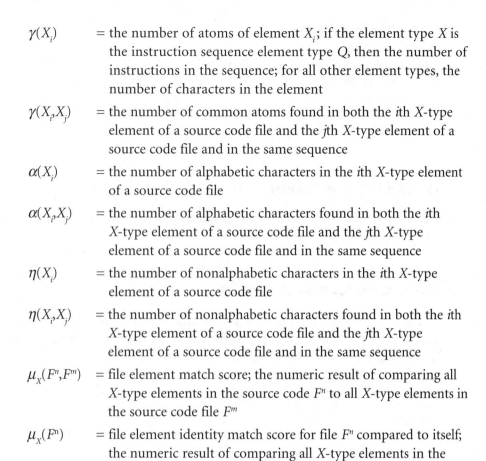

$\gamma(X_i)$ = the number of atoms of element X_i; if the element type X is the instruction sequence element type Q, then the number of instructions in the sequence; for all other element types, the number of characters in the element

$\gamma(X_i,X_j)$ = the number of common atoms found in both the ith X-type element of a source code file and the jth X-type element of a source code file and in the same sequence

$\alpha(X_i)$ = the number of alphabetic characters in the ith X-type element of a source code file

$\alpha(X_i,X_j)$ = the number of alphabetic characters found in both the ith X-type element of a source code file and the jth X-type element of a source code file and in the same sequence

$\eta(X_i)$ = the number of nonalphabetic characters in the ith X-type element of a source code file

$\eta(X_i,X_j)$ = the number of nonalphabetic characters found in both the ith X-type element of a source code file and the jth X-type element of a source code file and in the same sequence

$\mu_X(F^n,F^m)$ = file element match score; the numeric result of comparing all X-type elements in the source code F^n to all X-type elements in the source code file F^m

$\mu_X(F^n)$ = file element identity match score for file F^n compared to itself; the numeric result of comparing all X-type elements in the source code file F^n to themselves

15.4 SOURCE CODE CORRELATION MATHEMATICS

For each element (statement, comment/string, identifier, or instruction sequence), we calculate a match score that is the result of comparing all elements in one source code file to all elements in another source code file. For the match score to be useful, it must meet certain criteria that are the source code correlation axioms.

15.4.1 COMMUTATIVITY AXIOM

First, the match score must not be dependent on the order of comparing two files. In other words, the correlation value for any element we examine must be commutative, as represented by Equation 15.1:

$$\mu_X\left(F^n,F^m\right) = \mu_X\left(F^m,F^n\right) \tag{15.1}$$

15.4.2 IDENTITY AXIOM

The maximum match score must be equivalent to the identity match score. In other words, a file cannot match another file more than it matches itself. This is represented by Equation 15.2:

$$\mu_x\left(F^n\right) = \mu_x\left(F^n, F^n\right) \qquad (15.2)$$

15.4.3 LOCATION AXIOM

The location of the files in a file system should have no bearing on the correlation measurement.

15.4.4 CORRELATION DEFINITION

To normalize the correlation, we must calculate the maximum possible match score and then calculate the correlation of these two files by normalizing the match score using Equation 15.3:

$$\rho_x\left(F^n, F^m\right) = \frac{\mu_x\left(F^n, F^m\right)}{max\left(\mu_x\left(F^n, F^m\right)\right)} \qquad (15.3)$$

15.4.5 LEMMA

The maximum possible match score between any two files must be the smaller of the identity match scores for each file. If not, we would be violating equation 15.2. This is represented by Equation 15.4:

$$max\left(\mu_x\left(F^n, F^m\right)\right) = min\left(\mu_x\left(F^n\right), \mu_x\left(F^n\right)\right) \qquad (15.4)$$

15.5 SOURCE CODE EXAMPLES

To better understand the equations that follow, we will consider two small source code files to be compared. The listings for these files are presented in this section for reference later in the chapter.

Listing 15.1   Source Code File 1

```
1  int example_routine(float newVal)
2  {
3    float simVal;    // Similarity value to be calculated
4    int   i;         // Integer variable
5    int   j;         // Integer variable
6
7    printf("Starting.");
8
9    // Initialize variables
10   simVal = 1.0;
11   i = 0;
12   j = 0;
13
14   while (j < NUM_VALS)
15   {
16     j++;
17     simVal = simVal * 10;
18     if (simVal == newVal)
19     {
20       j = 0;
21       break;
22     }
23     printf("Done!");
24   }
25   return(j);
26 }
```

Listing 15.2   Source Code File 2

```
1  int example_routine2(float newVal)
2  {
3    float simVal;    // Similarity value to be calculated
4    int   i;         // Integer variable
5    int   j;         // Integer variable
6
7    simVal = 1.0;
8    i = 0;
9    j = 0;
10
```

Continues

Listing 15.2   Source Code File 2 *(Continued)*

```
11   while (i < NUM_VALS)
12   {
13     i++;
14     simVal = simVal * 10;
15     if (simVal == newVal)
16     {
17       i = 0;
18       break;
19     }
20   }
21   return(i);
22 }
```

15.6 UNIQUE ELEMENTS

Note that in some of the equations that follow I discuss "the *i*th *unique* element of a source code file." By this I mean the *i*th element of a source code file when all duplicate elements are removed. Consider the source code file of Listing 15.1 showing the routine `example_routine()`.

The unique statement, comment, and identifier elements are shown in Table 15.1. Altogether there are 26 lines in the source code file of Listing 15.1; there are 3 blank lines, 6 lines containing only the bracket symbol, which can be considered blank lines, 1 line containing only a comment, and 16 statements. However, Table 15.1 shows that there are only 14 unique statements because the statements `j = 0;` and `printf();` are repeated in the code (note that the string inside the statement is stripped out and considered separately). There are 4 comments in the code snippet, but only 3 of them are unique because the comment `Integer variable` is repeated. There are 2 strings in the code, and each of them is unique. Identifiers are used 18 times in the code snippet, but there are only 6 unique identifiers in the code.

To evaluate the term $N(S_i)$ for the statement `float simVal;`, we would count the number of times that the statement appears in the source code file. In this case it appears once, so $N(\texttt{float simVal;}) = 1$.

To evaluate the term $N(C_i)$ for the comment `Integer variable`, we would count the number of times that the comment appears in the source code file. In this case it appears twice, so $N(\texttt{Integer variable}) = 2$.

Table 15.1 Unique Source Code Elements

Statements	Comments/strings	Identifiers
int example_routine (float newVal)	Similarity value to be calculated	example_routine
float simVal;	Integer variable	newVal
int i;	Initialize variables	simVal
int j;	Starting	i
printf();	Done!	j
simVal = 1.0;		NUM_VALS
i = 0;		
j = 0;		
while (j < NUM_VALS)		
j++;		
simVal = simVal * 10;		
if (simVal == newVal)		
break;		
return(j);		

To evaluate the term $N(I_i)$ for the identifier simVal, we would count the number of times that the identifier appears in the source code file. In this case it appears five times, so $N(\text{simVal}) = 5$.

15.7 STATEMENT CORRELATION

The statement correlation is the result of comparing functional lines in the source code of the file pair. Unique statements are extracted from the two files being compared. All sequences of whitespace characters (spaces and tabs) are reduced to a single space, and leading and trailing whitespace is removed. All statements consisting entirely of programming language keywords and operators are ignored because these would be commonplace in many programs.

15.7.1 STATEMENT CORRELATION EQUATIONS

The file match score is then calculated according to Equation 15.5, which states that the file match score is equal to the sum of the match scores of each unique statement that can be found in both files multiplied by the least number of times that statement appears in one of the two files.

$$\mu_S\left(F^n, F^m\right) = \sum \mu\left(S_i\right) \cdot \min\left(N^n\left(S_i\right), N^m\left(S_i\right)\right) \forall \text{ unique } S_j : S_i \in F^n \cap F^m \quad (15.5)$$

This equation simply creates a one-to-one match for the statements in the two files being compared. For example, compare the code in the file of Listing 15.1 to that in the file of Listing 15.2 showing routine `example_routine2()`. In Listing 15.1 the statement `i = 0;` appears only once, but it appears twice in Listing 15.2. When calculating the statement correlation score, the match score for the statement `i = 0;` would be multiplied by 1, the least number of times it appears in either of the two files, in Listing 15.1. The second instance of statement `i = 0;` in Listing 15.2 cannot be matched to any statement in Listing 15.1, so it is not considered in calculating the statement correlation score.

The statement identity match score $\mu(S_i)$ can be calculated in many different ways that can be justified. The match score that I have found to work best is given by Equation 15.6. The multipliers k_α and k_η, where $k_\alpha > k_\eta$, are used to give more significance to alphabetic characters over numbers, operators, and symbols.

$$\mu\left(S_i\right) = k_\alpha \cdot \alpha\left(S_i\right) + k_\eta \cdot \eta\left(S_i\right) \quad (15.6)$$

The statement identity match score for a file is then simply given by Equation 15.7, which states that the identity match score is given by the sum of the match scores of each unique statement multiplied by the number of times that statement appears in the file.

$$\mu_S\left(F^n\right) = \sum \mu\left(S_i\right) \cdot N^n\left(S_i\right) \forall S_i : S_i \in F^n \quad (15.7)$$

Then the statement correlation $\rho_S(F^n, F^m)$ can easily be calculated by combining Equation 15.3, Equation 15.4, Equation 15.5, Equation 15.6, and Equation 15.7.

15.7.2 CALCULATING THE STATEMENT CORRELATION

Let us go through the calculation for the files given in Listing 15.1 and Listing 15.2, using $k_\alpha = 10$ and $k_\eta = 1$. In the first column, Table 15.2 shows each unique statement from the source code file of Listing 15.1. The next two columns show the count of alphabetic characters and nonalphabetic characters in each statement. In the fourth column each statement's identity match score is calculated from Equation 15.6. The fifth column shows the number of occurrences of each statement in the file. The rightmost column contains the product of the statement

Table 15.2 Statement Match Scores for File 1 (with $k_\alpha = 10$ and $k_\eta = 1$)

Statements	Alphabetic characters	Nonalphabetic characters	Statement identity match score	Occurrences	Score
`int example_ routine(float newVal)`	28	5	280 + 5 = 285	1	285
`float simVal;`	11	2	110 + 2 = 112	1	112
`int i;`	4	2	40 + 2 = 42	1	42
`int j;`	4	2	40 + 2 = 42	1	42
`printf();`	6	3	60 + 3 = 63	2	126
`simVal = 1.0;`	6	7	60 + 7 = 67	1	67
`i = 0;`	1	5	10 + 5 = 15	1	15
`j = 0;`	1	5	10 + 5 = 15	2	30
`while (j < NUM_VALS)`	13	7	130 + 7 = 137	1	137
`j++;`	1	3	10 + 3 = 13	1	13
`simVal = sim-Val * 10;`	12	9	120 + 9 = 129	1	129
`if (simVal == newVal)`	14	7	140 + 7 = 147	1	147
`break;`	5	1	50 + 1 = 51	1	51
`return(j);`	7	3	70 + 3 = 73	1	73
Statement identity match score for the file					**1269**

identity match score and the number of occurrences, which is then summed as required by Equation 15.7 to give the statement identity match score for the entire file at the bottom right of the table.

Table 15.3 shows the statements from the source code file of Listing 15.2, their statement identity match scores, and the statement identity match score for the file at the bottom right.

Now we look at the statements that exist in both files and use Equation 15.5 to calculate the statement match score for the two files in Table 15.4. The fifth column shows the minimum number of occurrences of each statement in the two files. While some statements appear twice in one file,

Table 15.3 Statement Match Scores for File 2 (with $k_\alpha = 10$ and $k_\eta = 1$)

Statements	Alphabetic characters	Nonalphabetic characters	Statement identity match score	Occurrences	Score
int example_ routine2 (float newVal)	28	6	280 + 6 = 286	1	286
float simVal;	11	2	110 + 2 = 112	1	112
int i;	4	2	40 + 2 = 42	1	42
int j;	4	2	40 + 2 = 42	1	42
simVal = 1.0;	6	7	60 + 7 = 67	1	67
i = 0;	1	5	10 + 5 = 15	2	30
j = 0;	1	5	10 + 5 = 15	1	15
while (j < NUM_VALS)	13	7	130 + 7 = 137	1	137
i++;	1	3	10 + 3 = 13	1	13
simVal = simVal * 10;	12	9	120 + 9 = 129	1	129
if (simVal == newVal)	14	7	140 + 7 = 147	1	147
break;	5	1	50 + 1 = 51	1	51
return(i);	7	3	70 + 3 = 73	1	73
Statement identity match score for the file					**1144**

that same statement appears only once in the other file, so the multiplier is always 1. The statement match score for the two files is at the bottom right of the table.

Equation 15.4 tells us that the maximum statement match score between the two files, $\mu_S(F^n, F^m)$, is simply the smaller of the statement identity match scores for the two files, in this case 1144. From Equation 15.2, the statement correlation score $\rho_S(F^n, F^m)$ for the two files is the statement match score of the two files divided by the maximum statement match score of the two files. In this case the result is 620/1144 or 0.54.

Table 15.4 Statement Match Scores for File 1 Compared to File 2 (with $k_\alpha = 10$ and $k_\eta = 1$)

Statements	Alphabetic characters	Nonalphabetic characters	Statement element match score	Minimum no. of occurrences	Score
`float simVal;`	11	2	$110 + 2 = 112$	1	112
`int i;`	4	2	$40 + 2 = 42$	1	42
`int j;`	4	2	$40 + 2 = 42$	1	42
`simVal = 1.0;`	6	7	$60 + 7 = 67$	1	67
`i = 0;`	1	5	$10 + 5 = 15$	1	15
`j = 0;`	1	5	$10 + 5 = 15$	1	15
`simVal = simVal * 10;`	12	9	$120 + 9 = 129$	1	129
`if (simVal == newVal)`	14	7	$140 + 7 = 147$	1	147
`break;`	5	1	$50 + 1 = 51$	1	51
Statement match score for the files					**620**

15.8 COMMENT/STRING CORRELATION

The comment/string correlation is the result of comparing unique nonfunctional lines in the source code of the file pair. All sequences of whitespace characters (spaces and tabs) are reduced to a single space, and leading and trailing whitespace is removed.

15.8.1 COMMENT/STRING CORRELATION EQUATIONS

The file match score is then calculated according to Equation 15.8, which states that the file match score is equal to the sum of the match scores of each unique comment or string that can be found in both files multiplied by the least number of times that comment or string appears in one of the two files.

$$\mu_c\left(F^n, F^m\right) = \sum \mu\left(C_i\right) \bullet min\left(N^n\left(C_i\right), N^m\left(C_i\right)\right) \ \forall \ unique \ C_i : C_i \in F^n \cap F^m \quad (15.8)$$

The comment/string element identity match score $\mu(C_i)$ can be calculated in many different ways that can be justified. The match score that I have found to work best is given by Equation 15.9, where the number of characters is used.

$$\mu\left(C_i\right) = \gamma\left(C_i\right) \quad (15.9)$$

The comment/string identity match score for a file is then simply given by Equation 15.10, which states that the identity match score is given by the sum of the match scores of each unique comment or string multiplied by the number of times that comment or string appears in the file.

$$\mu_C\left(F^n\right)=\sum \mu\left(C_i\right)\bullet N^n\left(C_i\right)\ \forall\ C_i:C_i\in F^n \tag{15.10}$$

Then the comment/string correlation $\rho_C(F^n, F^m)$ can easily be calculated by combining Equation 15.3, Equation 15.4, Equation 15.8, Equation 15.9, and Equation 15.10.

15.8.2 Calculating the Comment/String Correlation

Let us go through the calculation for the files given in Listing 15.1 and Listing 15.2. In the first column, Table 15.5 shows each unique comment or string from the source code file of Listing 15.1. The next column shows the count of characters in each comment or string. In the third column the identity match score for each comment or string is calculated from Equation 15.9, which is simply the character count. The fourth column shows the number of occurrences of each comment or string in the file. The rightmost column is the product of the comment/string identity match score and the number of occurrences, which is then summed as required by Equation 15.10 to give the comment/string identity match score for the entire file at the bottom right of the table.

Table 15.6 shows the statements from the source code file of Listing 15.2, their comment/string identity match scores, and the comment/string identity match score for the file at the bottom right.

Table 15.5 Comment/String Match Scores for File 1

Comments and strings	No. of characters	Comment/string identity match score	Occurrences	Score
Similarity value to be calculated	33	33	1	33
Integer variable	16	16	2	32
Initialize variables	20	20	1	20
Starting	9	9	1	9
Done!	5	5	1	5
Comment/string identity match score for the file				**99**

Table 15.6   Comment/String Match Scores for File 2

Comments and strings	No. of characters	Comment/string identity match score	Occurrences	Score
Similarity value to be calculated	33	33	1	33
Integer variable	16	16	2	32
Comment/string identity match score for the file				**65**

Table 15.7   Comment/String Match Scores for File 1 Compared to File 2

Comments and strings	No. of characters	Comment/string identity match score	Minimum no. of occurrences	Score
Similarity value to be calculated	33	33	1	33
Integer variable	16	16	2	32
Comment/string match score for the file				**65**

Now we look at the comments and strings that exist in both files and use Equation 15.8 to calculate the comment/string match score for the two files in Table 15.7. The fourth column shows the minimum number of occurrences of each comment or string in the two files. The comment/string match score for the two files is at the bottom right of the table.

Equation 15.4 tells us that the maximum comment/string match score between the two files, $\mu_C(F^n, F^m)$, is simply the smaller of the comment/string identity match scores for the two files, in this case 65. From Equation 15.2, the comment/string correlation score $\rho_C(F^n, F^m)$ for the two files is the comment/string match score of the two files divided by the maximum comment/string match score of the two files. In this case the result is 65/65 or 1.00.

15.9 IDENTIFIER CORRELATION

The identifier correlation is the result of comparing identifiers in the source code of the file pair. Identifiers are extracted from the two files being compared. If exact matching is used, then the equation for calculating the identifier match score would be comparable to that for calculating the statement match score or the comment/string match score. However, it is much easier, and much more common, for identifiers to be changed via a global search and replace. For this reason, it is more accurate to use a partial match score for identifiers. In other words, the match score is calculated not only for identifiers that match exactly, but also for those that match only partially. This makes the calculation for the identifier match score more complex than that for the statement match score or the comment/string match score. The match score is then calculated according to Equation 15.11.

$$\mu_I\left(F^n, F^m\right) = max\left(\sum_{i,j} \mu\left(I_i, I_J\right)\right) \forall\left(unique\ I_i, unique\ I_j\right) : I_i \in F^n, I_j \in F^m \quad (15.11)$$

This means the file match score is calculated by summing the match score between pairs of unique identifiers in the two files such that for each pair there is no other pairing that would produce a larger file match score. When identifiers do not have exact matches, they are paired with identifiers that most closely match, based on maximizing the longest common string or longest common subsequence between the two identifiers, or whatever method is used for calculating partial matches. The difficulty in calculating this exactly is illustrated in Table 15.8. File 1 has two unique identifiers and File 2 has two unique identifiers. It might be tempting to match identifier abc with identifier abcxy because the first identifier is a complete subset of the second identifier. This results in an identifier match score of 30 and leaves identifier xy to be paired with identifier ab, which have nothing in common and therefore an identifier match score of 0. The total file match score is then 30. However, if the identifiers are matched in the other way, then the total file match score is 40, which is maximized.

The pairing of similar but not identical identifiers covers cases where identifiers are similar but with some modifications, such as the variables `CurrentIndex` and `CurrentIndex1` or `RxSum` and `ArSum`. Because identifiers typically contain significant information about their use, similar though not exactly matching

Table 15.8   Pairing Identifiers to Maximize the File Match Score (with $k_\alpha = 10$ and $k_\eta = 1$)

File 1 identifiers	File 2 identifiers	Identifier match score
abc	abcxy	30
xyz	ab	0
Identifier match score for the file		**30**
abc	ab	20
xyz	abcxy	20
Identifier match score for the file		**40**

identifiers are correlated. Note that each identifier must belong to one and only one pair that produces the highest match score.

The identifier identity match score $\mu(I_i)$ can be calculated in many different ways that can be justified. The match score that I have found to work best is given by Equation 15.12:

$$\mu\left(I_i\right)=k_\alpha \cdot \alpha\left(I_i\right)+k_\eta \cdot \eta\left(I_i\right) \tag{15.12}$$

Similarly, the identifier match score $\mu(I_i, I_j)$ can be calculated in many different ways that can be justified. The match score I have found to work best is given by Equation 15.13:

$$\mu\left(I_i,I_j\right)=k_\alpha \cdot \alpha\left(I_i,I_j\right)+k_\eta \cdot \eta\left(I_i,I_j\right) \tag{15.13}$$

The multipliers k_α and k_η, where $k_\alpha > k_\eta$, are used to give more significance to alphabetic characters over numbers and delimiter characters in identifiers. The reason different weighting is used is that a matching alphabetic character in two identifiers is more significant than matching numbers or delimiters. Alphabetic characters give identifying information from the programmer, whereas numbers are quantities that are rarely identifiable as unique unless they represent a well-known constant such as *pi* or *e*. The identifier identity match score for a file is then simply given by Equation 15.14.

$$\mu_I\left(F^n\right)=\sum\mu\left(I_i\right) \ \forall \ I_i:I_i\in F^n \tag{15.14}$$

The identifier correlation $\rho_i(F^n,F^m)$ can be calculated by combining Equation 15.3, Equation 15.4, Equation 15.11, Equation 15.12, Equation 15.13, and Equation 15.14. The difficult part of this calculation is finding the pairs of identifiers whose identifier match scores maximize the file identifier match score. Methods for accomplishing this are discussed in Chapter 16.

15.10 INSTRUCTION SEQUENCE CORRELATION

The instruction sequence correlation is the result of comparing the sequence of instructions in the source code of the file pair. Statements are extracted from the two files being compared. Then the first instruction in the statement is extracted. The match score is then calculated according to Equation 15.15:

$$\mu_Q\left(F^n,F^m\right)=max\left(\mu\left(Q_i\right)\right) \ \forall \ Q_i:Q_i\in F^n\cap F^m \tag{15.15}$$

This means the file match score is calculated by taking the largest match score for all sequences of instructions that can be found in both files. The instruction sequence identity match score $\mu(Q_i)$ can be calculated in many different ways that can be justified. The match score that I have found to work best is given by Equation 15.16, which means that the instruction sequence match score is simply the number of instructions in any instruction sequence.

$$\mu\big(Q_i\big)=\gamma\big(Q_i\big) \tag{15.16}$$

The instruction sequence identity match score for a file is then simply given by Equation 15.17, which is the count of the longest instruction sequence in the file.

$$\mu_Q\big(F^n\big)=max\big(\mu\big(Q_i\big)\big)\;\forall\,Q_i:Q_i\in F^n \tag{15.17}$$

Then the instruction sequence correlation $\rho_Q(F^n,F^m)$ can easily be calculated by combining Equation 15.3, Equation 15.4, Equation 15.15, Equation 15.16, and Equation 15.17.

15.11 OVERALL CORRELATION

Each element correlation can be considered to be a single dimension that can be used to calculate a multidimensional overall correlation. This overall source code correlation ρ is a single measure of the similarity of the file pairs. We will now examine three calculations that combine the individual element correlations into one correlation score: a square root of sum-of-squares correlation, the maximum correlation, and the average correlation. I have performed studies to compare the three different methods of combining element correlation scores, and based on these studies I recommend one of the methods over the others, but I will explain each method first.

15.11.1 S-CORRELATION

S-correlation can be considered a normalized total correlation distance where each element correlation is an orthogonal measure of correlation. In this case, correlation is calculated according to Equation 15.18:

$$\rho=\frac{1}{2}\sqrt{\big(\rho_S\big)^2+\big(\rho_C\big)^2+\big(\rho_I\big)^2+\big(\rho_Q\big)^2} \tag{15.18}$$

S-correlation seems aesthetically more elegant than the other methods. S-correlation creates a four-dimensional space where each dimension is an orthogonal measure of the correlation of a specific source code element. The overall correlation is then simply the overall distance between two source code files in this four-dimensional space.

15.11.2 A-CORRELATION

A-correlation consists of simply averaging the correlation scores, as shown in Equation 15.19:

$$\rho = \frac{\rho_S + \rho_C + \rho_I + \rho_Q}{4} \tag{15.19}$$

It is interesting to note that in statistics, correlation ranges from −1 to 1, whereas the correlation defined here ranges from 0 to 1, which corresponds to the statistical definition of correlation squared. If our software source code correlations are considered the square of the dimension in a multidimensional space, then A-correlation is actually the normalized square of the distance.

15.11.3 M-CORRELATION

M-correlation takes the maximum of each element correlation, as shown in Equation 15.20:

$$\rho = max\left(\rho_S, \rho_C, \rho_I, \rho_Q\right) \tag{15.20}$$

When developing these methods for combining element correlation scores into an overall correlation score, I thought that M-correlation would end up being the superior method for finding copied files because if some file pairs resulted in low correlation scores for some source code elements but there was a significant correlation score for even one source code element, that would result in a high overall correlation score for the file pair. This high correlation score would make it particularly difficult for copiers to hide copying because they would need to address each source code element. However, it turns out that much software has some elements with relatively high correlation scores just because of the nature of the software. As a result, in my study, M-correlation ended up giving scores that were too high for unrelated files, so it is less effective at focusing on the pairs of copied files that I wanted to find.

15.11.4 RECOMMENDED CORRELATION METHOD

An argument can be made for each of these methods of combining element correlation scores into an overall correlation score. In the study that I performed, S-correlation and A-correlation were significantly better than M-correlation at giving high scores to file pairs that were known beforehand to be modified copies of each other. S-correlation performed slightly better than A-correlation, and so that is the algorithm that I recommend. However, I have put all three methods in this book because I believe there may be situations where one of the other methods is preferable.

FALSE NEGATIVES VERSUS FALSE POSITIVES

Source code correlation was originally designed to help pinpoint plagiarized source code in copyright infringement cases. This design required it to favor the reporting of false positives over false negatives. In other words, it is likely to point out correlation that is due to many factors including plagiarism, and it almost certainly reports all cases of plagiarism and rarely, if ever, misses any cases. It is then up to the user to explain the reasons for correlation and eliminate those that are not important. For example, if the user is attempting to detect plagiarism, the user must filter out those reasons for correlation that are not due to plagiarism. This process has been formalized and is explained later in this book.

This purposeful design of source code correlation also means that there are few, if any, false negatives. To date I have not personally been involved in any cases where code has been shown to be plagiarized but the source code correlation did not report a correlation. In litigation, it is the role of the other party's expert to dispute my results, and no expert has so far found copying where the source code correlation indicated no correlation.

In my design of source code correlation I thought that this was a positive feature of the analysis. In the case of a lawsuit, for example, the parties are eager not to miss any examples of copyright infringement, even if the analysis takes longer or is more expensive to perform. I have been involved in lawsuits involving over $1 billion, and so missing a case of copied code could be very harmful to a client. Even defendants in a case want to make sure that their code is clean, or, if not, they prefer to have knowledge beforehand that will help them prepare for court and possibly negotiate a reasonable settlement.

I noticed, however, that most existing algorithms traded speed for accuracy. These other programs were more likely to process code and return a result quickly but often missed much copied code. One time I saw a comparison of various "plagiarism detection" programs on a university website and noticed that CodeMatch, my program that implements source code correlation, was given a low grade. The review stated that CodeMatch produced many more file pairs with high scores than the other programs, and that was a disadvantage.

I contacted the professor who supervised the study and told him that CodeMatch was accomplishing its objectives by producing a larger number of file pairs. The professor explained that academics use these tools to compare students' programming assignments for signs of cheating. A professor does not have time to examine many files and so prefers a tool that reports fewer results. He explained that merely having a tool that detects plagiarism is, in most cases, enough to deter students, and consequently a tool that produces false negatives is all that is really needed. I contemplated whether a tool that only pretended to compare files was the optimal tool for academia because it could accomplish its goal of deterring students from cheating while requiring minimal development time and maintenance.

16

IMPLEMENTATION

Now that I have discussed the theory behind source code correlation, I will discuss ways of practically and efficiently implementing that theory.[1] The particular implementation discussed in this chapter is based on the implementation used in the commercial CodeMatch tool that is a function of the CodeSuite program available from S.A.F.E. Corporation. This tool focuses on finding software copyright infringement, so many of the implementation choices are based on optimizing that use of source code correlation.

The implementation I describe here makes use of a basic knowledge of programming languages and program structures to simplify the task of comparing and identifying matching program elements. It is not necessary to implement a full programming language parser because the exact functionality of the statements does not need to be known (this will not be the case, however, when functional correlation is developed). The implementation must only recognize programming language keywords that are specific to the programming language of the program being examined. In addition, this implementation needs to know the characters that are used to delimit comments, the characters that are used to delimit strings, and the characters called "separators," which are the characters that cannot be used in identifier names. For example, operators (such as * / + −) are separators because when parsing a statement, reaching one of these means

---

1. Note that some of the concepts discussed in this chapter may be covered by patents that have been issued or are pending.

the end of an identifier has been reached (typically, though not always, whitespace is reached first). On the other hand, the underscore character (_) is valid within an identifier name in many programming languages, so it is not a separator.

The implementation needs to separate programs into five elements: statements, comments, strings, instructions, and identifiers. Note that these are not mutually exclusive; statements can include instructions, identifiers, and strings. It is useful to put these elements of code into arrays.

16.1 CREATING ARRAYS FROM SOURCE CODE

The first step in creating the arrays is to create two arrays for each source code file being examined. Consider the small snippet of C code shown in Listing 16.1.

Listing 16.1 Code Snippet I

```
// ---- begin routine ----
void fdiv(
    char *fname,        // file name
    char *pathString)   // path
{
    int Index1, j;
    printf("Hello world!\n");

    if (strlen(pathString) == 0)
        strcpy(pathString, "C:\\Windows\\");
    else
        strcat(pathString, "\\");

    while (Index1 < 100)
    {
        printf("Getting results.\n");
        j = strlen(fname);
        j += strlen(PathString);
        /* find the file extension */
```

Table 16.1 shows how this small sample would lead to two arrays of statements and comments/strings. Note that whitespace has been reduced. This involves trimming all whitespace characters on the right and left of each string and

Table 16.1   Initial Arrays Created from Code Snippet 1

Line	Statements	Comments/Strings
1		`---- begin routine ----`
2	`void fdiv`	
3	`char fname`	`file name`
4	`char pathString`	`path`
5		
6	`int Index1 j`	
7	`printf`	`Hello world!\n`
8		
9	`if strlen pathString`	
10	`strcpy pathString`	`C:\\Windows\\`
11	`else`	
12	`strcat pathString`	`\\`
13		
14	`while Index1 100`	
15		
16	`printf`	`Getting results.\n`
17	`j strlen fname`	
18	`j strlen pathString`	
19		`find the file extension`

reducing all sequences of whitespace to a single space. This allows comparisons that are not obscured by the amount or placement of whitespace characters in the program lines of code, something that malicious plagiarists have been known to do to fool the detection software.

Also note that within the statements all separator characters have been treated like whitespace so that the elements are easier to compare. With the comments and strings, the separator characters remain except for the comment delimiters and string delimiters. This produces a correlation score that is more difficult to mask with small changes such as switching between the // comment delimiters and the /* */ comment delimiters, for example, which can easily be accomplished with a global search and replace or a short macro.

Note that lines 7 and 16 are identical, producing identical statements and identical strings. Both identical statements go into the statement array, and both identical strings go into the comment/string array. When correlation is determined, a file that also has two copies of these statements or strings will justifiably be more highly correlated to this file than one that has only one copy of these statements or strings.

Two more arrays are created from the code snippet, an identifier array and an instruction array, both shown in Table 16.2 where the null statements and null comments and strings are not shown (or may have been eliminated).

Note that blank lines are preserved as null strings in the array. This is done so that the index in each array corresponds to the line number in the original file and matching lines can easily be mapped back to their original files. There are other ways to accomplish this, such as creating a secondary array for line numbers.

Table 16.2 Arrays Created from Code Snippet I

Statements	Comments/Strings	Identifiers	Instructions
`void fdiv`	`---- begin routine ----`	`fdiv`	`void`
`char fname`	`file name`	`fname`	`char`
`char pathString`	`path`	`pathString`	`char`
`int Index1 j`	`Hello world!\n`	`Index1`	`int`
`if strlen pathString`	`C:\\Windows\\`	`100`	`printf`
`strcpy pathString`	`\\`		`if`
`strcat pathString`	`Getting results.\n`		`strcpy`
`while Index1 100`	`find the file extension`		`else`
`j strlen fname`			`strcat`
`j strlen pathString`			`while`
			`printf`
			`set`
			`set`

Also note that lines 7, 11, and 16 are not listed in the array of statements. This is done because these lines contain only programming language keywords, which is a common occurrence. For statements to be considered matching in the two files, they must contain at least one non-keyword such as a variable name or function name. In this implementation, these commonly occurring statements would otherwise generally raise all the file pair correlation scores so that truly interesting highly correlated file pairs might be missed.

Next, the statements in each file are examined to obtain a list of all identifiers in the source code. This is done by finding all words between whitespace in a statement (but not in a comment or string) and comparing them to a list of known keywords for the particular programming language. All words that are not in that list are identifiers and are put into an array of identifiers. In some programming languages like C and Java, keywords are case-sensitive. In other programming languages like BASIC, keywords are not case-sensitive. For a case-sensitive language like C, words are excluded from the identifier array only if they match the characters and the letter case of a programming language keyword. The word `while` is a keyword in the C programming language, but because the C programming language is case-sensitive, the word `While` would not be considered a language keyword and would be entered into the identifier array. The word `while` is also a keyword in the BASIC programming language, but BASIC is a case-insensitive language, so the word `While` would be considered a language keyword and would be ignored.

An identifier goes into the identifier array once, regardless of the number of times it appears in the source code file. An argument can be made that it should go into the array once for each instance, as is done with statements, comments, and strings. Identifiers typically appear many times within a source code file, and even one instance of a unique identifier can be a significant clue to copying, so including only one copy of each identifier in the array has turned out, in practice, to work well.

Note that in this implementation, identifier j is not listed as an identifier because all one-character identifiers are ignored as too common to consider. Also note that the number 100 is listed as an identifier. In this implementation, numbers are considered identifiers because large numbers may represent code or constants that are unique to the program. As explained later, numeric characters in an identifier name are given less weight than nonnumeric characters because they can be much more common and may simply represent basic numbers rather than unique information in the program.

An array of initial instructions is also created from the source code statements. Even statements that are not included in the statement array, because they consist of only programming language keywords, are still considered for the instruction array, which records only the first instruction that is found on each statement. Note that the last instruction is set even though the keyword set does not appear in the code. This is because the last statement sets a variable to a value and the set is implied by the = operator.

At this point, this implementation is ready for the various algorithms to be applied to compare each element of two source code files to obtain correlation scores. Every source code file in one program is compared to every source code file in another program such that every file pair is compared. Listing 16.2 shows a second code snippet that I will use to compare to Listing 16.1 to demonstrate how each correlation score is calculated.

Listing 16.2   Code Snippet 2

```
// FileDivide routine
   int FileDivide(
   bool allowWildcards;          // Allow wildcards in file names?
   int fileNumber;               // number of file being examined
   char Filename[_MAX_PATH+1],   // file name
{
   int i, j;
   printf("---- begin routine ----");

   if (PathString[0] == '\0')
       strcpy(PathString, "C:\\Windows\\");
   else
       strcpy(PathString, "\\");

   for (i = 0; i < 100; i++)
   {
       strcat(PathString, "C:\\NewPath\\");
       printf("Getting results.\n");
       j = strlen(Filename);
       // Find the file extension.
```

The specific implementation algorithms are described in the following sections.

16.2 STATEMENT CORRELATION

The statement correlation is determined by a statement-matching algorithm that compares each source code statement in the statement arrays for both files. In this implementation, regardless of whether or not the programming language is case-sensitive, the comparison is not case-sensitive; this provides a higher degree of correlation but also foils attempts by programmers to hide correlation by simply changing the letter case of identifier names. Note that a statement line may have a comment embedded in it, in which case the comment is stripped off for this comparison. Strings may also be embedded in the statement, and different implementations may or may not strip out the string. I recommend stripping out the string because simple changes to a string do not affect the program's functionality but do lower the correlation.

For each file pair, this algorithm yields a statement match score μ_s that is the number of exactly matching statements in the statement arrays generated from the pair of files. A statement in one array can be matched only once, so if the first array has two instances of identical statements S and the second array has only one instance of statement S, this implementation considers that as a single matching statement. The correlation score for each file pair, ρ_s, is the match score divided by the number of statements in the smaller statement array of the two files.

Table 16.3   Statement Arrays Created from Code Snippets 1 and 2

Code Snippet 1	Code Snippet 2
void fdiv	int FileDivide
char fname	bool allowWildcards
char pathString	int fileNumber
int Index1 j	char Filename _MAX_PATH 1
if strlen pathString	int i j
strcpy pathString	if strlen pathString
strcat pathString	strcpy pathString
while Index1 100	strcpy pathString
j strlen fname	for i i i
j strlen pathString	Strcat pathString
	j strlen Filename

As a practical example, consider the code snippet in Listing 16.2 compared to the code snippet in Listing 16.1. The statement arrays from these two snippets of code are shown in Table 16.3. The matching instructions in the two tables are shaded. The statement match score μ_s, the number of matching statements in the two files, is 3. If these code snippets were actually complete files, the first snippet would have 10 statements and the second snippet would have 11 statements. The statement correlation score ρ_s is thus 3/10 or 0.3.

16.3 COMMENT/STRING CORRELATION

The comment/string correlation is determined by a comment/string-matching algorithm that simply compares each source code comment and string in the comment/string arrays for both files. In this implementation, regardless of whether or not the programming language is case-sensitive, the comparison is not case-sensitive; this again provides a higher degree of correlation but also foils attempts by programmers to hide correlation by simply changing the letter case of words in comments. The entire comment or string is compared, regardless of whether there are programming language keywords in the comment or not, because programming language keywords have no function in a comment or string.

While the implementation described here compares comments and strings in a single array, it is conceivable that comments and strings could have their own arrays. It might also make sense that comment correlation would be one correlation element and string correlation would be another correlation element, and both could be combined into the overall correlation score as two separate elements rather than one. My experience has shown that combining them into a single correlation element produces good results. An implementation that uses separate arrays, however, can have advantages because comments and strings have slightly different characteristics. For example, an escape sequence consisting of a backslash and the letter n in most languages is interpreted in a string as a newline character or sequence of characters but is simply a backslash followed by the letter n in a comment.

For each file pair, this algorithm yields a comment/string match score μ_C that is the number of exactly matching comments and strings in the comment/string arrays generated from the pair of files. As with statements, comments and strings in one array can be matched only once, so if the first array has two instances of an identical comment, and the second array has only one instance of that same comment, this implementation considers that as a single matching comment. The correlation score for each file pair, ρ_C, is the match score divided by the number of comments/strings in the smaller comment/string array of the two files.

As a practical example, consider the code snippet in Listing 16.2 compared to the code snippet in Listing 16.1. The comment/string arrays from these two snippets of code are shown in Table 16.4. The matching comments and strings in the two tables are shaded. The comment/string match score μ_C, the number of matching comments and strings in the two files, is 6. If these code snippets were actually complete files, the first snippet would have 8 comments/strings and the second snippet would have 11 comments/strings. The statement correlation score ρ_C is thus 6/8 or 0.75.

16.4 IDENTIFIER CORRELATION

The identifier correlation is determined by an identifier-matching algorithm that simply compares each source code identifier in the identifier arrays for both files. In this implementation, regardless of whether or not the programming language is case-sensitive, the comparison is not case-sensitive; this again provides a higher degree of correlation but also foils attempts by programmers to hide correlation

Table 16.4 Comment/String Arrays Created from Code Snippets 1 and 2

Code Snippet 1	Code Snippet 2
```---- begin routine ----```	```FileDivide routine```
```file name```	```allow wildcards in file names?```
```path```	```number of file being examined```
```Hello world!\n```	```file name```
```C:\\Windows\\```	```---- begin routine ----```
```\\```	```\0```
```Getting results.\n```	```C:\\Windows\\```
```find the file extension```	```\\```
	```C:\\NewPath\\```
	```Getting results.\n```
	```find the file extension```

by simply changing the letter case of identifier names. Also, for this comparison, the implementation considers fully matching and partially matching identifiers, because a common way of masking copying is to simply perform a global search-and-replace operation that tacks a prefix or a suffix onto each identifier or changes one common sequence of characters to another sequence of characters.

For each file pair, this algorithm first calculates a match score μ_I that is the number of exactly matching identifiers in the identifier arrays generated from the pair of files. As noted in Chapter 15, the match score is a weighted match score that gives higher weight to longer identifiers and smaller weight to numeric characters within an identifier.

Once the identifier-matching algorithm is complete, the partial identifier-matching algorithm examines each identifier in the array of one file for which no exactly matching identifier was found in the array of the second file. For these non-matching identifiers, the partial identifier matching calculates a partial match score. There are a number of ways to define the partial match score, as described later, but whichever method is used, this partial identifier-matching algorithm must perform an optimization such that the pairing of unmatched identifiers from the two identifier arrays produces the highest possible overall partial match score. Given the large number of identifiers that can be found in a single source code file, this optimization may be too slow to be practical, so approximations can be calculated that are not ideal but get close to the ideal value within a reasonable amount of time.

The partial identifier-matching algorithm can find the longest common subsequence algorithm or the longest common substring algorithm, both of which are described in Chapter 10. In either case, the subsequence or substring must use the same weighting for numeric and nonnumeric characters as the identifier-matching algorithm. In this implementation, I use the longest common substring.

In theory, only the partial identifier-matching algorithm is really needed, because two identical identifiers will produce the highest possible match scores regardless of whether the partial identifier-matching algorithm relies on the longest subsequence or the longest substring. In practice, however, these partially matching algorithms tend to be slower than a simple one-to-one comparison of strings, and so it is faster to create these two matching algorithms. The identifier match score and the identifier partial match score are added together to produce μ_P the overall identifier match score. The correlation score for each file pair, ρ_P, is the match score divided by the smaller total match score calculated when each file's identifiers have exactly one complete match. In other words,

Table 16.5   Identifier Arrays Created from Code Snippets 1 and 2

Code Snippet 1	Code Snippet 2
fdiv	FileDivide
fname	allowWildcards
pathString	fileNumber
Index1	Filename
100	PathString
	100

each identifier array can be compared against itself using the identifier-matching algorithm. The smaller of the two match scores for the two files is the denominator for the identifier correlation between the two files.

As a practical example, consider the code snippet in Listing 16.2 compared to the code snippet in Listing 16.1. The identifier arrays from these two snippets of code are shown in Table 16.5. The matching identifiers are shown in the shaded cells. The partially matching identifiers have their longest common substrings highlighted. In this implementation, all numeric characters are given a weight of 1.0, and all nonnumeric characters are given a weight of 0.1. The identifier match score μ_I, the weighted value of all matching characters, is 17.3. If these code snippets were actually complete files, the weighted value of all characters of all the identifiers in the first file would be 24.4, and the weighted value of all characters of all the identifiers in the second file would be 52.3. The identifier correlation score ρ_I is therefore 17.3/24.4, or about 0.71.

16.5 INSTRUCTION SEQUENCE CORRELATION

The instruction sequence correlation is determined by an instruction-sequence-matching algorithm that finds the longest contiguous sequence of initial instructions common to both files. This algorithm finds sequences of code that appear to perform the same functions despite changed comments and string and identifier names.

For each file pair, this algorithm yields an instruction sequence match score μ_Q that is the longest common sequence of instructions within both files. The instruction sequence correlation score for each file pair, ρ_Q, is the instruction sequence match score divided by the length of the entire instruction sequence in the smaller of the two files.

As a practical example, consider the code snippet in Listing 16.2 compared to the code snippet in Listing 16.1. The instruction arrays from these two snippets of code are shown in Table 16.6. The longest common contiguous sequence of instructions is shown in the shaded cells. The instruction sequence match score μ_Q, the length of the longest common sequence of contiguous instructions in the two files, is 6. If these code snippets were actually complete files, the first snippet would have a sequence of 13 instructions and the second snippet would have a sequence of 14 instructions. The instruction sequence correlation score ρ_Q is thus 6/13, or about 0.46.

Other sequence-matching algorithms can be envisioned that are more complex or less complex than the one described in this implementation. For example, an alternative version could find the longest common sequence without requiring contiguity. Regardless of which specific algorithm is implemented, it is necessary to include some kind of sequence comparison in the overall correlation score for most applications of source code correlation and, in particular, for detecting copyright infringement, because malicious programmers can, with some effort, change all identifiers, all comments, and all strings. These changes would also effectively change many statements in the source code.

Table 16.6   Instruction Arrays Created from Code Snippets 1 and 2

Code Snippet 1	Code Snippet 2
void	int
char	bool
char	int
int	char
printf	int
if	printf
strcpy	if
else	strcpy
strcat	else
while	strcpy
printf	for
set	strcat
set	printf
	set

However, source code is, by its nature, a series of sequential instructions, and it is this sequence of instructions that performs the functions that make source code valuable. Until there is an efficient means of calculating functional correlation, instruction sequence correlation is the closest element correlation and the most difficult to fool.

16.6 OVERALL CORRELATION

The entire sequence, applying all five algorithms, is shown in Figure 16.1. In the first step, the statement, comment/string, identifier, and instruction arrays for the two source code files are created. In the second step, the statement arrays of the two files are compared using the statement-matching algorithm. In the third step, the comment/string arrays of the two files are compared using the comment/string-matching algorithm. In the fourth step, the identifier arrays of the two files are compared using the identifier-matching and partial identifier-matching algorithms. In the fifth step, the instruction arrays of the two files are compared using the instruction-sequence-matching algorithm. In the final step, the results of all matching algorithms are combined into a single correlation score.

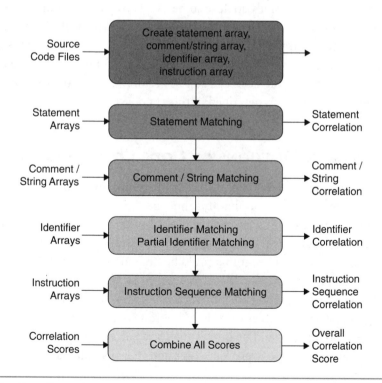

Figure 16.1 Overall correlation process

As discussed in Chapter 15, there are several ways of combining element correlation scores into an overall correlation score, including S-correlation, A-correlation, and M-correlation. S-correlation has been found to be most useful for detecting copyright infringement. S-correlation can be considered a normalized total correlation distance where each element correlation is an orthogonal measure of correlation.

16.7 COMPARING PROGRAMS IN DIFFERENT PROGRAMMING LANGUAGES

As mentioned in Chapter 15, nothing in the definition of source code correlation precludes comparing programs in different languages. As noted in that chapter, without transformational matches to match programming language statements and instructions in different languages, comparing two languages is limited in practice. Without some kind of transformational matching, statement correlation and instruction sequence correlation generally produce low scores unless the programming languages are similar in syntax. Fortunately, many programming languages do have similar syntax, so the statement correlation and instruction sequence correlation values do have some use. In any case, comment correlation and identifier correlation are still useful when comparing different programming languages. Because the relative correlation values are important in most applications of source code correlation, rather than the absolute values, comparing different programming languages can still be accomplished and yield useful results with the implementation described in this chapter.

16.8 COMPARING SECTIONS OF CODE OTHER THAN FILES

The implementation described in this chapter compares programs on a file-by-file basis. There is no reason that this must be the case, but files are convenient and logical containers of source code. For this reason, it makes sense to compare file pairs. However, it is certainly conceivable that programs could be compared in their entirety or that programs could be broken at other boundaries such as classes or functions. The way that a program is sliced and diced to calculate correlation affects the run time of the calculation and the ability of a user to focus on the particular lines of code of interest. While comparing file pairs has been useful so far, it would be interesting to research how other partitioning of source code affects the correlation scores and their usefulness.

17

APPLICATIONS

There are many potential applications for source code correlation. In this chapter I discuss some of the ones that I have identified, though there are likely many more than these. Table 17.1 shows the applications that I discuss in this chapter and the most useful element correlations to emphasize in each case; each application is likely to emphasize certain element correlations over others, though these are not hard-and-fast rules.

Table 17.1 Applications of Source Code Correlation

Type of application	Emphasized correlations
Identifying authorship	Comment/string correlation Identifier correlation
Identifying origin	Comment/string correlation Identifier correlation
Detecting copyright infringement (plagiarism)	Statement correlation Comment/string correlation Identifier correlation Instruction sequence correlation
Detecting trade secret theft	Statement correlation Comment/string correlation Identifier correlation Instruction sequence correlation Functional correlation

Continues

Table 17.1 Applications of Source Code Correlation *(Continued)*

Type of application	Emphasized correlations
Locating third-party (open source) code	Statement correlation
	Comment/string correlation
	Identifier correlation
	Instruction sequence correlation
Compiler optimization	Statement correlation
	Instruction sequence correlation
	Functional correlation
Refactoring	Statement correlation
	Comment correlation
	Instruction sequence correlation
	Functional correlation
Detecting patent infringement	Functional correlation

17.1 FUNCTIONAL CORRELATION

Note that Table 17.1 mentions "functional correlation." This correlation involves functional elements of the code. I do not discuss the particulars of functional correlation in the book because it is a wide-open topic. Many techniques have been developed to define and analyze the functionality of programs. As of yet, I have not come across a tool that meets the following four criteria:

1. Is completely automatic
2. Is programming-language-independent
3. Completes in a reasonable amount of time
4. Produces scores that can fit into the source code correlation framework

The first criterion means that source code files are compared without human intervention. Once the tool is pointed at two sets of source code files, it calculates functional correlation without the need for the user to intervene. Certainly it is possible for a useful tool to calculate functional correlation and still require human intervention, but ideally such operator interference would not be necessary.

The second criterion means that two programs in two different programming languages could be compared. This is particularly important because functional correlation should be comparing program functionality independently of the programming language. A starting point could be a tool that requires the programs being compared to be written in the same programming language. Such a tool could be useful but would be limited. Practical uses of functional correlation such as detecting trade secret theft and patent infringement would be most useful if one were able to compare programs written in different programming languages.

The third criterion has been a difficult goal to reach so far. Analyzing the functionality of a program seems to take exponential time with respect to the size of the program. Comparing two programs involves creating an abstract representation of the functionality of each program (something not well defined at this time and for which there is currently no standard) and comparing the two abstract representations. Many of the efforts to date attempt to create a representation of the entire program, which certainly makes a lot of sense. However, given the computational time constraints, perhaps it makes more sense to break the functionality down file by file and simply compare files as is done for the other correlation elements (statements, comments/strings, identifiers, and instruction sequences).

Once functionality can be automatically extracted from a program in a reasonable amount of time and independently of the programming language, the final criterion is to compare two functional representations in such a way that a normalized score is created. It is an open question how to accomplish this.

17.2 IDENTIFYING AUTHORSHIP

To use source code correlation to determine authorship of a program or an algorithm within a program, it would be most useful to find correlation between those elements that would be most likely to be unique to particular programmers. These elements are the comments, strings, and identifier names. Obviously any correlation used to determine authorship would emphasize comment/string correlation and identifier correlation.

There are instances when it is important to identify the author of source code. This could occur during legal disputes when two or more parties claim to have written a particular program. It could occur when two parties have jointly developed code for a program and, because of a contractual dispute or a royalty determination, must figure out which code was written by which party. While this may seem like an unusual scenario, I have been personally involved in several cases where a large software manufacturer has asked me to search for its own programs online, in surplus software stores, and in my own private computer software collection because the company cannot find an earlier version of its software. This occurs more often than you might think in the software industry, sometimes because of the lack of strict procedures at many companies. It also happens because many modern software companies start very small and grow very large in a short period of time, and the emphasis is on getting products out faster than their larger competitors. The limited resources and short market windows mean that developing software quickly takes precedence over installing and using version control systems to keep track of software changes.

Determining authorship can also be useful in tax cases. Tax rates vary according to jurisdictions (for example, city, county, state, country). When software is partially developed overseas, for example, the IRS of the U.S. government can tax the foreign-developed code at a different rate from the domestically developed code. When multiple versions of code have been developed in multiple countries by multiple teams using various tools, the company may not have kept track of which code was developed where. Again, source code correlation can be used to help make this determination.

Identifying authorship can be useful to computer historians to determine whether certain programmers are responsible for writing certain programs or portions of programs. Historians use this kind of technique to determine authorship of works of literature and works of art. As computers become a part of history, computer historians may need to do something similar to correctly attribute code to its authors. Literary works are almost always published with the author's name on the work, yet there are still controversies and there are known cases of fraud. There are those who believe that William Shakespeare was the pseudonym for writer Christopher Marlowe, philosopher and scientist Francis Bacon, or Edward de Vere, the 17th Earl of Oxford and Lord Great Chamberlain of England. There have also been famous forgeries of artwork. One such example is three Etruscan terra-cotta warriors. They were purchased in the years 1915 through 1918 and put on display in 1933 as examples of the work of the ancient Etruscans, a people that lived in Italy around 800 BCE. It was not until 1960 that chemical tests determined that modern materials were used and that, in fact, the pieces were created at the time of their sale by Italian brothers Pio and Alfonso Riccardi and their sons.

While it seems unlikely that source code would ever be as valuable as a historical artifact to warrant the attention of forgers, historians have already begun collecting, studying, and storing computer hardware and software in places like the Computer History Museum in Mountain View, California. It is conceivable that these historians may want to determine or even locate the programmer for a particular piece of code, and source code correlation can help.

Another use for identifying authorship is for tracking viruses, spyware, and other kinds of cyber-security threats. Identifying the origin of software, as described in the next section, as well as authorship is useful in this important field. Comparing source code for a computer virus against source code from known programmers, particularly those with a history of such illicit activity, can help catch these criminals and convict them at trial.

17.3 IDENTIFYING ORIGIN

As with determining authorship of a program or an algorithm within a program, identifying origin focuses on the correlation between those elements that would most likely be unique to programmers in particular companies or countries. These elements are the comments, strings, and identifier names. Any correlation used to determine origin would emphasize comment/string correlation and identifier correlation.

Identifying the origin of a program or a piece of a program can be useful for the same reasons as identifying authorship is useful. Because many modern programs are written by teams of engineers, it may not be possible to identify the actual author, but it may be possible to identify the company where the software was developed. Different companies have different coding standards and different corporate cultures that could result in higher correlation between programs developed within the company than between programs developed at different companies.

Similarly, it may be possible to identify the country of origin of a program. In particular, not only might coding standards and coding styles be similar among programmers in a particular country, but there would obviously be language differences in the identifier names and particularly in the comments and strings. Even in countries where programmers use the same language, idioms, colloquialisms, and slang would differentiate countries or areas within countries where the software was developed.

Identifying the country of origin can be useful in legal disputes, as described previously. Country of origin may be even more useful in tracing software intended to infiltrate another country's in an act of cyber warfare, a growing and dangerous threat in the modern world that can potentially bring down an entire nation without a single missile or weapon of mass destruction.

17.4　Detecting Copyright Infringement (Plagiarism)

The most common use of source code correlation to date is to find copyright infringement, which is essentially the legal term for plagiarism. Source code correlation was initially designed to help detect copyright infringement, and it has been successfully used in over 50 cases at the time of this writing.

To find copyright infringement, it is necessary to find all signs of copying, especially considering that modifications may have been made subsequent to the unauthorized copying. The modifications may be explained by the normal development process, including debugging and feature enhancements and additions. The modifications may also be the result of deliberate attempts to hide the copying. For these reasons, source code correlation used to detect copyright infringement must emphasize correlation of all literal elements: statements, comments and strings, identifiers, and instruction sequences.

17.5　Detecting Trade Secret Theft

Another common use of source code correlation is the detection of trade secret theft. When literal elements of a program's source code are copied, not only does that constitute copyright infringement, but it is also often a case of trade secret theft. This is because much software source code, other than open source software, meets the requirements of being a trade secret that were discussed in Chapter 8:

1. It is not generally known to the public. Programmers may know how to implement particular functions using source code, but each program has many unique functions that are implemented in ways that are not generally known because they are specific to the particular program.

2. It confers some sort of economic benefit on its holder, where the benefit is from not being known to the public. Most software is difficult to write, taking years of education and experience to do correctly. Most code has an economic benefit to its owner because of the knowledge and effort that went into creating it. Also, it can be argued that understanding source code allows a competitor to learn a program's weaknesses that can be exploited, lowering the program's value.

3. The owner of the trade secret makes reasonable efforts to maintain its secrecy. Software source code is almost always kept secret.

Consequently, in the case of literal copying, not only is source code correlation useful for detecting copyright infringement, but it is also useful for finding trade secret theft using all four algorithms—statement correlation, comment/ string correlation, identifier correlation, and instruction sequence correlation.

However, trade secret theft can also involve copying a method for accomplishing some function without copying the actual source code that implements that function. For this reason, source code correlation that would find all forms of trade secret theft would include functional correlation. As of today, there is not an efficient method for determining functional correlation in a reasonable amount of time. A tool for computing a correlation that can accurately detect trade secret theft is still in the future, as of this writing.

17.6 LOCATING THIRD-PARTY CODE (OPEN SOURCE)

As open source code is finding its way into more and more products, it is becoming a more complex issue. Open source code is covered by different licenses, the most common one being the GNU Public License (GPL) that has certain strict requirements, particularly about making source code available to the public. In many cases, open source code has crept into software projects without the managers or many of the programmers being aware. Sometimes open source code has been used in a project even though the project owners do not intend to abide by the licensing terms. Companies are now getting nervous about this phenomenon, especially because several successful lawsuits have been brought by the open source community of developers against commercial companies. Many companies now employ sophisticated means of determining whether their own software products contain open source code, and source code correlation can be used to help make that determination.

The issues associated with detecting open source code are really a subset of the issues associated with finding any third-party source code in a project. There may be instances of commercial third-party code for which the license has expired or that was obtained by unlawful means. Source code correlation can be a useful tool for detecting the use of such third-party code, whether it is open source or commercial.

In most cases, the third-party code has not been modified, or has not been modified significantly, because typically the source code is used unintentionally and so there is no attempt to obscure its use in the program. Even when the source code is used with the knowledge that it is not lawful, the users do not expect it to be uncovered because they are not releasing their source code (see Part VI). Also, third-party code is often not modified, or modified only slightly, because an advantage of third-party code is that it has been written and vigorously tested, and modifying the code would require further testing and debugging. In these cases, source code correlation may be overkill, and techniques that look for exact matches, like source code differentiation (see Part IV) or comparing hashes of the source code, may be sufficient.

However, if an attempt has been made to hide the third-party code, or it is believed that such an attempt was made, then source code correlation used to detect third-party code must emphasize the same elements as those used for detecting plagiarism. This involves all literal elements: statements, comments and strings, identifiers, and instruction sequences.

17.7 COMPILER OPTIMIZATION

It is possible that source code correlation can be used to eliminate redundancy in code during the compilation process, thereby optimizing the compilation. In this case, it seems that the correlation should emphasize statement correlation and instruction sequence correlation and, of course, functional correlation when that becomes available. By using source code correlation, a compiler could find highly correlated sections of code. Once a compilation has been completed for one of these sections of code, the compiler may be able to speed up the effort on highly correlated sections of code without needing to perform another full, time-consuming optimization process.

17.8 REFACTORING

An area of growing interest in computer science, and in industry, is refactoring. This is the process of cleaning up and simplifying software source code to make it more readable and maintainable, without changing its functionality. According to Martin Fowler, one of the early gurus of refactoring, "Refactoring is the process of changing a software system in such a way that it does not alter the external behavior of the code yet improves its internal structure."

One particular aspect of refactoring is clone detection and elimination. A clone is a copy of a section of code that performs a function that is identical to that of the original code. In an early paper on clone detection entitled "Using Clone Detection to Manage a Product Line," Ira Baxter and Dale Churchett describe clone detection and its benefits as follows:

Clone detection finds code in large software systems that has been replicated and modified by hand. Remarkably, clone detection works because people copy conceptually identifiable blocks of code, and make only a few changes, which means the same syntax is detectably repeated. . . . Clones can thus enhance a product line development in a number of ways: removal of redundant code, lowering maintenance costs, identification of domain concepts for use in the present system or the next, and identification of parameterized reusable implementations.

Obviously it is unnecessary and inefficient to have cloned code within a single product because it just increases the code size and increases the maintenance effort without providing significant additional functionality. Eliminating clones is a useful exercise if it can be done efficiently, and source code correlation can be an efficient method of doing so. Correlation used for clone detection and elimination would emphasize the following elements of source code correlation: statement correlation, comment correlation, instruction sequence correlation, and functional correlation.

Notice that I refer to comment correlation rather than comment/string correlation. It might not seem obvious at first to include comment correlation. Here we are concerned mostly about the descriptions provided in the comments, and this may be one area where comments and strings should be treated differently rather than combined into a single correlation score. Comments, particularly headers that describe the functionality of a routine in the program, could provide important details about the correlation of two functions in the program. For example, it is possible that two functions, written by two different programmers, would differ significantly in their implementation but in fact implement the same function. Depending on the efficiency, and availability, of a functional correlation measure, comment correlation could be a way of determining that two or more functions perform the same operation and can be replaced with a single function, even though their other correlation scores are low.

17.9 DETECTING PATENT INFRINGEMENT

Patent infringement essentially involves the creation of a program that uses a patented method by someone other than the person or entity that owns the patent and has not been given that right by the patent owner. Patent infringement occurs even when the infringer has never seen the source code of the patented invention. For this reason, calculating the correlation of the literal elements of a program is generally not useful unless source code was also copied. For the vast majority of patent cases, source code correlation would emphasize functional correlation, which, as explained above, is not yet available. When an efficient, accurate method of functional correlation is found, there will be many uses for it.

PART VI

OBJECT AND SOURCE/OBJECT CODE CORRELATION

"It is of the highest importance in the art of detection to be able to recognize, out of a number of facts, which are incidental and which vital. Otherwise your energy and attention must be dissipated instead of being concentrated."
—Sherlock Holmes in *The Adventure of the Reigate Puzzle*

In this part I discuss object code correlation and source/object code correlation. Object code correlation is the result of comparing object code files to other object code files. Source/object code correlation is the result of comparing source code files to object code files. Both object code correlation and source/object code correlation have the same mathematical framework as source code correlation.

Object code correlation and source/object code correlation have limitations that will be discussed. Despite these limitations, object code correlation and source/object code correlation have been found to be useful for the following tasks when no source code is available or source code is available from only one party:

- Initiating a copyright infringement case
- Determining common authorship

- Finding third-party code
- Detecting software licensing agreement violations (for example, open source licenses)

Object code correlation and source/object code correlation are designed to yield high scores even when only a small portion of code is correlated or only specific elements of code are correlated. They are designed to lead the user to suspicious sections of code, regardless of how small those sections are, and enable the user to decide whether source code should be obtained to do a more rigorous analysis. As with source code correlation, object code correlation and source/object code correlation cannot determine the reason for the correlation, but only whether the correlation exists.

In Chapter 18, I explain the theory behind object code correlation and source/object code correlation, which will get a little mathematical, but anyone with an understanding of basic algebra should be able to follow. In Chapter 19, I discuss implementations of object code correlation and source/object code correlation. In other words, I describe algorithms for creating a program to measure object code correlation and source/object code correlation. In Chapter 20 I describe applications of object code correlation and source/object code correlation, including existing applications and possible future applications.

Much of the mathematics and algorithms described in this section are used in the BitMatch function of the CodeSuite program developed and distributed by S.A.F.E. Corporation.

OBJECTIVES

The objective of this part of the book is to give theoretical, mathematical foundations for software object code correlation and source/object code correlation that can be used for basic comparisons of software, and I also describe applications and implementations of object code correlation and source/object code correlation. In particular, software object code correlation and source/object code correlation are used to compare elements of software in order to detect similarities that might be hidden from a basic bit-by-bit comparison. Although object code correlation and source/object code correlation can include a functional correlation element, such a functional correlation can be extremely time-consuming and very error-prone. Object code correlation measures and source/object code correlation measures that compare only certain literal code elements turn out to be very useful and can be calculated in a reasonable amount of time.

INTENDED AUDIENCE

Computer scientists and *computer programmers* will find this part useful for understanding the theory, implementation, and application of object code correlation and source/object code correlation, and they will be able to build upon this theory and practice for a variety of uses. *Technical consultants and expert witnesses for litigation* will find this part useful for understanding the theory, implementation, and application of object code correlation and source/object code correlation and will be able to use it in software IP litigation, particularly copyright infringement cases, certain kinds of trade secret theft cases, and possibly patent infringement cases. *Intellectual property lawyers* and *corporate managers* with an understanding of algebra will find this part useful, especially to get a deep understanding of the theory, implementation, and application of object code correlation and source/object code correlation and the associated tools that can be used in software IP litigation. *Software entrepreneurs* will find this part useful for understanding object code correlation and source/object code correlation to apply it to new software products and new businesses.

18 THEORY

Many experts believe that decompiling object code back into source code is required before an accurate determination of copying can take place. However, consider the original source code for the small routine in Listing 18.1 and compare it to the decompiled version of that routine in Listing 18.2. The comments in Listing 18.1 of course are gone, but worse, the decompiler has inserted its own comments on lines 1 through 4, 6, and 16 through 19. This is worse because for purposes of finding similarity, the decompiler itself creates correlation between two sets of unrelated code because of the comments it inserts. Note that the strings are unchanged, as we would expect, and the function names are unchanged, though variables have been given standard names that have no correlation to the original names and convey no useful information. Again, comparing unrelated decompiled source code would result in identifier correlation because the decompiler assigned variable names. Comparing the sequences of instructions would show little if any correlation because the decompiler has organized the code differently from the original code. Also note, incidentally, that the decompiled code in this example is incorrect and would not actually compile because the functions do not have the correct arguments. For example, the routine _findfirst() in the original code on lines 36 and 55 in Listing 18.1 correctly takes two arguments, while the same function on lines 23 and 49 of the decompiled code in Listing 18.2 incorrectly takes no arguments.

Listing 18.1 Original Source Code File `CleanExt.c`

```
1   /*****************************************************/
2   /*****************************************************/
3   /*****                 CleanExt               *****/
4   /***** File: CleanExt.c                       *****/
5   /***** Utility to clean extraneous characters *****/
6   /***** after the file name extension          *****/
7   /*****                                        *****/
8   /***** Written by Bob Zeidman                 *****/
9   /***** Copyright 2005 by Zeidman Consulting   *****/
10  /*****************************************************/
11  /*****************************************************/
12
13  /***** Library Include Files *****/
14
15  /* Microsoft C libraries */
16  #include <stdlib.h>   /* standard library */
17  #include <string.h>   /* string library */
18  #include <stdio.h>    /* stream (files) library */
19  #include <dos.h>      /* DOS system calls */
20  #include <errno.h>    /* DOS error number definitions */
21  #include <io.h>
22
23  /********** MAIN ROUTINE **********/
24  void main()
25  {
26      struct _finddata_t finfo;  // file info
27      struct _finddata_t finfo2; // file info
28      long   handle;             // file handle
29      char   filestr[257];       // file string
30      unsigned int i;
31
32      printf("\nCleanExt Utility Version 1.0\n");
33      printf("(C) 2005 Zeidman Consulting (TM)\n");
34      printf("Public Domain Software\n\n");
35
36      handle = _findfirst("*.*", &finfo);
37      if (handle != -1)
38      {
```

```
39       do
40       {
41         if (!(finfo.attrib & _A_SUBDIR))
42         {
43           /* Get the name of the file to rename. */
44           strcpy(filestr, finfo.name);
45
46           /* Find the first occurrence of '.' in the file name. */
47           i = strchr(filestr, '.') - filestr + 1;
48           if (i < strlen(filestr)-3)
49           {
50             /* Chop off the end. */
51             filestr[i+3] = '\0';
52           }
53
54           /* Check if the new file already exists. */
55           if (_findfirst(filestr, &finfo2) != -1)
56           {
57             /* If so, give a warning and continue. */
58             printf("File %s exists - not renaming file %s.\n",
59             filestr, finfo.name);
60           }
61           else
62           {
63             /* Else rename the file. */
64             printf("Renaming %s to %s\n", finfo.name, filestr);
65             rename(finfo.name, filestr);
66           }
67         }
68       } while (_findnext(handle, &finfo) == 0);
69     }
70     _findclose(handle);
71  }
```

Listing 18.2   Decompiled Source Code File `CleanExt.c`

```
1  /*
2   * Input file   : CleanExt.exe
3   * File type    : EXE
4   */
```

Continues

Listing 18.2   Decompiled Source Code File `CleanExt.c`   *(Continued)*

```
5
6  // Proc: _tmain
7  int _tmain(int argc, _TCHAR argv)
8  {
9    int loc1;
10   int loc2;
11   int loc3;
12   int loc4;
13   int loc5;
14   int loc6;
15   int loc7[0];
16   int loc8;    /* edi */
17   int loc9;    /* ecx */
18   int loc10;   /* eax */
19
20   printf ("\nCleanExt Utility Version 1.0\n");
21   printf ("(C) 2005 Zeidman Consulting (TM)\n");
22   printf ("Public Domain Software\n\n");
23   _findfirst ();
24   loc2 = &loc1;
25   if (loc2 != 0xFFFFFFFF) {
26     do {
27       loc8 = &loc3;
28       loc9 = ((loc1 & 16) | 0xFFFFFFFF);
29       loc10 = 0;
30       loc9 = ( ~ loc9);
31       loc8 = (loc8 - loc9);
32       loc10 = loc9;
33       loc8 = &loc4;
34       loc9 = (loc9 >> 2);
35       loc9 = loc10;
36       loc9 = (loc9 & 3);
37       strchr ();
38       loc10 = (loc10 - &loc4);
39       loc10 = (loc10 + 1);
40       loc5 = loc10;
41       loc8 = &loc4;
42       loc9 = (&loc4 | 0xFFFFFFFF);
43       loc10 = 0;
```

```
44        loc9 = ( ~ loc9);
45        loc9 = (loc9 + 0xFFFFFFFC);
46        if (loc5 < loc9) {
47        loc7[loc5] = 0;
48        }
49      _findfirst ();
50      if (loc5 != 0xFFFFFFFF) {
51        printf ("File %s exists - not renaming file %s.\n",
52          loc4, &loc3);
53
54        _findnext ();
55      }
56      else {
57        printf ("Renaming %s to %s\n", &loc3, &loc4);
58        rename ();
59      }
60      } while ((&loc1 == 0));
61    }
62    _findclose ();
63    return (&loc1);
64 }
```

These listings illustrate the difficulty of comparing even two very small routines. For entire programs, comparing original source code to decompiled source code is a very difficult task, somewhat akin to taking the wreckage of a house destroyed by a tornado and reassembling the original structure nearly perfectly from the scattered bricks and shards of wood. It can be done, but there are so many variables—such as the manufacturer and the version of the compiler used, the optimization switches set during compilation, and the third-party libraries that were linked into the object code—that the code resulting from the decompilation effort is certain to have many differences from the original code.

I have also seen attempts to compare functionality of object code by mapping data flow or by diagramming the overall software architecture and using these artifacts for a comparison to a similar mapping of another program's object code or source code. This too is a nearly impossible task because there are so many ways and so many levels at which object code can be mapped, all of which are essentially equivalent. Optimizing compilers rearrange and reorganize code so that the final structure usually has little resemblance to what the programmer wrote in the original source code. And when multiple source code files are compiled into a single object code file, there is no information remaining about how the original source code was organized into files or what the file names were.

18.1 PRACTICAL DEFINITION

In Chapter 4 I discussed how object code is derived from source code through the use of a compiler to translate human-readable text statements into machine-readable instructions consisting of ones and zeros. However, that compilation process still leaves some parts of the human-readable code embedded in the binary object code. Typically, comments are stripped out of the object code, but some compilers have the option of leaving comments in the binary object for debugging purposes. While the debug option is not recommended for creating code that gets released to customers, in my experience it is sometimes left turned on, often unintentionally, when compiling release versions of a program. Strings are left in the code so that they can be displayed to the user at the appropriate time while the program is executing. Labels may be left in the object code if the debug option of the compiler is used. Identifier names can be embedded in the object code by a compiler in debug mode, but even when a program is compiled for a release version, identifiers for APIs, those functions that are called by other programs, are usually embedded in the object code.

Figure 18.1 shows a small section of object code. Figure 18.1a shows the code displayed as text. Note that many of the characters are "garbage" characters. In other words, the text editor attempts to display a character but uses an unusual Unicode symbol that is almost certainly just a binary value in the code rather than a text character. Many of the bytes cannot even be displayed as symbols and so they are displayed as spaces. However, about halfway down we see real

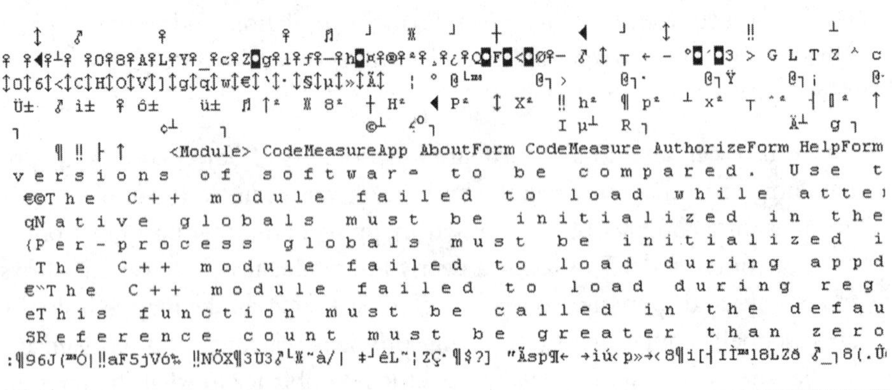

Figure 18.1a A section of raw object code

text that spells out words and functions that appear to be names of files and routines and messages to users. Figure 18.1b shows the same section of code displayed as hex and text. The leftmost column gives a memory location. The next four columns show the binary represented as hexadecimal words. The rightmost column shows the ASCII text value of the binary data wherever there is a printable ASCII character (Figure 18.1a goes off the screen to the right but Figure 18.1b wraps, which is why the two figures do not appear to be equivalent).

Essentially there is much text information that remains in object code. In Chapter 14, I defined source code as consisting of statements, from which we can derive a control structure, and comments and strings (see Table 14.1). Statements can be further divided into instructions, identifiers, and labels.

```
29350:  34000200  00000000  00000000  00004900   4 ┐              I
29360:  B5150000  52000200  00000000  00000000   µ┴   R ┐
29370:  00000100  C4150000  67000200  00000000     Ä┴   g ┐
29380:  00000000  00000100  D9150000  7C000800         Ù┴   | ▯
29390:  00000000  00000000  00004900  E4150000          I ä┴
293A0:  91000000  00000100  00007367  000050CE   `         sg  PÎ
293B0:  05000100  00009367  0000DCD5  05000100   |      `g  ÙÕ|
293C0:  0000B767  00004CDC  05000100  0000D667      ·g  LÜ|      Ög
293D0:  0000A8AE  0B000100  0000F567  0000F800      ¨®♪    õg   ø
293E0:  F700F900  F8000201  01010301  02010401   ÷ ù ø ┐    └ ┐ ┘
293F0:  03010501  04010801  07010901  08010A01   └ | ┘ ▯ • ▯
29400:  09011401  13011901  18010000  003C4D6F   ¶ ‼ ├ ↑    <Mo
29410:  64756C65  3E00436F  64654D65  61737572   dule> CodeMeasur
29420:  65417070  0041626F  7574466F  726D0043   eApp AboutForm C
29430:  6F64654D  65617375  72650041  7574686F   odeMeasure Autho
29440:  72697A65  466F726D  0048656C  70466F72   rizeForm HelpFor
29450:  6D005374  61747573  466F726D  004D6169   m StatusForm Mai
29460:  6E466F72  6D005965  734E6F4D  61796265   nForm YesNoMaybe
29470:  0076635F  61747472  69627574  65730041   vc_attributes A
29480:  63636573  73547970  65005F45  58434550   ccessType _EXCEP
29490:  54494F4E  5F444953  504F5349  54494F4E   TION_DISPOSITION
294A0:  005F5349  445F4E41  4D455F55  5345005F   _SID_NAME_USE _
294B0:  41434C5F  494E464F  524D4154  494F4E5F   ACL_INFORMATION_
294C0:  434C4153  53005F41  55444954  5F455645   CLASS _AUDIT_EVE
294D0:  4E545F54  59504500  5F534543  55524954   NT_TYPE _SECURIT
294E0:  595F494D  50455253  4F4E4154  494F4E5F   Y_IMPERSONATION_
294F0:  4C455645  4C005F54  4F4B454E  5F545950   LEVEL _TOKEN_TYP
29500:  45005F54  4F4B454E  5F454C45  56415449   E _TOKEN_ELEVATI
```

Figure 18.1b   A section of object code displayed as hex and text

Instructions are made up of control words, specifiers, and operators. Identifiers include variables, constants, functions, and labels. A single line of source code may include one or more statements and one or more comments and strings. Object code correlation and source/object code correlation consider only comment/string correlation and identifier correlation, which are calculated essentially in the same way as for source code correlation. As with source code correlation, a correlation between 0 and 1 should be determined for each element individually. The correlation for a particular element should represent a single dimension of a multidimensional correlation that is orthogonal to the correlation of the other elements. The individual correlation scores are then combined into a single overall correlation score between 0 and 1. As with source code correlation, each correlation is determined on a file-to-file basis, but nothing precludes comparing object code on a program-to-program basis or some other basis. Files are convenient and available, though a large number of source code files are typically compiled into a single object code file anyway. The element correlations and overall source/object code correlation are defined using these symbols:

- Comment/string correlation (ρ_C)
- Identifier correlation (ρ_I)
- Overall source code correlation (ρ)

In the frameworks of object code correlation and source/object code correlation, there is room to add a functional correlation just as can be done within the source code correlation framework. In theory, a functional representation of an object code file could be compared to a functional representation of another object code file, for determining object code correlation, or a functional representation of a source code file could be compared to a functional representation of an object code file for determining source/object code correlation. At this writing I am unaware of any such representation that can be calculated reliably in a reasonable amount of time for either object code or source code in a way that would facilitate such a calculation, so for now, there is no functional element in the framework of object code correlation or source/object code correlation.

18.2 EXTRACTING ELEMENTS

Extracting elements from source code has already been covered in Chapter 14. One challenge with object code correlation is identifying the elements in object code. How is a comment or string differentiated from an identifier when both consist simply of sequences of text embedded in a file of binary? This is done in a way such that all possibilities of strings, comments, and identifiers are taken into account.

18.2.1 COMMENT/STRING ELEMENTS

Typically comments are discarded when a program is compiled into object code, but it is possible that some compilers keep comments when the program is compiled in debug mode. However, strings are always embedded in object code so that the program can display them to the user.

Comments and strings within object code are identified as sequences of text characters that may include characters that are normally used to separate words, such as spaces and tabs, but do not include any non-text characters. Every maximal-size continuous sequence of text characters, beginning with a printable text character (not a space or tab) and ending with a printable text character (not a space or tab), is considered to be a comment or string. So the whitespace is trimmed from both ends of the sequence but kept inside the sequence of characters.

In Figure 18.2 we see a small snippet of object code that can commonly be found in Windows programs. The sequence of text is

```
!This program cannot be run in DOS mode.
```

This entire line would be considered to be one comment/string element. In fact, this is a message that is displayed to a user who attempts to run this Windows program from a DOS command line.

18.2.2 IDENTIFIER ELEMENTS

Often, function names are left in a program's object code files, especially when the program allows an external program to call functions within it. This occurs in programs like dynamic link libraries (DLLs). In debug mode, compilers may also leave variable names, constant names, and label names in order to facilitate debugging the code while relating the compiled code back to the original source code.

```
40:  0E1FBA0E 00B409CD 21B8014C CD215468  ♪ °♪ ´ í!  Lí!Th
50:  69732070 726F6772 616D2063 616E6E6F  is program canno
60:  74206265 2072756E 20696E20 444F5320  t be run in DOS
70:  6D6F6465 2E0D0D0A 24000000 00000000  mode.    $
```

Figure 18.2   Snippet of object code displayed as hex and text

Identifiers within object code are identified as sequences of text characters but do not include spaces or tabs within them. Typically they can contain underscores, but not other symbols. This varies with different programming languages, and so to accurately perform a comparison may require some knowledge, if possible, of the programming language that was used to create the object file. Without that knowledge it is safest to not include any symbols other than underscores.

Thus identifiers would be sequences of characters that include only alphanumeric characters and some limited symbols. In the example from Figure 18.2, the line that was included as a string/comment would also be considered as a list of the following identifiers (sorted):

```
be
DOS
cannot
in
mode
program
run
This
```

18.3 COMPARING DIFFERENT PROGRAMMING LANGUAGES

As with source code correlation, nothing in the definition of object code correlation or source/object code correlation precludes comparing programs in different languages. All modern programming languages use strings and identifiers that typically end up being compiled into text sequences in object code files, so unlike with source code correlation, comparing programs in different languages does not necessarily result in lower overall correlation scores than comparing programs in the same language.

18.4 MATHEMATICAL DEFINITIONS

Let us define the various mathematical terms and symbols used throughout this chapter for calculating object code correlation and source/object code correlation. These definitions are a subset of those used for source code correlation in Chapter 15, but I repeat them here for convenience.

F^n	=	the nth object code file in a set of files being compared
$\rho_C(F^n, F^m)$	=	comment/string correlation between files F^n and F^m
$\rho_I(F^n, F^m)$	=	identifier correlation between files F^n and F^m
$\rho(F^n, F^m)$	=	overall correlation between files F^n and F^m

The following are the more specific definitions that apply to all elements being examined for correlation. Note that there is currently only one type of element defined, and that is a text substring. However, I define a generic object code element X for the case where more object code elements, such as a functional element, are defined at some future time.

X_i	=	the ith element of an object code file
$N^n(X_i)$	=	the number of times the ith element X_i appears in source code file n
$\mu(X_i, X_j)$	=	element match score, a measure of the similarity between the ith X-type element of an object code file and the jth X-type element of an object code file, not necessarily the same files
$\mu(X_i)$	=	element identity match score, the match score for the ith X-type element of an object code file; in other words, the match score if that element is also exactly found in another file
$\gamma(X_i)$	=	the number of "atoms" of element X_i; for text substrings, the number of characters in the substring
$\gamma(X_i, X_j)$	=	the number of common atoms found in both the ith X-type element of an object code file and the jth X-type element of an object code file and in the same sequence
$\alpha(X_i)$	=	the number of alphabetic characters in the ith X-type element of an object code file
$\alpha(X_i, X_j)$	=	the number of alphabetic characters found in both the ith X-type element of an object code file and the jth X-type element of an object code file and in the same sequence
$\eta(X_i)$	=	the number of nonalphabetic characters in the ith X-type element of an object code file
$\eta(X_i, X_j)$	=	the number of nonalphabetic characters found in both the ith X-type element of an object code file and the jth X-type element of an object code file and in the same sequence
$\mu_X(F^n, F^m)$	=	file element match score, the numeric result of comparing all X-type elements in the object code file F^n to all X-type elements in the object code file F^m

$$\mu_X(F^n) \quad = \quad \text{file element identity match score for file } F^n \text{ compared to itself;}$$

the numeric result of comparing all X-type elements in the object code file F^n to themselves

18.5 OBJECT AND SOURCE/OBJECT CODE CORRELATION MATHEMATICS

For each element (comment/string or identifier), we will calculate a match score that is the result of comparing all elements in one source code file or object code file to all elements in another object code file. For the match score to be useful, it must meet certain criteria that are the axioms. These axioms are the same as those for source code correlation and are repeated here.

18.5.1 COMMUTATIVITY AXIOM

First, the match score must not be dependent on the order of comparing two files. In other words, the correlation value for any element we examine must be commutative, as represented by Equation 18.1:

$$\mu_X \left(F^n, F^m \right) = \mu_X \left(F^m, F^n \right) \tag{18.1}$$

18.5.2 IDENTITY AXIOM

The maximum match score must be equivalent to the identity match score. In other words, a file cannot match another file more than it matches itself. This is represented by Equation 18.2:

$$\mu_X \left(F^n \right) = \mu_X \left(F^n, F^n \right) \tag{18.2}$$

18.5.3 LOCATION AXIOM

The location of the files in a file system should have no bearing on the correlation measurement.

18.5.4 CORRELATION DEFINITION

In order to normalize the correlation, we must calculate the maximum possible match score and then calculate the correlation of these two files by normalizing the match score using Equation 18.3:

$$\rho_x\left(F^n, F^m\right) = \frac{\mu_x\left(F^n, F^m\right)}{max\left(\mu_x\left(F^n, F^m\right)\right)} \qquad (18.3)$$

18.5.5 Lemma

The maximum possible match score between any two files must be the smaller of the identity match scores for each file. If not, we would be violating equation 18.2. This is represented by Equation 18.4:

$$max\left(\mu_x\left(F^n, F^m\right)\right) = min\left(\mu_x\left(F^n\right), \mu_x\left(F^m\right)\right) \qquad (18.4)$$

18.6 Comment/String Correlation

The comment/string correlation is the result of comparing unique nonfunctional lines in one source code file or object code file with those extracted from another object code file. All sequences of whitespace characters (spaces and tabs) are reduced to a single space, and leading and trailing whitespace is removed.

18.6.1 Comment/String Correlation Equations

The file match score is then calculated according to Equation 18.5, which states that the file match score is equal to the sum of the match scores of each unique comment or string that can be found in both files multiplied by the least number of times that comment or string appears in one of the two files:

$$\mu_C\left(F^n, F^m\right) = \sum \mu\left(C_i\right) \bullet min\left(N^n\left(C_i\right), N^m\left(C_i\right)\right) \;\forall\; unique\; C_i : C_i \in F^n \cap F^m \quad (18.5)$$

The comment/string element identity match score $\mu(C_i)$ can be calculated in many different ways that can probably be justified. The match score that I have found to work best is given by Equation 18.6, where the number of characters is used:

$$\mu\left(C_i\right) = \gamma\left(C_i\right) \qquad (18.6)$$

The comment/string identity match score then is simply given by Equation 18.7, which states that the identity match score is given by the sum of the match scores of each unique comment or string multiplied by the number of times that comment or string appears in the file:

$$\mu_c\left(F^n\right)=\sum\mu\left(C_i\right)\cdot N^n\left(C_i\right)\ \forall\, C_i:C_i\in F^n \tag{18.7}$$

Then the comment/string correlation $\rho_c(F^n, F^m)$ can easily be calculated by combining Equation 18.3, Equation 18.4, Equation 18.5, Equation 18.6, and Equation 18.7. An example of calculating comment/string correlation is given in Chapter 15.

18.7 IDENTIFIER CORRELATION

The identifier correlation is the result of comparing identifiers in the first source code file or object code file with those extracted from another object code file. If exact matching is used, then the equation for calculating the identifier match score would be comparable to that for calculating the statement match score or the comment/string match score. However, it is much easier, and much more common, for identifiers to be changed via a global search and replace. For this reason, it is more accurate to use a partial match score for identifiers. In other words, the match score is calculated not only for identifiers that match exactly, but also for those that match only partially. This makes the calculation for the identifier match score more complex than that for the statement match score or the comment/string match score. The match score is then calculated according to Equation 18.8:

$$\mu_I\left(F^n, F^m\right)=\max\,(\sum_{i,j}\mu\left(I_i, I_j\right))\ \forall\left(unique\,I_i, unique\,I_j\right):I_i\in F^n, I_j\in F^m \tag{18.8}$$

This means the file match score is calculated by summing the match score between pairs of unique identifiers in the two files such that for each pair there is no other pairing that would produce a larger file match score. When identifiers do not have exact matches, they are paired with identifiers that most closely match, based on maximizing the longest common string or longest common subsequence between the two identifiers, or whatever method is used for calculating partial matches.

The pairing of similar but not identical identifiers covers cases where identifiers are similar but with some modifications, such as the variables CurrentIndex and CurrentIndex1 or RxSum and ArSum. Because identifiers typically contain significant information about their use, similar though not exactly matching identifiers are correlated. Note that each identifier must belong to one and only one pair that produces the highest match score.

The identifier identity match score $\mu(I_i)$ can be calculated in many different ways that can probably be justified. The match score that I have found to work best is given by Equation 18.9:

$$\mu\left(I_i\right)=k_\alpha \cdot \alpha\left(I_i\right)+k_\eta \cdot \eta\left(I_i\right) \tag{18.9}$$

Similarly, the identifier match score $\mu(I_i,I_j)$ can be calculated in many different ways that can probably be justified. The match score I have found to work best is given by Equation 18.10:

$$\mu\left(I_i,I_j\right)=k_\alpha \cdot \alpha\left(I_i,I_j\right)+k_\eta \cdot \eta\left(I_i,I_j\right) \tag{18.10}$$

The multipliers k_α and k_η, where $k_\alpha > k_\eta$, are used to give more significance to alphabetic characters over numbers and delimiter characters in identifiers. The reason different weighting is used is that a matching alphabetic character in two identifiers is more significant than matching numbers or delimiters. Alphabetic characters give identifying information from the programmer, but numbers are quantities that are rarely identifiable as unique unless they represent a well-known constant such as the square root of 2 or the Avogadro constant. The identifier identity match score then is simply given by Equation 18.11:

$$\mu_l\left(F^n\right)=\sum\mu\left(I_i\right) \; \forall \, I_i:I_i\in F^n \tag{18.11}$$

The identifier correlation $\rho_l(F^n,F^m)$ can be calculated by combining Equation 18.3, Equation 18.4, Equation 18.8, Equation 18.9, Equation 18.10, and Equation 18.11. The difficult part of this calculation is finding the pairs of identifiers whose identifier match scores maximize the file identifier match score. Methods for accomplishing this are discussed in Chapter 16.

18.8 OVERALL CORRELATION

Each element correlation can be considered to be a single dimension that can be used to calculate a multidimensional overall correlation. This overall correlation ρ is a single measure of the similarity of the file pairs. As with source code correlation, I have considered three calculations that combine the individual element correlations into one correlation score: a square root of sum-of-squares correlation, the maximum correlation, and the average correlation. Given the research I have performed, I recommend S-correlation.

18.8.1 S-CORRELATION

S-correlation can be considered a normalized total correlation distance where each element correlation is an orthogonal measure of correlation. In this case, correlation is calculated according to Equation 18.12:

$$\rho = \sqrt{\frac{\left(\rho_C\right)^2 + \left(\rho_I\right)^2}{2}} \qquad (18.12)$$

As I said when discussing source code correlation, S-correlation seems to me to be aesthetically more elegant than the other methods. S-correlation creates a two-dimensional space where each dimension is an orthogonal measure of the correlation of a specific object code element. The overall correlation is then simply the overall distance between two object code files in this two-dimensional space.

18.8.2 A-CORRELATION

A-correlation consists of simply averaging the correlation scores, as shown in Equation 18.13:

$$\rho = \frac{\rho_C + \rho_I}{2} \qquad (18.13)$$

It is interesting to note that in statistics, correlation ranges from -1 to 1, whereas the correlation defined here ranges from 0 to 1, which corresponds to the statistical definition of correlation squared. If our software source code correlations are considered the square of the dimension in a multidimensional space, then A-correlation is actually the normalized square of the distance.

18.8.3 M-CORRELATION

M-correlation takes the maximum of each element correlation, as shown in Equation 18.14:

$$\rho = max\left(\rho_C, \rho_I\right) \qquad (18.14)$$

18.9 FALSE NEGATIVES

It should be noted that source/object code correlation and object code correlation produce a high degree of false negatives. In other words, there can be correlation between two files that is not found using source/object code correlation or object code correlation. When a fast, accurate means of comparing the functionality of files is developed, it can be combined with comment/string correlation and identifier correlation to reduce the number of false negatives and make object code correlation and source/object code correlation more accurate.

As it is, though, source/object code correlation and object code correlation are very useful before litigation in the case of finding copyright infringement when one party suspects copying but does not have access to the other party's source code. A low correlation may mean that copying occurred but could not be found. However, high correlation often means that copying did in fact occur, in which case it can be used to convince a party to begin a lawsuit or to convince a judge that there is reasonable belief that copying occurred and a litigation should move forward.

19

IMPLEMENTATION

Now that I have discussed the theory behind object code correlation and source/object code correlation, I will discuss ways of practically and efficiently implementing the theory.[1] The particular implementation discussed in this chapter is based on the implementation used in the commercial BitMatch tool that is a function of the CodeSuite program, available from S.A.F. E. Corporation. This tool focuses on finding software copyright infringement, so many of the implementation choices are based on optimizing that particular use of object code correlation or source/object code correlation.

19.1 CREATING TEXT SUBSTRING ARRAYS FROM OBJECT CODE

To extract comments, strings, and identifiers from object code, it is necessary to extract text strings, which are found simply by reading the object code files byte by byte and looking for bytes that represent text. The two most common standard representations of text are ASCII and Unicode. ASCII represents up to 128 characters, using 7 of the 8 bits in a byte, shown in Table 19.1. Of those 128 characters, there are 95 printable ASCII characters. The other characters are unprintable characters such as backspace or carriage return. I use the terms "printable characters" and "text characters" interchangeably.

---

1. Note that some of the concepts discussed in this chapter may be covered by patents that have been issued or are pending.

Table 19.1 Printable ASCII Characters (Text Characters)

Char.	Hex	Char.	Hex	Char.	Hex	Char.	Hex
	20	8	38	P	50	h	68
!	21	9	39	Q	51	i	69
"	22	:	3A	R	52	j	6A
#	23	;	3B	S	53	k	6B
$	24	<	3C	T	54	l	6C
%	25	=	3D	U	55	m	6D
&	26	>	3E	V	56	n	6E
'	27	?	3F	W	57	o	6F
(	28	@	40	X	58	p	70
)	29	A	41	Y	59	q	71
*	2A	B	42	Z	5A	r	72
+	2B	C	43	[	5B	s	73
,	2C	D	44	\	5C	t	74
-	2D	E	45	]	5D	u	75
.	2E	F	46	^	5E	v	76
/	2F	G	47	_	5F	w	77
0	30	H	48	`	60	x	78
1	31	I	49	a	61	y	79
2	32	J	4A	b	62	z	7A
3	33	K	4B	c	63	{	7B
4	34	L	4C	d	64			7C
5	35	M	4D	e	65	}	7D
6	36	N	4E	f	66	~	7E
7	37	O	4F	g	67		

There is also a definition for extended ASCII, which consists of the other 128 characters, shown in Table 19.2. These characters are not typically used in the English language, nor are they typically used in programming languages, but they may be used in the code being examined, depending on the language of the programmers and the language of the intended users.

Unicode is a much more comprehensive standard than ASCII and can represent up to 107,000 characters from many different languages. Unicode is represented by 1 to 4 bytes and can thus handle up to 4,294,967,296 characters. Unicode is a superset of ASCII, which means that the ASCII value for any character is the same in Unicode. A more precise and specific definition of Unicode can be found on the website of the Unicode Consortium at www.unicode.org.

Creating the text substring array simply requires going though the bytes in the object code file and determining if they could represent a text character. If the object code file uses ASCII, then each byte is examined and compared to the ASCII text characters. If the object code file uses Unicode, then a sliding window of 1, 2, 3, and 4 bytes should be used to look for text characters because Unicode defines different-byte-length characters. If it is not known which standard is being used in the object code file, Unicode is more inclusive and should be used to search for text substrings.

Looking for ASCII characters is fairly simple and requires simply reading a byte at a time and comparing it to the values of text characters. Looking for Unicode characters requires a sliding window of varying size from 1 to 4 bytes. Some intelligence in the algorithm is required to determine which sequences of bytes could represent text characters. This is particularly difficult because there are so many valid Unicode printable characters. Any information about the program being examined, such as the language of the intended users, would help narrow down the number of possible characters and make this process easier.

A sequence of text characters is considered to be a substring when a sequence of bytes that can represent text characters is found, followed by a byte or series of bytes that does not represent a text character. We find the longest such sequences and put them into an array of text substrings. There are many cases where bytes just happen to look like text characters when in fact they are some other data.

Table 19.2 Printable Extended ASCII Characters (Text Characters)

Char.	Hex	Char.	Hex	Char.	Hex	Char.	Hex	Char.	Hex
€	80	š	9A	´	B4	Î	CE	è	E8
	81	›	9B	µ	B5	Ï	CF	é	E9
‚	82	œ	9C	¶	B6	Ð	D0	ê	EA
ƒ	83		9D	·	B7	Ñ	D1	ë	EB
„	84	ž	9E	¸	B8	Ò	D2	ì	EC
…	85	Ÿ	9F	¹	B9	Ó	D3	í	ED
†	86		A0	º	BA	Ô	D4	î	EE
‡	87	¡	A1	»	BB	Õ	D5	ï	EF
ˆ	88	¢	A2	¼	BC	Ö	D6	ð	F0
‰	89	£	A3	½	BD	×	D7	ñ	F1
Š	8A	¤	A4	¾	BE	Ø	D8	ò	F2
‹	8B	¥	A5	¿	BF	Ù	D9	ó	F3
Œ	8C	¦	A6	À	C0	Ú	DA	ô	F4
	8D	§	A7	Á	C1	Û	DB	õ	F5
Ž	8E	¨	A8	Â	C2	Ü	DC	ö	F6
	8F	©	A9	Ã	C3	Ý	DD	÷	F7
	90	ª	AA	Ä	C4	Þ	DE	ø	F8
'	91	«	AB	Å	C5	ß	DF	ù	F9
'	92	¬	AC	Æ	C6	à	E0	ú	FA
"	93		AD	Ç	C7	á	E1	û	FB
"	94	®	AE	È	C8	â	E2	ü	FC
•	95	¯	AF	É	C9	ã	E3	ý	FD
–	96	°	B0	Ê	CA	ä	E4	þ	FE
—	97	±	B1	Ë	CB	å	E5	ÿ	FF
˜	98	²	B2	Ì	CC	æ	E6		
™	99	³	B3	Í	CD	ç	E7		

Single characters are not significant for several reasons. The chances of finding a byte or set of bytes that does not represent a text character but appears to represent a valid text character are pretty high. Programmers rarely use single characters for variable names or strings because they contain so little information.[2] The chance of matching single-character substrings in two programs is high even when the programs are completely unrelated. It makes sense to set some lower threshold for string lengths such that any string with a length below that threshold is ignored in the comparison. I define that threshold as the text length threshold τ_T:

$$\tau_T = \text{text length threshold}$$

The text length threshold should be at least 2 because, as discussed previously, single characters are not significant. Arguments can be made for the threshold to be 3 or 4 or possibly other numbers. The particular number could depend on the kind of object file being examined and how much information is available about the file.

Each text substring can be considered to be a comment or string and placed into a comment/string array for comparison with other comments and strings to calculate the comment/string correlation. In addition, these text substrings must be parsed into identifiers. Identifiers are separated by whitespace—spaces or tabs—so that characters between whitespace are considered identifiers and are placed in identifier arrays for comparison with other identifiers to calculate the identifier correlation. Note that it may be possible to refine the identification of identifiers further because in most programming languages, only alphanumeric characters and underscores are allowed in identifier names. Any character that is not an alphanumeric character or underscore can be considered to be an identifier delimiter.

19.2 Creating Arrays from Source Code

19.2.1 Extracting Identifiers

Identifier arrays are created from source code in the same way that they are created for determining source code correlation. Because this process is described in detail in Chapter 16, I will not repeat the description here.

---

2. In the early days of computing, some languages like BASIC allowed only single-character variable names or single characters followed by a number. Correlation due to these variable names would have little significance anyway because the language forced the use of these simple names, and so we would expect to find matches in unrelated programs.

19.2.2 EXTRACTING COMMENTS AND STRINGS

Comment/string arrays are created from source code by extracting comments and strings from the source code. It is arguable that comments are very unlikely to be found in object code, and computation time can be decreased by ignoring comments in the source code, making this array simply consist of strings.

There is an important difference between how the strings are extracted from source code and put into the comment/string array for source/object code and how they are put into the comment/string array for source code correlation. In particular, special attention must be paid to string delimiters, escape characters, and substitution characters, as described in the following sections.

19.2.3 STRING DELIMITERS

When creating strings for the string array for the purpose of calculating source code correlation or source/object code correlation, everything between string delimiters constitutes the string. String delimiters are those characters used to mark the beginning and end of the string. Typically the string delimiters are double quotes or single quotes. Some languages allow other kinds of delimiters, including special instructions or user-defined characters. Parsing the source code for these delimiters can be complex but is necessary for creating the string/comment arrays. Listing 19.1 shows some examples of string delimiters in different programming languages.

Listing 19.1   Examples of Strings and String Delimiters

```
"Double quote is the string delimiter in the C programming language."
'single quote in JavaScript allows "double quotes" in the string.'
"Double quote in JavaScript allows 'single quotes' in the string."
<<<EOT
PHP allows multiple line strings that start with
        three "less than" signs followed by a sequence of characters.
        The string ends when those three characters are encountered
again.
EOT;
```

19.2.4 ESCAPE CHARACTERS

Identifying and dealing with escape characters are important for source/object code correlation calculations but not for source code correlation calculations.

Escape characters are characters or character combinations that represent a different character or combination of characters. For example, some programming languages that use double quotes as string delimiters interpret two double quotes inside a string to be a double quote character. Most languages use the backslash followed by a character to represent a special character. The backslash is called an "escape character," and the combination of the backslash and another character is called an "escape sequence." The escape characters for the C programming language are common to many programming languages and are shown in Table 19.3.

The interpretation of these special characters can get a bit complex. In particular, note that the escape sequence for the newline character (\n) varies depending on which operating system the program has been compiled for. Also note that

Table 19.3 Escape Sequences in C

Escape sequence	Character	ASCII value
\\	backslash	0x5C
\ '	single quote	0x27
\"	double quote	0x22
\0	null (string terminator)	0x00
\ooo	octal number where o is an octal digit	
\ a	alert (or bell)	0x07
\ b	backspace	0x08
\ f	form feed	0x0C
\ n	newline UNIX: LF DOS: CR+LF MAC: CR	UNIX: 0x0A DOS: 0x0D0A MAC: 0x0D
\ r	carriage return (CR)	0x0D
\ t	tab	0x09
\ uhhhh	Unicode number where h is a hex digit	
\ v	vertical tab	0x0B
\ xhh	hex number where h is a hex digit	0xhh
\ xhhhh	hex number where h is a hex digit	

some escape sequences result in nonprintable characters that would not be included in the text substring array. These nonprintable characters should not be included in the string array because they will never result in a match. One simple solution, if the escape sequence represents a deterministic printable character, is to substitute that printable character in the string. If the escape sequence represents a nonprintable character, or it is not possible to determine exactly which character it represents, simply divide the string into two strings, the first before the escape character and the second after the escape character. However you deal with these escape characters, splitting up strings implies that the comment/string correlation calculation for source/object correlation should use partial matching (i.e., looking for longest common subsequences or substrings) just as identifier correlation calculation does. Partial matching compensates for strings that are split up or for places where the escape character could not be determined with certainty.

19.2.5 SUBSTITUTION CHARACTERS

Parsing strings for creating the string array also requires dealing with substitution characters, examples of which are given in Listing 19.2. Often strings in source code include characters or sequences of characters that represent a variable value that should be placed in the string. For example, in the C programming language, the `printf` function takes a string and any number of variables, the values of which are placed in the string at run time.

Listing 19.2   Examples of Substitution Characters

```
printf("Print the value of string nameStr: %s", nameStr);
printf("Print the value of the integer Index: %i", Index);
printf("Print the value of the floating point number fp1: %4.2f", fp1);
printf("Print all these values: %s %i %4.2f", nameStr, Index, fp1);
```

The format for these substitution characters can be very complex. Because these substitution characters are substituted at run time, it is not possible to know from static source code what value will be substituted. Also, the strings are stored in some format in the binary object code without the substituted characters. How these strings are stored may differ with different compilers. Again, a good way to deal with the issue of substitution characters is to simply remove them from the string, thus dividing the string into multiple strings. Dividing the strings also implies that partial matching should be used when comparing strings in source code to strings in object code because the string may be stored differently in the object code from the way it is divided in the comment/string array.

19.3 IDENTIFIER CORRELATION

The identifier correlation is determined by an algorithm that compares each entry in the identifier array of the object code file to each entry in the identifier array of the source code file or another object code file. The comparison is case-insensitive, because changing case is a common way to hide copying, so it makes sense to do a case-insensitive comparison. As stated before, my philosophy is to favor false positives over false negatives and to filter out the false positives after correlation has been calculated, in order not to miss any important correlation. For each file pair, this algorithm yields an identifier match score μ_I that is calculated from the number of exactly matching and partially matching text substrings in the object code file and identifiers in the source code file.

19.4 COMMENT/STRING CORRELATION

The comment/string correlation is determined by an algorithm that compares each entry in the comment/string array of the object code file to each entry in the comment/string array of the source code file or another object code file. Again, the comparison is not case-sensitive, because changing case is a common way to hide copying, so it makes sense to do a case-insensitive comparison. For each file pair, this algorithm yields a comment/string match score μ_C that is calculated from the number of exactly matching and partially matching text substrings in the object code file and comments and strings in the source code file.

19.5 OVERALL CORRELATION

As discussed in Chapter 18, there are several ways of combining source/object element correlation scores into an overall source/object correlation score, including S-correlation, A-correlation, and M-correlation. I prefer an implementation that uses S-correlation, because that combination has been found to be most useful for detecting copyright infringement.

20 APPLICATIONS

As with source code correlation, there are many potential applications for object code correlation and source/object code correlation, in particular when there is no access to one party's source code but only the object code. There are certain times when source code is rarely available or never available. At these times, source/object code correlation or object code correlation is useful. Following is a list of some applications for which object code correlation or source/object code correlation is particularly useful. I describe these applications in more detail in the sections that follow.

- Pre-litigation detective work
- Tracking malware
- Locating third-party code
- Detecting open source code license violations

20.1 PRE-LITIGATION DETECTIVE WORK

To bring a case to court, a plaintiff (in a civil case) or a prosecutor (in a criminal case) must argue that there is a reasonable belief that an action took place that justifies the plaintiff's complaint. In other words, in a criminal case a judge or grand jury must be convinced that there is a reasonable possibility that a crime was committed. In a civil case, a judge must be convinced that some action took place that justifies a civil complaint. Typically the party bringing the case has source code available but does not have the other party's source code available to it. Only after the judge or grand jury has been convinced that there is a reasonable possibility that code was stolen or misappropriated will there be an order issued for both parties to turn over their source code to an independent expert for comparison. Therefore, before litigation can occur, source/object code correlation is a good measure for determining whether litigation is worthwhile and can be used to convince a judge or grand jury that litigation should proceed. Because source/object code correlation has a high rate of false negatives, a positive result can be very convincing, but a negative result cannot rule out theft or misappropriation, and other methods should be used to help find clues to theft or misappropriation.

There are situations when the party bringing the action does not have the source code, in which case object code correlation is the required comparison method. Some possible reasons that a party may not have any source code to compare include the following, each of which is described in more detail in the next sections:

- The code in dispute is distributed as object code.
- A third party is bringing the suit.
- The original source code cannot be located.

20.1.1 THE CODE IN DISPUTE IS DISTRIBUTED AS OBJECT CODE

Many companies license object code libraries to their customers that can be linked into a program after the compilation phase. The customer never has access to source code but rather gets only object code. There is typically a limitation on these licenses. For example, the object code libraries may be used in only certain applications or for a limited period of time. In these cases, comparing the company's object code to the customer's object code, using object code correlation, would be an efficient way of determining whether the object code was in use in the customer's program. Of course, if the object code is being used in its entirety, a simple byte-by-byte comparison could be even more useful.

20.1.2 A THIRD PARTY IS BRINGING THE SUIT

Sometimes a party that brings a lawsuit does not have the source code. One scenario, for example, is that company A hires consulting company B to develop custom software for company A to use or sell. Company A then notices that company C has software that looks suspiciously like its own software.

OBJECTIONABLE OBJECT CODE

I was contacted by an attorney a few years ago for a case where a small software development company had licensed its object code to a very large company for use in its Web-based application. The software developer had licensed the code to the customer for one year, at which time the customer complained that the code was unusable and refused to renew the license. The software developer wondered why it took the customer so long to complain about the code and why the customer paid for the first year if it didn't work. In other words, the software developer was suspicious.

The attorney gave me the URL of the website and also sent me the client's source code and object code files. I said that for a start I would download the company's application and take a look at the object code. When I downloaded the application, I found a file with the exact name and size of the software developer's object file. Doing a bit-by-bit comparison, I found the files to be 100 percent identical.

"Well, this was an easy job," I told the attorney. "I guess you don't need me or my sophisticated tools for this one." The attorney thanked me, I submitted a very small bill for my services, and I was paid quickly.

About a year later I got a call from that same attorney. He told me that the case was still going on and he needed my help. The customer had continued to deny that the object code was being used and found an expert witness to confirm that. I was pretty surprised.

Initially the "expert" had claimed that the two files were identical only by coincidence. I laughed, but unfortunately people make ridiculous claims in court all the time and it's my job to debunk them in a way that a nontechnical judge or jury will understand. I started on my rebuttal by showing two things. First, there is a time and date stamp in the object code, so that at the very least, unless these two programs were coincidentally compiled on the exact same date and at the exact same time, this stamp would differ between the two programs. Second, given the number of bits in the programs, if a program were to be compiled once every minute since the beginning of the universe, there was still only a remote possibility that they would be 100 percent identical (I gave some rough astronomically large numbers in the expert report I ended up writing).

After this, the defendant's "expert" stated that the object code file was still in the download folder but was not actually being used. The simple test for this, of

Continues

course, is to simply remove the file and see if the program still runs. It took all of five minutes to perform this test, and when I executed the program, there was immediately an error message stating that the file could not be found and the program could not run. Being confronted with this at her deposition, the "expert" replied that she would have to try that test when she had an opportunity before she could verify my results.

Silly arguments like this continued throughout the case, and I'm happy to say my client survived, though the company needed bridge loans to cover legal expenses, and is thriving today. I bring this up mainly to illustrate the fact that object code files do indeed become critical in some litigation. I also bring this up to show another reason why quantifiable measures and standard methodologies are needed to ensure that experts are honest and competent and that rulings are fair.

Company A may not have the source code, or the source code may be kept in an escrow account that can be accessed only under strict conditions. In this case, company A could obtain company B's program object code and compare it.

Another thing to note is that company A can be in legal trouble if it is infringing on company C's software, even if company C got the software from company B. In that case company C could sue company B, but if company B is small, it might not have enough money to cover a potential damages award to company C, so company C may sue company A instead—or in addition. There are many ways this scenario can play out, all of which result in risks to the company that has copyrighted software for which it doesn't have the rights and may not have the source code.

20.1.3 THE ORIGINAL SOURCE CODE CANNOT BE LOCATED

Although this sounds strange, I have worked for several large software companies that could not locate their own source code. Sometimes they did not even have copies of their object code, but that can often be obtained at places that sell used, surplus, or "vintage" software. This seems to happen more often than I originally expected, particularly in Silicon Valley where so many companies start out in garages and apartments and college dormitories. The companies grow so quickly, move to ever larger office spaces, and never keep track of where everything is. By the time the company becomes a billion-dollar company, no one knows the whereabouts of the original source code. In many cases, the programmers do not know exactly how their program works, particularly if the original programmers are multimillionaires and have retired to the Bahamas, the Seychelles, Monaco, Albania, or some other luxurious tax haven.

20.2 TRACKING MALWARE

Malware such as viruses and spyware is becoming a significant problem. A significant amount of malware source code is actually available on the Web and can be purchased through numerous websites. In many cases, though, the source code is not readily available. However, it has been suggested that object code correlation can be used to compare the executable code for various malware programs, once they have been detected, and look for correlation with databases of malware object code that would identify the author or the country of origin based on the naming conventions, the strings, and the language used in the object code. Even malware that has mutated, either automatically as it spreads or manually as different programmers design their own variations, might be correlated in such a way, as is the case with DNA, that the malware's evolution can be tracked. I am not aware that anyone is currently using source/object code correlation or object code correlation to categorize and fingerprint malware, but it is an exciting application with great potential commercial success.

20.3 LOCATING THIRD-PARTY CODE

Source/object code correlation and object code correlation could be used by parties wanting to determine whether certain executable programs contain certain third-party libraries. If one party has source code available, then obviously source/object code correlation would be the way to go. If the party does not have source code, then object code correlation makes sense.

This use is essentially the same as that described in the previous section about pre-litigation detective work, but there are other reasons to do this besides litigation. One reason would involve research at a university, in which case the university might or might not have access to its own source code. Another reason might be market analysis by an independent marketing firm that does not have access to any source code but wants to determine which programs that are available on the market incorporate which other companies' object code libraries. Source/object code correlation and object code correlation could even be useful for a competitive analysis where one company wants to find out how prevalent is the use of its competitors' object code libraries, and again it would typically not have access to its competitors' source code.

20.4 DETECTING OPEN SOURCE CODE LICENSE VIOLATIONS

Source/object code correlation could be used by parties wanting to determine whether certain executable programs contain certain third-party source code. In particular, source/object code can be very helpful for locating programs that use open source code yet do not meet the open source licensing obligations. For example, many open source providers release their code under a GNU Public License (GPL) that requires the party using the code to make the source code for the entire program available to the public for free. Several companies have been caught in recent years for having used open source code without meeting the license requirements. Typically these companies get caught only through the testimony of employees who are aware of the license violation or other nontechnical means. The Free Software Foundation successfully sued Cisco Systems with the help of the Software Freedom Law Center. According to its website, the Software Freedom Law Center was specifically created to "provide legal representation and other law-related services to protect and advance Free, Libre and Open Source Software (FLOSS)." It does not charge for its services. It successfully sued Monsoon Multimedia, Inc., over its use of the open source BusyBox software. Later it successfully sued Verizon Communications, Bell Microproducts, and a number of other companies. Some of those lawsuits are still pending as of this writing. Object/source code correlation can be used to make the process of finding open source license violators more efficient and more exact.

PART VII
SOURCE CODE CROSS-CORRELATION

"We balance probabilities and choose the most likely. It is the scientific use of the imagination."
—Sherlock Holmes in *The Hound of the Baskervilles*

Source code cross-correlation measures the amount of code in one file that appears as comments in another file and vice versa. When copying source code, programmers sometimes place the code in a new file and "comment out" the code in order to use the code as a guide for writing a similar function in the new file. This is often done for legitimate reasons, such as when a programmer wants to rewrite a function in a different programming language or requires a certain function but needs to make changes to it to enhance it or to integrate it into an existing program. When such commenting out is done in a case of copyright infringement, the programmer may change the functional code to make it more difficult to detect that it was copied but may also neglect to change the commented-out code or forget to remove it, because this code is nonfunctional and does not affect the operation of the program. For this reason, source code cross-correlation is a useful tool in software forensics to find copied code.

In fact, source code cross-correlation is the only measure of those discussed in this book that can, by itself, give a strong clue as to which program was developed first. Source code correlation, object code correlation, and source/object code correlation can determine that files are similar despite modifications that have occurred. The measure says nothing about those modifications. With source code cross-correlation, unless there is some other reasonable explanation, the file that contains commented-out statements almost certainly was copied from the file in which those statements represent functioning code. Of course, each situation is different and there are other possible explanations. For example, both files may have been copied from a third file. Or the commented-out code may have existed in the original file that was then copied, and the commented-out statements were subsequently removed from the copied file. But the fact that functional code in one file shows up as commented-out code in another file is something that deserves close attention.

Source code cross-correlation is an odd measurement compared to source code differentiation, source code correlation, object code correlation, and source/object code correlation. These other four measures are basic measures of software that compare code to code and calculate a number that allows one to determine how much one program is like or unlike another program. Source code cross-correlation is different because it measures something that is used only to find clues to indicate whether one program was copied from another. While a nonzero source code cross-correlation measure means almost certainly that one program was copied from another, it has no other use of which I am aware. Maybe someone will find another use for it.

Much of the mathematics and algorithms described in this part are used in the CodeCross function of the CodeSuite program developed and distributed by S.A.F.E. Corporation.

OBJECTIVES

The objective of this part of the book is to give a theoretical, mathematical foundation for software source code cross-correlation that can be used for basic comparisons of software to find copying. In particular, software source code cross-correlation is used to compare functional lines of software source code to nonfunctional comments of software source code in order to detect copying.

INTENDED AUDIENCE

Computer scientists and *computer programmers* will find this part useful for understanding the theory, implementation, and application of source code cross-correlation, and they will be able to build upon this theory and practice for a variety of uses. *Technical consultants and expert witnesses for litigation* will find this part useful for understanding the theory, implementation, and application of source code cross-correlation and will be able to use it in software IP litigation, particularly copyright infringement cases, certain kinds of trade secret theft cases, and possibly patent infringement cases. ***Intellectual property lawyers*** and ***corporate managers*** with an understanding of algebra will find this part useful, especially to get a deep understanding of the theory, implementation, and application of source code cross-correlation and the associated tools that can be used in software IP litigation. ***Software entrepreneurs*** will find this part useful for understanding source code cross-correlation to apply it to new software products and new businesses.

THEORY, IMPLEMENTATION, AND APPLICATIONS

In Chapter 14 I defined source code as comprising functional statements and nonfunctional comments and strings (see Table 14.1). A single line of source code may include one or more statements and one or more comments and strings. Source code cross-correlation is a measure of the correlation of comments and string to statements and vice versa. As with the other code correlation measures, a source code cross-correlation between 0 and 1 should be determined for an individual correlation measure. Each correlation should represent a single dimension of a multidimensional correlation that is orthogonal to the other correlations. The individual correlation scores can then be combined into a single overall correlation score between 0 and 1. These individual correlations and the overall source code cross-correlation are defined using these symbols:

- Statement-to-comment/string correlation (ρ_{SC})
- Comment/string-to-statement correlation (ρ_{CS})
- Overall source code cross-correlation (ρ)

The statement-to-comment/string correlation ρ_{SC} is the result of comparing nonfunctional comments and strings in a first file to functional statements in a second file. The comment/string-to-statement correlation ρ_{CS} is the result of comparing functional statements in a first file to nonfunctional comments and strings in a second file. As with the other code correlation measures, each correlation is determined on a file-to-file basis, though nothing precludes comparing code on a program-to-program or other basis.

21.1 COMPARING DIFFERENT PROGRAMMING LANGUAGES

As with the other code correlation measures, nothing in the definition of source code cross-correlation precludes comparing programs in different languages. All modern programming languages use comments and strings. In fact, there are times when a programmer copies code from one language into a file to use it as a guide for writing code in another language, so source code cross-correlation is a good method for finding such copying between programming languages.

21.2 MATHEMATICAL DEFINITIONS

In this section, I take a more rigorous mathematical look at correlation. First let us define the various mathematical terms and symbols used throughout this chapter. These are the most basic definitions:

F^n = the nth source code file in a set of files being compared

$\rho_{SC}(F^n, F^m)$ = statement-to-comment/string correlation between files F^n and F^m

$\rho_{CS}(F^n, F^m)$ = comment/string-to-statement correlation between files F^n and F^m

$\rho(F^n, F^m)$ = overall source code cross-correlation between files F^n and F^m

The following definitions apply to all elements being examined for correlation. These are described in more detail later in this chapter. As with other correlation measures, I define a generic code element X. In the case of source code cross-correlation, the element consists of two source code elements and a direction. One element is statements compared to comments and strings. The other element is comments and strings compared to statements.

X_i = the ith element of a source code file

$N^n(X_i)$ = the number of times the ith element X_i appears in source code file n

$\mu(X_i, X_j)$ = element match score, a measure of the similarity between the ith X-type element of a source code file and the jth X-type element of a source code file, not necessarily the same files

$\mu(X_i)$ = element identity match score, the match score for the ith X-type element of a source code file; in other words, the match score if that element is also exactly found in another file

$\gamma(X_i)$	=	the number of "atoms" of element X_i; for comment and statement elements, this is the number of characters in the element
$\gamma(X_i, X_j)$	=	the number of common atoms found in both the ith X-type element of a source code file and the jth X-type element of a source code file and in the same sequence
$\alpha(X_i)$	=	the number of alphabetic characters in the ith X-type element of a source code file
$\alpha(X_i, X_j)$	=	the number of alphabetic characters found in both the ith X-type element of a source code file and the jth X-type element of a source code file and in the same sequence
$\eta(X_i)$	=	the number of nonalphabetic characters in the ith X-type element of a source code file
$\eta(X_i, X_j)$	=	the number of nonalphabetic characters found in both the ith X-type element of a source code file and the jth X-type element of a source code file and in the same sequence
$\mu_X(F^n, F^m)$	=	file element match score, the numeric result of comparing all X-type elements in the source code file F^n to all X-type elements in the source code file F^m
$\mu_X(F^n)$	=	file element identity match score for file F^n compared to itself; the numeric result of comparing all X-type elements in the source code file F^n to themselves

21.3 SOURCE CODE CROSS-CORRELATION MATHEMATICS

For each cross-correlation element (statements to comments/strings and comments/strings to statements), we calculate a match score that is the result of comparing all elements in one source code file to all elements in another source code file. For the match score to be useful, it must meet certain criteria that are the source code correlation axioms. These axioms are a bit different from those for the other correlation measures.

21.3.1 COMMUTATIVITY AXIOM

For source code cross-correlation there is no element-level commutativity. Because two different types of elements are being compared, the statement-to-comment/string match score and the comment/string-to-statement match score are not commutative. In other words, comparing the statements in a first file to the comments and strings in a second file yields entirely different results from comparing the comments and strings in the first file to the statements in the second file except in unusual, contrived situations. However, the combined cross-correlation match score must be commutative. In other words, the combined source code cross-correlation match score must be the same regardless of which file is the first file and which is the second file being compared. So the commutativity axiom for source code cross-correlation is expressed in Equation 21.1:

$$\mu\left(F^n, F^m\right) = \mu\left(F^m, F^n\right) \tag{21.1}$$

21.3.2 Identity Axiom

For source code cross-correlation, unlike other code correlation measures, a file actually can match another file more than it matches itself. This is because we are comparing one kind of element to another kind of element. The highest correlation would be between one file consisting of all instructions and no comments and another file consisting only of those instructions but commented out. Comparing the first file to itself would have no cross-correlation because there are no comments in the file. Comparing the second file to itself would have no cross-correlation because there are no instructions.

So for software source code cross-correlation there is no element-level identity. However, the combined cross-correlation match score must have an identity. In other words, the overall source code cross-correlation match score for a single file must be equal to the source code cross-correlation match score for a file compared to itself. So the commutativity axiom for source code cross-correlation is expressed in Equation 21.2:

$$\mu\left(F^n\right) = \mu\left(F^n, F^n\right) \tag{21.2}$$

21.3.3 Location Axiom

The location of the files in a file system should have no bearing on the correlation measurement.

21.3.4 Correlation Definition

As with the other correlation measures, to normalize the correlation, we must calculate the maximum possible match score for each individual measure (statement to comment/string and comment/string to statement) and then calculate the correlation of these two files by normalizing the match score using Equation 21.3. Specifically how this is done, though, is different from how it is done for the other correlation measures, as we will see in the next section on the lemmas.

$$\rho_X\left(F^n, F^m\right) = \frac{\mu_X\left(F^n, F^m\right)}{max\left(\mu_X\left(F^n, F^m\right)\right)} \tag{21.3}$$

21.3.5 LEMMAS

The first lemma is that the maximum possible statement-to-comment/string match score between any two files must be the smaller of the statement identity match score for the first file and the comment/string identity match score for the second file; the statement and comment/string identity match scores are defined in Chapter 15 where I discussed source code correlation. This is represented by Equation 21.4:

$$max\left(\mu_{SC}\left(F^n, F^m\right)\right) = min\left(\mu_S\left(F^n\right), \mu_C\left(F^m\right)\right) \tag{21.4}$$

Another way to say this is that the statement-to-comment/string match score cannot be larger than the case where every statement in the first file has a corresponding comment or string in the second file, and the statement-to-comment/string match score cannot be larger than the case where every comment and string in the second file has a corresponding statement in the first file.

The second lemma is that the maximum possible comment/string-to-statement match score between any two files must be the smaller of the comment/string identity match score for the first file and the statement identity match score for the second file. This is represented by Equation 21.5:

$$max\left(\mu_{CS}\left(F^n, F^m\right)\right) = min\left(\mu_C\left(F^n\right), \mu_S\left(F^m\right)\right) \tag{21.5}$$

The comment/string-to-statement match score cannot be larger than the case where every comment and string in the first file has a corresponding statement in the second file, and the statement-to-comment/string match score cannot be larger than the case where every statement in the second file has a corresponding comment or string in the first file.

21.4 SOURCE CODE EXAMPLES

To better understand the equations that follow, we consider two small source code files to be compared, shown in Listing 21.1 and Listing 21.2.

Listing 21.1 Source Code File 1

```
1    int example_routine(float newVal)
2    {
3      float simVal;      // similarity value to be calculated
4      int i;             // integer variable
5      int j;             // integer variable
6
7      printf("Starting.");
8
9      // Initialize variables.
10     simVal = 1.0;
11     i = 0;
12     j = 0;
13
14     while (j < NUM_VALS)
15     {
16       j++;
17       simVal = simVal * 10;
18       if (simVal == newVal)
19       {
20         j = 0;
21         break;
22       }
23       printf("Done!");
24     }
25     return(j);
26   }
```

Listing 21.2 Source Code File 2

```
1    long example_routine2(double Value)
2    {
3      float similarity;
4      long p
5      long q
6
7      similarity = 1.0;
8      p = 0;
9      q = 0;
```

```
10
11 /*  while (j < NUM_VALS)
12     {
13       j++;
14       simVal = simVal * 10;
15       if (simVal == newVal)
16       {
17         j = 0;
18         break;
19       }
20       printf("Done!");
21     }
22     */
23     for (p = 1; p <= VALNUMS; p++)
24     {
25       similarity = similarity * 10;
26       if (similarity == Value)
27       {
28         p = 0;
29         break;
30       }
31     }
32     return(p);
33 }
```

The statements and comments/strings that are extracted from these source code files are shown in Tables 21.1 and 21.2. As with other correlation measures, we consider only unique elements. In other words, we do not count an element more than once even if it appears in the file more than once. Also, we convert symbols to whitespace, we reduce all sequences of whitespace to a single space, and we trim off the leading and trailing whitespace.

Table 21.1 Unique Source Code Elements from Source Code File 1

Statements	Comments/Strings	Identifiers
int example_routine (float newVal)	Similarity value to be calculated	example_routine
float simVal;	Integer variable	newVal
int i;	Initialize variables	simVal

Continues

Table 21.1 Unique Source Code Elements from Source Code File 1 *(Continued)*

Statements	Comments/Strings	Identifiers
`int j;`	`Starting.`	`i`
`printf();`	`Done!`	`j`
`simVal = 1.0;`		`NUM_VALS`
`i = 0;`		
`j = 0;`		
`while (j < NUM_VALS)`		
`j++;`		
`simVal = simVal * 10;`		
`if (simVal == newVal)`		
`break;`		
`return(j);`		

Table 21.2 Unique Source Code Elements from Source Code File 2

Statements	Comments/Strings	Identifiers
`int example_routine2 (double Value)`	`while (j < NUM_VALS)`	`example_routine2`
`float similarity;`	`{`	`Value`
`long p;`	`j++;`	`similarity`
`long q;`	`simVal = simVal * 10;`	`p`
`similarity = 1.0;`	`if (simVal == newVal)`	`q`
`p = 0;`	`j = 0;`	`VALNUMS`
`q = 0;`	`break;`	
`for (p = 1; p <= VALNUMS; p++)`	`}`	
`while (j < NUM_VALS)`	`printf("Done!");`	
`similarity = similarity * 10;`		
`if (similarity == Value)`		
`break;`		
`return(p);`		

The tables show that there are no matches between statements in the two source code files. We can also see that there are no matches between the strings or comments in the two files. There are some partial matches between the identifiers in the two files, but nothing that could be considered to be significant and that could be explained by the use of common terms. However, the second file contains a sequence of commented-out instructions that are identical to actual instructions in the first file, nearly certain evidence that the second file was copied from the first file.

21.5 STATEMENT-TO-COMMENT/STRING CORRELATION

The statement-to-comment/string correlation is the result of comparing functional lines in the source code of a first file to nonfunctional lines in the source code of a second file. Statements are extracted from the first file being compared and are processed just as they are for calculating statement correlation. Comments and strings are extracted from the second file being compared and are processed just as they are for calculating comment/string correlation. The match score is then calculated according to Equation 21.6:

$$\mu_{SC}\left(F^n, F^m\right) = \sum \mu\left(S_i\right) \bullet min\left(N^n\left(S_i\right), N^m\left(C_i\right)\right) \ \forall \ unique \ S_i, C_j : S_i \in F^n, C_j \in F^m$$
(21.6)

This means the match score is calculated by summing the match score for each unique statement that is found in the first file that is also found as a comment or string in the second file and multiplying by the least number of occurrences in either file. The statement element identity match score $\mu(S_i)$ is the same as for source code correlation and is calculated in the same way, given by Equation 21.7. The multipliers k_α and k_η, where $k_\alpha > k_\eta$, are used to give more significance to alphabetic characters over numbers, operators, and symbols.

$$\mu\left(S_i\right) = k_\alpha \bullet \alpha\left(S_i\right) + k_\eta \bullet \eta\left(S_i\right)$$
(21.7)

The statement file identity match score then is simply given by Equation 21.8:

$$\mu_S\left(F^n\right) = \sum \mu\left(S_i\right) \bullet N^n\left(S_i\right) \ \forall S_i : S_i \in F^n$$
(21.8)

Then the statement-to-comment/string correlation $\rho_{SC}(F^n, F^m)$ can easily be calculated by combining Equation 21.3, Equation 21.4, Equation 21.5, Equation 21.6, and Equation 21.8.

21.6 COMMENT/STRING-TO-STATEMENT CORRELATION

The comment/string-to-statement correlation is the result of comparing non-functional lines in the source code of a first file to functional lines in the source code of a second file. Comments and strings are extracted from the first file being compared and are processed just as they are for calculating comment/string correlation. Statements are extracted from the second file being compared and are processed just as they are for calculating statement correlation. The match score is then calculated according to Equation 21.9:

$$\mu_{CS}\left(F^n, F^m\right) = \sum \mu\left(C_i\right) \cdot min\left(N^n\left(C_i\right), N^m\left(S_i\right)\right) \forall \, unique \; C_i, S_j : C_i \in F^n, S_j \in F^m$$

$$(21.9)$$

This means the match score is calculated by summing the match score for each unique comment or string that is found in the first file that is also found as a statement in the second file and multiplying by the least number of occurrences in either file. The comment/string element identity match score $\mu(C_i)$ can be calculated in many different ways that can probably be justified. The match score I have found to work best is given by Equation 21.10, where the number of characters is used:

$$\mu\left(C_i\right) = \gamma\left(C_i\right)$$

$$(21.10)$$

The comment/string identity match score then is simply given by Equation 21.11:

$$\mu_c\left(F^n\right) = \sum \mu\left(C_i\right) \cdot N^n\left(C_i\right) \quad \forall \, C_i : C_i \in F^n$$

$$(21.11)$$

Then the comment/string-to-statement correlation $\rho_{CS}(F^n, F^m)$ can easily be calculated by combining Equation 21.3, Equation 21.5, Equation 21.9, Equation 21.10, and Equation 21.11.

21.7 OVERALL CORRELATION

Each element correlation can be considered a single dimension that can be used to calculate a multidimensional overall correlation. This overall source code cross-correlation ρ is a single measure of the cross-similarity of the file pairs. As with the other correlation measures, I have considered three calculations that combine the individual element correlations into one cross-correlation score: a square root of sum-of-squares correlation, the maximum correlation, and the average correlation. Given the research I have performed, I again recommend S-correlation.

21.7.1 S-CORRELATION

S-correlation can be considered a normalized total correlation distance where each element correlation is an orthogonal measure of correlation. In this case, correlation is calculated according to Equation 21.12:

$$\rho = \sqrt{\frac{\left(\rho_{SC}\right)^2 + \left(\rho_{CS}\right)^2}{2}} \tag{21.12}$$

S-correlation creates a two-dimensional space where each dimension is an orthogonal measure of the correlation of a specific source code element. The overall correlation is then simply the overall distance between two source code files in this two-dimensional space.

21.7.2 A-CORRELATION

A-correlation consists of simply averaging the correlation scores, as shown in Equation 21.13:

$$\rho = \frac{\rho_{SC} + \rho_{CS}}{2} \tag{21.13}$$

It is interesting to note that in statistics, correlation ranges from -1 to 1, whereas the correlation defined here ranges from 0 to 1, which corresponds to the statistical definition of correlation squared. If our software source code correlations are considered the square of the dimension in a multidimensional space, then A-correlation is actually the normalized square of the distance.

21.7.3 M-CORRELATION

M-correlation takes the maximum of each element correlation, as shown in Equation 21.14:

$$\rho = max\left(\rho_{SC}, \rho_{CS}\right) \tag{21.14}$$

21.8 IMPLEMENTATION AND APPLICATIONS

The implementation of source code cross-correlation is essentially the same as that of source code correlation. Statements are extracted from source code in the same way that they are extracted for source code correlation. Comments and strings are extracted from source code in the same way that they are extracted for source code correlation. The only difference is that with source code correlation, statements are compared to statements, and comments and strings are compared to comments and strings. For source code cross-correlation, statements are compared to comments and strings, and comments and strings are compared to statements.

Software source code cross-correlation is very specialized, and its one application of which I am aware is finding clues about copying, typically for use in software copyright infringement cases. I invented software source code cross-correlation for the simple reason that throughout my career I have continually come across cases where a programmer copied code from one program to another, commented out that code to use it as a guide to write a similar function, and left in the original commented-out code. As you know from Chapter 6, it is perfectly fine to reverse engineer code to understand how it works and then write something similar without using the original code as a reference (assuming that you have the right to the original code). However, it is not OK to refer to the original code when creating the new code because the new code is then considered to be a derivation of the original code, which constitutes copyright infringement if the original code's owner has not given permission.

I suspect that once this book is published, the incidences of commented-out code will diminish. If not, it means my book is not being widely read or not being widely read by those stealing code. In any case, my experience is that commented-out code will continue to remain in some copied programs, and source code cross-correlation will continue to be a useful tool for detecting software copyright infringement.

DO PEOPLE REALLY LEAVE IN COMMENTED-OUT CODE?

I often get asked this question when I talk about source code cross-correlation. The answer is yes. Even I am surprised by how often this occurs. I think it happens for two reasons. First, many programmers who copy think that by copying the code and changing it, they're not doing anything wrong. Wrong! Second, many programmers are just not slick, sophisticated criminals. Whether they believe they are legally entitled to copy code or they believe they are doing something illicit, or they just don't think anyone will find the code, they are usually anxious to move on to more important matters like debugging the code and getting their program to work. While debugging, they may even ignore the comments because comments are nonfunctional and they're trying to get the functional code to work.

In one particular case on which I worked, a programmer moved from one company to a competitor of that company, and the first company sued the programmer for copyright infringement. As an expert in the case, I examined the source code from both companies and, using source code correlation, found multiple examples of copied code. However, this alone did not enable me to determine definitively which code was the original code and which was copied (though that could be inferred from the timeline of the programmer's job hopping). The programmer, when confronted with the copied code, claimed that he had independently developed the code in common between the two programs on his own time. However, my analysis using code cross-correlation found that the second program also contained code from the first program that had been commented out. What I found particularly interesting was that the commented-out statements included a reference to a function that could not be found in the second company's code but did exist in the first company's code. To me this was clear and convincing evidence not only that the code was copied, but that the code was copied from the first company's program to the second company's program.

PART VIII

DETECTING SOFTWARE IP THEFT AND INFRINGEMENT

"Once you eliminate the impossible, whatever remains, no matter how improbable, must be the truth."
—Sherlock Holmes in *The Sign of the Four*

As mentioned earlier in this book, software intellectual property theft is a problem of growing concern. Now that various aspects of software intellectual property have been defined and various mathematical frameworks for comparing software and measuring software IP have been presented, we are ready to examine methods for detecting software IP theft and infringement.

In this part I describe techniques for investigating software to determine whether IP theft or infringement has occurred. I discuss these techniques from the point of view of an independent expert, also known as an expert witness. Such experts are engineers with special expertise in the technologies involved in the case who are hired by the parties to a lawsuit, or sometimes by the court, to uncover the truth regarding the technologies at issue. These experts investigate the software and any other technical issues in the case and reach conclusions based on accepted scientific and engineering principles.

While experts are typically paid by one party in the litigation, they are expected to be unbiased and cannot have a stake in the outcome of the case. For this reason experts cannot be paid on commission or in any other way in which the pay is dependent upon a particular result.

Experts are expected to report the truth, but there are always areas where things can be represented in a manner that is more favorable to the client. This is why both parties hire experts and both experts file "expert reports" with the court to explain their findings. This is also why experts are deposed and testify in court and are cross-examined. The idea is that if both experts perform an analysis and present their results under oath in court, and both experts are rigorously questioned to find the basis for their conclusions and to reveal any biases, then the judge or jury will have all of the information required to make a fair judgment.

There have been times when I have performed an investigation and found the facts to be contrary to what my client claimed. I have been hired by plaintiffs and informed them that I could find no sign of wrongdoing by the defendant. I have been hired by defendants and informed them that someone at their company did in fact misappropriate a trade secret, or infringe a copyright or a patent. This is the ethical requirement of the job. In the cases where I was hired by the plaintiff, the attorneys typically thanked me for the information, paid me, and gave me no further work on the case. At that point the client may have dropped the lawsuit or entered into settlement negotiations, but I was no longer involved in the case. This is entirely appropriate and ethical. In the cases where I was hired by the defendant, the attorneys often used my knowledge to terminate any employees who acted unethically or illegally and to clean the source code in order to limit damages. Again, the client may have entered into settlement negotiations at that time. And again, this is entirely appropriate and ethical.

What is not ethical is for experts to simply echo the position of the client and make unsound statements that support the client's claims. Unfortunately I have seen this behavior on the part of some experts. Usually their statements are easy to disprove by someone who understands the technology and can explain it in simple terms, two cornerstone attributes of any expert witness. Unfortunately, some judges and some juries are fooled by a steady onslaught of the technical jargon at which some experts are adept. However, if an expert is found by a court to be misleading or lying or even using techniques that are not generally accepted by those in the expert's field of expertise, the expert's testimony can be fully excluded, leaving the client unable to rebut any technical arguments. Also, if an expert's testimony has been excluded once from a trial, that person's career as an expert witness is almost certainly over for good.

OBJECTIVES

The objective of this part is to explain methods and tools used by expert witnesses and technical consultants involved in intellectual property litigation for examining software in order to determine whether IP infringement or theft occurred.

INTENDED AUDIENCE

Computer scientists, computer programmers, corporate managers, and *entrepreneurs* will find this part of the book useful for understanding the tools and processes that are used for detecting software intellectual property theft and infringement, which is especially valuable if they are ever involved in protecting software IP or involved in software IP litigation. *Technical consultants and expert witnesses for litigation* will find this part invaluable for practicing their craft, for improving their skills, and for furthering their careers. *Lawyers whose practice is not intellectual property* will find this part important for developing criteria for evaluating and hiring engineering consultants and expert witnesses, for working with these people, for preparing experts for testimony, and for preparing cross-examination of an expert.

DETECTING COPYRIGHT INFRINGEMENT

Now that I have discussed how copyrights pertain to software and have given a mathematical framework for comparing software to find correlation, in this chapter I delve into the practical aspects of finding copyright infringement. We have the definitions and the mathematical tools, but more is needed.

For several years now I have been working as an expert witness in intellectual property disputes, specializing in software copyright infringement and trade secret theft cases. When I began working in this area, I found that most experts used a combination of off-the-shelf computer code analysis programs, homegrown analysis programs, and lots of long hours and late nights poring over thousands of lines of computer code. Some experts also used tools available from academia and billed as "software plagiarism detection tools." Expert reports were then written and rebutted. When code from one program looked similar to code from another program, questions arose about whether the code was actually copied or there were other reasons for the similarities. Arguments often got very technical and detailed and could easily confuse a nontechnical judge or jury. Different experts often had different definitions of plagiarism or found different signs that they considered markers for copied code.[1] It is important to note that code is

---

1. Programmers have had the idea for some time that whitespace patterns—unusual patterns of spaces and tabs—can be used to identify sections of copied code. When two files have matching whitespace patterns but nothing else in common, this is a sign that code was copied and later extensively modified to hide the copying. I am aware of this technique being used in court to assert claims of copyright infringement. At Zeidman Consulting we performed extensive research on this previously untested notion, which we presented at conferences. (Continues)

rarely copied verbatim, but it is often copied and then modified, sometimes to make feature changes and sometimes to hide detection. Some clients—and some experts they hired, I am sad to say—seemed to purposely cloud the issues to justify illicit or at least questionable behavior.

Finding a correlation between the source code files for two different programs does not necessarily mean that illicit behavior occurred. Over the years I have determined that there are exactly six reasons for correlation between two different programs. These reasons are summarized in the next section.

22.1   REASONS FOR CORRELATION

Finding a correlation between different programs does not necessarily imply that illicit behavior occurred. There can be correlation between programs for a number of reasons, as enumerated here:

- Third-party source code
- Code generation tools
- Commonly used elements
- Common algorithms
- Common author
- Copying (plagiarism, copyright infringement)

These reasons for correlation are described in more detail in the following sections.

22.1.1   THIRD-PARTY SOURCE CODE

It is possible that widely available open source code is used in both programs. Open source code is software source code that has been created by programmers around the world and can be used by any person or any company at no charge as long as the appropriate license terms are met. Typically the license terms require that the code contain notification of the author's name. Licenses often put other restrictions on the use of the code that vary by the particular license that the original programmer chose, but typically no fees are required. Open

---

To date, our conclusion is that whitespace patterns, even unusual ones, are very common and cannot, by themselves, be used to determine that copying occurred. Some of our recent research shows that matching whitespace in sequential lines of code may be useful for showing that copying occurred. In all cases, whitespace can be useful for providing further evidence of the extent of copying when other methods are used to initially locate copying.

source code is described in more detail in Chapter 26. If two different programs use the same open source code, the programs will have correlation.

Also, libraries of source code can be purchased from third-party software vendors. Typically a programmer pays a one-time fee or a royalty per use, but either way any customer who makes the appropriate payments has the right to use the code within whatever license restrictions may apply. If two different programs use this same third-party library code, the programs will have correlation.

22.1.2 CODE GENERATION TOOLS

Automatic code generation tools generate software source code using similar or identical identifiers for variables, classes, methods, and properties. Code generation tools often use a template to generate code, and so code generated using these tools will have the structure of the template, with an identifiable pattern. For example, look at the code fragments in Listings 22.1 and 22.2, written in the C++ programming language. They are nearly identical. Both fragments are source code generated automatically by Microsoft Visual Studio when a user creates a standard Windows form. Both files have high correlation.

Listing 22.1   C++ Source Code Fragment 1 Generated by Microsoft Visual Studio

```
#pragma once

namespace Whitespace {

using namespace System;
using namespace System::ComponentModel;
using namespace System::Collections;
using namespace System::Windows::Forms;
using namespace System::Data;
using namespace System::Drawing;
using namespace System::IO;

/// <summary>
/// Summary for MainForm
///
/// WARNING: If you change the name of this class, you will need to
/// change the 'Resource File Name' property for the managed resource
/// compiler tool associated with all .resx files this class depends
```

Continues

Listing 22.1   C++ Source Code Fragment 1 Generated by Microsoft Visual Studio *(Continued)*

```
/// on. Otherwise, the designers will not be able to interact
/// properly with localized resources associated with this form.
/// </summary>
public ref class MainForm : public System::Windows::Forms::Form
{
public:
  MainForm()
{

    InitializeComponent();
    //
    //TODO: Add the constructor code here
    //

}
```

Listing 22.2   C++ Source Code Fragment 2 Generated by Microsoft Visual Studio

```
#pragma once

namespace CodeMeasure {

using namespace System;
using namespace System::ComponentModel;
using namespace System::Collections;
using namespace System::Windows::Forms;
using namespace System::Data;
using namespace System::Drawing;
using namespace System::IO;

/// <summary>
/// Summary for MainForm
///
/// WARNING: If you change the name of this class, you will need to
/// change the 'Resource File Name' property for the managed resource
/// compiler tool associated with all .resx files this class depends
/// on. Otherwise, the designers will not be able to interact
/// properly with localized resources associated with this form.
/// </summary>
public ref class MainForm : public System::Windows::Forms::Form
{
```

```
public:
  MainForm(String^ CMCfilename)
  {
    InitializeComponent();
    //
    //TODO: Add the constructor code here
    //
    this->openConfigFileDialog->FileName = CMCfilename;
  }
```

Thus we see that two different programs that were developed using the same code generation tool have correlation.

22.1.3 COMMONLY USED ELEMENTS

Certain source code elements can be shared by two independently developed programs. Certain identifier names are commonly taught in schools or commonly used by programmers in certain industries. For example, the identifier result is often used to hold the result of an operation, and the identifier count is often used to hold the number of items that have been counted in a loop. It is standard programming practice to use a routine called main or some variation of the word main, such as MainFunction or MainForm, as the name of the routine of a program that is called when a program begins executing and from which all other routines are called to perform the various functions of the program. These identifiers can be found in many unrelated programs but result in correlation between the programs. The statement for (i = 0; i < count; i++) is a very common programming statement for creating a simple counting loop. The string "out of memory" is commonly used, with some variation, to signal to the user that a program has run out of memory and cannot continue. The comment // initialize variables is a common way to note where variables are being set to their initial values in the code.

Programmers in certain industries commonly use particular comments, strings, and statements. For example, the function name CreditCard, not surprisingly, is used in many financial transaction programs.

These types of common identifiers, statements, strings, and comments are found in many unrelated programs but result in these programs having correlation.

22.1.4 COMMONLY USED ALGORITHMS

An algorithm is a procedure or a set of instructions for accomplishing some task. In one programming language there may be an easy or well-understood way of writing a particular algorithm that most programmers use. For example, there might be a way to calculate the square root of a number. Perhaps this algorithm is taught in most programming classes at universities or is found in a popular programming textbook.

Listing 22.3, taken from Chapter 13 of my book *Verilog Designer's Library*, shows a source code listing in the Verilog hardware description language for implementing a linear feedback shift register (LFSR). Verilog is a programming language used to design hardware such as application-specific integrated circuits (ASICs) and field-programmable gate arrays (FPGAs), but for our purposes it is a programming language like any other. LFSRs are used extensively in encryption and decryption circuits. When designed correctly, they create encryption schemes that are very difficult or practically impossible to break. They are difficult to design correctly, and when they are designed incorrectly, they create encryption schemes that are very easy to break. I spent considerable time tracking down a design that worked correctly, expanded it to generate more complex patterns, and used a computer simulation to test that the circuit was indeed correct. It would not surprise me to learn that this code is being used, with various modifications, in many chip designs. This is a fair use of the code in my book; the source code from programs that implement LFSRs using the algorithm described here could correlate highly with my code if the files implement the same algorithm that I used but were not copied from my code.

Listing 22.3 Verilog Source Code for a Linear Feedback Shift Register (LFSR)

```
/**********************************************************/
// MODULE: linear feedback shift register (LFSR)
//
// FILE NAME: lfsr_rtl.v
// VERSION: 1.1
// DATE: January 1, 2003
// AUTHOR: Bob Zeidman, Zeidman Consulting
//
// CODE TYPE: Register Transfer Level
//
// DESCRIPTION: This module defines a linear feedback shift
// register (LFSR) using a single XOR gate.
//
/**********************************************************/
```

```
// DEFINES
`define DEL 1           // Clock-to-output delay. Zero
                        // time delays can be confusing
                        // and sometimes cause problems.

                        // These are good tap values for 2 to 32 bits
`define TAP2   2'b11
`define TAP3   3'b101
`define TAP4   4'b1001
`define TAP5   5'b10010
`define TAP6   6'b100001
`define TAP7   7'b1000001
`define TAP8   8'b10001110
`define TAP9   9'b100001000
`define TAP10 10'b1000000100
`define TAP11 11'b10000000010
`define TAP12 12'b100000101001
`define TAP13 13'b1000000001101
`define TAP14 14'b10000000010101
`define TAP15 15'b100000000000001
`define TAP16 16'b1000000000010110
`define TAP17 17'b10000000000000100
`define TAP18 18'b100000000001000000
`define TAP19 19'b1000000000000010011
`define TAP20 20'b10000000000000000100
`define TAP21 21'b100000000000000000010
`define TAP22 22'b1000000000000000000001
`define TAP23 23'b10000000000000000010000
`define TAP24 24'b100000000000000000001101
`define TAP25 25'b1000000000000000000000100
`define TAP26 26'b10000000000000000000100011
`define TAP27 27'b100000000000000000000010011
`define TAP28 28'b1000000000000000000000000100
`define TAP29 29'b10000000000000000000000000010
`define TAP30 30'b100000000000000000000000101001
`define TAP31 31'b1000000000000000000000000000100
`define TAP32 32'b10000000000000000000000001100010
`define BITS 8         // Number of bits in the LFSR
```

Continues

Listing 22.3   Verilog Source Code for a Linear Feedback Shift Register (LFSR) *(Continued)*

```verilog
`define TAPS `TAP8    // This must be the taps for the
                      // number of bits specified above
`define INIT 1        // This can be any non-zero value
                      // for initialization of the LFSR
// TOP MODULE
module LFSR(
  clk,
  reset,
  data);

// PARAMETERS

// INPUTS
input clk;         // Clock
input reset;       // Reset

// OUTPUTS
output [`BITS-1:0] data;        // LFSR data

// INOUTS

// SIGNAL DECLARATIONS
wire clk;
wire reset;
reg [`BITS-1:0] data;


// ASSIGN STATEMENTS

// MAIN CODE

// Look at the rising edge of clock or reset
always @(posedge clk or posedge reset) begin
  if (reset)
    data <= #`DEL `INIT;
  else begin
    // Shift all of the bits left
    data[`BITS-1:1] <= #`DEL data[`BITS-2:0];
```

```
`ifdef ADD_ZERO          // Use this code if data == 0 is required
                         // Create the new bit 0
    data[0] <= #`DEL ^(data & `TAPS) ^ ~|data[`BITS-2:0];
`else                    // Use this code for a standard LFSR
                         // Create the new bit 0
    data[0] <= #`DEL ^(data & `TAPS);
`endif


  end
end
endmodule              // LFSR
```

Commonly used algorithms show up in many different programs, resulting in a high degree of correlation between the programs even though the programs are different and there was no direct contact between the programmers.

22.1.5 Common Author

It is possible that one programmer or "author" of a program created two programs that have correlation simply because that programmer tends to write code in a certain way. This is the programmer's style of coding. There are many different styles for writing code that are all legitimate. When it comes to strings, different programmers have distinct styles for writing messages to the user. With comments, some programmers write brief comments and others write long, elaborate comments. Some programmers write no comments at all (unfortunately, because this is bad programming practice). Some programmers subscribe to very strict coding standards that prescribe where to put brackets, how to write comments, or how to name variables. For example, CreditApplication, creditApplication, credit_application, and iCreditApplication are all ways to create the same variable but according to different, recognized coding standards.

Thus two programs written by the same programmer can have high correlation because the style is similar, even though there was no copying and the functionality of the programs is different.

22.1.6 Copying (Plagiarism, Copyright Infringement)

If all of the previous reasons for correlation are ruled out, then the only remaining reason for the correlation is that code was copied from one program to another. If the copying was unauthorized or represented as one's own work, then the code was plagiarized. To determine that copyright infringement occurred, however, there are several other requirements. The copied code needs to be creative and it needs to be substantial. Determining whether copied code is substantial or creative requires further analysis, as described in section 22.2.6 below.

22.2 STEPS TO FIND CORRELATION DUE TO COPYING

For someone attempting to find copyright infringement, there is a series of steps to go through to eliminate each of the other five reasons for correlation, as depicted in Figure 22.1. If the other five reasons can be eliminated and there is still correlation, the correlation must be due to copying.

Note that there is no correlation value that by itself indicates that copying occurred. Anyone who asserts otherwise is simply wrong. After the other five reasons for correlation are filtered out, if any correlation remains, no matter how small the value, it is the result of copying. If the copying was unauthorized, then copyright infringement must have occurred.

22.2.1 FILTERING OUT CORRELATION DUE TO THIRD-PARTY CODE

The most accurate way to check for third-party code is to put the matching statements, comments, and strings of the source code of two programs into a general Internet search engine and count the number of times each of them shows up. Any elements that show up frequently are almost certainly not copied but are simply common usages. These elements could be part of third-party

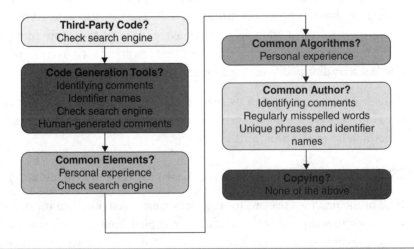

Figure 22.1   Software copyright infringement methodology

code, though they could also be automatically generated or commonly used elements. In any case, they are used often in other programs by other programmers, and the correlation of these elements in the two programs cannot be attributed to copying, at least without other evidence. Any elements that show up nowhere on the Internet, but show up in both programs, are almost certainly due to copying.

It might not be apparent why I suggest checking a general Internet search engine rather than an open source database search engine. There are some sites on the Internet that allow searching of open source code. However, there are many sources of code on the Internet, including code from individual programmers whose code may not be incorporated into any of the databases. Similarly, we are looking not just for open source code, but also for third-party code that may not be available without paying a fee. One of these specialized search engines would not find this commercial code. However, a good general-purpose search engine indexes the specialized databases and also indexes the code of the many small programmers who post their code to only a few sites. Also, while we would not expect to find commercial code anywhere on the Web, we would expect to find user's guides and white papers and discussions on bulletin boards about the code. Only the general-purpose search engine would index this information.

SourceDetective is a function of CodeSuite, the program developed by S.A.F.E. Corporation. SourceDetective reads in a database containing the matching elements from two sets of source code that was generated by the CodeMatch function of CodeSuite. It sends these matching elements to a general-purpose Internet search engine and records in the database how many "hits" were found. The elements with a large or nonzero number of hits can then be filtered out of the database to eliminate correlation due to third-party code.

22.2.2 FILTERING OUT CORRELATION DUE TO AUTOMATICALLY GENERATED CODE

Checking for code that was automatically generated by a code generation tool involves a number of things. Identifier names in code that has been automatically generated often have a noticeable pattern. For example, variable names that are random collections of letters and numbers are more likely to have been automatically generated because programmers use mnemonics for their variable names to remember what they represent. Thus variable names like `count`, `MyIndex2`, and `TempString` are likely to be generated by a programmer, whereas a variable name like `C_ASSERT_H_3803b949_b422_4377_8713_ce606f29d546` is more likely to be automatically generated.

Searching the Internet using a general-purpose search engine can be useful for finding automatically generated code also. Some of the patterns found in automatically generated code will show up in other code samples and in other documentation on the Web, though we would not expect entire code segments to show up unless the particular automatically generated code is available as third-party code. So SourceDetective is a useful tool for helping determine whether correlation is due to automatically generated code.

The comments can also be used to determine whether code was automatically generated. Comments consisting of long explanations, particularly if they mention things like programmers' names, company names, or information specific to the program or to the industry in which the program is being used would imply that the comments were human-generated and thus the code in which the comments are embedded is likely to be human-generated. Spelling and grammar mistakes would indicate that the comments were likely human-generated. Automatically generated code usually, though not always, is free of spelling and grammar mistakes. Often, automatically generated code states that it is automatically generated and may also specify the name of the tool that was used and the company that provides the tool.

Note that if two programs were developed using the same code generation tools, we would expect similarities and correlation due to those similarities. However, we would not expect significant sections of code to be completely matching. If that is the case, it is unlikely that all of the correlation can be explained by the code generation tools, which would tend to generate slightly different code according to the requirements of the project and the settings provided by the programmer. Identical major sections of the automatically generated code would point toward copying.

Identifying automatically generated code requires paying attention to the details of the code, performing research on tools that are available and how they generate code, and looking for clues that are specific to factors such as the nature of the program, the industry in which it is used, the programmers who developed it, and other things that will vary on a case-by-case basis.

22.2.3 FILTERING OUT CORRELATION DUE TO COMMON ELEMENTS

Common elements are those that are commonly used by programmers in general or by programmers in the industry in which the program is being used. Sometimes element names are dictated by standards within an industry or general programming standards, but these standards typically apply only to interfaces with other programs. For example, standards rarely, if ever, dictate the names of variables or functions within a program because these are arbitrary. Standards may dictate the names of functions that are exported from a program so that other programs can use them. This is most common with databases where a standard may state that specific names must be used for the database table names and field names so that the database can be accessed by different programs that need to use the data.

Determining that such elements are common and are correlated simply for this reason can require someone who is very familiar with programming or familiar with programming in the specific industry in which the programs are used. Extensive research may be needed to find various standards documents that spell out such requirements. Of course, submitting the elements to a general-purpose search engine is a very good way of finding that elements are common and then filtering them out of the analysis.

22.2.4 Filtering Out Correlation Due to Common Algorithms

Many algorithms are described in programming textbooks or taught at many schools, and thus we would expect to find correlation for programs containing these algorithms, even if the programs were developed independently. Finding common algorithms can require extensive research and deep knowledge of programming, particular in the relevant industry. Again, a general-purpose search engine can help, though such common algorithms may be difficult to uncover using a search engine.

22.2.5 Filtering Out Correlation Due to Common Author

A single programmer or "author" has a certain style of writing code. If the same person wrote the code for two different programs, without having literally copied any code, there will still be correlation. A single programmer may have a preferred way of formatting the code, such as where to put tabs and spaces or how to align brackets, and may favor certain programming instructions over other equivalent instructions. A single programmer may comment in a particularly unique and identifiable way. A programmer may have favorite variable names or function names that would match in two independently developed programs.

Comments can be particularly telling. Things to look for include phrases that a programmer likes to use. These can be spotted especially if there are consistent spelling mistakes, punctuation errors, or incorrect grammar.

It is important, though, to recognize when a mistake is a sign of copying rather than a common author. One sure sign of this is when a spelling, grammar, or punctuation mistake appears in both programs in similar or identical places in the code, but this same mistake does not appear elsewhere. For example, suppose in one comment in both programs, the word *generate* is spelled "generat" but is spelled correctly in other comments throughout the code. This fact shows that the programmer actually knew how to spell the word, so what are the chances that she would spell it incorrectly only once and in the same comment in functionally similar or identical sections of code? Not very likely at all. In this case the misspelling is not a sign of a common author (though the author is in fact common to both programs) but is a sign that the code was copied.

22.2.6 ANY CORRELATION REMAINING IS DUE TO COPYING

When all of the other reasons for correlation have been eliminated, any correlation that remains must be due to copying.[2] The actual correlation number may be very small but nonetheless indicates copying. Whether that copying constitutes infringement depends upon three issues: whether the copier had the right to copy the code, whether the copying was substantial, and whether the code was creative.

Usually factors including the circumstances of the copying, the functionality of the code that was copied, the difficulty in creating the code from scratch, and the importance of the code to the entire program need to be understood. Often the assistance of a lawyer and sometimes an expert in the particular subject matter at issue is required to determine whether copied code constitutes copyright infringement.

---

2. Occasionally someone claims that there can be reasons for correlation other than the six listed here, and so eliminating the first five reasons does not necessarily mean copying has occurred. However, people are often hard pressed to find a reason that does not fall into one of the other categories. One hypothetical scenario that was described to me is two programmers who work very closely and adopt each other's styles—styles that no other programmers use—then one moves to a new company. The coding style of the programmer who moved correlates highly with that of the ex-colleague whose code the programmer is accused of misappropriating. In my opinion, this very unlikely scenario falls into the category of common author because the two programmers adopted the same style, so the accused programmer is using a style that he shares with the other programmer.

   The other category that I have considered but not included here is that of coincidence. There is a tiny but nonzero chance that two programmers wrote similar code without having had any contact. Realistically, how likely is this possibility? Certainly not likely enough to create reasonable doubt in the case of litigation.

22.2.6.1 The Right to Copy

The copier had the right to copy if the copier owned the copyright to the code, the copying was a fair use of the code, or the copier was given the authority by the owner of the code. These rights were discussed in Chapter 6.

22.2.6.2 Substantial

What constitutes substantial code is often open to argument. Some parties argue that it is the percentage of code that determines whether the copied code is substantial. Usually this is argued most vehemently by parties who have copied code. This argument is not very strong because code can be critical to a particular program's operation but consist of a relatively small percentage of the total lines of code. For example, a critical algorithm in a very large, complex program would be a small percentage of the number of lines of code and yet still be considered to be substantial.

One can argue that nearly all lines of code, with the possible exception of nonfunctional comments, are substantial. Removing any line of code from a program will cause it to execute incorrectly if it executes at all.

22.2.6.2 Creative

Only creative works can be protected by copyright. For example, a listing of positive integers less than 1,000 is not creative—nearly anyone can count and produce such a list—and therefore it cannot be copyrighted. What is considered creative with regard to computer program code is a bit of a gray area. Some would argue that all code is creative because it is difficult to write and even the most mundane operations can cause a program to fail entirely if the code is written incorrectly. Others argue that well-known algorithms that are literally copied are not creative because any minimally skilled programmer could look up the algorithm and write code for it.

22.3 ABSTRACTION FILTRATION COMPARISON TEST

In 1992, the case of *Computer Associates International Inc. v. Altai Inc.* raised important questions about how copyrights protect software. The background of the case is as follows.

22.3.1 BACKGROUND

Computer Associates (CA) had developed a job-scheduling program called CA Scheduler that, in some form, is still in use today. The program runs on large mainframe computers; it sorts, executes, and controls jobs that are given to a computer. Modern operating systems often control the scheduling of various tasks like backup or antivirus scanning, but with little if any input from the user. Some operating systems include simple mechanisms for scheduling jobs; for example, Linux and UNIX include a simple job scheduler called "cron." CA Scheduler was a more sophisticated job scheduler.

CA Scheduler was written to run on IBM System 370 computers that could use any one of three different operating systems: DOS/VSE, MVS, and VM/CMS. Rather than create three different versions of the program, one for each operating system, Computer Associates created a software component called Adapter that translated messages from CA Scheduler for use by whichever operating system was in use on the computer. Adapter allowed one version of CA Scheduler to be developed and maintained yet run on any IBM 370 computer.

Altai was a competitor of Computer Associates and set out to develop its own job scheduler, a program called Zeke that was to run on the MVS operating system. Claude Arney was an employee of Computer Associates who was recruited to Altai by his friend James Williams. Arney left CA and took with him the Adapter source code, using about 30 percent of it to create a program called OSCAR 3.4 that performed the same function as CA's Adapter program.

In 1988, CA discovered that Altai's OSCAR 3.4 program used code from CA's Adapter program and filed a copyright infringement and trade secret misappropriation lawsuit against Altai. In response, Altai rewrote the OSCAR 3.4 program in a clean room environment where the program is developed without any person having access to or knowledge of some other program code, to ensure that copyright infringement does not occur (see Chapter 25 for information about a software clean room). The new program, developed in the clean room, was released as OSCAR 3.5.

In the United States District Court for the Eastern District of New York, the Honorable George C. Pratt, United States Circuit Judge, decided that OSCAR 3.4 constituted copyright infringement of the CA Scheduler program because of the copied code. The district court ruled that the OSCAR 3.5 rewrite, though, did not infringe.

Computer Associates appealed the judgment of noninfringement by Altai's OSCAR 3.5. CA claimed that OSCAR 3.5 did have substantial similarity to Adapter because there was copying of nonliteral elements of the computer software. Copyright of written works such as novels protects not only the literal words of the novel but such nonliteral elements as plot, plot devices, and characters. An earlier case of *Whelan v. Jaslow* had determined that nonliteral elements of a program are protectable. Despite the clean room rewrite, according to CA, there was still substantial similarity in the flowcharts, intermodular relationships, parameter lists, macros, and services obtained from the operating system.

Judge John Walker of the United States Court of Appeals for the Second Circuit agreed with Computer Associates that nonliteral elements of the code of CA's Adapter program had been infringed by Altai's OSCAR 3.5 program. The court created a test to determine whether there was "substantial similarity" between the nonliteral elements of the two programs, a requirement for finding copyright infringement. The test is called the "abstraction-filtration-comparison test."

The abstraction-filtration-comparison test has three parts. The first part of the test involves "abstracting" the source code into a representation of a higher level of functionality than just the individual lines of code. The second part of the test involves filtering out protectable elements of the code from unprotectable elements. Such unprotectable elements include those required by efficiency (e.g., known optimization techniques), elements required by external factors (e.g., interfacing with an operating system), and elements taken from the public domain (e.g., open source functions). In the third step a comparison is performed between the high-level functional representations that remain after filtering. If there is similarity between these abstract, filtered functions, copyright infringement is determined to have occurred even though none of the source code statements may match between the two programs.

22.3.2 HOW CODESUITE IMPLEMENTS THE TEST

The CodeSuite program from S.A.F.E. Corporation is able to perform the abstraction-filtration-comparison test for nonliteral elements while it also compares literal elements of the programs.

22.3.2.1 Abstraction

CodeSuite performs abstraction by extracting instruction sequences from the source code. This extraction effectively abstracts a higher level of functionality from the code. Instruction sequences consider the sequences of instructions, but not the exact data that is being operated upon. Also, instruction sequences consider only the basic functionality of the instruction. For example, the following statement within a sequence

```
if (x > y)
```

is considered a match to the following statement within a sequence

```
if (sqrt(abc) + len(xyx) == 3.1415926)
```

because both use the same instruction (`if`) even though the details of the instructions are significantly different.

22.3.2.2 Filtration

CodeSuite has built-in filtering functionality that allows the user to filter out those source code elements that are not protectable. Also, the SourceDetective function of CodeSuite allows automatic filtering of any elements that are found on the Internet and thus are most likely not protectable because of their common usage.

22.3.2.3 Comparison

The main function of CodeSuite is comparing the source code of two programs. This comparison includes comparing instruction sequences.

22.3.3 PROBLEMS WITH THE TEST

It is important to note that many people have pointed out problems with the abstraction-filtration-comparison test. The main problem resides in the concept upon which the test is founded—that an idea, which is not protected by copyright law, can be separated from its expression, which is protected by copyright law. In the case of *Nichols v. Universal Pictures Corp.* about copyright infringement of the play of *Abie's Irish Rose*, Judge Learned Hand wrote an opinion in which he stated that ideas are not protected by copyright law but the expression of ideas is protected. However, he famously said that "nobody has ever been able to fix that boundary, and nobody ever can."

22.3.3.1 Abstraction Level

The abstraction process is an attempt to separate these two things within the embodiment of software source code. However, consider Figure 22.2, which shows a block diagram of roughly 20 percent of the main functionality of the CodeSuite program itself. This main functionality is the computation engine that performs all of the source code file analyses, including dividing files into their constituent elements, comparing the elements, and calculating the correlation. Only 20 percent is shown because the entire diagram would not fit on a

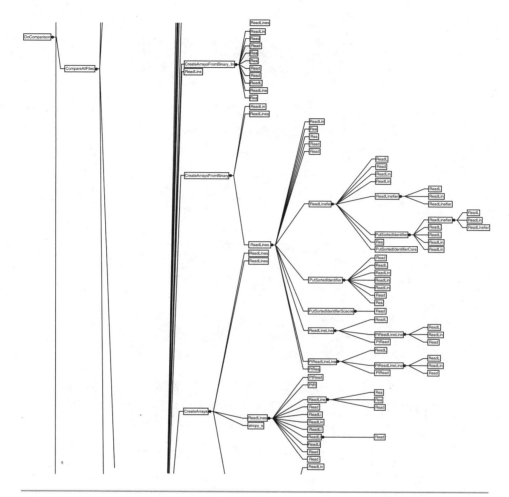

Figure 22.2   Block diagram of about 20 percent of the CodeSuite computation engine

page; even at this scale it is barely legible. This main functionality does not include any parts of the user interface implementation.

Now look at Figure 22.3, which shows a much higher-level abstracted block diagram. This is the block diagram of the CodeMatch function of CodeSuite from U.S. Patent 10/720,636, which also represents roughly this same 20 percent of the CodeSuite functionality.

The second diagram was used to represent not the expression of the CodeSuite program but the underlying invention. At what point does an abstraction become so high-level that it no longer represents an expression but rather represents an invention, which is covered under patent law or trade secret law rather than copyright law?

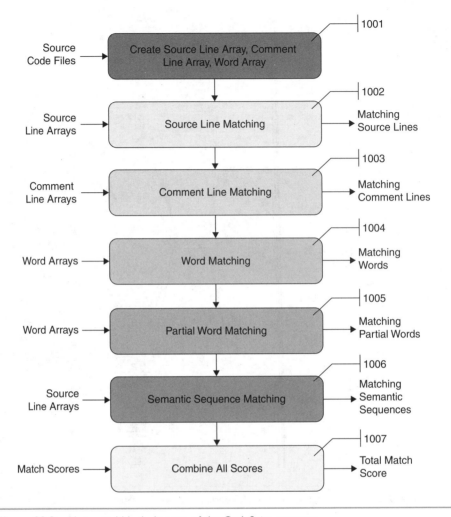

Figure 22.3 Abstracted block diagram of the CodeSuite program

Now consider Figure 22.4, a very high-level block diagram of the CodeSuite program. This diagram represents the program at such a high level that a huge number of computer programs can be boiled down to this exact functionality. An abstraction at this level is worthless for determining copyright infringement (though I must say I have been involved in cases where experts have attempted to "prove" copyright infringement by using abstractions nearly this extreme).

In fact, in the case of *Computer Associates v. Altai*, Judge Walker gives a warning about this when he quotes in his opinion from Steven R. Englund, *Idea, Process, or Protected Expression? Determining the Scope of Copyright Protection of the Structure of Computer Programs*:

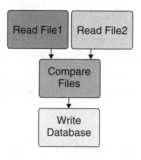

Figure 22.4   Very high-level block diagram of the CodeSuite program

At the lowest level of abstraction, a computer program may be thought of in its entirety as a set of individual instructions organized into a hierarchy of modules. As a higher level of abstraction, the instructions in the lowest-level modules may be replaced conceptually by the functions of those modules. At progressively higher levels of abstraction, the functions of higher level modules conceptually replace the implantation of those modules … until finally one is left with nothing but the ultimate function of the program. … A program has structure at every level of abstraction at which it is viewed. At low levels of abstraction, a program's structure may be quite complex; at the highest level it is trivial.

22.3.3.2 Software Architecture

Attorneys and expert witnesses have sometimes attempted to represent a computer program in terms of its "software architecture" to perform this abstraction. The idea is that such an architectural representation is a standard way of abstracting software, and thus it would be a more acceptable way of creating the abstract representation. In reality, though "software architecture" is a common term used by programmers and computer scientists to describe the high-level operation of a computer program, there is no accepted standard for determining a program's architecture. Architecture may refer to the low-level diagram of Figure 22.2 or the high-level diagram of Figure 22.4 or anything in between. It may refer to a use case document for describing the software using diagrams and text. It may refer to something like a specification that cannot be directly mapped to the expression of the source code itself and is thus not covered by copyright law.

When a plaintiff hires me to opine on a software copyright case based on software architecture, I first suggest that a detailed source code correlation analysis be performed. Sometimes plaintiffs are surprised to find that actual lines of code have been copied, which makes the case much easier to present and prove. If no lines of copied code can be found, then I can move on to examining software architecture, keeping in mind the difficulty of proving such a case. When a defendant hires me for a software copyright case and tells me that the plaintiff is claiming infringement of software architecture, I usually reassure the client because this is a difficult case to win.

22.4 COPYRIGHT INFRINGEMENT CHECKLIST

At Zeidman Consulting we have developed a checklist of steps to test for copyright infringement that I include here. These steps rely on the use of CodeMatch from S.A.F.E. Corporation as well as manual inspection.

1. Unzip all files to be examined to make sure that there are no compressed directories or files that would otherwise escape analysis.

2. When examining binary files, check for and run any installers so that their output executables can be examined directly.

3. Search the entire directory tree and note all file types, looking for all source code files.

4. Perform global searches of the directories with a tool that can examine text and binary files to

    a. Check for the string "Copyright" in all of the files

    b. Check the files for the names of all companies involved in the litigation

    c. Check the files for the names of programmers at all companies involved in the litigation

    d. Check the files for any technical or business terms that may directly relate to the technology or industry at issue in the case

5. Check for any third-party files among the code being examined. If it can be determined that third-party code exists, it may be possible to eliminate these files from the analysis to save time and money. Be careful, though, because the copying of modified third-party code may represent copyright infringement.

6. Set up CodeSuite and report the indicated cost to the client, for approval, before running the analysis.

7. Run CodeSuite with a high file threshold of at least 64 files to compensate for future filtering.

8. Export the CodeSuite database to an HTML report; browse the report and create a filter to filter out any obvious source code elements, files, and folders that are not of interest.

9. Examine the file pairs with the highest scores to make an initial determination of whether copying occurred.

10. Run SourceDetective on the CodeSuite database to identify commonly used identifiers, statements, and comments. Use the CodeSuite filter to filter out those commonly used elements.

    a. Produce the search spreadsheets that show the frequency of Internet hits for each element once SourceDetective is complete to determine an appropriate hit level to filter.

    b. Filter the high hit count matches out of the database.

    c. If some of the elements with low hit counts seem unimportant and should be filtered out, copy and paste the individual matches that should be filtered from the search spreadsheet into a filter file and filter the database again.

    d. If some of the elements with high hit counts seem important, then filtering may have to be done by cutting and pasting elements into a filter rather than filtering according to hit value.

11. Continue filtering the results, eliminating elements that correlate because of third-party source code, code generation tools, commonly used elements, commonly used algorithms, and common author.

12. Examine the code around every remaining matching element after filtering to get an idea of the functionality of the code.

13. Report preliminary findings to the client, especially the identifiers, statements, and comments with zero Web matches that strongly indicate that copying occurred. Manually confirm the matching elements in the files before reporting to the client.

14. Ask the client if there are certain elements (e.g., screen shots, identifier lists, etc.) in which they may be interested at this point, or to keep in mind for an expert report in the future.

15. For each file in a folder of files being compared, examine the detailed report for the file that has the highest correlation with that file. Remember that relative correlation scores are more important than absolute correlation scores.

16. Examine all detailed reports for file pairs with correlation scores over a certain threshold. The threshold will vary depending on the resulting correlation scores after filtering. Remember that relative correlation scores are more important than absolute correlation scores.

17. Compile a list of file pairs that require further examination. Report the findings to clients and work with them to determine what the next steps should be

and what format they would like for the final report. Suggestions include the following:

a. Compile side-by-side screen shots of interesting code snippets.

b. Create lists of interesting identifiers, statements, and comments.

c. Create lists of interesting files.

18. Manually recheck the lines of interest inside the actual files before submitting a final report to the client.

DETECTING PATENT INFRINGEMENT

23

In this chapter I discuss techniques for detecting whether a program infringes on a patent. Unlike the detection of copyright infringement, the detection of patent infringement has few hard-and-fast rules. Patents can cover broad technologies and categories of software, or they can cover a small individual function within a program. In this chapter I share my experience and the general process that we have at my consulting company, Zeidman Consulting, for going about this work.

23.1 INTERPRETING THE CLAIMS

Initially the most important part of determining whether a product infringes on a patent is to determine what the patent means. This may sound easy but it is not, and companies spend lots of dollars on lawyers to argue about what a particular patent means.

This first phase of a patent litigation is called "claim construction." The claims make up the essence of a patent. The rest of the patent is basically used as a reference for interpreting the claims. Consider, for example, the famous "Head patents" (U.S. 4,884,674 and U.S. 5,216,613) held by Texas Instruments (so called because the inventor was Claude Head). These patents are very important to Texas Instruments and probably strike fear in the hearts of every other semiconductor company. That is because TI owns the patents for dynamic random access memories (DRAMs), perhaps the most common device used in every personal computer and manufactured by most if not all semiconductor companies. Semiconductor companies pay TI an annual license fee for the right to manufacture DRAMs. These licenses are negotiated every ten years, and every ten years, some of the licensees attempt to avoid another decade of payments. That is when TI pulls out its Head patents. Claim 1 of U.S. 4,884,674 reads as follows:

> 1.   A method for transferring a workpiece within an asynchronously operating assembly line provided with at least first and second work stations comprising the steps of:
>
> (a) indicating at said first work station that said workpiece is ready for transfer from said first work station to said second work station;
>
> (b) indicating when said work station is prepared to receive said workpiece;
>
> (c) assuring said workpiece exits from said first work station responsive to said indications in steps (a) and (b);
>
> (d) preparing said first work station to receive another workpiece after assuring said workpiece exits from said first work station; and
>
> (e) repeating steps (a) through (d).

These patents cover almost every conceivable wafer-handling machine in existence. The diagram in Figure 23.1 is from this patent and shows an assembly line of wafers being processed. I was fortunate enough to get a start on my litigation consulting career when I was asked to join the engineering team for Texas Instruments, assembled from around the world, to work on the case for TI against Samsung. During that time I examined several wafer-handling machines, and there was only one machine, as I recall, that did not infringe.[1]

However, whether infringement of a claim has occurred depends on the meaning of the claim. Look at claim 1(d) and note that it states "after assuring said workpiece exits from said first work station." What does it mean for a workpiece (i.e., the semiconductor wafer) to exit from the work station? Does it mean the wafer must have physically been fully removed from the work station?

---

1. Although the wafer-handling machines were manufactured by other companies, the method claims for these patents are infringed if the method is used. Thus the semiconductor companies that used the wafer-handling machines to process semiconductor wafers were infringing on the method. A patent holder can sue only one company for one act of infringement—the company performing the method or the company inducing the method. And while the wafer-handling machine manufacturers could have been sued, their revenues were "only" in the hundreds of millions of dollars, whereas the semiconductor manufacturers had revenues in the billions.

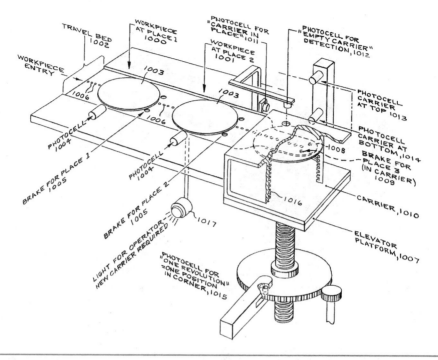

Figure 23.1 Head patent 4,884,674, Figure 10

Does it mean that less than 50 percent of it is still within the physical boundaries of the work station? What defines the boundary of the work station? Can exiting be construed to mean that it is being prepared for exit even though it has not physically begun to exit? The claims refer to "indicating" something happening. Was an electrical signal an "indication"? Could a software event be an "indication"?

One of the machines that we examined looked more like the one in Figure 23.2, consisting of a robot arm with two "hands," one above the other, each of which moves around the wafer. In this particular machine, one used extensively by many semiconductor manufacturers including Samsung (and Texas Instruments), the indicators occur before and after the wafer rests in the middle of the machine but outside any processing area such as a spinner or oven. Could a robot hand be considered a "work station" even though no processing work is being performed? Could a location in space be considered a "work station"?

I have raised a lot of questions with no answers. Before a patent litigation can proceed, a Markman hearing is required to answer these kinds of questions.

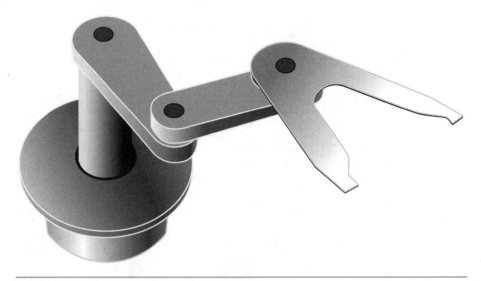

Figure 23.2 A robot arm for a wafer-handling machine

MY FIRST PATENT CASE

In early 1996 I approached Professor Mike Flynn of Stanford University about investing in my remote backup start-up. He wasn't interested, but he told me he needed a consultant to do research on a trade secret case in which he was the testifying expert. When I heard what I was going to be paid, I quickly agreed.

Shortly after that case ended, I was asked to join the team of experts working for Texas Instruments in the Head patents case against Samsung. I had just closed down my remote backup company for lack of customers (always a good reason to close a company) and the draining of my bank account (another good reason) and was happy to accept. I did not know at the time that my career path would change for good.

My first week on the case I was sent to Lubbock, Texas, to examine a wafer-handling machine at a small wafer fabrication facility ("fab") owned by TI. The attorneys for TI had discovered that Samsung used the same equipment in its own fab, so it was more effective to examine the equipment at TI's fab where we could, in theory, get unrestricted access to it. In reality, the engineers who ran the equipment had good reason to resent our use of it. First, TI ran many wafers through the fab, and any interruption meant a loss of revenue. I was told that bringing down the machines for an hour resulted in about a $50,000 loss. Also, the engineers running the equipment were judged on the amount of uptime, so we were potentially reducing their own income. And, of course, good engineers feel an affinity for the equipment they maintain and don't like other people poking around. And we were performing some pretty obtrusive tests such as removing hard drives to copy the software and removing circuit boards and soldering wires to examine specific signals. One little-known fact is that one of the engineers, while examining a circuit board, actually blew out an integrated circuit on it. This engineer had amazing intuition in addition to great engineering skills. After examining the circuit schematics, which were labeled in Japanese, and he knew no Japanese, he decided that the chip was a standard TTL logic gate and rushed to Radio Shack to buy a replacement. To my amazement, he plugged in the 25-cent chip and the multimillion-dollar wafer handler came back to life before anyone knew there was a problem.

Texas Instruments flew an impressive team of engineers from around the world into Dallas for about three months. We worked 80 to 100 hours a week, shuttling between TI fabs and our hotel rooms, with few breaks and little time off. It was exciting and exhilarating because we were under tremendous time pressure to reverse engineer complex hardware and software and determine whether it operated in a way that infringed TI's Head patents (it did). I found myself working with the smartest and hardest-working engineers I had met in my career. The lawyers were also very sharp. Most had undergraduate engineering degrees and were much better engineers than I would have expected. We were given a virtually unlimited budget to order test equipment. Someone added up the money spent on equipment, engineering consultants, lawyers, and other expenses and estimated that TI was spending millions of dollars a month. We worried about justifying that expense.

One day, as several of us were suiting up in head-to-toe protective outfits ("bunny suits") to enter the TI fab, exhausted from working late into the previous night, we got a phone call from the lawyers telling us that it was over. Samsung and Texas Instruments had settled. Samsung had agreed to pay TI over $1 billion over a ten-year period. Suddenly our consulting rates seemed insignificant and we realized our work had been worthwhile. We also realized that we had never before been directly and personally responsible for so much money changing hands.

23.1.1 MARKMAN HEARING

In 1996, the U.S. Supreme Court in the case of *Markman v. Westview Instruments, Inc.* decided that the courts should interpret the claims of the patent. Prior to this decision, a jury typically interpreted the claims based on the testimony of an expert witness. Whereas the claims were previously determined during the proceedings of the patent infringement trial, there is now an initial trial, known as a "Markman hearing," in which attorneys argue about the meaning of the claims and a judge makes the determination.

Another landmark case about patent claims was *Phillips v. AWH Corporation*. There have been hundreds of court decisions regarding how to interpret patent claims, and it would not surprise me to find out there are hundreds more, even possibly changing the guidelines for interpretation significantly. However, for now, the hierarchy determined in *Phillips v. AWH Corporation* is the one that stands; it considers both intrinsic evidence (interpretations of terms used in the claims as referenced in the patent documents themselves) and extrinsic evidence (interpretations of terms by using common definitions). We can categorize this hierarchy as follows:

- Intrinsic evidence
- Patent
- Prosecution history
- Foreign and related patents and their prosecution histories
- Prior art that is cited or incorporated by reference in the patent and prosecution history
- Extrinsic evidence
- Inventor testimony
- Expert testimony
- Other documentary evidence
- Dictionaries
- Treatises

This hierarchy is intended as a guideline, not hard-and-fast rules. According to this, intrinsic evidence is generally given more weight. In other words, an inventor can define a term to be something other than what it normally means as long as the term is used consistently. For example, an inventor can state that an "automobile" has two wheels and is pedaled by a rider. Throughout the patent claims, then, the term "automobile" would mean what is commonly referred to as a bicycle.

Intrinsic evidence consists not only of definitions in the patent itself, but also of definitions used in communications with the patent examiner before the patent is issued. These communications are referred to as the "prosecution history."

Similarly, definitions can be used from related patents and prior art that is cited or simply mentioned in the patent or prosecution history.

Extrinsic evidence typically carries less weight than intrinsic evidence. This makes sense because there is no requirement that the inventor be a competent communicator, or that the inventor communicate ideas to experts in the field, but only that the communications are consistent. Extrinsic evidence includes testimony by the expert about what the inventor meant. Courts have noted, though, that an inventor may not be the best interpreter of the patent mainly because she has such in-depth knowledge of the invention that she may not be able to generalize it or explain it well to an audience of laypeople.

Extrinsic evidence also includes the testimony, oral or written, of experts as well as other evidence such as dictionaries or articles, papers, or books.

23.1.2 THE ROLE OF EXPERTS AT A MARKMAN HEARING

Typically, a Markman hearing is held without experts; attorneys from both parties argue the claim construction in front of a judge. Both sides want a claim construction that helps their case. The plaintiff want claims to be construed such that they are not so broad that the other side will find prior art that invalidates the patent (that is, showing that the invention already existed and the patent should not have been granted in the first place). The plaintiff also wants claims to be construed such that it is easy to show that the defendant's product infringes. The defendant wants claims that are so broad that the patent can be shown to be invalid or are construed such that their product does not infringe.

I have attended only a few Markman hearings and have not yet testified at one. I think that not having expert testimony at these hearings is a huge mistake on the part of most judges who are not engineers and cannot understand the intricacies of technical patents. Once the patent claims are construed, the experts must work within those constraints, which sometimes seem unworkable.

Though it is difficult to change the mind of a judge, with whom I have little contact during litigation, I try to convince the attorneys to work with me on claim construction so that the claims make sense to me and do not conflict with prior art of which I am aware. Sometimes the attorneys bring an expert into a patent case after the Markman hearing, and I believe this is a strategic mistake. While this saves initial costs, it also puts limitations on the analysis done by the technical consultants that make their job harder or even impossible. Thus in the long run it can raise costs and can result in an argument from the retaining party that is difficult for an expert to support.

23.2 EXAMINING THE SOFTWARE

As I said earlier, patents can cover very broad technologies and categories of software, or they can cover a small individual function within a program. Because of this, investigating software for patent infringement is a difficult task and there is no set procedure for doing it. There are some general techniques that I have found to work, in particular

- Searching for comments
- Searching for identifier names
- Reviewing from a high level
- Instrumenting running software

Each of these techniques is described in a subsequent section. All of these techniques alone or in combination are useful for finding infringing code.

23.2.1 SEARCHING FOR COMMENTS

Searching for comments within source code is a really good starting point for finding patent infringement. Well-written code includes comments that describe the functionality of the code. Ironically, while managers want well-written code extensively commented because it makes debugging and maintenance of the program much easier, such well-commented code makes it easier to find and demonstrate patent infringement when that software is examined. So poorly written code, devoid of comments, can often hide patent infringement and help shield a company from a patent infringement lawsuit.

Of course, comments by themselves represent only circumstantial evidence, and it is not possible to use comments alone to show patent infringement. The comments lead an expert to sections of code that, judging by the descriptions in the comments, may infringe on a patent. The comments may constitute a lengthy description of the behavior of the software, or there may simply be one or two lines that hint at a method or apparatus in a claim of the patent at issue. Once the comment clues are discovered, it is necessary to understand the functionality of the code.

Remember that comments can be completely wrong. It may be that the programmer's comments represent functionality that existed in the program at one time but were later modified. It is not uncommon for programmers to update code and neglect to update the comments.

23.2.2 Searching for Identifier Names

Identifier names can also be good clues to patent infringement. Relying solely on identifier names is probably not a good argument to show patent infringement. However, they are slightly better than comments in that identifiers represent real functionality, and their names are more likely to represent the actual function being performed.

Still, a significantly better argument is made when the functional code is located that infringes on the patent. Identifiers that have descriptive names can help locate the infringing code.

23.2.3 Reviewing from a High Level

There are software tools that can be used to look at software from a high-level perspective. Diagrams can be created that show high-level, basic functionality or fine-grained, low-level functionality. Which level is more important depends on the breadth or narrowness of the patent claims, though in my experience it takes a view of many different levels of abstraction to get a good enough understanding of the software's functionality to comprehend whether the software infringes on the patent at issue and, if so, where the infringement is located.

23.2.4 Instrumenting Running Software

It is usually a good idea, though not a requirement, that the software at least be examined while running to determine that it does indeed infringe. Screen shots can make good trial illustrations to show the abstract concepts embodied by the software and by the patent claims.

Strong claims of patent infringement can be made by instrumenting the software while it is running and demonstrating the functionality of the patent by associating specific lines of code with specific actions by the software. By "instrumenting" the software I mean attaching equipment to the computer or other hardware that the software is controlling and observing effects. It may also involve inserting code that triggers the instrumentation, such as print statements that display on a monitor or on a printer, or code that writes to memory so that a logic analyzer can trigger on the memory access. At a simple level, instrumenting can mean observing what is happening on the computer screen. This can be useful, but the vast majority of computer functions have to do with calculations or low-level hardware control, which are not visible on a screen, so instrumenting these functions can mean attaching an oscilloscope or logic analyzer to observe and record changing voltage levels and sequences of electronic signals at various points in hardware.

There are a couple of caveats about doing this, though. First, it is nearly impossible to instrument code without first getting at least a basic understanding of the source code. Software is generally so complex that attempting to figure out what it is doing while it is running is akin to understanding the principles of a combustion engine by driving a car. I can assure you that the vast majority of automobile drivers do not understand how their engines work, despite years of driving experience.

The second caveat is that instrumenting code can be a very time-consuming task requiring expensive equipment. In the Texas Instruments case against Samsung, a team of about ten experts worked on instrumenting equipment for about 80 hours a week for two months straight, burning up I would estimate about $1.5 million. We also rented or purchased about $50,000 worth of equipment. On a follow-up case in which TI asserted the Head patents against Hyundai, I transferred software from a wafer handler to a PC and created a virtual wafer-handling machine in my house. I could run various jobs and convince the PC that it was controlling a wafer handler by sending back packets that I had reverse engineered to understand that they meant things like "wafer has entered the oven" and "wafer is ready to be taken out of the spinner." This effort took nine months to get to the point where I could understand only the small portion of code that was relevant to the patent. Another expert then took over the work to further reverse engineer the binary object code to obtain source code.

23.3 TOOLS

There are a number of tools that can be useful for finding patent infringement. In particular, many static analysis tools (tools that analyze software code without the need to execute the code) can be used to help find patent infringement because the key task is to understand the functionality of the code in question. Some of the tools that I have come across for this purpose and that I can recommend are described in the following sections.

23.3.1 UNDERSTAND

Understand is a tool from Scientific Toolworks that be downloaded for a free trial from the company's website at www.scitools.com. Understand is a reverse-engineering tool for source code. It offers code navigation using a detailed cross-reference, a syntax-colorizing "smart" editor, and a variety of graphical reverse-engineering views. Understand is an interactive development environment designed to help maintain and understand large amounts of legacy or newly created source code. Its usefulness for detecting patent infringement is that it can show relationships, graphically and textually, between various functions, routines, objects, and other programming data and control structures. When Understand is run on an unknown body of source code, details of the code's functionality become apparent, though it can require a significant amount of human intervention to understand the code well enough to pinpoint patent infringement.

Understand can parse very large projects in a very short time. Very little is needed to get started—you just point it to the top of your source tree. For more parsing accuracy you can add any externally defined macro definitions and include paths. All of this is done from the Understand GUI, allowing users to do an initial analysis of their project in minutes.

Understand documents class inheritance hierarchies (base class and derived classes), call and call by trees, include and include by trees, as well as where and how everything in the source code is used in an automatically generated cross-reference. This tool creates detailed automatic documentation about the source code in HTML and text reports. Using the PERL and C API, you can write your own documentation generators.

23.3.2 KLOCWORK INSIGHT

Klocwork is provided by Klocwork Inc. A free trial version can be downloaded from the URL www.klocwork.com/freetrial, and your software can be uploaded to the Klocwork website for a free code evaluation.

Klocwork Insight allows individual developers and development organizations to apply static analysis to their application source code, to reverse engineer the application's real architecture. Klocwork combines its breadth of analysis features with reporting and management capabilities, including architectural analysis and optimization, metrics and trending tools, and Web-based defect management and reporting capabilities—all designed to support large and complex software development teams.

23.3.3 DMS SOFTWARE REENGINEERING TOOLKIT

The DMS Software Reengineering Toolkit (SRT) is a set of tools from Semantic Designs. Although there is no free trial version or temporary license, Semantic

Designs offers a 60-day money-back guarantee. The company website is at the URL www.semdesigns.com.

The DMS Software Reengineering Toolkit is used for automating customized source program analysis, modification or translation, or generation of software systems containing arbitrary mixtures of languages ("domains"). The term "software" for DMS is broad and covers any formal notation, including programming languages, markup languages, hardware description languages, design notations, and data descriptions. The DMS technology supports deep semantic analysis and understanding of software. It is fundamentally a tool-building technology, engineered to support arbitrary programming languages and designed for scale, so that very large software systems can be effectively handled.

23.3.4 STRUCTURE101

Structure101 is a tool from Headway Software and can be downloaded from the URL www.headwaysoftware.com/downloads/structure101. You can request a trial license key from the company. With regard to patent infringement discovery, Structure101 is specifically useful for reverse engineering, architecture specification, and visualization. Architecture requirements and deviations can be accessed. Structure101 currently provides support for the Java, C, and C++ programming languages.

23.4 DETERMINING PATENT VALIDITY

This chapter is devoted to detecting patent infringement. Obviously, an expert working for the defendant in a patent litigation wants to show noninfringement, meaning demonstrating that the functionality of a program does not infringe a patent. Typically, this argument is done in rebuttal to an argument by the plaintiff that the product does infringe. It is difficult to prove a negative. However, in some cases it is useful for a defendant to make an active effort to show that a product does not infringe, and the analysis would be similar, and use the same tools, as the analysis showing patent infringement.

The defendant is typically more active in trying to prove invalidity. To prove invalidity, it is required to show either that the patent is non-enabling (that is, the patent does not describe to someone "of ordinary skill in the art" how to make or use the invention) or that the invention existed prior to the filing of the patent. There is a bit of an obstacle to overcome for the defendant because the U.S. Patent and Trademark Office, in granting the patent, has determined that the patent is valid. Therefore, the defendant must refute a presumption of validity. Again, the same kinds of tools described previously can be used, but in much different ways. Often these tools are used to examine prior art to show that some previously known invention "anticipated" the invention in question by performing the same function or including the same mechanism as the invention before the filing of the patent.

Invalidity is typically shown by proof based on Sections 102, 103, and/or 112 of the *Manual of Patent Examining Procedure* (MPEP) issued by the U.S. Patent and Trademark Office.

23.4.1 INVALIDITY BASED ON MPEP 35 U.S.C. § 102

MPEP 35 U.S.C. § 102 is entitled "Conditions for Patentability; Novelty and Loss of Right to Patent" and describes conditions for an invention to be patented:

A person shall be entitled to a patent unless—

(a) the invention was known or used by others in this country, or patented or described in a printed publication in this or a foreign country, before the invention thereof by the applicant for patent, or

(b) the invention was patented or described in a printed publication in this or a foreign country or in public use or on sale in this country, more than one year prior to the date of the application for patent in the United States, or

(c) he has abandoned the invention, or

(d) the invention was first patented or caused to be patented, or was the subject of an inventor's certificate, by the applicant or his legal representatives or assigns in a foreign country prior to the date of the application for patent in this country on an application for patent or inventor's certificate filed more than twelve months before the filing of the application in the United States, or

(e) the invention was described in - (1) an application for patent, published under section 122(b), by another filed in the United States before the invention by the applicant for patent or (2) a patent granted on an application for patent by another filed in the United States before the invention by the applicant for patent, except that an international application filed under the treaty defined in section 351(a) shall have the effects for the purposes of this subsection of an application filed in the United States only if the international application designated the United States and was published under Article 21(2) of such treaty in the English language; or (**f**)   he did not himself invent the subject matter sought to be patented, or

(**g**)(**1**) during the course of an interference conducted under section 135 or section 291, another inventor involved therein establishes, to the extent permitted in section 104, that before such person's invention thereof the invention was made by such other inventor and not abandoned, suppressed, or concealed, or (2) before such person's invention thereof, the invention was made in this country by another inventor who had not abandoned, suppressed, or concealed it. In determining priority of invention under this subsection, there shall be considered not only the respective dates of conception and reduction to practice of the invention, but also the reasonable diligence of one who was first to conceive and last to reduce to practice, from a time prior to conception by the other.

Any patent found to be in violation of these conditions is invalid. The major invalidity defenses derived from Section 102 are anticipation, on sale, and public use.

- **Anticipation**. A patent claim is considered anticipated if every limitation of the claim is found either expressly or inherently in a single prior art reference. Also, the prior art reference must enable one of ordinary skill in the art to make and use the claimed invention.

- **Public use or on sale**. A patent claim is invalid if the claimed invention was publicly used or offered for sale more than one year before the filing date of the application. It must be shown that the device fully anticipated the claimed invention or would have rendered it obvious to one of ordinary skill in the art.

23.4.2 INVALIDITY BASED ON MPEP 35 U.S.C. § 103

MPEP 35 U.S.C. § 103 is entitled "Conditions for Patentability; Non-Obvious Subject Matter" and states:

(**a**) A patent may not be obtained though the invention is not identically disclosed or described as set forth in section 102 of this title, if the differences between the subject matter sought to be patented and the prior art are such that the subject matter as a whole would have been obvious at the time the invention was made to a person having ordinary skill in the art to which said subject matter pertains. Patentability shall not be negatived by the manner in which the invention was made.

(b)

(1) Notwithstanding subsection (a), and upon timely election by the applicant for patent to proceed under this subsection, a biotechnological process using or resulting in a composition of matter that is novel under section 102 and nonobvious under subsection (a) of this section shall be considered nonobvious if-

    (A) claims to the process and the composition of matter are contained in either the same application for patent or in separate applications having the same effective filing date; and

    (B) the composition of matter, and the process at the time it was invented, were owned by the same person or subject to an obligation of assignment to the same person.

(2) A patent issued on a process under paragraph (1)-

    (A) shall also contain the claims to the composition of matter used in or made by that process, or

    (B) shall, if such composition of matter is claimed in another patent, be set to expire on the same date as such other patent, notwithstanding section 154.

(3) For purposes of paragraph (1), the term "biotechnological process" means-

    (A) a process of genetically altering or otherwise inducing a single- or multi-celled organism to-

        (i) express an exogenous nucleotide sequence,

        (ii) inhibit, eliminate, augment, or alter expression of an endogenous nucleotide sequence, or

        (iii) express a specific physiological characteristic not naturally associated with said organism;

    (B) cell fusion procedures yielding a cell line that expresses a specific protein, such as a monoclonal antibody; and

    (C) a method of using a product produced by a process defined by sub-paragraph (A) or (B), or a combination of subparagraphs (A) and (B).

(c)

(1) Subject matter developed by another person, which qualifies as prior art only under one or more of subsections (e), (f), and (g) of section 102 of this title, shall not preclude patentability under this section where the subject matter and the claimed invention were, at the time the claimed invention was made, owned by the same person or subject to an obligation of assignment to the same person.

(2) For purposes of this subsection, subject matter developed by another person and a claimed invention shall be deemed to have been owned by the same person or subject to an obligation of assignment to the same person if -

(A) the claimed invention was made by or on behalf of parties to a joint research agreement that was in effect on or before the date the claimed invention was made;

(B) the claimed invention was made as a result of activities undertaken within the scope of the joint research agreement; and

(C) the application for patent for the claimed invention discloses or is amended to disclose the names of the parties to the joint research agreement.

(3) For purposes of paragraph (2), the term "joint research agreement" means a written contract, grant, or cooperative agreement entered into by two or more persons or entities for the performance of experimental, developmental, or research work in the field of the claimed invention.

In other words, the invention must not be obvious. Being the first person to write it down on paper does not entitle someone to a patent if everyone else already knew how to make the invention. The law regarding obviousness has been changing according to court rulings in recent years, but generally an invention is considered obvious when prior art teaches, suggests, or motivates ("TSM") something that would have led a person of ordinary skill in the art to select the references and combine them in such a fashion so as to produce the claimed invention.

23.4.3 INVALIDITY BASED ON MPEP 35 U.S.C. § 112

MPEP 35 U.S.C. § 112 is entitled "Specification" and states:

The specification shall contain a written description of the invention, and of the manner and process of making and using it, in such full, clear, concise, and exact terms as to enable any person skilled in the art to which it pertains, or with which it is most nearly connected, to make and use the same, and shall set forth the best mode contemplated by the inventor of carrying out his invention.

The specification shall conclude with one or more claims particularly pointing out and distinctly claiming the subject matter which the applicant regards as his invention.

A claim may be written in independent or, if the nature of the case admits, in dependent or multiple dependent form.

Subject to the following paragraph, a claim in dependent form shall contain a reference to a claim previously set forth and then specify a further limitation of the subject matter claimed. A claim in dependent form shall be construed to incorporate by reference all the limitations of the claim to which it refers.

A claim in multiple dependent form shall contain a reference, in the alternative only, to more than one claim previously set forth and then specify a further limitation of the subject matter claimed. A multiple dependent claim shall not serve as a basis for any other multiple dependent claim. A multiple dependent claim shall be construed to incorporate by reference all the limitations of the particular claim in relation to which it is being considered.

An element in a claim for a combination may be expressed as a means or step for performing a specified function without the recital of structure, material, or acts in support thereof, and such claim shall be construed to cover the corresponding structure, material, or acts described in the specification and equivalents thereof.

Essentially this section discusses the requirements of how the patent should be written to convey the necessary information to one of ordinary skill in the art. Invalidity of a patent can be based on an inventor's failure to comply with these requirements. The most commonly raised invalidity issues based on Section 112 include an inadequate written description, a lack of enablement, a failure to disclose the best mode of implementing the invention known to the inventor, and indefiniteness.

DETECTING TRADE SECRET THEFT

In this chapter I discuss techniques for detecting whether a program incorporates another's trade secret. In many respects trade secret theft detection is more difficult than copyright infringement detection or patent infringement detection. Like patents, trade secrets can cover broad technologies and categories of software, or they can cover a small individual function within a program. Unlike patents, trade secrets require that the owner's code meet the three requirements for being a trade secret:

1. It is not generally known to the public.

2. It confers some sort of economic benefit on its holder, where the benefit results from not being known to the public.

3. The owner of the trade secret makes reasonable efforts to maintain its secrecy.

In addition, trade secrets are typically not well defined in a detailed document as is a patent. No government agency has previously confirmed the validity of a trade secret, as is the case with a patent. No hearing is held early on in the case to specifically determine the meaning or scope of the trade secret as there is for a patent. In practice, the specifics of the trade secret are often not actually determined until after discovery when the plaintiff has the defendant's source code to examine, at which point the plaintiff can know what was stolen, if anything.

24.1 IDENTIFYING TRADE SECRETS

It is the plaintiff's responsibility to identify the trade secrets that the defendant has allegedly misappropriated. Although the burden of proof is on the plaintiff, it is the defendant's de facto responsibility to refute these charges. The defendant must show either that its software does not implement the trade secrets identified by the plaintiff or that the technology at issue does not meet the requirements to be a trade secret. Essentially a plaintiff uses the techniques described in this section to attempt to show that the claimed technology in the defendant's code is a trade secret, and the defendant uses the same techniques to attempt to show that the technology identified in its code cannot qualify as a trade secret of the plaintiff.

24.1.1 TOP-DOWN VERSUS BOTTOM-UP

The process for determining trade secrets in software can be generally described as falling into one of two categories: top-down or bottom-up. A top-down approach involves starting at the highest-level description of the behavior of the software to find functions, algorithms, or organizations of the software that fit the criteria for being a trade secret. This can be a very time-consuming process because software can be considered on many different levels of functionality and can be divided and subdivided in many different ways. For example, a particular algorithm can be described within a dozen lines of code within a single source code file or can be distributed over many lines of code in many different files. A trade secret may be embodied in the way some lines of source code are organized to produce a particular result or may be embodied in the way a set of routines are interconnected, each routine consisting of many lines of code. A particular algorithm may be well known in general, but the way it is used in a particular program may be unique and qualify as a trade secret. For example, a distance in n-dimensional space is typically calculated by taking the square root of the sum of the squares of all the distances along each of n axes; the distance calculation by itself would not be considered a trade secret. However, using such a calculation to determine a software source code correlation value could be a trade secret if source code correlation is not generally calculated in this way.

A bottom-up approach compares two sets of source code to find lines of code that are literally or functionally similar. Once those lines of code are identified, it is necessary to understand the functions that the lines of code perform to determine whether that functionality qualifies as a trade secret.

The difficulty of a top-down approach is that because software can be divided in so many ways and considered at so many levels of abstraction, there is a huge number of possibilities to consider. The difficulty of a bottom-up approach is that trade secrets can be misappropriated even though not a single line of source code was copied. Therefore, input from the owner of the code is critical. To represent the plaintiff in a trade secret theft case it is critical to get the owner's input to identify the trade secrets. To represent a defendant in a trade secret theft case it is critical to wait for the plaintiff to specify the trade secrets before performing any analysis.

24.1.2 INPUT FROM OWNER

For the investigator who is working for a plaintiff trying to determine the trade secrets to bring a lawsuit, one critical ingredient is input from the client. There have been a few occasions when I have been asked to enumerate trade secrets within a plaintiff's source code without input from the plaintiff itself. In some cases the original software developers had left the company. In other cases the plaintiff had hired an outside software development company to write the code. In these cases it is crucial to have documentation of some kind that describes the important and valuable features of the software. In at least one case, my client had no contact with the original software developers and had no access to any documentation. I will not say that this is always an impossible situation, but in that case I told the client that I could not move forward on the case without more information.

The reason the input from the owner is required, if it is not obvious, is that two of the conditions to be a trade secret are that it has value to the owner and that the owner makes reasonable efforts to keep it secret. It is difficult, if not impossible, for an independent expert to show that the technology had value to the client without confirmation from the client. An independent expert also cannot confirm that the client took reasonable measures to keep the technology secret without documents or evidence from the client.

24.1.3 STATE WITH SPECIFICITY

A requirement for bringing a trade secret theft lawsuit is that the plaintiff must show just cause for believing that the defendant has stolen trade secrets. Part of that just cause requires stating the trade secrets in a trade secret claim with "specificity."

Just what constitutes "specificity"? This is an interesting question. There are no laws on the matter or even guidelines provided by the courts. In fact, courts in various jurisdictions have issued rulings on similar trade secret identification issues but with an entire spectrum of results. Most courts have required more detailed identification, and a few courts have allowed the plaintiff to proceed with only general descriptions of the alleged trade secrets.

In reality, trade secrets are nebulous. The entire program will not work correctly, if at all, when even one functional statement out of hundreds of thousands is removed. So how does one claim software trade secrets with specificity? This aspect of trade secret law, with respect to software, needs improvement in my opinion. Charles Tait Graves and Brian D. Range of the law firm Wilson, Sonsini, Goodrich & Rosati, in their paper entitled "Identification of Trade Secret Claims in Litigation: Solutions for a Ubiquitous Dispute," offer five proposals constituting a standard for identification of alleged secrets in litigation that they hope the courts will adopt:

1. Courts should first separate the question of whether the plaintiff has identified an alleged secret from the question of whether the information is, in fact, a trade secret;

2. Courts should require a reasonably detailed identification of the alleged secrets before a plaintiff can proceed with discovery—a rule already required by statute in California, and by common law in several other states;

3. Perhaps most importantly, if a defendant properly requests a precise identification during discovery, the court should require a precise, complete identification of whatever type of information is at issue—including an identification of alleged "combination trade secrets";

4. No trade secret plaintiff should obtain an injunction or avoid summary judgment without a precise identification of alleged secrets;

5. Trade secret plaintiffs should not be permitted to alter or amend an identification of trade secret claims without a showing of good cause.

To date, though, neither these standards nor any others have been adopted, and so we must deal with the law the way it is written, interpreted, and implemented now, not the way we would like it to be.

One simple way to state trade secrets with specificity is for the plaintiff to simply turn over all of its code. This is a risk, though. Any party that gives out its source code so early in the process, without reciprocal receipt of source code from the other party, gives the other party an advantage of having much more time to examine the code and rebut the trade secret theft assertion. If the source code is released during the discovery process that occurs later in the process, as is typically the case, both parties give their code to both parties' experts at the same time, setting a level playing field with no inherent advantage for either party.

HOW SPECIFIC IS SPECIFICITY?

I was hired by the plaintiff for a case where the judge was inexperienced in trade secret law and unfamiliar with software source code and software development. The attorney representing the plaintiff was the brother of the company owner and had not previously tried an intellectual property case. The attorney, with my help, wrote a description of the misappropriated trade secrets based on the observable behavior of the defendant's program. Of course, without the defendant's source code, it was impossible to determine which of the many trade secrets embodied in the program were actually stolen, if any. The defendant, however, kept demanding that the plaintiff state its trade secrets with more specificity. We wrote several descriptions of our best understanding of the misappropriated trade secrets, using increasingly detailed explanations of the plaintiff's software and sections of actual source code, but each description was attacked by the defendants as inadequate and rejected by the judge, without giving us any details of what they considered to be missing from the descriptions. We ended up submitting five drafts of our client's trade secret claims. The risk to the plaintiff at such a point is that the trade secrets are described in enough detail that the defendant can show there is a small change between what was claimed and what the defendant actually implemented. While the plaintiff can later amend the trade secrets, that requires time and delays the judgment. And unscrupulous defendants can even examine the plaintiff's source code in detail and remove any suspicious artifacts from their own code before turning it over to the plaintiff's experts.

By the fifth trade secret declaration the plaintiff's attorney decided to turn over all of the plaintiff's source code. The judge agreed that the source code gave enough specificity to the identified trade secrets and the case was allowed to continue. Unfortunately, the defendant had gotten a big advantage in that it received all of the plaintiff's source code to examine and could prepare a defense before the plaintiff received any code from the defendant.

At the other extreme was a case in which I was hired by a large Internet-based company that was a defendant in a case. The company was being sued by a small

Continues

company consisting of a programmer, a manager, and a few part-time employees. The small company claimed that a short PowerPoint presentation it had given to executives at the large company contained trade secrets that the large company had subsequently stolen. The case was a ridiculous effort to extort money. Most of the dozen or so slides were available on the small company's website until shortly before the lawsuit was filed. The small company was evasive in describing its alleged trade secrets, saying that they included things like alphabetized lists of emails and the ability to click on a link to send an email. The presentation was given in 2006, many years after these kinds of functions were developed and were well known not only to programmers, but probably to the millions of Web browser users around the world. The small company claimed that while these technologies were well known, the trade secret was their combination in their specific application in their specific industry where, according to the company, programmers had obviously been isolated from the rest of society for a few decades. Unfortunately, the judge allowed the plaintiff to continue without requiring it to specify its trade secrets with any specificity whatsoever. Eventually the large company settled the case by paying a small sum of money to the small company. While the outcome was a little disappointing, my understanding was that the sum only covered the small company's legal expenses.

I often spend the most time on trade secret cases where the trade secrets are not well defined or where they involve well-known technologies. In this case I created a 302-page expert report that documented all of the technologies that were well known at the time of the presentation and showed them being used in combinations and in the industry with which these two companies were involved. I like to think that my work on the case prevented the small company from making any kind of profit from the lawsuit.

24.1.4 REASONABLE EFFORTS TO MAINTAIN SECRECY

An investigator must determine whether reasonable steps were taken to maintain the secrecy of the source code in question. The main effort here is to see the written policies of the company regarding source code. There are most likely employment agreements that employees are required to sign when starting employment that specify that confidential materials are to be kept confidential. Employees sometimes sign separate nondisclosure agreements (NDAs) that specify how to handle confidential materials. Programmers may sign documents that spell out how source code is to be handled, maintained, and transferred.

Confidential documents should be consistently marked as confidential, and company policies should spell out how confidential documents are to be handled. These policies should be in writing. There may be several levels of confidentiality, and the written policies should discuss all of the levels, how they differ, and how employees should handle materials at each level of confidentiality.

There may be electronic security systems such as email scanners and firewalls that prevent confidential electronic documents, including software source code, from being transmitted over networks outside the company or to people who do not have the appropriate level of responsibility to possess these things.

There may also be physical security such as guards at entrances to buildings who check things going in or out. There may be sign-in sheets or databases used to record when software source code and other trade secrets are taken from a building by employees. It is difficult, if not impossible, to use physical methods to prevent software source code from leaving a building, but such physical security can be considered part of a reasonable effort to stop software source code from leaving without permission.

An investigator should look into whether a plaintiff in a trade secret case has implemented these precautions. It may be difficult to determine exactly what constitutes "reasonable efforts," but the lack of these kinds of precautions gives weight to the argument that the company cannot claim its software source code as trade secrets. Similarly, if policies are not in writing or are not applied consistently, there is a good argument against the software source code being regarded as containing trade secrets.

24.1.5 COPIED CODE AS TRADE SECRETS

It is important to note that while copied source code often constitutes copyright infringement, it almost always constitutes trade secret theft, assuming it meets the criteria of being a trade secret.

1. **Not generally known.** It is rare for any company to not protect its software.
2. **Economic benefit.** That the code was stolen implies that it had an economic benefit to the owner; otherwise, why steal it and risk a lawsuit? The benefit may be that it implements an important function but may also be as simple as the fact that redeveloping the code, even a simple function, would take time. The value of having the code is the time saved by not needing to develop it from scratch.

3. **Secrecy.** Most companies take normal precautions to protect the secrecy of their software source code, as described previously.

Consequently, an investigator finding literally copied source code can almost always make the case that the code constitutes trade secrets.

24.1.6 PUBLIC SOURCES

An investigator in a software trade secret theft case must look into public sources to determine whether the claimed trade secrets were known to the public. Public sources include textbooks, journal papers, magazine articles, newspapers, and other such printed materials. Of course, the Internet should probably be the first place to look and would most likely uncover nearly all such sources. The trick is to know which search terms to use and how to narrow the search.

A particularly useful site is the WayBack Machine that is maintained by the nonprofit Internet Archive with the URL www.archive.org. This description of the Internet Archive can be found at that website:

> The Internet Archive is a 501(c)(3) non-profit that was founded to build an Internet library. Its purposes include offering permanent access for researchers, historians, scholars, people with disabilities, and the general public to historical collections that exist in digital format. Founded in 1996 and located in San Francisco, the Archive has been receiving data donations from Alexa Internet and others. In late 1999, the organization started to grow to include more well-rounded collections. Now the Internet Archive includes texts, audio, moving images, and software as well as archived web pages in our collections, and provides specialized services for adaptive reading and information access for the blind and other persons with disabilities.

The WayBack Machine is an extensive historical collection of Web pages. When you enter a URL into the WayBack Machine, you are given a snapshot of the pages of the website at various dates in the past. Not all websites are maintained in the database, and many websites include dynamic pages that cannot be captured by the WayBack Machine. However, there have been many times when documents have been found that describe a claimed trade secret but that were subsequently removed from the Web. More than once I have found that an unscrupulous plaintiff in a trade secret case had removed a document from its website shortly before bringing a trade secret theft lawsuit. Consequently, the claimed trade secret had been publicly known and its secrecy had not been protected.

It appeared that the plaintiff in those cases had brought a case that it knew was not valid and attempted, but failed, to hide its knowledge of that fact.

Note that trade secret laws vary slightly in different jurisdictions in the United States. Most states subscribe to the concept that if some intellectual property is publicly known, then it is not a trade secret. However, some states have a looser definition where IP must be "readily ascertainable" to disqualify it from being a trade secret. In other words, if the IP was made public but in a way that was difficult for most practitioners to obtain, then it can still qualify as a trade secret. In those jurisdictions it can be argued, for example, that a Web page describing the technology but that had little traffic, was not publicized, and required registration to access does not qualify as readily ascertainable.

24.2 Tools

There are a number of tools that can be useful for detecting trade secret theft of software. The tools described in Chapter 23 for detecting patent infringement are equally useful for detecting trade secret theft, because essentially the same kind of investigation of the software is required. Also, the tools described in Chapter 22 for finding copied code can be used for detecting trade secret theft because, as described earlier, most cases of software copyright infringement also constitute trade secret theft.

PART IX
MISCELLANEOUS TOPICS

"In my profession all sorts of odd knowledge comes useful, and this room of yours is a storehouse of it."
—Sherlock Holmes in *The Adventure of the Three Garridebs*

In this part I introduce a number of topics that are important for anyone involved in the field of software forensics. In particular, I discuss a software clean room, open source code, and the Digital Millennium Copyright Act.

A software clean room development process is a method for developing software in a manner such that copyright infringement of a specific program does not occur. Software clean rooms are often used when two companies are partnering and wish to share certain code but not inadvertently share other code. Software clean rooms are also often used as result of a software copyright infringement litigation where copyright infringement was found to have occurred and the infringing party agrees to remove the infringing code and replace it with code developed in a software clean room.

Open source software is increasingly important in all aspects of software development. Open source software is software for which source code is easily available for free use in other programs but that usually requires license terms to be met in return for its use. Open source licenses range from very simple, allowing unrestricted use of the code, to very complex with very specific limitations on the use of the code. All software developers need to understand open source code and the licensing issues. Those involved with intellectual property theft need to understand when open source code can be used and when it cannot be used, as well as how to identify when two programs are correlated because of their use of the same open source code rather than from copying.

The Digital Millennium Copyright Act, implemented in 1996, extends U.S. copyright law to cover production and dissemination of technology, devices, or services that circumvent encryption measures and other digital rights management (DRM) measures that control access to copyrighted works. In other words, copyright law protects original works from being copied. The DMCA introduced laws that protect the methods used to protect works from being copied.

OBJECTIVES

The objective of this part of the book is to discuss important areas that are not directly related to software intellectual property or software forensics but that anyone involved in the field of software forensics will no doubt come across and should be informed about.

INTENDED AUDIENCE

Computer scientists, computer programmers, corporate managers, and ***entrepreneurs*** will find this part useful for understanding issues that will probably affect them at some time in their careers. ***Technical consultants and expert witnesses for litigation*** will find this part valuable for understanding issues that are likely to come up in some of the litigation in which they will be involved. ***Lawyers*** will find this part important for obtaining an introductory explanation of some very important topics regarding software licensing and software intellectual property that will no doubt be critical to certain intellectual property cases and software contract cases.

IMPLEMENTING A SOFTWARE CLEAN ROOM

In this chapter I discuss the software clean room development process, a method for developing software in such a way that copyright infringement and trade secret misappropriation of a specific program do not occur. A software clean room is named after a semiconductor manufacturing "clean room" where the manufacturing area is filtered to keep it free of small particles that could contaminate the semiconductor wafers, introducing defects into the integrated circuits that would render them unreliable or unusable. In a similar way, a software clean room is kept free of the source code of certain other programs that could contaminate it with copyrighted code or trade secrets from those other programs. Software clean rooms are often used when two companies are partnering and wish to share certain code but not inadvertently share other code or certain trade secrets. Software clean rooms are also often used as the result of a software copyright infringement case or a software trade secret case when one party's IP was found to have been used without permission and the accused party agrees to remove the code in question and replace it with code developed independently. Note that a software clean room, as discussed here, is not to be confused with the Cleanroom Software Engineering development process created by Harlan Mills at IBM in the 1980s as a way to minimize software defects but having nothing to do with intellectual property.

25.1 Background

Chapter 6 on copyrights includes a discussion of the landmark cases of *Atari Games Corp. v. Nintendo of America Inc.* and *Sega Enterprises Ltd. v. Accolade Inc.* The precedent of these cases is that it was made clear that the copying of software concepts does not violate copyright laws as long as the specific expression is not copied. Of course, copyright does not protect ideas, only the expression of those ideas. Software embodies many abstract concepts, and this makes it particularly difficult to draw the line between idea and expression. This was demonstrated in the case of *Computer Associates International Inc. v. Altai Inc.*, described in Chapter 22, where the abstraction-filtration-comparison test was defined by the court. The question from a practical point of view is how one party can develop code legally, abiding by the judgments handed down by the courts, without infringing copyrights or misappropriating trade secrets. You will recall that Atari was reprimanded, and found liable by the court, because it did not follow an acceptable procedure. The software clean room is an acceptable procedure, if followed carefully.

One of the first successful uses of a clean room was by Columbia Data Products to create an IBM PC clone. In the wild and woolly early days of the personal computer revolution in the late 1970s, compatibility was not an issue. Each computer had such a small share of the market, and anyway the customers were primarily hobbyists and tinkerers who preferred the latest technology over compatibility with older technology. That changed with the introduction of the Apple II from Apple Computer in 1977. It immediately became the fastest-selling personal computer to date, at least partly because it was available completely assembled, instead of in kit form, and was marketed to business people, educators, and other non-technical people. As sales took off, competitors wanted to copy it, but Apple then, as now, fought hard to keep others from using its intellectual property. Franklin Computer created an Apple clone by making a literal copy of the Apple ROM that contained its operating system. As discussed in Chapter 6, Apple sued Franklin for copyright infringement and won, setting a legal standard for computer object code copyright.

In 1981 IBM introduced its own personal computer, the PC, and created yet another surge in personal computer sales. The computer was made with off-the-shelf parts and was easy to reverse engineer, and clone makers jumped on the bandwagon in large numbers. However, to be compatible with the IBM PC and run all of the available software required that the Basic Input/Output System (BIOS) be identical to that of the IBM PC. The BIOS controlled access to the keyboard, the printer port, the monitor, and the floppy disk drives. Like the Apple operating system, the IBM BIOS was stored in a ROM. IBM published the BIOS source code but also threatened, and often took legal action against, clone makers who literally copied the BIOS.

In 1982, Columbia Data Products introduced the first IBM PC clone, the MPC 1600 "Multi Personal Computer," which had a BIOS that had been developed in a clean room. One set of engineers in a "dirty room" read the IBM BIOS source code and wrote a high-level specification that was then given to engineers in the "clean room," who wrote the new BIOS code from scratch. While Columbia Data Products is still around, as of this writing it no longer manufactures personal computers but produces products for data security that can be used for digital forensics.

In 1983, Phoenix Technologies successfully created a clean room version of the IBM BIOS that it began selling to personal computer vendors. This became a highly successful product for Phoenix, leading to an IPO in 1988 and its purchase by Hewlett-Packard in 2010. Although IBM seemed poised to sue BIOS makers for copyright infringement, it appears that they rarely brought a lawsuit.

There are no standards and few documented procedures for implementing a software clean room. In 2008 in the case of *Nordstrom Consulting, Inc. et al. v. M&S Technologies, Inc. et al.*, Judge John W. Darrah confirmed that a software clean room is a viable procedure for learning functionality from a program and duplicating that functionality to create a compatible or interoperable program, while avoiding copyright infringement.[1] According to the court:

> Defendants claim to have used a "clean room" procedure to develop the new software. "Clean room" procedure attempts to avoid violations of the copyright laws by using two separate teams of developers to create a competing product. . . . The first team describes the functional aspects of a product to the second team; the second team then uses those descriptions to write the code for a competing product. . . . Defendants claim to have instituted a clean room procedure in which Marino and Butler fulfilled the role of the first team, while the second team was composed of three independent programmers who worked offsite and had no access to the program code. If Defendants did indeed follow clean room procedures, then Plaintiffs would be unable to make the necessary showing that Defendants had access to the copyrighted work.

---

1. This particular case is muddied a bit by the fact that the defendant did not follow procedures that are acceptable in a software clean room. There was contamination between the two sets of developers—the ones who examined the competitor's program and the ones developing the new program. However, the plaintiff did not effectively challenge the software clean room process because it did not show that substantially similar code was transferred and did not call an expert witness on this point. Because of this, the judge accepted the process as legitimate.

25.2 THE SETUP

The setup for clean room development basically involves three entities: a dirty room, a clean room, and a monitor (see Figure 25.1). The setup for this development is such that a reasonable person would not doubt that the procedure was followed correctly. A reasonable person would include a judge or a jury member, should the process be challenged in court. Also remember that the process is set up so that violations of the procedure, while not at all impossible, would be noticed and recorded.

25.2.1 THE DIRTY ROOM

The dirty room is a physical place where programmers can examine copyrighted code to understand its functionality and how to interface to it. Here programmers can have full access to all code and all documents that are legally available to them in any form. It is important that the dirty room be a physical place where access can be monitored and verified. It must be certain that those who do not have official access to the dirty room have not accessed the code or documents in the dirty room surreptitiously and transferred that knowledge to those in the clean room.

In the dirty room the programmers can examine the original source code and any hardware and documents that they are legally entitled to access. Note that this may include access to confidential, nonpublic documents. It may even include trade secrets if the programmers have been given legal access to such trade secrets. The clean room development process is often implemented between parties that wish to share some information, for the purpose of a joint venture, but restrict other information. In this case one party may give certain proprietary documents and equipment to programmers in the dirty room but withhold other documents and equipment that do not directly relate to the software being developed.

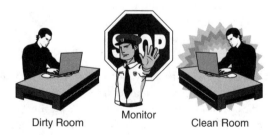

Dirty Room   Monitor   Clean Room

Figure 25.1   Clean room setup

It is important in a situation when companies share proprietary information that a detailed written contract be drawn up and signed by both parties that explicitly states which materials can be shared, including specific copyrighted materials and specific trade secrets. It should also specify which proprietary information cannot make its way into the new software and therefore cannot be transmitted from the dirty room to the clean room.

Programmers in the dirty room must have no official communication with programmers in the clean room. All communication between the dirty room programmers and the clean room programmers should be minimized, and communications about specific technical matters should be prohibited. Programmers in both rooms should agree in writing that any inadvertent communication about specific technical matters should be reported to the monitor, who should record the fact and verify that no protected IP was shared.

25.2.2 The Clean Room

The clean room is a physical place where programmers have no access to the copyrighted code or trade secrets or to any of the documents that describe this protected intellectual property. It is important that the clean room be a physical place where access can be monitored and verified. It must be certain that those who do not have official access to the clean room have not accessed the code or documents in the clean room surreptitiously.

In the clean room, programmers produce the functionally equivalent code that does not infringe the copyright or misappropriate trade secrets of the original code. People with close contact with the programmers who wrote the original code or with employees of the company that produced the original code should not have access to the clean room. This includes former employees of the original company that developed the original code or independent contractors of that company. Essentially, access to the clean room should be denied to anyone who may reasonably be thought to be familiar with the original software development. Note that this includes not only those who had direct access to the original software development team or the original code, but also those who might reasonably be thought to have had access, including employees of the original company who worked on a different project, for example. The goal is to make sure that a reasonable person would not suspect that someone in the clean room might have had such access and such knowledge to contaminate the new code.

25.2.3 THE MONITOR

The monitor is a trusted third party, not directly related to the company or people attempting to copy code, who verifies that what is passed between the dirty room and the clean room does not violate any copyrights or trade secrets. The monitor should be a party that is independent from the company developing the new code and that does not have a stake in whether the new code works or whether it violates or does not violate a copyright or trade secret. The monitor is often an independent contractor, and the monitor's payment cannot depend on the success of the product being developed. There should be no incentive, or appearance of incentive, for the monitor to give an OK to code that has not been developed cleanly.

The monitor has access to the software, documents, and equipment in both the dirty room and the clean room. Every piece of code, every document, and every piece of equipment that is passed or communicated between the programmers in one room to the programmers in the other room must pass through the monitor, who first determines that the materials contain no copyrights or trade secrets of the company that produced the original code. Any materials containing such intellectual property are blocked from going to the other room.

The monitor also verifies that the final software produced in the clean room does not contain protected intellectual property of the original software. This can be done using a tool that measures software source code correlation or software source/object code correlation to determine whether any correlation is due to copyright infringement. In the case of trade secrets, tools for examining and comparing software functionality should be used.

25.3 THE PROCEDURE

In his book *Software and Intellectual Property Protection*, Professor Bernard Galler gives seven specific guidelines for implementing a software clean room. While Geller's guidelines are very useful and form the basis for my own procedure (see Figure 25.2), they include requirements that are simply impractical to implement. For example, Galler states that all contact between programmers in the dirty room and those in the clean room must be avoided, including social contact. Given that both sets of programmers most likely work at the same company, and that all kinds of electronic communication are not only prevalent but in some cases unavoidable, this kind of separation is not possible. It is also not necessary if reasonable precautions against sharing intellectual property are put in place.

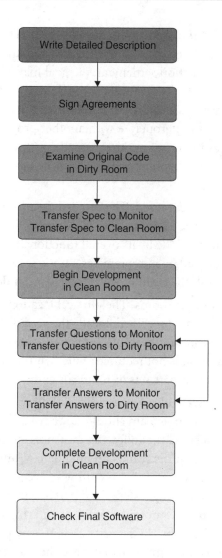

Figure 25.2 Clean room procedure

25.3.1 WRITE A DETAILED DESCRIPTION

As with all critical procedures, the first step is to write a detailed description of the procedure. This document is especially critical for clean room software development should the new code created in the clean room ever be challenged in court. This document is to be shared with everyone involved in the project: the clean room developers, the dirty room developers, the monitors, and the project managers. The detailed description should include all of the following things:

1. **The purpose of the clean room development.** This should be well defined from the beginning so that all parties involved know what the goal is. For example, in a litigation settlement, the goal may be to rewrite specific sections of code that have already been determined to hold infringing code. In another case, the clean room development may be required to produce a program that can interoperate with another program or with a particular piece of hardware. In yet another case, the purpose may be to reverse engineer and copy the functionality of some other party's program without literally copying it.

2. **The code to be understood.** The detailed description should make clear which code is being understood to be copied or interfaced. This section should refer to the code by its overall functionality but should not include anything that could be interpreted as a trade secret because this document is to be shared with the clean room and dirty room developers.

3. **Physical location of rooms.** The physical locations of the clean room and the dirty room should be specified. Ideally the rooms should be as physically separate as possible, for example, by a continent or an ocean, though such extreme separation is not required. Note that the clean room and dirty room may actually encompass sets of rooms or entire buildings.

4. **Security measures.** Ideally the clean and dirty rooms should be in different locations, and one team should not have access to the other team's buildings. Otherwise the following measures should be put in place: Locks on doors leading to the rooms are mandatory, and security systems requiring electronic access and that record who accesses the room and when they access the room are suggested. Each person entering or leaving the room should be required to note the times of entering and leaving if this is not done automatically by the security system. Any people who are removed from the teams must immediately have their access to their room revoked.

5. **Designate programmers in each room.** The programmers in the dirty room and those in the clean room should be designated by name. Any programmers who are brought onto one team or let go from a team should immediately be noted in this document.

6. **Designate monitor.** The person or persons designated as monitors for the process should be named in this document. If a company is designated as a monitor, only specific employees of that company should be allowed to act as monitors, and those persons should be named in this document. Any people who are subsequently named as monitors or who are removed as monitors should immediately be noted in this document.

7. **Communications methods and procedures.** This section of the document should specify how dirty room and clean room programmers are to communicate with the monitor. This section should also specify how communication is to take place, whether it is by written documents, printed documents, flash drives, other removable drives, email, or some other method or combination of methods. Whenever possible, encryption methods should be used for any information coming out of either the clean room or the dirty room. Direct communication between the two sets of programmers should be severely restricted, though it is usually not possible to curtail all communications, especially when they are located in the same building or nearby corporate location. The programmers should not be assigned to any other projects that might require business-related communication to the other team.

8. **Activity report format for each room.** Programmers in each room should prepare regular reports on their activities. This section of the detailed description should specify the format of those reports, the media used for the reports, and the frequency of the reports. It should also specify whether each individual programmer is responsible for producing a report or whether a team leader is responsible for producing a report for the entire team.

9. **Documents relied upon.** This detailed description should list those documents that will be relied upon. Each room will rely on a different set of documents, each to be listed in this detailed description. Any documents discovered later or determined to be necessary during the development process should be added to this list.

10. **Hardware and software.** A detailed description of the hardware and software that will be relied upon should be in the document. In the case of the dirty room, this includes all hardware and software used to examine and reverse engineer the original code. In the case of the clean room, this includes all hardware and software used to develop the new code. This can be particularly useful in the future if the tools introduce artifacts that appear to be infringement but in fact are not, because they can be shown to have been introduced by the tools.

25.3.2 SIGN AGREEMENTS

All parties should sign agreements not to violate the clean room procedure. All programmers, managers, monitors, and any others involved in the process should commit to following the documented procedures. All people involved must be impressed with the importance of the development project and the seriousness of the endeavor. They must be made to understand that violations of the procedures will have serious consequences for the company and, in turn, for them.

25.3.3 EXAMINE THE ORIGINAL CODE IN THE DIRTY ROOM

The programmers in the dirty room now can begin the process of reverse engineering or otherwise understanding the functionality of the original code. They must write a description of the functionality to be developed in the clean room at a high level, including only those details necessary for creating the new software and nothing else.

25.3.4 TRANSFER SPECIFICATION TO THE MONITOR AND THEN TO THE CLEAN ROOM

The programmers in the dirty room then transfer the specification to the monitor, who examines it for any of the original code's protected intellectual property. If the monitor determines that the specification does not contain any protected IP, he then transfers it to the clean room. If the monitor finds some protected IP, he sends the specification back to the dirty room with markup showing the problems to be resolved. The dirty room programmers continue to rework the specification and transfer it to the monitor until the monitor verifies it as containing no protected IP and transfers it to the clean room.

25.3.5 BEGIN DEVELOPMENT IN THE CLEAN ROOM

Using the specification that was sent to them from the dirty room via the monitor, the clean room programmers begin development of the new code. Any communications between the two groups relating to the software are written up and transferred to the monitor. This is a way of ensuring that there are no communications between the clean room and the dirty room that go unmonitored—for every question that the monitor receives from either room, he should have a corresponding reply from the other room.

25.3.6 TRANSFER QUESTIONS TO THE MONITOR AND THEN TO THE DIRTY ROOM

The programmers in the clean room transfer any questions to the monitor, who examines them for any issues that may potentially divulge protected IP by the programmers in the dirty room. If that is the case, the monitor marks those questions with a warning not to divulge any protected IP in answering the question before transferring the questions to the dirty room.

25.3.7 Transfer Answers to the Monitor and Then to the Clean Room

The programmers in the dirty room then transfer the answers to the questions to the monitor, who examines them for any of the original code's protected intellectual property. If the monitor determines that the answers do not contain any protected IP, she then transfers them to the clean room. If the monitor finds some protected IP, she sends the answers back to the dirty room with markup showing the problems to be resolved. The dirty room programmers continue to rework the answers and transfer them to the monitor until the monitor verifies them as containing no protected IP and transfers them to the clean room.

25.3.8 Continue Process Until New Software Is Completed

This entire process continues until the new software has been developed and tested in the clean room.

25.3.9 Check Final Software for Inclusion of Protected IP

The monitor performs a final check to confirm that no protected IP has contaminated the new code. In the case of a copyright issue, a source code correlation tool or a source/object correlation tool can be used to determine that any correlation between the original code and the new code is not due to copyright infringement. In the case of a trade secret issue, tools to examine and analyze the functionality of the original code and the new code can be used to help the monitor check for trade secret misappropriation.

25.3.10 Violations of the Procedure

Any violations of the procedure must be reported to the monitor, who will determine whether any protected IP was shared. If so, the monitor must determine how to best resolve the situation. Resolutions may include removing certain programmers from the team who have willfully violated the procedure. Resolutions may also include removing clean room programmers from the team who have received protected intellectual property to ensure that this information is not shared with other programmers in the clean room. In cases where the intellectual property has significantly contaminated the clean room, it may be necessary to start the procedure from the beginning with a new team of clean room programmers.

OPEN SOURCE SOFTWARE

In this chapter I discuss open source software, increasingly important in all aspects of software development. Open source software is software for which the source code is easily available for free use in other programs but that usually requires the user to abide by a specific license.

Open source licenses range from very simple, allowing unrestricted use of the code, to very complex, with very specific limitations on the use of the code. Software developers should understand open source code and the licensing issues that go along with it before using the code in their projects. Those involved with intellectual property theft need to understand when open source can be used and when it cannot be used, as well as how to identify when two programs are correlated because of their use of the same open source code rather than from copying.

26.1 DEFINITION

Essentially open source code is code that can be freely used in other projects. Programmers from around the world contribute code to any program or proj-ect. Also, many corporations donate code developed internally to open source proj-ects to get widespread adoption. If the code is developed through an official open source program, such as SourceForge, owned and operated by Geeknet, Inc., a publicly traded U.S.-based for-profit company, then there are strict testing and release procedures that ensure that the code is reliable. One colleague told me that most of the programmers on his team could not develop open source software because the development and testing requirements and standards were so tough.

The Open Source Initiative (OSI) is a nonprofit corporation that was founded in February 1998 by Bruce Perens and Eric S. Raymond. The organization was initiated by Netscape Communications Corporation, the browser company that started the browser wars, popularized the Internet, woke Microsoft up to the commercial possibilities of the Internet, and eventually died a slow but spectacular death. Netscape used OSI to publish the source code for its flagship Netscape Communicator product when it decided to open it to developers. According to the OSI website, the OSI was "formed to educate about and advocate for the benefits of open source and to build bridges among different constituencies in the open-source community." The OSI is generally considered the keeper of open source standards, the repository for all open source licenses, and the advocate for all things open source. OSI has created a good, formal definition of open source code that reads as follows:

(1) Free Redistribution

The license shall not restrict any party from selling or giving away the software as a component of an aggregate software distribution containing programs from several different sources. The license shall not require a royalty or other fee for such sale.

(2) Source Code

The program must include source code, and must allow distribution in source code as well as compiled form. Where some form of a product is not distributed with source code, there must be a well-publicized means of obtaining the source code for no more than a reasonable reproduction cost, preferably downloading via the Internet without charge. The source code must be the preferred form in which a programmer would modify the program. Deliberately obfuscated source code is not allowed. Intermediate forms such as the output of a preprocessor or translator are not allowed.

(3) Derived Works

The license must allow modifications and derived works, and must allow them to be distributed under the same terms as the license of the original software.

(4) Integrity of the Author's Source Code

The license may restrict source-code from being distributed in modified form only if the license allows the distribution of "patch files" with the source code for the purpose of modifying the program at build time. The license must explicitly permit distribution of software built from modified source code. The license may require derived works to carry a different name or version number from the original software.

(5) **No Discrimination Against Persons or Groups**

The license must not discriminate against any person or group of persons.

(6) **No Discrimination Against Fields of Endeavor**

The license must not restrict anyone from making use of the program in a specific field of endeavor. For example, it may not restrict the program from being used in a business, or from being used for genetic research.

(7) **Distribution of License**

The rights attached to the program must apply to all to whom the program is redistributed without the need for execution of an additional license by those parties.

(8) **License Must Not Be Specific to a Product**

The rights attached to the program must not depend on the program's being part of a particular software distribution. If the program is extracted from that distribution and used or distributed within the terms of the program's license, all parties to whom the program is redistributed should have the same rights as those that are granted in conjunction with the original software distribution.

(9) **License Must Not Restrict Other Software**

The license must not place restrictions on other software that is distributed along with the licensed software. For example, the license must not insist that all other programs distributed on the same medium must be open-source software.

(10) **License Must Be Technology-Neutral**

No provision of the license may be predicated on any individual technology or style of interface.

Distributed software that has a license that meets these criteria can be approved by the OSI board of directors and is then considered "OSI Certified open source software." The OSI's influence is such that to gain widespread adoption, open source software effectively requires OSI certification. Organizations such as SourceForge will not support any software unless it has an OSI-approved license.

26.2 FREE SOFTWARE

Free software is often confused with open source software, but they are not the same thing. Free software is informally explained on the website of the nonprofit GNU organization:

> "Free software" is a matter of liberty, not price. To understand the concept, you should think of "free" as in "free speech," not as in "free beer."

Free software is the brainchild and passionate motivation of Richard Stallman, creator of the GNU Operating System open source project, main author along with Eben Moglen of the GNU Public License (GPL) for open source software, and founder of the Free Software Foundation (FSF) that promotes free software. Stallman believes that it is immoral to reserve rights such as intellectual property rights for software. He feels that one can charge for software but must not restrict any rights regarding copying expressions or ideas. He is a strong opponent of any kind of proprietary rights to software, including intellectual property rights such as copyrights and patents. According to the Free Software Foundation, free software allows users to run, copy, distribute, study, change, and improve the software. This in turn allows society to improve rapidly and fairly. Of course, the obvious implication of this thinking is that capitalism is bad and socialism is the way to improve society. Maybe that is a discussion for another book.

More precisely, the FSF states that a free program's users have the four essential freedoms (counting from 0 in the tradition of a computer program):

0. The freedom to run the program, for any purpose

1. The freedom to study how the program works, and change it to make it do what you wish

2. The freedom to redistribute copies so you can help your neighbor

3. The freedom to distribute copies of your modified versions to others

Of course, as any lawyer will tell you, any license, by definition, has restrictions, so it is unclear how the FSF reconciles the idea of a restrictionless license. Most people in the open source movement, even those who believe in the value of some software being free, see Stallman as an extremist. There is no question, however, that he is a great programmer, a tireless activist, and the father of a movement that has had significant ramifications for software development.

26.2.1 COPYLEFT

The Free Software Foundation has coined the word *copyleft* to refer to its GPL agreement. The concept is that a copyright protects the programmer's rights to restrict usage of a program. A programmer could simply not claim a copyright on a program, but some other programmer could make changes to the program and claim a copyright on the changes, putting restrictions on the use of the new version that includes the original version. The GPL, as well as many other open source licenses, not only allows the original programmer the ability to make the program and its source code available to everyone freely to use and change as they wish, but this freedom to use and change gets transferred down the line of programmers from the original programmer to any other programmers who continue to develop the code. In other words, the software source code and derivative works are available to all and free to use forever.

The copyleft does not replace the copyright. In fact, the first step for copyleft is to claim a copyright on the code. Then distribution terms are added to the copyright through a legal agreement that gives everyone the rights to use, modify, and redistribute the program's code, or any program derived from it, but only if the distribution terms are unchanged. Thus, according to the FSF, "the code and the freedoms become legally inseparable."

26.2.2 CREATIVE COMMONS

A more generic version of the copyleft is the Creative Commons license (or "CC license"), advanced by Creative Commons, a nonprofit organization founded in 2001 by Larry Lessig, Hal Abelson, and Eric Eldred. Like the copyleft, the CC license requires and builds upon a copyright. Whereas a copyright reserves all rights for the owner, and a copyleft gives up most, and very specific, rights by agreement of the copyright owner, the CC license gives up some rights at the discretion of the copyright owner. The copyright owner can choose which rights he wants to preserve and which to abandon. The Creative Commons can then help him choose an appropriate license. Creative Commons has also developed a number of marks similar to the "circle c" © copyright symbol to identify the rights that the CC license owner has preserved.

26.2.3 PATENT RIGHTS

Open source licenses allow one to copy a program's source code with a variety of restrictions ranging from strict to none. However, initially none of them dealt explicitly with patents. The United States is one of the few countries that allow software patents, but obviously significant development goes on here and developers and end users of open source software have not been protected from patent infringement. Remember that a user who runs a program can be liable for infringing a method claim of a patent even though that user did not develop the software.

The Free Software Foundation believes that software patents are immoral but acknowledges that they exist. The GPL version 3 (GPL3), created in 2007, includes a new protection for patent infringement. Essentially, developers of any open source software or any software that incorporates open source software must give up the right to license any patents embodied by the software or sue any users of the software for patent infringement. This somewhat controversial change to the GPL means that many companies still release their open source software under the terms of the GPL2 or other open source licenses to avoid the risk of perhaps contaminating all of their software and thus giving up all IP rights to their entire software portfolio. Many individual open source developers believe that there should be no IP rights and do release their code under GPL3, which is becoming increasingly popular.

26.3 OPEN SOURCE LICENSES

A large and growing number of organizations produce and support open source licenses. Each of them has its own terms, requirements, restrictions, and uses. As of this writing, 66 licenses have been approved by the OSI:

- Academic Free License 3.0 (AFL 3.0)
- Adaptive Public License
- Affero GNU Public License
- Apache License, 2.0
- Apple Public Source License
- Artistic License 2.0
- Attribution Assurance License
- Boost Software License (BSL1.0)
- BSD License
- Common Development and Distribution License
- Common Public Attribution License 1.0 (CPAL)

- Computer Associates Trusted Open Source License 1.1
- CUA Office Public License Version 1.0
- Eclipse Public License
- Educational Community License Version 2.0
- Eiffel Forum License Version 2.0
- Entessa Public License
- EU DataGrid Software License
- European Union Public License (link to every language's version on their site)
- Fair License
- Frameworx License
- GNU General Public License (GPL)
- GNU General Public License Version 3.0 (GPLv3)
- GNU Library or "Lesser" General Public License (LGPL)
- GNU Library or "Lesser" General Public License Version 3.0 (LGPLv3)
- Historical Permission Notice and Disclaimer
- IBM Public License
- IPA Font License
- ISC License
- Lucent Public License Version 1.02
- Microsoft Public License (Ms-PL)
- Microsoft Reciprocal License (Ms-RL)
- MirOS Licence
- MIT License
- Motosoto License
- Mozilla Public License 1.1 (MPL)
- Multics License
- NASA Open Source Agreement 1.3
- Naumen Public License
- Nethack General Public License
- Nokia Open Source License
- Non-Profit Open Software License 3.0 (Non-Profit OSL 3.0)
- NTP License

- OCLC Research Public License 2.0
- Open Font License 1.1 (OFL 1.1)
- Open Group Test Suite License
- Open Software License 3.0 (OSL 3.0)
- PHP License
- PostgreSQL License
- Python License (CNRI Python License)
- Python Software Foundation License
- Qt Public License (QPL)
- RealNetworks Public Source License Version 1.0
- Reciprocal Public License 1.5 (RPL1.5)
- Ricoh Source Code Public License
- Simple Public License 2.0
- Sleepycat License
- Sun Public License
- Sybase Open Watcom Public License 1.0
- University of Illinois/NCSA Open Source License
- Vovida Software License Version 1.0
- W3C License
- wxWindows Library License
- X.Net License
- zlib/libpng License
- Zope Public License

26.4 OPEN SOURCE LAWSUITS

When the open source movement began, the founders had little, if any, belief in intellectual property rights. Also, they consisted of informal groups of programmers that were not large enough or organized well enough to confront any violators of open source licenses. Additionally, they did not have any financial resources, and, more important, it was difficult to assign monetary damages to a group or person who did not derive any income from their products. Finally, it was difficult if not impossible to detect the use of open source code in a project once the code had been compiled into a binary executable and distributed to customers.

Given this situation, many companies incorporated open source software into their products without abiding by the licensing terms. Also, a movement that promotes the concept that software should be free and "unrestricted" had a difficult time restraining programmers from using this free software. After many years of this kind of incorporation of open source software in commercial products, things began to change when the number of open source programmers reached a critical mass, commercial companies saw the advantage of forcing competitors to reveal their source code or otherwise expend capital and manpower on lawsuits, and nonprofit open source organizations got significant funding to pursue litigation.

26.4.1 SCO v. LINUX

The most famous case, and potentially the most damaging to Linux, the open source operating system that competes with Microsoft, is the case of *SCO v. IBM*.[1] This case was a straightforward software copyright case (though other issues between SCO and IBM and SCO and Novell were also litigated) and did not have any aspects that were unique to open source code, except that a very major open source program was under attack.

SCO began life as the Santa Cruz Operations, Inc., in 1979, a consulting company founded by Larry Michels and Doug Michels. In 1983 they delivered the first version of the UNIX operating system, originally developed by AT&T, to run on an IBM PC. It was called Xenix. Microsoft was an early partner of SCO and later invested in the company. AT&T also partnered with SCO, which became a premier provider of UNIX and grew through the 1990s and expanded its product line. In 1993 SCO went public. In 1995 SCO acquired Novell Corporation's UNIX system source technology business and its UnixWare 2 operating system. In 1996 SCO introduced Tarantella network management software. By the year 2000, the Internet boom was under way and SCO, like many other high-tech companies, was seduced by its riches and hype. SCO changed its name to Tarantella and began moving toward Web applications and away from UNIX, selling its two UNIX divisions to Caldera Systems, Inc., which subsequently changed its name to SCO and later to the SCO Group.

---

1. For the sake of full disclosure, I was hired by SCO for a month in 2004 as a consultant and potential testifying expert witness in this case. The code analysis had already been under way for a while by other consultants on the case. My CodeMatch tool for measuring source code correlation was fairly new at that time. I was really excited and saw this as an opportunity to prove my tools and "make my reputation in this field." The SCO attorneys gave me some code samples from SCO UNIX and Linux to compare. CodeMatch chugged along for days before generating a report showing very little correlation. The attorneys thanked me, paid me my very generous retainer (that they had put into my contract), and I never heard from them again.

In the meantime, in 1983 Richard Stallman announced the GNU operating system. GNU is a "recursive acronym" that stands for "GNU's not UNIX," a clever but obscure acronym implying that GNU would be a UNIX-like operating system that was different from UNIX. In 1991, Linus Torvalds, a student in Helsinki, Finland, began work on Linux, a UNIX-like kernel that worked with GNU. It is difficult to track exact dates for Linux as it was among the first open source projects and intermediate code was continually being released, shared, and modified. In September 1991 Torvalds "released" version 0.01 of Linux.

In 2003 the SCO Group announced that it had received U.S. copyright registrations for UNIX System V source code and claimed that Linux "contained SCO's UNIX System V source code and that Linux was an unauthorized derivative of UNIX." SCO filed suit against IBM for an unprecedented $1 billion, later increased to $3 billion and again later to $5 billion, and demanded that Linux end users pay license fees. SCO also filed suit against large Linux end users AutoZone and DaimlerChrysler as well as Novell, which distributed its own version of Linux and claimed that it, not SCO, owned the copyrights to UNIX. SCO also sent letters to members of the Fortune 1000 and Global 500 companies warning them of the possibility of liability if they used Linux. The largest distributor of Linux, Red Hat Systems, joined the fray with its own suit against SCO.

The case continued for years, with SCO claiming it had found proof that code in Linux was copied from UNIX, but never presenting the proof publicly or in court. On August 10, 2007, the court ruled that Novell, not SCO, was the owner of the UNIX operating system copyrights. Shortly thereafter, SCO filed for bankruptcy, but in business as in horror movies, the dead don't stay dead for long. Two years later, on August 24, 2009, the U.S. Court of Appeals reversed a part of the district court decision and permitted SCO to pursue its claim of ownership of the UNIX copyrights at a new trial. On March 30, 2010, the jury in that trial returned the verdict that Novell owned the copyrights. For now, the case seems truly stake-in-the-heart dead, and Linux users and distributors no longer need fear litigation.

Two major results can be traced to the SCO lawsuits. First, the open source groups became more powerful and were able to raise money, and garner influence, that enabled them to bring their own lawsuits to ensure that open source licensing was upheld by users of open source code. Second, an industry of companies, led by Black Duck Software, sprang up that examined source code, searching for open source code that might be buried, unknowingly, within a commercial software package. Commercial software providers were now worried about litigation and legal liability; they needed to know whose code was incorporated in their products and what their legal responsibilities were with respect to the appropriate open source licenses.

26.4.2 THE BUSYBOX LAWSUITS

In the early days of personal computers, to boot an operating system required a boot floppy, a disk that contained a driver for the CD-ROM drive, and a mouse, as well as other small utility programs that would allow some basic functions to get the entire operating system loaded. One such open source set of drivers and utility programs for booting Linux became known as BusyBox. Embedded systems are systems that have processors and software embedded inside them, but this fact is invisible to the user. For example, a smart refrigerator may have a processor that runs software to control temperature and displays information on a screen on the front. The user is not aware that the refrigerator contains a process and runs small programs on top of a limited operating system based on Linux, nor is it relevant. The user cannot edit programs or add or remove programs—they are fixed by the manufacturer. Such fixed software is called "firmware." Over the years, BusyBox became a popular set of tools for booting up such an embedded system because it used a small amount of memory—had a "small memory footprint"—which reduced the overall costs of the device.

On September 20, 2007, the Software Freedom Law Center (SFLC) filed the first U.S. lawsuit over a GPL violation. The lawsuit was filed on behalf of Erik Andersen and Rob Landley, two of the many programmers who worked on BusyBox over the years, against Monsoon Multimedia, Inc. BusyBox code had been discovered in the firmware of a Monsoon product, and letters to Monsoon had gone unanswered. Over the next few years, the SFLC brought similar lawsuits on behalf of Andersen and Landley against other companies, including Xterasys, High-Gain Antennas, Verizon Communications, Bell Microproducts, Super Micro Computer, Best Buy, JVC, Samsung, and others.

In every suit, the plaintiffs alleged that products sold by the defendants included BusyBox source code in violation of the GPL license. According to each complaint, to comply with the GPL, when parties distribute an object code or executable form of BusyBox, they must include either (1) the "complete corresponding machine readable source code," or (2) a written offer to give any third party a complete machine-readable copy of the corresponding source code. Failure to do this is a failure to fulfill the terms of the copyright license and thus that distribution is a violation of copyright. Each lawsuit was settled in a similar way. In each case the defendant was required to make the BusyBox software source code available publicly and pay an undisclosed amount of money to the two developers.

The lawsuits served as a warning to companies that use open source software, in whole or in part, that is covered by the GPL. The GPL simply requires that when parties distribute a program that includes GPL source code, or a binary derivative of such source code, they must include either (1) the source code to that GPL-licensed software, or (2) a written offer to give any third party a complete machine-readable copy of the source code. This written offer can simply be a link on a website for downloading the source code.

It is important to note that the GPL does not require any company to make its own proprietary source code available. The GPL requires only that the GPL-licensed code itself be distributed. There are easy ways for a company to separate the GPL code from its own proprietary code, for example, by including them in separate files.

Another lesson from the BusyBox lawsuits is the importance of responding to pre-suit complaint letters alleging a violation of the GPL. The SFLC claims that it sent notification letters to all of the defendants prior to filing the lawsuit, and all of the companies either ignored SFLC's notice or did not respond to the notice in a meaningful way. The BusyBox website itself states that the authors "don't want monetary awards, injunctions, or to generate bad PR for a company, unless that's the only way to get somebody that repeatedly ignores us to comply with the license on our code."

26.4.3 *IP INNOVATION LLC V. RED HAT AND NOVELL*

Patents present a particular problem for open source developers because, unlike copyrights, a patent can be infringed unintentionally and without knowledge of the infringement. The patent holder may not be obligated to the GPL and may not be friendly to the open source community. The first such case was *IP Innovation v. Red Hat and Novell* over U.S. Patents 5,072,412, 5,394,521, and 5,533,183 that are all titled "User Interface with Multiple Workspaces for Sharing Display System Objects." IP Innovation is a subsidiary of Acacia Technologies, one of the best-known "non-practicing entities" or NPEs, otherwise known derogatorily as "patent trolls."[2]

The case was filed on October 9, 2007, and the verdict was issued by the jury about two and a half years later, on April 30, 2010. Both sides presented their cases to the best of their abilities, the lawyers for each side giving the best spin

---

2. Again for the sake of full disclosure, I should state that I myself am a non-practicing entity (as well as being a practicing entity). See Chapter 7 for more about that.

for their client. The jury deliberated just over two hours, a sign that they felt the case was not complex and the issues were fairly obvious to resolve. The jury decided that the patents were invalid—that the prior art presented by the defendants had anticipated the patents and thus the patents should not have been issued.

Many in the open source community celebrated this verdict with headlines like "Total Victory for Open Source Software in a Patent Lawsuit." The fact is that while this was an important case, it should not be considered a definitive victory against patents. The patents-in-suit were determined to be invalid, and so the case ended without really testing the consequences of open source code that infringes a patent. The more interesting battle will be resolved when an open source provider is sued by a company with patents that are found to be valid and where the open source software is found to infringe. Then the monetary amount of the judgment to the patent holder and the effect on the open source community and open source software distributors may significantly change the open source landscape.

26.4.4 NETWORK APPLIANCE, INC. v. SUN MICROSYSTEMS, INC.

The next open source patent lawsuit to watch is *Network Appliance* (NetApp) *v. Sun Microsystems* (Sun). Sun created the Zettabyte File System (ZFS), a method of storing files on a hard disk, for Sun's Solaris operating system. While a file system is mostly invisible to a user, how files are stored tells how they can be read and written, the maximum size of files, how fast they can be accessed or searched, and what kind of information is kept with each file, such as date created, dates modified, and other features that are manipulated by the operating system. In 2005 Sun donated the ZFS to the open source community, publishing the file system method and making it an open standard that anyone can use.

On November 30, 2007, NetApp filed suit against Sun for infringement of seven U.S. patents relating to file systems. Dave Hitz, founder and executive vice president of NetApp, explained his company's position in a declaration for the court asking for an injunction against Sun:

> Sun has open-sourced ZFS and thereby given away for free NetApp's patented technology to anyone that wants to download a copy. That means Sun has created infringing computer code and made it easy for software users and software companies everywhere to infringe, instead of having users compensate NetApp for its technology through normal product purchases. This is not much different from the problems caused when an entity builds a business by distributing for free infringing copies of music. In both cases, there are practical problems in any attempt to recover the

infringing copies of music. In both cases, there are practical problems in any attempt to recover the infringing copies or to enforce rights against everyone that has downloaded copies of the infringing software. One difference is that adoption of ZFS requires time because it is a software program and not just a song. The next two or three years are very significant for the proliferation of ZFS and it is vital to shut down Sun's distribution promptly.

Sun, of course, countersued NetApp for infringement of a number of its own patents. As of this writing, the case is ongoing. The court ruled that Sun does not infringe one of NetApp's patents. Another of NetApp's patents was reexamined by the U.S. Patent Office at Sun's request and received a final rejection; NetApp has appealed the rejection. All of Sun's patents for which NetApp requested reexamination successfully made it through the reexamination process without being invalidated. No doubt the case will go on for some time, with reexamination requests and summary judgment requests and appeals. If any of NetApp's patents is eventually upheld and ZFS is found to infringe, that is when the excitement will begin. If that happens, it will be very interesting to see what kind of settlement is reached or what kind of damages are awarded, and how that affects all of the open source users of ZFS.

26.5 THE PERVASIVENESS OF OPEN SOURCE SOFTWARE

Based on my own personal experience as a software developer for many years, much of today's software still uses significant amounts of open source code in violation of license agreements, but the code is difficult to find once it has been compiled. Of course, source/object code correlation is a tool that can possibly find many such cases, but it may be impractical to do such a comparison on the vast amounts of code in existence. This is especially true for embedded software that is particularly difficult to examine because it is embedded, as the name suggests, in hardware and is not generally accessible without disassembling the product in which it is embedded. I have seen a significant amount of embedded software that includes open source code, and much of it likely violates the licensing requirements.

Enforcing the license agreements on all of this software would require resources well beyond what any open source organization is likely to ever have. However, the threat of future lawsuits has made companies more sensitive to the issue, and they are now taking many more proactive steps to check for open source code creeping into their program's source code and steps to understand the many different license requirements and to meet those requirements or eliminate the open source code.

OPEN SOURCE SOFTWARE: I DON'T COMPLETELY GET IT

The whole open source movement is, I have to admit, a bit beyond my comprehension. I understand wanting to work on large projects with lots of smart people from around the world. I understand wanting to get recognition for that work. I understand the excitement of creating something ingenious and unique that has never been done before. I understand the pride of having something I've developed being used by millions of people around the world. I even understand that in many countries, such as third-world countries and those with oppressive regimes and leaders, there are few other ways to get these opportunities. What I don't understand is why these people don't want money for their work.

I'm a strong believer in capitalism, an ideology under which most of the great innovations throughout time have been created. I also believe that people deserve to be compensated for their time. On the occasions when people have come to me asking to work for free, to gain experience or prove their abilities, I couldn't comply. If they were qualified to work for me, I compensated them to some extent.

When the open source movement began, I believed it would remain relatively small, consisting of the kinds of people described above plus a small group of anticapitalist radicals. I was wrong. Of course, it helped that large corporations began supporting the movement. And I understand that. Big corporations have a lot to gain from software developed for free, rather than by paid employees. That certainly helps their profitability greatly. Also, distributing open source software reduces their chances of being charged with copyright infringement. And software distributed freely cannot be patented, so they are protected against patent suits. I should note that these large companies still keep their crown jewels—the programs containing patented methods and critical functions—under tight security and do not contribute these very valuable assets to the open source community.

As the movement grew, I was certain that it would eventually collapse, and maybe that will still happen in the future. The critical moment, I believe, was when companies that distribute and support open source software, like Geeknet (formerly VA Linux) and Red Hat Software, started reaping huge profits and making their shareholders, officers, and employees extremely wealthy from the work of unpaid programmers. At that time, I believed that these programmers working for free, and particularly those who objected to any profits derived from software whatsoever, would split off and form new movements that would further restrict the rights of use. Well, the open source distributors are generating huge profits and the open source community has continued its pro bono support. It will be interesting to see what happens in the future.

DIGITAL MILLENNIUM COPYRIGHT ACT

The Digital Millennium Copyright Act (DMCA) was passed by unanimous vote of the U.S. Senate and signed into law by President Clinton on October 28, 1998. It implemented treaties signed in December 1996 at the World Intellectual Property Organization (WIPO) Geneva conference. It also amended Title 17 of the United States Code to extend the reach of copyright while limiting the liability of online service providers for copyright infringement by their users.

27.1 WHAT IS THE DMCA?

The DMCA is divided into five titles:

Title I, the "WIPO Copyright and Performances and Phonograms Treaties Implementation Act of 1998," implements the WIPO treaties.

Title II, the "Online Copyright Infringement Liability Limitation Act," creates limitations on the liability of online service providers for copyright infringement when engaging in certain types of activities.

Title III, the "Computer Maintenance Competition Assurance Act," creates an exemption to copyright law to allow the creation of a copy of a computer program by activating a computer for purposes of maintenance or repair.

Title IV contains six miscellaneous provisions, relating to the functions of the Copyright Office, distance education, the exceptions in the Copyright Act for libraries and for making ephemeral recordings, "webcasting" of sound recordings on the Internet, and the applicability of collective bargaining agreement obligations in the case of transfers of rights in motion pictures.

Title V, the "Vessel Hull Design Protection Act," creates a new form of protection for the design of vessel hulls.

The specific issues addressed in the DMCA that are relevant to software and the Internet are these:

- The act makes it a crime to circumvent antipiracy measures (commonly known as "digital rights management" or DRM) built into most commercial software but provides exemptions for nonprofit libraries, archives, and educational institutions under certain circumstances.

- It outlaws the manufacture, sale, and distribution of code-cracking devices used to illegally copy software but permits the cracking of copyright protection devices to conduct encryption research, assess product interoperability, and test computer security systems.

- It creates a "safe harbor" for Internet service providers by limiting their copyright infringement liability for simply transmitting information over the Internet, though service providers are expected to remove material from users' websites that appears to constitute copyright infringement.

- The act limits the liability of nonprofit institutions of higher education, when they serve as online service providers and under certain circumstances, for copyright infringement by faculty members or graduate students.

- It requires webcasters to pay licensing fees to record companies for distributing copyrighted recordings.

- It requires that the Register of Copyrights, after consultation with relevant parties, submit to Congress recommendations regarding how to promote distance education through digital technologies while "maintaining an appropriate balance between the rights of copyright owners and the needs of users."

- It states explicitly that "[n]othing in this section shall affect rights, remedies, limitations, or defenses to copyright infringement, including fair use."

27.2 FOR AND AGAINST THE DMCA

The music industry, the movie industry, and the software industry all see the DMCA as a means to protect their intellectual property while still being able to distribute it in electronic format. Some people say that the advent of audio and video tape and tape players that allowed copying was also initially fought by the record and movie industries. When these industries eventually embraced the technology, they found that the new technology became a new sales method that actually increased rather than decreased revenue and profits. I would argue that this analogy is not quite right. Those companies did not face the near-instant worldwide communication combined with the availability of computers and other media devices that exists today. In the past it was difficult for anyone to copy a work and distribute it to more than a few friends. Nowadays, distribution can easily reach millions of people within a very short time. I would also remind readers that the majority of artists and writers make a minimal amount of money from their effort. For every J. K. Rowling or Stephen King there are tens of thousands of people like Michael Barr and Gary Stringham who rely on their book income to supplement their regular income. You can see which side of the argument this author and filmmaker is on.

The Free Software Foundation, not surprisingly, is strongly against the DMCA. The following statement is taken from its website:

> Since they were enacted in 1998, the "anti-circumvention" provisions of the Digital Millennium Copyright Act ("DMCA") have not been used as Congress envisioned. Congress meant to stop copyright pirates from defeating DRM restrictions (aka content or copy protections) added to copyrighted works and to ban the "black box" devices intended for that purpose.
>
> In practice, the DMCA and DRM have done nothing to stop "Internet piracy." Yet the DMCA has become a serious threat that jeopardizes fair use, impedes competition and innovation, chills free expression and scientific research, and interferes with computer intrusion laws. If you circumvent DRM locks for non-infringing fair uses or create the tools to do so, you might be on the receiving end of a lawsuit.

Note that at least some of these fears are unfounded because the DMCA specifically exempts the work of researchers, libraries, nonprofits, and academic institutions. Also, the Librarian of Congress is required to issue exemptions from the prohibition against circumvention of access-control technology when it is shown that such technology has had a substantial adverse effect on the ability of people to make non-infringing uses of copyrighted works. The current exemptions, issued in July 2010,[1] are:

---

1. Exemptions to the DMCA are supposed to be considered and voted upon by Congress every three years beginning in 2000. Congress created exemptions in 2000, 2003, and 2006, but the latest exemptions were only approved on July 23, 2010.

1. Motion pictures on DVDs that are lawfully made and acquired and that are protected by the Content Scrambling System when circumvention is accomplished solely to accomplish the incorporation of short portions of motion pictures into new works for the purpose of criticism or comment, and where the person engaging in circumvention believes and has reasonable grounds for believing that circumvention is necessary to fulfill the purpose of the use in the following instances:

(i) Educational uses by college and university professors and by college and university film and media studies students;

(ii) Documentary filmmaking;

(iii) Noncommercial videos

2. Computer programs that enable wireless telephone handsets to execute software applications, where circumvention is accomplished for the sole purpose of enabling interoperability of such applications, when they have been lawfully obtained, with computer programs on the telephone handset.[2]

3. Computer programs, in the form of firmware or software, that enable used wireless telephone handsets to connect to a wireless telecommunications network, when circumvention is initiated by the owner of the copy of the computer program solely to connect to a wireless telecommunications network and access to the network is authorized by the operator of the network.

4. Video games accessible on personal computers and protected by technological protection measures that control access to lawfully obtained works, when circumvention is accomplished solely for the purpose of good faith testing for, investigating, or correcting security flaws or vulnerabilities, if:

(i) The information derived from the security testing is used primarily to promote the security of the owner or operator of a computer, computer system, or computer network; and

(ii) The information derived from the security testing is used or maintained in a manner that does not facilitate copyright infringement or a violation of applicable law.

5. Computer programs protected by dongles that prevent access due to malfunction or damage and which are obsolete. A dongle shall be considered obsolete if it is no longer manufactured or if a replacement or repair is no longer reasonably available in the commercial marketplace; and

6. Literary works distributed in ebook format when all existing ebook editions of the work (including digital text editions made available by authorized entities) contain access controls that prevent the enabling either of the book's read-aloud function or of screen readers that render the text into a specialized format.

---

2. Colloquially referred to as "jailbreaking" or "rooting," this was strenuously objected to by Apple and other smartphone manufacturers.

Also note that there is little controversy among world governments regarding the issues addressed by the DMCA. On May 22, 2001, the European Union passed the Copyright Directive (EUCD) that, along with the Electronic Commerce Directive, addresses the same issues as the DMCA.

27.3 Noteworthy Lawsuits

There have been a number of lawsuits resulting from the DMCA, and there will certainly be more in the future. As of this writing there are three specific cases that are important to consider.

27.3.1 Adobe Systems Inc. v. Elcom Ltd. and Dmitry Sklyarov

The case of *Adobe Systems Inc. v. Dmitry Sklyarov* was the first major test of the criminal provisions of the Digital Millennium Copyright Act that make it a crime to manufacture, sell, or distribute encryption software used for illegally copying software. Russian programmer Dmitry Sklyarov was arrested in 2001, for alleged infringement of the DMCA. While working for ElcomSoft in Russia, he developed the Advanced eBook Processor, a software application allowing users to strip usage restriction information from ebooks produced by Adobe Systems. ElcomSoft presented the software for sale to the public on its website.

Sklyarov was arrested in the United States after presenting a speech at the Defcon-9 conference in Las Vegas, Nevada. The Defcon-9 conference website describes the conference as "an annual computer underground party for hackers in Las Vegas," and it states that Mr. Sklyarov's speech was about "security aspects of electronic books and documents."

In this case, Federal Judge Ronald Whyte instructed the jury that to produce a guilty verdict, they must agree that the company acted willfully or with knowledge of the DMCA and intent to break it. According to the attorney for the government, Assistant U.S. Attorney Scott Frewing, ElcomSoft representatives knew about the DMCA and willfully violated it by developing and selling the Advanced eBook Processor program. "The only point of the program was to remove protections from eBooks," he said.

Adobe Systems initially informed the government about Elcom's publication and brought the copyright charges after insisting that ElcomSoft remove the Advanced eBook Processor from its website, which it did. However, Adobe was on the wrong end of a significant amount of bad publicity in newspapers, particularly among software developers whom they were courting to support their formats and their programs. At some point, Adobe withdrew its complaint against Sklyarov but not against ElcomSoft. The government continued to prosecute both ElcomSoft and Sklyarov, as is its prerogative when it feels a crime has been committed.

Government prosecutors dropped charges against Sklyarov in return for his testimony, though he had already spent nearly a month in jail. In the end, the jury came back with a verdict of not guilty for ElcomSoft because, according to jury foreman Dennis Strader, the jurors agreed that ElcomSoft's product was illegal but acquitted the company because they believed the company didn't mean to violate the law. In an interview after the verdict he said, "We didn't understand why a million-dollar company would put on their Web page an illegal thing that would [ruin] their whole business if they were caught." Strader added that the jury was confused by the DMCA language, and that if they found it confusing, ElcomSoft executives from Russia were probably also confused by it.

The result, I believe, is disturbing. Being confused by a law has never been a valid excuse for breaking it. It would set a lot of bad precedents, including fewer convictions of mentally impaired, or presumably mentally impaired, criminals and those from other countries who have a poor knowledge, or no knowledge, of English. Essentially, defense attorneys were successful in getting jurists to side with the little guy against the big corporation. In this day and age of hackers who wield a lot of technical knowledge and very little ethical knowledge, this kind of resolution can have serious consequences. The effect of the prosecution, though, seems to be the desired one as there have been few other developers who have created encryption-cracking software and offered it to the public since that time.

27.3.2 *MPAA v. RealNetworks Inc.*

In August 2009, the Motion Picture Association of America won a lawsuit against RealNetworks for violating copyright law by selling its RealDVD software that allowed users to copy DVDs and store them on a hard drive. The MPAA claimed that RealNetworks violated the DMCA by circumventing antipiracy measures ARccOS Protection and RipGuard, as well as breaking RealNetworks' licensing agreement with the MPAA's Content Scrambling System.

27.3.3 *Viacom Inc. v. YouTube, Google Inc.*

On March 13, 2007, Viacom filed a lawsuit against YouTube and its corporate parent, Google, for copyright infringement, seeking more than $1 billion in damages. Viacom claimed that the popular video-sharing site was engaging in "massive intentional copyright infringement" for making available a contended 160,000 unauthorized clips of Viacom's entertainment programming. Google lawyers say they are relying on the safe harbor provisions of the 1998 Digital Millennium Copyright Act to shield them from liability. On March 11, 2008, the judge ruled that Viacom could not seek punitive damages against YouTube, but that statutory damages, which could amount to significant money, could be pursued. On June 23, 2010, U.S. District Judge Louis Stanton granted a summary judgment in favor of YouTube, confirming that YouTube is protected by the safe harbor of the DMCA. Viacom has said that it will appeal the verdict.

PART X

CONCLUSION: PAST, PRESENT, AND FUTURE

"Education never ends, Watson. It is a series of lessons with the greatest for the last."
—Sherlock Holmes in *The Red Circle*

I would like to close by going over some of the areas that were developed in the book and encouraging others to take the information here and expand on it. My own work in software forensics began originally just as a way to make some good money while I was working on other projects. In fact, almost a decade ago I started a company, Zeidman Technologies, and developed SynthOS, which I still believe is a great new way to automatically generate or "synthesize" a real-time operating system. I put together a prototype, filed for some patents, and wrote some papers. Then I formed a corporation, hired a team of programmers, rented an office, found a marketing/sales person (actually, I went through several of them), and the work began in earnest. Whether I was ahead of my time or I was simply wrong about my invention (I still believe RTOS synthesis in particular and software synthesis in general will end up being very valuable ways to develop complex software at a high level with more reliability and fewer bugs), the company's revenue was not enough to pay the rent. Or the salaries. So I went back to work as a technical consultant supporting IP litigation to fund the company. I was asked to compare source code from the programs of two parties in litigation. Because I was getting paid by the hour, I was tempted to take as much time as necessary. But the work was also boring, so I created a little utility program to help me out.

I shared that little utility program with other technical consultants and expert witnesses and incorporated their feedback. In a short while, I found myself being recommended for copyright infringement and trade secret cases, mostly based on this little program I had developed. Being the brilliant businessman that I am, it took me all of a year to figure out that I should shutter the business that was losing money (or at least put it on hold) and focus on the little utility program that was making money. I called the program CodeMatch and handed it to a new corporation I had formed called Software Analysis and Forensic Engineering, while expanding my consulting business, Zeidman Consulting.

New cases required new functionality, and eventually CodeMatch got combined with CodeDiff into a program called CodeSuite. These functions were later joined by BitMatch, CodeCLOC, CodeCross, and SourceDetective, all of which were functions that I incorporated into CodeSuite.

What seemed initially like a simple utility program has proven to be very valuable. An entire set of theories and equations has been developed around it. I feel that I have been able to formalize processes and procedures that previously were more art than science. I also feel that there is a long way to go. Each case that we work on at Zeidman Consulting uncovers new issues that need to be considered. As programming languages change and evolve, the methods and mathematics for examining these programs must change and evolve also. I am a strong believer in formal procedures, and those described in this book must be continually improved and tested.

I also feel that the mathematical frameworks described in this book can be applied to many things outside of software forensics, including image recognition, search engine optimization, malware detection, and cyber security. Most likely there are other applications that I do not yet see, but that you will discover and implement. As you do, please write to me and let me know how you apply the information in this book to the field of software forensics or other fields. I wish you much success.

Bob Zeidman
Zeidman Consulting
Bob@ZeidmanConsulting.com

GLOSSARY

ABC   *See* Atanasoff-Berry Computer.

abstraction   Starting from a computer program's source code and creating a representation of a high level of functionality.

abstraction-filtration-comparison test   The test to find nonliteral copyright infringement of a computer program's source code by abstracting the code to a high level of functionality, filtering out those source code elements that are not protectable, and then comparing two computer programs to find copying. Put forth by Judge John Walker in his opinion for the case of *Computer Associates International Inc. v. Altai Inc.*

ACM   *See* Association for Computing Machinery.

A-correlation   The method of combining source code element correlation scores into an overall correlation score by averaging the element correlation scores.

Agreement on Trade-Related Aspects of Intellectual Property Rights (TRIPs)   A multilateral agreement signed in 2000 by the member nations of the World Trade Organization (WTO) that creates uniform principles and enforcement of intellectual property rights.

algorithm   A method for solving a problem in a limited sequence of steps.

American Standard Code for Information Interchange (ASCII)   A standard representation of characters using a single byte (8 bits).

anticipate   With respect to patents, to describe a patent claim before the patent is filed.

API   *See* application program interface.

application program interface (API)   A function in a first computer program that allows a second computer program to access the data or the functionality of the first computer program in the second computer program's source code.

ASCII   *See* American Standard Code for Information Interchange.

assembler   A computer program for translating assembly language code into object code.

assembly language   A low-level computer programming language that describes simple instructions that are closely mapped to object code.

Association for Computing Machinery (ACM)   An international nonprofit organization of computer scientists and engineers that advances computing as a science and a profession.

Atanasoff-Berry Computer (ABC)   The first digital computer, conceived in 1937 and tested in 1942 at Iowa State University by John Atanasoff and Clifford Berry.

atom   The basic division of a source code element type. If the element type is the instruction sequence, the atom is the number of instructions in the sequence. For the statement, comment/string, and identifier element types, the atom is the number of characters in the element.

axiom   A mathematical principle that cannot be proven, but from which mathematical results can be derived and proven.

BASIC   Popular computer programming language created by John George Kemeny and Thomas Eugene Kurtz in 1964 at Dartmouth University to teach computer programming to students outside of computers or science. Stands for **B**eginner's **A**ll-purpose **S**ymbolic **I**nstruction **C**ode.

Basic Input/Output System (BIOS)   Firmware in a personal computer that controls the hardware for entering information into the computer, such as the keyboard and mouse, and the hardware for displaying information, such as the monitor.

binary   A representation using only ones and zeros.

BIOS   *See* Basic Input/Output System.

bit   The smallest binary piece of information, a one or a zero.

BitMatch   The function of CodeSuite that calculates object code correlation and source/object code correlation.

Board of Patent Appeals and Interferences (BPAI)   An administrative law body of the United States Patent and Trademark Office to which patent applicants can appeal decisions by the USPTO; in making such decisions the board decides issues of patentability.

Boolean algebra   The algebra used by programmers to describe the operations performed by modern digital computers. Invented by mathematician George Boole and first used to describe computer circuits by electrical engineer Claude Shannon.

BPAI   *See* Board of Patent Appeals and Interferences.

BSD   Berkeley Source Distribution.

build   With respect to software, the process to create an executable computer program from source code.

byte   Eight bits.

bytecode   A representation of a computer program that is simpler than typical source code but more complex than assembly code. Source code for the Java programming language is compiled into bytecode, rather than object code, and executed on an interpreter called a "virtual machine."

C One of the most popular computer programming languages in use today. Developed by Dennis Ritchie at AT&T Bell Labs in 1972.

C++ An extension of the C programming language that was one of the first, and certainly the most popular, object-oriented languages. Developed by Bjarne Stroustrup at AT&T Bell Labs in 1979.

CAFC *See* Court of Appeals for the Federal Circuit.

call by diagram A diagram that shows which functions are called by other functions in a computer program.

changing lines of code (CLOC) A method for comparing computer programs to measure the evolution of the source code and changes in its intellectual property.

CIP *See* continuation-in-part patent.

claim With respect to a patent, the most basic description of an invention.

claim chart A chart that shows how a particular product implements (or infringes on) the claims of a patent.

clean room *See* software clean room.

CLOC *See* changing lines of code.

clone With respect to software, a copy of a section of code that performs a function identical to that of the original code.

COBOL One of the earliest high-level computer programming languages. Stands for COmmon Business Oriented Language.

CodeCLOC The function of CodeSuite that calculates changes in software using the CLOC method.

CodeCross The function of CodeSuite that calculates source code cross-correlation.

CodeDiff The function of CodeSuite that calculates source code differentiation.

CodeMatch The function of CodeSuite that calculates source code correlation.

CodeMeasure A computer program from Software Analysis and Forensic Engineering Corporation that calculates changes in software using the CLOC method.

CodeSuite A computer program from Software Analysis and Forensic Engineering Corporation that calculates the various kinds of source code and object code correlation for use in IP litigation.

comment A line of source code that does not specify an operation for the computer to execute but is used to give a description to someone reading the source code.

comment out To turn functional source code into a comment, typically by adding comment delimiters.

commutativity A mathematical principle. A function is commutative if an operation on two elements does not depend on the order of the elements.

compile With respect to software, to turn source code into object code.

compiler With respect to software, the computer program that takes in source code and outputs object code.

computer forensics The study of digital computer data for the purpose of presenting evidence in court.

conditional   With respect to software, a line of source code that tests a condition and performs one of two or more options depending on the test result.

constant   With respect to software, a number that, once defined, cannot change.

continuation patent   A patent that has claims that describe aspects of an invention that was previously described in an earlier patent.

continuation-in-part patent (CIP)   A patent that has some claims that describe aspects of an invention that was previously described in an earlier patent and other claims that describe new aspects of the previous invention.

copyleft   Term coined by the Free Software Foundation (FSF) to refer to its GNU Public License (GPL) agreement. Protects the programmer's rights to restrict usage of a computer program and is used in addition to a copyright.

copyright   Legal term describing rights given to creators for their literary and artistic works, including computer software.

correlation   A mathematical representation of the similarity of two or more things.

Court of Appeals for the Federal Circuit (CAFC)   The federal court that hears appeals from the district courts located within its circuit, appeals from decisions of federal administrative agencies, and appeals in specialized cases such as those involving patent laws and cases decided by the Court of International Trade and the Court of Federal Claims.

cross compiler   A compiler that runs on one computer but produces object code for another computer.

cyber crime   Crime that involves computers as an integral part of the crime.

cyber security   Security measures for preventing cyber crime.

cyber theft   Theft that involves computers as an integral part.

cyber warfare   Warfare that involves computers as an integral part, such as attacking a country's computer infrastructure using a computer virus.

cyclomatic complexity   Invented by Thomas McCabe, a method of determining the complexity of a computer program by counting the number of individual execution paths through the program's source code.

database   A collection of data, typically in electronic format, that is organized so that its contents can easily be accessed, managed, and updated.

debug   To test and fix problems ("bugs") in a computer program.

debugger   Software that enables and improves the ability to test and fix problems in a computer program.

decompile   To reverse the compilation process by translating object code into source code.

decrypt   To reverse the encryption process by translating disguised information back into the original undisguised information.

delimiter   With respect to software, one or more characters used to specify the limits of a source code element. For example, a double quotation mark is a delimiter used at the beginning and the end of a string.

deposition   In law, an oral cross-examination of a witness, under oath, for later use at a trial.

design patent   A patent that covers a new, original, and ornamental design of an item.

deterministic   A value that can be exactly calculated.

digit   The smallest digital piece of information, a number from zero through nine.

digital   Strictly a representation using only zero through nine, though typically used to mean a computer that performs calculations using discrete values, usually binary.

digital forensics   The study of digital data for the purpose of presenting evidence in court. This area of study is not concerned with the meaning of the data.

Digital Millennium Copyright Act (DMCA)   A U.S. law that extends copyright protections by addressing encryption methods, Internet distribution, and other aspects of electronic works.

Digital Rights Management (DRM)   Electronic methods for controlling access to materials protected by intellectual property laws, including copyrights and patents.

disassemble   To reverse the assembly process by translating object code into assembly code.

Disk Operating System (DOS)   Refers generically to the earliest personal computer operating systems for computers that used disk drives such as Apple DOS, PC-DOS, and MS-DOS. Later came to be used to refer specifically to MS-DOS.

divisional patent   A patent that originally was a part of another patent that was divided up, usually at the request of a patent examiner who decided that the original patent described more than one invention.

DLL   *See* Dynamic Link Library.

DMCA   *See* Digital Millennium Copyright Act.

dongle   A hardware security device connected to a computer that allows the computer to run a specific computer program.

DOS   *See* Disk Operating System.

DRM   *See* Digital Rights Management.

Dynamic Link Library (DLL)   A small computer program that cannot run by itself but that provides functionality to other programs while they are running.

Economic Espionage Act   The 1996 federal law criminalizing commercial espionage and trade secret theft involving multiple states or foreign entities.

EFF   *See* Electronic Frontier Foundation.

Electronic Frontier Foundation (EFF)   A nonprofit organization with the mission of defending free speech, privacy, innovation, and consumer rights when these freedoms in the networked world come under attack.

embedded system   A software system that controls hardware and is not accessible for a user to modify.

embodiment   With respect to patents, an example of an invention.

enabling   With respect to patents, a term applied to a description of an invention that allows one to build the patented invention. If the description does not give enough information to build the patent, it is non-enabling.

encryption A method of disguising information so that only allowed parties are able to reverse the disguise (decrypt) the information and understand it.

ENIAC Built at the University of Pennsylvania in 1946 by Professors John Mauchly and J. Presper Eckert, the first digital electronic computer to be used for a practical purpose. Stands for **E**lectronic **N**umerical **I**ntegrator **a**nd **C**omputer. Often credited as the first digital electronic computer, which was actually the Atanasoff-Berry Computer, from which ENIAC was derived.

EUCD *See* European Union Copyright Directive.

European Union Copyright Directive (EUDC) Copyright law passed by the European Union that with the Electronic Commerce Directive addresses many of the issues covered by the DMCA in the United States.

European Union Electronic Commerce Directive Commerce law passed by the European Union that with the Copyright Directive addresses many of the issues covered by the DMCA in the United States.

executable file A binary object file that can be used to execute a computer program.

extrinsic evidence With respect to patents, interpretations of terms used in patent claims as referenced in the patent documents themselves.

factorial A mathematical operation. A product is produced by multiplying an integer by the next smallest integer, continuing until the integer 1 is reached. Represented by an exclamation point following the starting number. The exception is that 0! is equal to 1.

filtration With respect to analyzing software to determine copyright infringement, eliminating source code that is not protectable under copyright law.

fingerprint With respect to software, a small representation of a computer program, or section of a computer program, that can be used to identify that program or program section.

firmware Software that is built into a computer that is used to directly control the computer's hardware.

flowchart A diagram used to show flow of control and/or data within a computer program.

forensic engineering The investigation of things to determine their cause of failure, for presentation in a court of law.

forensics From the Latin word *forensis* meaning "of or before the forum," the science of examining evidence and drawing conclusions for presentation in a court of law.

Fortran Developed at IBM in 1957 by a team led by John W. Backus, the earliest high-level computer programming language still in use. Stands for "**For**mula **tran**slation."

Free Software Foundation (FSF) A nonprofit group that advocates for "free software ideals" whereby users should have the ability to run, copy, distribute, study, change, and improve all software. Works for the adoption of free software and free media formats and organizes activist campaigns against commercial software, digital rights management, and software patents.

FSF *See* Free Software Foundation.

GNU   A UNIX-like operating system. Stands for "GNU's not UNIX."

GNU Project   A nonprofit organization that was created to develop a complete UNIX-like open source operating system.

GNU Public License (GPL)   A software license supported by the GNU organization that allows a computer programmer to make a program and its source code available to everyone freely to use and change and that also requires that all derivative software and its source code remain available and free to use and change.

GPL   *See* GNU Public License.

Graphical User Interface (GUI)   A method for a computer to interact with a user with windows, check boxes, buttons, and other graphical representations.

GUI   *See* Graphical User Interface.

Halstead measure   One of the earliest methods of mathematically measuring software, developed by Maurice H. Halstead.

hardware description language (HDL)   A language similar to a computer programming language but that is used to create hardware, typically an integrated circuit.

HDL   *See* hardware description language.

header file   A small source code file that traditionally was used to hold common definitions but now often contains code generated by an automatic code generation tool.

hex   *See* hexadecimal.

hexadecimal (hex)   A base-16 representation of a number.

HTML   *See* Hypertext Markup Language.

HTTP   *See* Hypertext Transmission Protocol.

Hypertext Markup Language (HTML)   The language used to create Web page layouts and control interactions with a Web page user.

Hypertext Transmission Protocol (HTTP)   The communications protocol used to send and receive Web pages and other information over the Internet.

IDE   *See* interactive development environment.

identifier   A source code element that names a variable, constant, function, or label in a computer program.

IEEE   *See* Institute of Electrical and Electronics Engineers.

infringe   To encroach upon in a way that violates law or the rights of another.

initial public offering (IPO)   The first stock offering on a public market for a company.

Institute of Electrical and Electronics Engineers (IEEE)   An international nonprofit organization of engineers involved in developing and testing electrical and electronic devices.

instruction   A source code element that signifies the actions to take place in a computer program.

intellectual property (IP)   Property that is abstract rather than physical; specifically, anything created by the human mind.

interactive development environment (IDE)   A computer program or set of programs that provides interoperable tools for developing software.

Internal Revenue Service (IRS)   The U.S. government agency responsible for tax collection and tax law enforcement.

interpreter   A computer program that interprets each line of source code and commands the computer what to do.

intrinsic evidence   With respect to patents, interpretations of patent claim terms by using common definitions.

IP   *See* intellectual property.

IPO   *See* initial public offering.

IRS   *See* Internal Revenue Service.

jailbreaking   A process that allows users of personal digital assistants and cell phones to install their own software applications on their devices by unlocking the operating system that is locked by the manufacturer.

Java   A computer programming language developed at Sun Microsystems in 1995 by James Gosling to be run on a wide variety of computers with different operating systems residing on a common network.

JavaScript   A computer programming language developed by Brendan Eich of Netscape for programs to be run from a Web browser.

JPlag   A "plagiarism detection" computer program created by Guido Malpohl and Michael Phlippsen at the University of Karlsruhe.

keyword   With respect to software, a word that has a special meaning in a particular computer programming language.

label   With respect to software, a word used to give a name to a particular location in source code for reference by instructions in the source code.

LCCS   *See* longest common contiguous subsequence.

LCS   *See* longest common subsequence.

lemma   A short theorem used in proving a larger theorem.

LFSR   *See* linear feedback shift register.

linear feedback shift register (LFSR)   A hardware circuit for connecting flip-flops and exclusive OR logic gates to create a pseudorandom sequence of numbers.

lines of code (LOC)   The number of lines of software source code in a computer program. Also referred to as "SLOC" (source lines of code).

Linux   The UNIX-like kernel developed for the personal computer in 1991 by Linus Torvalds to work with the GNU operating system.

LISP   Programming language created by John McCarthy in 1958 at the Massachusetts Institute of Technology for artificial intelligence (AI) projects. Stands for **LIS**t **P**rocessing.

LLOC   *See* logical lines of code.

LOC   *See* lines of code.

logical lines of code (LLOC)   The number of functional lines of software source code in a computer program.

longest common contiguous subsequence (LCCS)   The longest contiguous sequence of things that can be found in two sequences of things. Also known as longest common substring.

longest common subsequence (LCS)   The longest sequence of things that can be found in two sequences of things, in the same order but not necessarily contiguous.

longest common substring   The longest contiguous sequence of things that can be found in two sequences of things. Also known as longest common contiguous subsequence.

MAC OS   Operating system for the Apple Macintosh computer.

macro   With respect to software, one or more lines of code that represent a much larger number of actions or lines of code. A static macro always represents a fixed set of source code statements. A context-dependent macro functionality that is synthesized into different source code statements depending on the context in which it is used (see primitive).

malware   Any malicious software that accesses a computer for the purpose of performing illegal or unapproved activities, including stealing information and invading privacy. Includes software viruses and spyware.

***Manual of Patent Examining Procedure* (MPEP)**   A document published by the United States Patent and Trademark Office that describes the laws and regulations for examination of U.S. patent applications.

MASM   An assembler and assembly language created for the personal computer by Microsoft.

McCabe measure   *See* cyclomatic complexity.

M-correlation   The method of combining source code element correlation scores into an overall correlation score by taking the maximum element correlation scores.

metadata   Data about a data file that gives information about such things as the creation or owner of the file, for example, the name of the person who created it, the creation date, the date last modified, and the file format.

microprocessor   A computer processor on a chip, the most common type of computer processor available.

misappropriate   A nicer word for "theft," usually used to describe intellectual property that was taken without appropriate permission, purposely or by accident.

MOSS   A plagiarism detection computer program developed at the University of California at Berkeley by Professor Alex Aiken. Stands for "**M**easure **o**f **S**oftware **S**imilarity."

Motion Picture Association of America (MPAA)   A United States nonprofit business and trade association for advancing the business interests of movie studios.

MPAA   *See* Motion Picture Association of America.

MPEP   *See Manual of Patent Examining Procedure.*

Multics   An early time-sharing operating system developed in 1962 at the MIT Computation Center by a team led by Professor Fernando J. Corbató.

multidimensional correlation   A correlation between two things determined by combining correlation values for individual aspects of these things into a single correlation value.

native code   Binary code that is directly executable by a computer processor without requiring any intermediate software.

NDA   *See* nondisclosure agreement.

nondisclosure agreement (NDA)   An agreement by one party that it will not disclose confidential information it learns from a second party.

non-practicing entity (NPE)   An entity that does not produce a product but holds patents and licenses them to other companies, often suing these other companies when a license payment cannot be agreed upon.

NPE   *See* non-practicing entity.

obfuscate   To make something unclear. With respect to software, changing source code comments, identifier names, and other code elements in such a way that the code still functions correctly but is difficult to understand.

object code   Binary code that can be executed directly by a computer processor.

object-oriented programming (OOP)   A computer programming paradigm where the code manipulates objects that comprise functions and the data upon which the functions operate.

one of ordinary skill in the art   See person having ordinary skill in the art.

OOP   *See* object-oriented programming.

OOSITA   One of ordinary skill in the art. See person having ordinary skill in the art.

open source   A type of software for which the source code is made available for use at no charge, but often with restrictions according to an open source license agreement.

Open Source Initiative (OSI)   A nonprofit corporation formed to educate about and advocate for the benefits of open source and to build bridges among different constituencies in the open source community.

orthogonal   In geometry, things that are at right angles to each other when mapped in a Euclidian space. Also used to refer to things that have no relation to each other.

OSI   *See* Open Source Initiative.

patent The grant of a property right to an inventor, issued by a government, for a limited-time monopoly on the use of an invention.

patent-in-suit A patent involved in a lawsuit.

patent troll Derogatory name for a non-practicing entity.

PERL A high-level, general-purpose, interpreted, dynamic computer programming language originally developed by Larry Wall in 1987.

person having ordinary skill in the art (PHOSITA) A hypothetical person who has average skills in an area to which an invention applies, such that the person should be able to know that an invention is or is not obvious and should be able to create the invention by reading the patent.

PHOSITA *See* person having ordinary skill in the art.

PHP A general-purpose scripting language created by Rasmus Lerdorf in 1995 and used mostly for back-end Web development to produce dynamic Web pages.

physical lines of code *See* lines of code.

piracy With regard to software, refers to stealing software by copying it and distributing it without paying the owner.

plagiarism The unauthorized use or close imitation of a work and the representation of it as one's own original work.

Plague One of the earliest plagiarism detection programs, developed by Professor Geoffrey Whale at the University of New South Wales.

plant patent A patent for the invention or discovery and asexual reproduction of a distinct and new variety of plant, other than a tuber-propagated plant or a plant found in an uncultivated state.

primitive A high-level statement in software source code that represents a complex function that is synthesized into source code statements (see macro).

prior art With regard to patents, documents and other materials that were publicly available before a patent was filed that are relevant to the patent's claims. If any prior art describes any patent claims for an invention, those claims are not patentable.

processor With regard to computers, the part of the computer that executes the instructions of a computer program.

programming language A human-readable language that is used to write source code for computer programs.

provisional patent An preliminary patent application that can be filed without any formal patent claims, oath or declaration, or information disclosure statement but establishes an effective filing date and allows the term "Patent Pending" to be applied to the invention.

PTO *See* United States Patent and Trademark Office.

Python A general-purpose high-level computer programming language created in December 1989 by Guido van Rossum at the National Research Institute for Mathematics and Computer Science in the Netherlands and designed to emphasize code readability.

Rabin-Karp algorithm   A string-searching algorithm created by Professors Michael O. Rabin of Hebrew University and Richard M. Karp of the University of California at Berkeley in 1987.

readily ascertainable   With regard to trade secrets, easy to obtain. Some states give trade secret status to things that are not readily ascertainable rather than simply not publicly available.

real-time operating system (RTOS)   A computer program that schedules execution within specified time constraints, manages system resources, and provides a consistent foundation for developing application code.

redact   To obscure or remove from a document.

refactor   With regard to software, to improve the maintainability of code without changing its functionality.

repository   With regard to software, an area used to store source code for different versions of a computer program.

reverse engineer   To examine an object to understand how it works in order to duplicate or enhance it.

rooting   *See* jailbreaking.

RTOS   *See* real-time operating system.

S-correlation   The method of combining source code element correlation scores into an overall correlation score by calculating the square root of the sum of squares of the element correlation scores.

script   The source code for a program written in a simple, interpreted language called a "scripting language."

scripting language   A simple, interpreted programming language.

SLOC   Source lines of code. *See also* lines of code (LOC).

software architecture   A vague term that generally refers to the overall structure and organization of a computer program.

software clean room   A method for developing one computer program based on a second computer program without infringing on the copyrights of the second computer program.

software forensics   The examination of software for producing results in court.

source code   Human-readable instructions for a computer program that are compiled into machine-readable instructions for the computer processor to execute.

source code differentiation   A method for determining the differences and similarities in two sets of computer source code.

SourceDetective   The function of CodeSuite that searches the Internet for common source code elements.

SourceForge   A large open source software development website that provides free services to help people build open source software and distribute it.

spyware   A type of malware that runs on a computer without the users' knowledge, collects information about users without their knowledge, and sends it to a remote site.

SQL   A computer programming language developed at IBM by Donald D. Chamberlin and Raymond F. Boyce in the early 1970s and designed for accessing a database. Stands for "Structured Query Language."

statement   A line of source code that specifies an operation for the computer to perform.

string   With regard to computer source code, a source code element that is a message to the user. With regard to analyzing text such as source code, simply a sequence of characters.

substring   A sequence of characters that is a contiguous subset of another sequence of characters that constitute a string of characters.

synthesis   With respect to software, the process of taking high-level source code primitives representing a complex function and producing source code statements to perform that function.

theory   A coherent group of general propositions used as principles of explanation for a class of phenomena and that can be derived or proved from axioms.

third party   A party that is not directly involved with the issue being evaluated. With regard to software development, a party that provides software either for free or for a price.

trademark   Protectable intellectual property comprising words, names, symbols, sounds, or colors that distinguish goods and services from those manufactured or sold by others.

transfer pricing   A means of pricing goods that are transferred from one tax jurisdiction to another.

TRIPs   *See* Agreement on Trade-Related Aspects of Intellectual Property Rights.

UML   *See* Unified Modeling Language.

Unicode   A comprehensive standard for representing up to 107,000 characters from many different languages.

Unified Modeling Language (UML)   A visual language for specifying, constructing, and documenting software systems.

Uniform Trade Secrets Act (UTSA)   A document adopted by many but not all states in the United States to create uniform definitions and enforcement of trade secret rights throughout the United States.

United States Patent and Trademark Office (USPTO)   The U.S. government agency for granting U.S. patents and registering trademarks.

universal resource locator (URL)   The unique address for a resource that is accessible on the Internet. For Web pages, it is the address of the Web page such as http://www.zeidman.net/index.htm.

UNIX   A computer operating system developed in 1969 by a group at AT&T Bell Labs that included Ken Thompson, Dennis Ritchie, Brian Kernighan, Douglas McIlroy, and Joe Ossanna.

URL   *See* universal resource locator.

USPTO   *See* United States Patent and Trademark Office.

utility patent   A patent for the invention of a new and useful process, machine, manufacture, or composition of matter, or a new and useful improvement thereof.

UTSA   *See* Uniform Trade Secrets Act.

variable   With regard to software, a name given to a holder for changing data.

Verilog   A hardware description language developed by Phil Moorby and Prabhu Goel in 1983 at Automated Integrated Design Systems, which later became Gateway Design Automation.

VHDL   A hardware description language developed by the U.S. Department of Defense to document the behavior of integrated circuits. Stands for "**VHSIC H**ardware **D**escription **L**anguage."

virtual machine   A software program that allows one computer to act like a second computer by executing code meant for the second computer on the first computer. The second computer may be virtual in that the computer does not physically exist but is rather a common platform for running programs.

Visual Basic   An event-driven computer programming language and integrated development environment (IDE) developed by Alan Cooper and introduced in 1991 by Microsoft that allows program graphical user interfaces (GUIs) to be drawn and the code for implementing them to be generated automatically.

whitespace   Characters in text that are used to separate characters but do not print (i.e., space and tab characters).

Windows operating system   The versions of personal computer operating systems developed by Microsoft.

World Trade Organization (WTO)   An organization of member nations that deals with the rules of international trade, including intellectual property trade, and provides a forum for governments to negotiate resolutions to trade disputes.

WTO   *See* World Trade Organization.

Xenix   A version of the UNIX operating system, licensed by Microsoft from AT&T in the late 1970s and later acquired by Santa Cruz Operations (SCO), which distributed it as SCO UNIX and later as SCO OpenServer.

YAP   One of the earliest plagiarism detection programs, developed by Professor Michael J. Wise at the University of Sydney. Stands for "**Y**et **A**nother **P**lague."

REFERENCES

Chapter 1   About This Book

World Intellectual Property Organization (WIPO), www.wipo.int, retrieved July 7, 2009.

Chapter 2   Intellectual Property Crime

McAfee, Inc., *Unsecured Economies: Protecting Vital Information*, http://resources.mcafee.com/content/NAUnsecuredEconomiesReport, 2009.

Ellen Messmer, "More than Half of Booted Workers Steal Data on Way Out, Survey Finds," *Network World*, February 23, 2009.

Matthew Forney and Arthur Kroeber, "Google's Business Reason for Leaving China," *Wall Street Journal*, April 6, 2010.

BBC News, "Russia Timeline," http://news.bbc.co.uk/2/hi/europe/country_profiles/1113655.stm, retrieved July 2, 2010.

Terry Macalister and Tom Parfitt, "$20bn Gas Project Seized by Russia," *The Guardian*, December 12, 2006.

Andrew Meier, "Who Fears a Free Mikhail Khodorkovsky?" *New York Times Magazine*, November 18, 2009.

"Sakhalin-II," Reference.com, www.reference.com/browse/wiki/Sakhalin-II, retrieved July 2, 2010.

Chapter 3   Source Code

The Language Guide, http://groups.engin.umd.umich.edu/CIS/course.des/cis400, University of Michigan, retrieved August 9, 2010.

"Verilog Resources," www.verilog.com, 2009, retrieved August 9, 2010.

Chapter 5   Scripts, Intermediate Code, Macros, and Synthesis Primitives

Arnold Berger, Mathew Hill, and Bob Zeidman, "Software and RTOS Synthesis: The Next Step in Software Development?" *EETimes* (www.pldesignline.com), February 27, 2008.

Bob Zeidman, "Software Synthesis for Embedded Systems," *Embedded Systems Programming*, February 2005, pp. 36–43.

Part III   Intellectual Property

Kenneth W. Dobyns, *The Patent Office Pony: A History of the Early Patent Office*, 1994, www.myoutbox.net/pohome.htm, retrieved August 24, 2010.

Rabbi Israel Schneider, "Jewish Law and Copyright," www.jlaw.com/Articles/copyright1.html, retrieved August 24, 2010.

Cornell University Law School Legal Information Institute, "Trademark," http://topics.law.cornell.edu/wex/Trademark, retrieved August 24, 2010.

Chapter 6   Copyrights

World Intellectual Property Organization (WIPO), "Intellectual Property—Some Basic Definitions," www.wipo.int/about-ip/en/studies/publications/ip_definitions.htm, retrieved August 11, 2010.

Case Law on Copyright of Computer Programs, Intellectual Property Rights (IPR), vol. 5, no. 7, a bulletin from Technology Information, Forecasting and Assessment Council (TIFAC) (New Delhi, India: Patent Facilitating Cell (PFC) 1999).

Benjamin Constant, translated by Biancamaria Fontana, *Constant: Political Writings (Cambridge Texts in the History of Political Thought)* (Cambridge: Cambridge University Press, 1988).

David Vaver, *Intellectual Property Rights: Critical Concepts in Law*, 1st ed. (London: Routledge, 2006).

Davoll et al. v. Brown, Massachusetts 1845, Case No. 3,662.

U.S. Copyright Office, Library of Congress, Circular 1, *Copyright Basics*, rev: 10/2008 print: 10/2008–75,000.

Lloyd L. Rich, *Benefits of Copyright Registration*, 2011, www.publaw.com/article/advantages-of-copyright-registration/, retrieved January 30, 2011.

U.S. Copyright Office, Library of Congress, Circular 92, *Copyright Law of the United States and Related Laws Contained in Title 17 of the United States Code*, October 2007.

Lee A. Hollaar, "Digital Law Online," http://digital-law-online.info, retrieved July 7, 2009.

"Statute of Anne, 1710," *The History of Copyright: A Critical Overview with Source Texts in Five Languages*, www.copyrighthistory.com/anne.html through www.copyrighthistory.com/anne6.html, retrieved August 11, 2010.

Edward Samuels, *The Illustrated Story of Copyright* (New York: St. Martin's Press, 2000).

Rob Hassett, "Impact of Apple vs. Franklin Decision," *Computer World*, December 5, 1983.

Apple Computer, Inc. v. Franklin Computer Corporation, U.S. Court of Appeals Third Circuit, August 30, 1983, Digital Law Online, http://digital-law-online.info/cases/219PQ113.htm, retrieved August 11, 2010.

U.S. Copyright Office, Library of Congress, Circular 61, *Copyright Registration of Computer Programs*, May 2009.

"Rule of Doubt," www.nolo.com/dictionary/rule-of-doubt-term.html, retrieved July 8, 2009.

U.S. Code Collection, Cornell University, LII/Legal Information Institute, Title 17—Copyrights, www.law.cornell.edu/uscode/17, retrieved July 8, 2009.

Williams Electronics, Inc. v. Artic International, Inc., U.S. Court of Appeals, Third Circuit, August 2, 1982.

William F. Patry, "Copyright and Computer Programs: A Failed Experiment and a Solution to a Dilemma," *New York Law School Law Review*, vol. 46, February 25, 2003.

Calvin N. Mooers, "Computer Software and Copyright," *Computing Surveys*, vol. 7, no. 1 (March 1975).

J. D. Salinger v. Fredrik Colting, U.S. District Court, Southern District of New York, July 7, 2009.

Paul Andrews, "Apple-Microsoft Lawsuit Fizzles to a Close—'Nothing Left' to Fight About," *The Seattle Times*, June 2, 1993.

Apple Computer, Inc. v. Microsoft Corporation, Nos. 93-16867, 93-16869, and 93-16883, United States Court of Appeals, Ninth Circuit. Argued and Submitted July 11, 1994. Decided September 19, 1994, http://bulk.resource.org/courts.gov/c/F3/35/35.F3d.1435 .93-16883.93-16869.93-16867.html.

Owen W. Linzmayer, *Apple Confidential* (San Francisco: No Starch Press, 1999).

Atari Games Corp. v. Nintendo of America Inc., U.S. Court of Appeals, Federal Circuit, September 10, 1992.

Sega Enterprises Ltd. v. Accolade Inc., U.S. Court of Appeals, Ninth Circuit, October 20, 1992.

Michaud Duffy Group LLP, "The Statue of Liberty: The Most Famous of Design Patents," www.michaud-duffy.com/news27.html, retrieved July 13, 2009.

Web Designer Depot, "Operating Interface Design Between 1981–2009," www.webdesignerdepot.com/2009/03/operating-system-interface-design-between-1981-2009, retrieved September 19, 2010.

Chapter 7   Patents

"The 212th Anniversary of the First American Patent Act," http://inventors.about.com/library/weekly/aa073100a.htm, retrieved August 24, 2010.

Kenneth W. Dobyns, *The Patent Office Pony: A History of the Early Patent Office*, 1994, www.myoutbox.net/pohome.htm, retrieved August 24, 2010.

Ladas & Perry LLP, "A Brief History of the Patent Law of the United States," www.ladas.com/Patents/USPatentHistory.html, retrieved August 24, 2010.

Roger A. Bruns, *A More Perfect Union: The Creation of the United States Constitution* (Washington, DC: Published for the National Archives and Records Administration by the National Archives Trust Fund Board, 1986), www.archives.gov/exhibits/charters/constitution_history.html, retrieved January 17, 2011.

Legal Information Institute, Cornell University Law School, "United States Code: Title 35, Title 35—Patents," www.law.cornell.edu/uscode/35, retrieved August 16, 2010.

United States Patent and Trademark Office, "Description on Patent Types," www.uspto.gov/web/offices/ac/ido/oeip/taf/patdesc.htm, retrieved August 16, 2010.

United States Patent and Trademark Office, "Patents," www.uspto.gov/patents/index.jsp, retrieved August 11, 2010.

World Intellectual Property Organization (WIPO), "Intellectual Property—Some Basic Definitions," www.wipo.int/about-ip/en/studies/publications/ip_definitions.htm, retrieved August 11, 2010.

Manual of Patent Examining Procedure (MPEP), 8th ed., August 2001, latest revision July 2008.

University of Cincinnati Intellectual Property Office, "Patent FAQs," www.ipo.uc.edu/index.cfm?fuseaction=overview.faq, retrieved August 16, 2010.

Diamond, Commissioner of Patents and Trademarks v. Diehr and Lutton, United States Supreme Court, March 3, 1981.

State Street Bank & Trust v. Signature Financial Group, United States Court of Appeals for the Federal Circuit, 149 F.3d 1368 (Fed. Cir. 1998).

D. A. Tysver, "The History of Software Patents," BitLaw, www.bitlaw.com/software-patent/history.html, retrieved July 7, 2009.

Jeffrey R. Kuester and Ann K. Moceyunas, "Patents for Software-Related Inventions," KuesterLaw, March 1995, www.kuesterlaw.com/swpat.html, retrieved August 16, 2010.

P. Heckel, "Debunking the Software Patent Myths," *Communications of the ACM*, vol. 35, no. 6 (1992), pp. 121–140.

"System and Method for Remote Mirroring of Digital Data from a Primary Network Server to a Remote Network Server," U.S. Patent 5,537,533, filed August 11, 1994, issued July 16, 1996.

Alice R. Burks and Arthur W. Burks, *The First Electronic Computer: The Atanasoff Story* (Ann Arbor: University of Michigan Press, 1989).

United States Circuit Court of Appeals, *In re Bernard L. Bilski and Rand A. Warsaw*, Appeal from the United States Patent and Trademark Office, Board of Patent Appeals and Interferences, 2007-1130 (Serial No. 08/833,892), January 3, 2007.

Fourth Annual Northwestern Journal of Technology & Intellectual Property Symposium, "Debate on *In re Bilski*," www.law.northwestern.edu/journals/njtip/symposium/2009/materials/Debate%20on%20In%20re%20Bilski.pdf, March 6, 2009.

Dennis Crouch, "Divided Infringement," Patently-O blog, www.patentlyo.com/patent/2007/03/divided_infring.html, retrieved January 18, 2011.

Chapter 8   Trade Secrets

Karl F. Jorda, "Jorda on: Trade Secrets Have a Long History," Franklin Pierce Law Center, www.jordasecrets.com/2007/10/jorda_on_trade_secrets_have_a.html, retrieved August 24, 2010.

Digital Business Law Group, P.A., "Trade Secrets: History," www.digitalbusinesslawgroup.com/ts-history.html, retrieved August 24, 2010.

Rainer M. Kohler, "Trade Secrets," *Boston College Law Review*, vol. 7, issue 2 (1966), Article 13, http://lawdigitalcommons.bc.edu/cgi/viewcontent.cgi?article=3025&context=bclr, retrieved August 24, 2010.

Vickery v. Welch, Supreme Judicial Court of Massachusetts, October Term, 1837, http://rychlicki.net/inne/19_Pick._523.doc, retrieved August 25, 2010.

World Intellectual Property Organization (WIPO), "Intellectual Property—Some Basic Definitions," www.wipo.int/about-ip/en/studies/publications/ip_definitions.htm, retrieved August 11, 2010.

Yield Dynamics, Inc. v. TEA Systems Corp. (2007) 155 Cal.App.4th 503a.

Uniform Trade Secrets Act, National Conference of Commissioners on Uniform State Laws, as amended 1985, www.law.upenn.edu/bll/archives/ulc/fnact99/1980s/utsa85.htm.

R. Mark Halligan, "The Economic Espionage Act of 1996: The Theft of Trade Secrets Is Now a Federal Crime," 1996–97, http://tradesecretshomepage.com/crime.html, retrieved August 17, 2010.

Economic Espionage Act of 1996, United States Code, Title 18, Chapter 90—Protection of Trade Secrets, www.tscm.com/USC18_90.html, retrieved August 17, 2010.

Chapter 9   Software Forensics

Midwest Forensics Resource Center at the U.S. Department of Energy's Ames Laboratory, Ames, IA, www.mfrc.ameslab.gov, retrieved August 17, 2010.

"Song Ci, Father of Forensic Medicine," *Cultural China*, http://history.cultural-china.com/en/37History279.html, retrieved August 17, 2010.

Gernet, Jacques, *Daily Life in China on the Eve of the Mongol Invasion, 1250–1276* (Stanford: Stanford University Press, 1962).

National Academy of Forensic Engineers, www.nafe.org, retrieved August 17, 2010.

United States Computer Emergency Readiness Team, Department of Homeland Security, "Computer Forensics," 2008, www.us-cert.gov/reading_room/forensics.pdf, retrieved August 17, 2010.

Richard P. Feynman with Ralph Leighton, *"What Do You Care What Other People Think?"* (New York: Bantam Books, 1989).

Marcia S. Smith, *NASA's Space Shuttle Columbia: Synopsis of the Report of the Columbia Accident Investigation Board*, National Aeronautics and Space Administration, September 2, 2003.

Michael G. Noblett, Mark M. Pollitt, and Lawrence A. Presley, "Recovering and Examining Computer Forensic Evidence," *Forensic Science Communications*, vol. 2, no. 4 (October 2000).

P. Sallis, A. Aakjaer, and S. MacDonell, "Software Forensics: Old Methods for a New Science," International Conference on Software Engineering: Education and Practice, January 24–27, 1996, Dunedin, New Zealand.

E. H. Spafford and S. A. Weeber, "Software Forensics: Can We Track Code to Its Authors?" *Purdue Technical Report* CSD–TR 92–010, Purdue University, West Lafayette, IN, 1992.

Chapter 10   Theory

The IEEE and The Open Group, "*Diff*," The Open Group Base Specifications Issue 7, IEEE Std 1003.1-2008, 2001–2008, www.opengroup.org/onlinepubs/9699919799/utilities/diff.html, retrieved August 21, 2010.

James W. Hunt and M. Douglas McIlroy, "An Algorithm for Differential File Comparison," Computing Science Technical Report 41, Bell Laboratories, June 1976.

P. Heckel, "A Technique for Isolating Differences between Files," *Communications of the ACM*, vol. 21, no. 4 (April 1978), pp. 264–268.

Robert Sedgewick and Kevin Wayne, *Algorithms*, 4th ed. (Boston: Addison-Wesley, 2011).

Dan Ellard, "The Rabin-Karp Algorithm," *S-Q Course Book*, Harvard University, www.eecs .harvard.edu/~ellard/Q-97/HTML/root, retrieved August 21, 2010.

Software Analysis & Forensic Engineering Corp., *CodeSuite User's Guide v 3.5*, August 2009.

Claude Shannon, *Claude E. Shannon: Collected Papers* (New York: Wiley-IEEE Press, 1993).

D. E. Knuth, *The Art of Computer Programming*, 2nd ed., vol. 3: *Sorting and Searching* (Reading, MA: Addison-Wesley, 1998).

Mikhail J. Atallah, ed., *Algorithms and Theory of Computation Handbook* (Boca Raton, FL: CRC Press, 1999).

Paul E. Black, "Longest Common Subsequence," *Dictionary of Algorithms and Data Structures*, online ed., U.S. National Institute of Standards and Technology, February 4, 2009, www.itl.nist.gov/div897/sqg/dads/HTML/longestCommonSubsequence.html, retrieved August 21, 2010.

Paul E. Black, "Longest Common Substring," *Dictionary of Algorithms and Data Structures*, online ed., U.S. National Institute of Standards and Technology, February 4, 2009, www.itl.nist.gov/div897/sqg/dads/HTML/longestCommonSubstring.html, retrieved August 21, 2010.

Chapter 12   Applications

"Software Metrics," *SQL Software Quality Assurance*, www.sqa.net/softwarequalitymetrics.html, retrieved October 2, 2008.

M. H. Halstead, *Elements of Software Science* (New York: Elsevier, 1977).

Virtual Machinery, "The Halstead Metrics," 2009, www.virtualmachinery.com/sidebar2.html, retrieved July 22, 2010.

Thomas J. McCabe, "A Complexity Measure," *IEEE Transactions on Software Engineering*, vol. SE-2, no. 4 (December 1976), pp. 308–320.

Kevin Groke, "How to Get Metrics with Understand 2.0," Scientific Toolworks, July 11, 2008, www.scitools.com/blog/2008/07/documentation-how-to-get-metrics-with-understand-20.html, retrieved October 2, 2008.

Robert E. Park, *Software Size Measurement: A Framework for Counting Source Statements* (Pittsburgh: Software Engineering Institute, Carnegie Mellon University, 1992).

N. Baer and B. Zeidman, "Measuring Software Evolution with Changing Lines of Code," 24th International Conference on Computers and Their Applications (CATA-2009), April 10, 2009.

L. Marco, "Measuring Software Complexity," *Enterprise Systems Journal*, April 1997.

Capers Jones, *Programming Productivity* (San Francisco: McGraw-Hill, 1986).

Capers Jones, *A New Business Model for Function Point Metrics, Version 7.0* (Minneapolis: Capers Jones & Associates LLC, 2008).

M Squared Technologies, "Metrics Definitions," 2009, http://msquaredtechnologies.com/m2rsm/docs/rsm_metrics_narration.htm, retrieved August 21, 2010.

Robert E. Park, *Software Size Measurement: A Framework for Counting Source Statements*, Technical Report CMU/SEI-92-TR-020, ESC-TR-92-020, Software Engineering Institute, Carnegie Mellon University, Pittsburgh, PA, 1996, www.sei.cmu.edu/reports/92tr020.pdf, retrieved August 21, 2010.

"*Veritas v. Commissioner*: Tax Court Decision Exposes Flaws in Common IRS Cost-Sharing Buy-In Theories," Morgan, Lewis & Bockius LLP, December 16, 2009, www.morganlewis.com/pubs/Tax_CostSharingBuyInTheories_LF_16dec09.pdf.

John Letzing, "Symantec Wins $545 Million Decision in Federal Tax Case," *MarketWatch.com*, December 10, 2009, www.marketwatch.com/story/symantec-wins-545-million-opinion-in-tax-case-2009-12-10, retrieved December 10, 2009.

Ceteris, "Transfer Pricing Times Legal Edition, Volume V Issue 1," www.ceterisgroup.com/index.php?option=com_content&task=view&id=219&Itemid=150, retrieved April 18, 2010.

Chapter 13 Software Plagiarism Detection

Qing Li with Caroline Yao, *Real-Time Concepts for Embedded Systems* (Lawrence, KS: CMP Books, 2003).

J. A. W. Faidhi and S. K. Robinson, "An Empirical Approach for Detecting Program Similarity and Plagiarism within a University Programming Environment," *Computer Education*, vol. 11 (1987), pp. 11–19.

M. H. Halstead, *Elements of Software Science* (New York: Elsevier, 1977).

H. T. Jankowitz, "Detecting Plagiarism in Student Pascal Programs," *Computer Journal*, vol. 31, no. 1 (1988), pp. 1–8.

A. Parker and J. O. Hamblen, "Computer Algorithms for Plagiarism Detection," *IEEE Transactions on Education*, vol. 32, no. 2 (1989), pp. 94–99.

Geoff Whale, "Identification of Program Similarity in Large Populations," *The Computer Journal*, vol. 33, no. 2 (1990).

Michael J. Wise, *String Similarity via Greedy String Tiling and Running Karp-Rabin Matching*, Department of Computer Science Technical Report, Sydney University, 1993.

Michael J. Wise, "YAP3: Improved Detection of Similarities in Computer Program and Other Texts," SIGCSE '96, Philadelphia, PA, February 15–17, 1996, pp. 130–134.

Lutz Prechelt, Guido Malpohl, and Michael Phlippsen, "Finding Plagiarisms among a Set of Programs with JPlag," *Journal of Universal Computer Science*, vol. 8, no. 11 (2002), pp. 1016–1038.

Saul Schleimer, Daniel Wilkerson, and Alex Aiken, "Winnowing: Local Algorithms for Document Fingerprinting," SIGMOD 2003, San Diego, CA, June 9–12, 2003.

Chapter 14   Source Code Characterization

R. Zeidman, "Multidimensional Correlation of Software Source Code," 2008 Third International Workshop on Systematic Approaches to Digital Forensic Engineering, IEEE, Oakland, CA, 2008, pp. 144–156.

R. Zeidman, "Software Source Code Correlation," 5th IEEE/ACIS International Conference on Computer and Information Science and 1st IEEE/ACIS International Workshop on Component-Based Software Engineering, Software Architecture and Reuse (ICIS-COMSAR'06), IEEE, Honolulu, HI, 2006, pp. 383–392.

Martin Fowler, *Refactoring: Improving the Design of Existing Code* (Reading, MA: Addison-Wesley, 1999).

Chapter 15   Theory

Wilbur B. Davenport and William L. Root, *An Introduction to the Theory of Random Signals and Noise* (New York: McGraw-Hill, 1958).

R. Zeidman, "Multidimensional Correlation of Software Source Code," 2008 Third International Workshop on Systematic Approaches to Digital Forensic Engineering, IEEE, Oakland, CA, 2008, pp. 144–156.

R. Zeidman, "Software Source Code Correlation," 5th IEEE/ACIS International Conference on Computer and Information Science and 1st IEEE/ACIS International Workshop on Component-Based Software Engineering, Software Architecture and Reuse (ICIS-COMSAR'06), IEEE, Honolulu, HI, 2006, pp. 383–392.

"'Smoking Gun' Presented at Avanti Restitution Hearing," *EETimes*, June 27, 2001.

Chapter 16   Implementation

Robert M. Zeidman, "Software Tool for Detecting Plagiarism in Computer Source Code," U.S Patent 7,503,035, filed November 5, 2003, issued March 10, 2009.

Robert M. Zeidman, "Software Tool for Detecting Plagiarism in Computer Source Code," U.S. Patent application number 12/217,711, filed July 7, 2008.

Chapter 17   Applications

Martin Fowler, *Refactoring: Improving the Design of Existing Code* (Reading, MA: Addison-Wesley, 1999).

I. Baxter and D. Churchett, "Using Clone Detection to Manage a Product Line," ICSR7 Workshop, Industrial Experience with Product Line Approaches, 2002.

Chapter 19   Implementation

Robert M. Zeidman, "Detecting Copied Computer Source Code by Examining Computer Object Code," U.S. Patent application number 12/214,128, filed June 17, 2008.

American National Standard for Information Systems—Coded Character Sets—7-Bit American National Standard Code for Information Interchange (7-Bit ASCII), ANSI X3.4-1986, American National Standards Institute, Inc., March 26, 1986.

ISO/IEC 8859-1:1998, 8-bit single-byte coded graphic character sets, Part 1: Latin alphabet No. 1 (draft dated February 12, 1998, published April 15, 1998).

The Unicode Consortium, *The Unicode Standard, Version 5.0*, 5th ed. (Boston: Addison-Wesley, 2006).

Chapter 20   Applications

Unicode, Inc., "The Unicode Standard: A Technical Introduction," 1991–2010, www.unicode .org/standard/principles.html, retrieved September 23, 2010.

Ronald B. Standler, "Differences between Civil and Criminal Law in the USA," 1998, www.rbs2 .com/cc.htm.

Chapter 21   Theory, Implementation, and Applications

Robert M. Zeidman, "Detecting Plagiarism in Computer Source Code," U.S. Patent application number 12/330,492, filed December 8, 2008.

Chapter 22   Detecting Copyright Infringement

William F. Patry, "Copyright and Computer Programs: A Failed Experiment and a Solution to a Dilemma," *New York Law School Law Review*, September 25, 2003.

Ladas & Perry, LLP, "The 'Abstraction, Filtration, Comparison' Test," www.ladas.com/Patents/ Computer/SoftwareAndCopyright/Softwa06.html, retrieved May 4, 2010.

Whelan Associates, Inc. v. Jaslow Dental Laboratory, Inc., et al., U.S. Court of Appeals, Third Circuit, August 4, 1986, 797 F.2d 1222, 230 USPQ 481.

Lee A. Hollaar, "Chapter 2: Copyright of Computer Programs, Legal Protection of Digital Information," http://digital-law-online.info/lpdi1.0/treatise22.html, retrieved September 21, 2010.

Computer Associates International Inc. v. Altai Inc., U.S. Court of Appeals, Second Circuit, June 22, 1992.

Bob Zeidman, "What, Exactly, Is Software Plagiarism?" *Intellectual Property Today*, February 2007.

Robert M. Zeidman, "Searching the Internet for Common Elements in a Document in Order to Detect Plagiarism," U.S. Patent application 12/253,249, filed October 17, 2008.

Ilana Shay, Nikolaus Baer, and Robert Zeidman, "Measuring Whitespace Patterns as an Indication of Plagiarism," ADFSL Conference on Digital Forensics, Security and Law, May 20, 2010.

Bob Zeidman, *Verilog Designer's Library* (Upper Saddle River, NJ: Prentice Hall, 1999).

Nichols v. Universal Pictures Corporation et al., Circuit Court of Appeals, Second Circuit, 45 F.2d 119; 1930 U.S. App. LEXIS 3587, November 10, 1930.

Steven R. Englund, "Idea, Process, or Protected Expression? Determining the Scope of Copyright Protection of the Structure of Computer Programs," *Michigan Law Review*, vol. 88, no. 4 (February 1990), pp. 866–909.

Chapter 23   Detecting Patent Infringement

"Segmented Asynchronous Operation of an Automated Assembly Line," U.S. Patent 4,884,674, filed January 30, 1985, issued December 5, 1989.

"Segmented Asynchronous Operation of an Automated Assembly Line," U.S. Patent 5,216,613, filed August 12, 1992, issued June 1, 1993.

"Patent Hawk—Claim Construction," http://patenthawk.com/claims.htm, retrieved May 12, 2010.

Peter S. Menell, Lynn H. Pasahow, James H. A. Pooley, and Matthew D. Powers, "Patent Case Management Judicial Guide," UC Berkeley Public Law Research Paper No. 1328659, June 1, 2009, http://ssrn.com/abstract=1328659.

Markman et al. v. Westview Instruments, Inc., et al., Supreme Court of the United States, 517 U.S. 370, April 3, 1996.

Phillips v. AWH Corporation, et al., United States Court of Appeals for the Federal Circuit, 03-1269, 03-1286, July 12, 2005.

J. Michael Jakes, "Using an Expert at a Markman Hearing: Practical and Tactical Considerations," *IP Litigator*, August 2002, www.finnegan.com/resources/articles/articlesdetail.aspx?news=e3962a13-b898-4102-8fca-171c656a6ed2, retrieved May 12, 2010.

Manual of Patent Examining Procedure (MPEP), 8th ed., August 2001, latest revision July 2008.

Jeanne M. Gills, "Crafting an Effective Patent Invalidity Opinion—Is It the Last Bastion of Defense?" *Practising Law Institute—Preparing Patent Legal Opinions* (New York: Foley & Lardner, 2003), www.foley.com/files/tbl_s31Publications/FileUpload137/1527/Gillsfinal.pdf, retrieved May 13, 2010.

Chapter 24   Detecting Trade Secret Theft

Bob Zeidman and Nikolaus Baer, "What, Exactly, Is Software Trade Secret Theft?" *Intellectual Property Today*, March 2008.

Charles Tait Graves and Brian D. Range, "Identification of Trade Secret Claims in Litigation: Solutions for a Ubiquitous Dispute," *Northwestern Journal of Technology and Intellectual Property*, vol. 5, no. 1 (Fall 2006).

Internet Archive WayBack Machine, www.archive.org.

Chapter 25   Implementing a Software Clean Room

Bernard A. Galler, *Software and Intellectual Property Protection: Copyright and Patent Issues for Computer and Legal Professionals* (Westport, CT: Quorum Books, 1995).

IEEE Computer Society Awards, "Tribute to Harlan D. Mills," www.computer.org/portal/web/awards/millsbio, retrieved September 25, 2010.

Mathew Schwartz, "Reverse-Engineering," *Computerworld*, November 12, 2001.

Atari Games Corp. v. Nintendo of America Inc., U.S. Court of Appeals, Federal Circuit, September 10, 1992.

Sega Enterprises Ltd. v. Accolade Inc., U.S. Court of Appeals, Ninth Circuit, October 20, 1992.

Mitchell Zimmerman, *Intellectual Property Bulletin*, Fenwick & West, Spring 2008.

Nordstrom Consulting, Inc. v. M&S Technologies, Inc., U.S. District Court, Northern District of Illinois, Eastern Division, March 4, 2008.

Chapter 26   Open Source Software

Open Source Initiative, "About the Open Source Initiative," http://opensource.org/about, retrieved September 24, 2010.

Open Source Initiative, "The Open Source Definition (Annotated)," http://opensource.org/docs/definition.php, retrieved September 24, 2010.

Todd R. Weiss, "Does the Open-Source Development Model Work for Business Users?" *Computerworld*, March 5, 2008.

David Boutcher and Bob Stankey, "Open Source's Dark Side," *Computing*, September 17, 2008.

Nichelle N. Levy, "Open Source Software License Enforcement Actions on the Rise," *Local Tech Wire*, December 4, 2009.

Grant Gross, "Open Source Group Sues Verizon," *IDG News*, December 8, 2007.

Lawrence Rosen, *Open Source Licensing* (Upper Saddle River, NJ: Prentice Hall, 2004).

Geeknet, Inc., "About Us," http://geek.net/about, retrieved September 25, 2010.

Free Software Foundation, www.fsf.org, retrieved July 10, 2010.

GNU Operating System, www.gnu.org, retrieved July 10, 2010.

Creative Commons, http://creativecommons.org, retrieved July 12, 2010.

Creative Commons, "Creative Commons FAQ," http://wiki.creativecommons.org/FAQ, retrieved September 25, 2010.

Funding Universe, "The Santa Cruz Operation, Inc.," www.fundinguniverse.com/company-histories/The-Santa-Cruz-Operation-Inc-Company-History.html, retrieved July 15, 2010.

Groklaw, "SCO," www.groklaw.net/staticpages/index.php?page=20061212211835541, retrieved September 25, 2010.

"The History of Linux," www.linux.org/info/linux_timeline.html, retrieved July 15, 2010.

SCO, "SCO Registers UNIX Copyrights and Offers UNIX License," press release, Lindon, UT, July 21, 2003, http://ir.sco.com/releasedetail.cfm?ReleaseID=114170, retrieved July 15, 2010.

Beth Z. Shaw, "Recent Lawsuits Reflect Open Source Software Users' Copyright Compliance Obligations," *Washington Legal Foundation*, vol. 25, no. 15 (May 7, 2010).

BusyBox, "BusyBox Is Licensed under the GNU General Public License, Version 2," http://busybox.net/license.html, retrieved July 24, 2010.

Rob Tiller (Red Hat), Opensource.com, "Total Victory for Open Source Software in a Patent Lawsuit," http://opensource.com/law/10/5/total-victory-patent-lawsuit-against-open-source-software, May 3, 2010.

Groklaw, "*IP Innovation v. Red Hat and Novell*—1 Year Later," www.groklaw.net/articlebasic.php?story=20081010043532860, October 11, 2008.

Sun Microsystems, "NetApp Patent Lawsuit against ZFS Open Source Technology," www.sun.com/lawsuit/zfs/index.jsp, retrieved July 16, 2010.

Groklaw, "Update on the NetApp-Sun Patent Litigation," www.groklaw.net/article.php?story=20080529163415471, June 04 2008

Chapter 27   Digital Millennium Copyright Act

U.S. Copyright Office, "The Digital Millennium Copyright Act of 1998," Summary, December 1998.

The UCLA Online Institute for Cyberspace Law and Policy, "The Digital Millennium Copyright Act," www.gseis.ucla.edu/iclp/dmca1.htm, February 8, 2001.

Electronic Freedom Foundation, "DMCA," www.eff.org/issues/dmca, retrieved July 16, 2010.

cnet news, "Adobe Hacking Case Goes to Jury," http://news.cnet.com/Adobe-hacking-case-goes-to-jury/2100-1023_3-977766.html, December 12, 2002.

U.S. Department of Justice, "Russian Man Charged in California under Digital Millennium Copyright Act with Circumventing Adobe eBook Reader," press release, www.justice.gov/criminal/cybercrime/Sklyarovindictment.htm, August 28, 2001.

Adobe FAQ, "ElcomSoft Legal Background," www.adobe.com/aboutadobe/pressroom/pressreleases/200108/elcomsoftqa.html, retrieved July 23, 2010.

cnet news, "ElcomSoft Verdict: Not Guilty," http://news.cnet.com/2100-1023-978176.html, December 17, 2002.

U.S. Copyright Office, "Fiscal Year 2011 Budget Request, Statement of the Librarian of Congress Relating to Section 1201 Rulemaking," www.copyright.gov/1201/2010/Librarian-of-Congress-1201-Statement.html, July 23, 2010.

INDEX

FREE Online Edition

Your purchase of *The Software IP Detective's Handbook* includes access to a free online edition for 45 days through the Safari Books Online subscription service. Nearly every Prentice Hall book is available online through Safari Books Online, along with more than 5,000 other technical books and videos from publishers such as Addison-Wesley Professional, Cisco Press, Exam Cram, IBM Press, O'Reilly, Que, and Sams.

SAFARI BOOKS ONLINE allows you to search for a specific answer, cut and paste code, download chapters, and stay current with emerging technologies.

Activate your FREE Online Edition at www.informit.com/safarifree

> **STEP 1:** Enter the coupon code: JBDLWWA.

> **STEP 2:** New Safari users, complete the brief registration form. Safari subscribers, just log in.

If you have difficulty registering on Safari or accessing the online edition, please e-mail customer-service@safaribooksonline.com